LABOR VERSUS EMPIRE

RACE, GENDER, AND MIGRATION

EDITED BY
GILBERT G. GONZALEZ, RAUL FERNANDEZ,
VIVIAN PRICE, DAVID SMITH, AND LINDA TRINH VÕ

Routledge
New York • London

Published in 2004 by
Routledge
270 Madison Avenue
New York, NY 10016
www.routledge-ny.com

Published in Great Britain by
Routledge
2 Park Square
Milton Park, Abingdon,
Oxon OX14 4RN U.K.
www.routledge.co.uk

Routledge is an imprint of the Taylor and Francis Group.

Printed in the United States of America on acid-free paper.

10 9 8 7 6 5 4 3 2 1

Library of Congress Cataloging-In-Publication data:

Labor versus empire : race, gender, and migration / edited by Gilbert Gonzalez with
    Raul Fernandez . . . [et al.].
        p.cm.
Includes bibliographical references.
    ISBN 0-415-94814-2 (hardcover : acid-free paper)—ISBN 0-415-94815-0
(pbk. : acid-free paper) 1. Imperialism—Social aspects—Congresses.
2. Working class—Congresses.
I. Gonzalez, Gilbert G., 1941-
    JC359.L26 2004
    306.3'6—dc22   2003025504

TABLE OF CONTENTS

PREFACE

This anthology mirrors several years of collegial effort by the faculty and graduate students at the University of California, Irvine. In spring 1996, a number of us who researched working class themes gathered informally to consider organizing a labor studies research unit that evolved into a formal organization known as the Focused Research Program in Labor Studies.

Over the years, participants have come from various programs and departments on campus, including Art History, Asian American Studies, Chicano Latino Studies, Education, History, Political Science, Sociology, and Women's Studies. Our collective efforts provided us with a critical interdisciplinary and comparative vision of working peoples and shaped our research around themes such as migration, musicology, gender, offshore production, racism, the state, unionization, working class communities, and films about the shared interests of working peoples across cultural and ethnic borders.

We could not escape the political reality of the time and the increasing popularity of the ideologies of *globalization* that rapidly emerged as favorite mantras of political leaders in advanced countries. Long before we were granted formal status as a Focused Research Program, a discourse critical of globalization matured within the group. Rather than study labor from a perspective that revolved around globalization, we engaged in theoretical interpretations that more adequately explained the political and economic realities of the contemporary world. It is apparent that the struggle for domination across the world pursued by economically advanced nations and led by the U.S. hid beneath the cover offered by globalization. It is our contention that the important questions facing labor today cannot be illuminated through recourse to globalization because it fails to explain the factors leading to the economic relations between nations and the social relations within nations. Rather, our frame of analysis is empire—which provides a theoretical foundation for examining the condition of the working class and more appropriately sets the stage for the struggles of working peoples for justice and democracy.

When the time came to plan our 2003 conference, we chose the title "Labor, Race, and Empire" to reflect the growing interest of the group in imperialism, particularly U.S. imperialism. Because gender and migration figured significantly into the conference presentations and writings, we titled this book *Labor versus Empire: Race, Gender, and Migration*. As co-editors, we worked together to plan the conference, gather the chapters, and write the introduction. Along the way, we engaged in lively debates that continually reshaped this project—it has been a truly collaborative process.

As with any undertaking of this nature, many people and organizations contributed to the success of the conference and the production of this book. Members of the program staff assisted significantly with logistical aspects of the conference, and special thanks are due to Leslie Bunnage, Roberto Gonzales, Matt Mahutga, and Rosaura Sanchez Tafoya, all graduate students in the Department of Sociology. They and Tryon Woods, a graduate of the Social Ecology program, also chaired panels at the conference. Raul Fernandez, Gilbert G. Gonzalez, John Liu, David Smith, and Linda Trinh Võ served as panel members. We also thank Dana Frank, David Kyle, Edna Bonacich, and Chris Chase-Dunn, whose research projects also contributed to the panels.

Over the years the program benefited from the cooperation of the Department of Asian American Studies, the Women's Studies Program, and the African American Studies Program in the School of Humanities and the Department of Sociology in the School of Social Sciences. The Chicano Latino Studies Program provided space for our program meetings. Anna Gonzalez, Director of the Cross-Cultural Center, offered generous assistance whenever requested. We are grateful to the School of Social Sciences for providing funds for luncheons as well as for the 1999 graduate conference and the successful all-UC conference hosted in spring 2001. In addition, we appreciate the financial assistance allocated by the University of California at Irvine's Office of Research, which granted us funding that made possible the various endeavors of the program including seed grants, seminars, conferences, and guest speakers. We are also indebted for the timely financial support from the Office of Student Affairs that aided our conferences.

We wish to express our deep appreciation to the University of California Institute of Labor and Employment for providing the funding over the past 2 years that made the conference and this book possible. Our special thanks are extended to Ruth Milkman, Director of the Institute, for her unflagging support for our endeavors. Finally, we owe a special debt to Gillian Kumm, Barbara Abell, and Stella Ginez, of the University of California School of Social Sciences at Irvine, for their assistance. We particulary wish to express our appreciation to Dorothy Fujita-Rony, Asian American Studies, for her many contributions to this work.

We wish to thank Karen Wolny, Editor, and Jaclyn Bergeron, Assistant to the Editor, at Routledge. They expressed enthusiasm about this book project when we were still organizing the conference and gave us the autonomy to develop our vision for it as well. In short, working with Routledge has been a pleasure. Special appreciation is also due to the exceptional contributors to this volume. The quality and merits of the book are due largely to their labor and we thank them for making this endeavor possible.

One person who figured prominently in the early phase of establishing the Labor Studies Program, Jeff Garcilazo, professor of History and Chicano Latino Studies, passed away tragically before he could finish his life's work. His commitment to the program and to working people inspired his colleagues and all who worked with him. In Jeff's honor, the editors will allocate all royalties from the sale of this book to the Jeff Garcilazo Fellowship/Scholarship Fund administered by Chicano Latino Studies at the University of California, Irvine.

INTRODUCTION

Globalization: Masking Imperialism
and the Struggles from Below
Raul Fernandez, Gilbert Gonzalez, Vivian Price,
David Smith, and Linda Trinh Võ

Background

In recent years, dramatic changes in economic processes have deepened the disparities between the rich and the poor on a worldwide basis and have undercut the power of working people everywhere. An imperialist agenda hidden under the aegis of *globalization* undergirds these widening rifts. The economic elite and political leadership of the U.S. pilot this process of polarization as the country continues its historic role of expansionism and domination on a greater scale than ever.

For the rest of the world, imperialism and militarism, mostly emanating from the U.S., are omnipresent realities and daily challenges. In the name of freedom and democracy, we are witnessing the increasing erosion of civil rights and economic justice for the working class at home and abroad along with inequities surrounding national origin, gender, race, class, and sexuality. No less constant and no less important are everyday struggles for basic necessities—earning a living wage, keeping one's family intact, providing for one's children, and living a life free of violence and discrimination. In the face of all these challenges, what is labor to do?

This question is at the very core of this anthology. Our title, *Labor versus Empire*, demonstrates our insistence on addressing the strategies of the working class, particularly in relation to imperialism and its accompanying systems of political, economic, and social domination. Our aim is to examine how the imposition of empire from above is resisted by the struggles for democracy from below, highlighting the ways that workers contest and shape the world around them. In doing so, we not only address the centrality of labor in the policies and economic debates that too often marginalize them, but also examine how workers in many areas of production affect the processes of empire, from peasant challenges against free-trade agreements to industrial workers' challenges of regulations in transnational corporations; from popular protests against the policies of nation–states to the organization of alliances by immigrant healthcare workers.

Our collective interests steered us toward analyzing the recent transformation popularly titled *globalization* (more accurately described as neoliberal economics on a world scale) and its relation to working peoples. Recent interest in globalization in both popular and official discourse spawned renewed interest in topics such as free trade, global economics, global assembly lines, global trade, global cities, global information, and global capital. Popular media repeat the official chant of globalization and the core of the neoliberal creed: free trade lifts all boats, globalization assures democracy, and globalization is inevitable; all nations must sign on or be left behind. This message was repeated endlessly by affluent nations, particularly by the U.S., the bastion of international financial agencies such as the International Monetary Fund (IMF), World Bank, and World Trade Organization (WTO). This unholy triumvirate controlled by the U.S. and other rich nations manages global "free" trade, negotiates debt regimes, oversees adjustment policies in poor countries, and performs other monetary functions.

Some scholars and pundits now declare that the nation–state is fading into oblivion because of large world political and economic shifts, as free trade overwhelms old national structures and previous state controls. However, despite its popularity in some quarters, under close scrutiny this "decline of the state" thesis does not hold up (Smith, Solinger, and Topik, 1999). In fact, the state did not wither away; on the contrary, some states emerged stronger than ever. This is particularly true of the U.S. government. Free trade in the U.S. under WTO auspices is merely old-fashioned protectionism in disguise. Steel and agriculture, both major large-scale industries, were accorded government largesse for decades in the form of stiff tariffs and sumptuous subsidies. In the geopolitical sphere, the most powerful of nations and unparalleled promoter of neoliberalism—the U.S.—constructed the most dominant and war-ready military machinery in history, all under the guidance of the highly centralized state.

Ideologies of Globalization

Globalization is a popular term today. Unfortunately, it obfuscates more than it illuminates, particularly in masking the processes of imperialism in the global arena. Wide-ranging discussions of globalization emerged in the late 1990s, and the concept soon became a mantra of political leaders throughout the world. Globalization became a familiar buzzword to anyone attuned to the global media, with proponents claiming that major transformations of the global system occurred in the past two or three decades. Major worldwide transformations occurred and many of them, including dramatic increases in indices of global inequality, are clearly *not* changes for the better. Globalization is left, perhaps conveniently, undefined.

Rising above the din of the debates about globalization are at least two basic insights. First is the notion that a basic feature of the current global economy is an increasing time–space compression (Mittleman, 1996; Arrighi, 1999). This involves a dramatic geometric surge in the sheer velocities of various types of global exchanges. The "global gambling casino" dynamics of today's international banking and finance system became especially transparent and quite alarming with the East Asian crisis of the late 1990s (Wade and Veneroso, 1998). Transformations happen very fast and the pace is constantly increasing. Even people as unlikely as transnational financier George Soros equate the contemporary global economy to a runaway train (Soros, 1997). The lords and high priests of capitalism, like Alan Greenspan and his contemporaries at the World Bank and IMF, may have trouble controlling and braking this locomotive, increasing the likelihood of a planetary train wreck.

Second, and perhaps even more critically, we must understand that current images of globalization are saturated with ideology. Epitomized by Margaret Thatcher's proclamation of TINA (there is no alternative) to global neoliberalism, the ideology emanates from the capitalist core nations and is relentlessly promoted by western conservative theorists, large corporations, and wealthy individuals and foundations (Cox, 1996; Gill, 1996). They claim that forces like deregulation and marketization are inevitable and in the long run beneficial. Such uses of the *globalization* term are ideological in the sense that they enshrine the values of free-market liberalism and legitimize the global domination of corporate capitalism.

Advocates of this global neoliberalism believe it is necessary to subordinate states and politics to the requirements of capital accumulation. Although this view rose to prominence in the early 1980s during Margaret Thatcher's and Ronald Reagan's time on the international stage, it has become widely shared among political and economic elites around the world. Invocation of the free-market mantra is *de rigueur* for western heads of state at G-8 summit meetings, and the ideology is now publicly embraced by leaders of many underdeveloped or Third World countries, too.

Globalization is an all-purpose elixir, offered with assurances that acceptance of the neoliberal prescription will not only cure economic problems (like the "Asian Flu" of "crony capitalism" in the years following the East Asian crisis) but will also ineluctably lead to democracy, human rights, improving the status of women, etc. It all sounds wonderful, particularly given the emphasis on *free* trade, *opening* markets, *liberalizing* states, etc. Like the tonics peddled at old-fashioned medicine shows that sounded too good to be true, globalization is another situation where the buyer should beware.

Globalization Masking Imperialism

On close inspection, it is clear that touted globalization schemes actually promote increasing disparity within nations, between labor and capital, and between poor and rich nations. Such schemes represent little more than new manifestations of imperialism. The contemporary U.S. is an imperialist power, an empire intent on domination of poor countries and economic and military supremacy across the globe.

A clarion call of this volume is the need to reformulate language. Imperialism must be moved from the margins to the center, and we must discard innocuous-sounding and romanticized labels such as globalization and global markets. Our reasoning parallels the cogent summary on the schemes of free traders offered by William Finnegan (2003) in the pages of *Harper's Magazine*: "[T]heirs is not an ideology of freedom or democracy. It is a system of control. It is an economics of empire." Elevating imperialism, particularly U.S. imperialism, to its central place leads to consideration of recent, triumphalist, neo-conservative discourse on the topic.

A growing, cynical, and disturbing consensus among neo-conservatives celebrates the U.S. as an imperialist power. Although this may seem like a strikingly unconventional perspective, it is a chic topic among pundits today who find the facts self-evident. For instance, Robert D. Kaplan in a 2003 *Atlantic Monthly* article titled "Supremacy by Stealth: Ten Rules for Managing the World," contends that "It is a cliché these days to observe that the United States possesses a global empire—different from Britain's and Rome's but an empire nonetheless. It is time to move beyond a statement of the obvious …. So how should we operate on a tactical level to manage an unruly world?"

Kaplan's unapologetic view of a world dominated by the U.S. is not unique. In the *Washington Post*, nationally syndicated columnist Charles Krauthammer (2002) noted the popularity of this view. Differing somewhat with Kaplan, he suggested "People are now coming out of the closet on the word *empire* …. We dominate every field of human endeavor from fashion to film to finance. We rule the world culturally, economically, diplomatically and militarily as no one since the Roman Empire." In case *empire* and *imperialism* sound a bit over the top, other neo-conservative pundits add qualifiers. William Kristol, William Rusher, Max Boot, and a host of others make the case for the U.S. as the first "benign" humanitarian imperialist power in history, unlike any previous empire. Max Boot (2001) writing in the pages of the neo-conservative *Weekly Standard*, argues that the U.S. differs from empires of the past because it is liberal and humanitarian.

In appropriating the term, neo-conservatives deliberately sanitize the meaning of *imperialism* by arguing that the U.S. simply wishes to extend the virtues of democracy and capitalism, thereby modernizing backward regions and lifting intermediate nations to higher levels. They concede, when necessary, that the U.S. will overthrow those governments (democratically elected or not) that close their borders to foreign capital and thereby oppose democracy through a process known as *regime change*. Unfortunately, those on the political right who currently monopolize this discourse on empire and imperialism applaud maintaining, if not expanding, an imperial reach that has already reached historically unmatched proportions. It is time for us to develop critical interpretations of empire and imperialism that are not squeamish about calling them what they truly are.

American Exceptionalism

Despite a barrage of news articles and television interviews applauding U.S. imperialism and calling for more of it, Americans remain uneasy about the use of the term. Most accept the mainstream myth that the U.S. relates to all nations on the basis of equality and reciprocity. This view is integral to an older version of "American Exceptionalism" that sees the country as anti-imperialist. The neo-conservative view of humanitarian or benign imperialism proposes a newer version of American Exceptionalism, contending that the U.S. empire is different from empires of the past. Generally, Americans are unwilling to see their nation as imperialist. It is becoming increasingly clear, though, that the identification of the U.S. as an imperialist power is generally accepted as a given throughout most of the world. Ironically, the residents of the main imperial power seem to be the last to fully grasp that sentiment.

Emily Eakins (2003) writes in the *New York Times* that "Americans are used to being told—typically by resentful foreigners—that they are imperialists. But lately some of the nation's own eminent thinkers are embracing the idea. More astonishing, they are using the term with approval. From the isolationist right to the imperialist-bashing left, a growing number of experts are issuing stirring paeans to American empire." The vast majority of Americans, many in academia, and most of the news media have found it difficult to incorporate U.S. imperialism into their political consciousness, research, and news reporting, respectively.

The rightward shift in national politics in recent years affected higher education. Conservative ideologues and corporate influence and funding succeeded in reconstructing large parts of U.S. academia into a bulwark of research governed by neo-liberal principles. Despite occasional neo-conservative rants about leftist bias in U.S. universities (often in tandem with an imagined liberal bias in mainstream media), plenty of evidence indicates this shift to the right on campuses motivated by perpetual searches for world-class standing, emphasis on commercially viable research, attacks upon tenure, hiring of part-time lecturers as major components of the teaching corps, various efforts to bust unions, etc. Despite this trend, a number of scholars in the humanities and social sciences continue to formulate research that incorporates a critical view of imperialism at its center. However, an appreciation of contemporary politics and economics dominated by imperialist policies remains beyond the scope of the vast majority of university research and instruction.

Similarly, serious discussions of these issues are absent from the narrow debates that pass for American political discourse. Our two main political parties, both infused with heavy doses of neo-liberalism and frequently offering voters a choice between Tweedledum and Tweedledee, shun the "I" word. They are willing to cite imperialism only when discussing foreign powers, particularly those in serious contention with the U.S., for example, the former Soviet Union. One rarely hears even the suggestion of American imperialism. Perhaps the mainstream politicos feel that the public cannot handle the harsh truth about U.S. foreign policy and corporate behavior overseas. We should probably thank the neo-conservative minions of the far right for resurrecting a crucial debate about the nature of empire.

This neo-conservative "outing" and celebration of U.S. imperialism, firmly grounded on a political bedrock for neo-liberal economic orthodoxy, threatens to pervert the meaning of the term. In this right-wing interpretation, imperialism comes to mean the triumph of good over everything evil. American troops and capital are seen as benign forces intervening around the world, and the U.S. is the standard bearer for the whole world. It is as if the "white man's burden" of 19th century colonialism has been transformed into a 21st century American empire. The lack of significant attention to U.S. imperialism in academic study, as Amy Kaplan (1993) convincingly demonstrated, and in political discourse and popular literature (certainly the case in labor studies), makes it imperative that U.S. imperialism—not the imperialism defined by Boot, Rusher, and Kaplan or the uncritical paeans to globalization—be placed on the national agenda.

The authors in this book, who hail from a variety of academic disciplines and activist approaches and whose studies differ in style and content, have no problem identifying the U.S. as an empire. Moreover, based on the arguments and evidence presented in the various chapters, imperialism is alive and far from benign. The argument that the U.S. is a humanitarian power interested only in spreading freedom, wealth, and health over the globe is thoroughly debunked. The authors discuss a number of substantive topics and historical periods and present an array of evidence ranging from personal narratives to detailed statistics that present a far different picture of the role of the U.S. across the world. Their studies counter the contention that the U.S. spreads in a disinterested manner the benefits that its own peoples enjoy. Indeed, the chapters in this book persuasively link the inequality, deprivation, and disempowerment of people in far-flung parts of the globe with growing poverty, unemployment, and disenfranchisement here in the U.S. where nearly 35 million people live in poverty (U.S. Census Bureau, 2000) and 3.5 million are homeless (Clementson, 2003; Gosselin, 2003; Johnston, 2003; Shulman, 2003).

This book should also challenge readers, forcing them to consider alternative understandings of the U.S. that move beyond both the official denial of imperialism and the emerging neo-conservative consensus about its humanitarian nature. In order to address the contemporary dilemmas of labor and working people, we must understand the concepts of world domination and global inequality.

Theory and the Imperial State

A vast literature in various fields discusses the theoretical natures of imperialism and globalization (Lenin, 1970; Moore, 1979; Marx and Engels, 1998). Here we need distinguish only three generic views. One contends that imperialism and globalization are consequences of policy choices and they can be fundamentally altered, reformed, pulled back, or dismissed by political and economic elites without altering the nation's capitalist system.

This view analytically separates the political from the economic and considers the possibility that they operate independently. In this version of historical events, the militaristic supremacy of the U.S. and its search for economic domination are influenced by various policy choices. Thus, for example, the military aggression against Iraq and Afghanistan expresses behavior by politically powerful groups in the U.S., but it is conceivable that different elites might have made different choices. This U.S. policy was neither preordained nor determined by the nature of American political economy. Consequently, another group of policy makers, part of a new Democratic administration, for example, might enter the policymaking arena and alter the imperial course.

The second approach argues that imperialism, in both its militaristic and economic expressions, is ultimately a manifestation of the capitalist order and therefore originates from the logical functioning of monopoly capitalism. In this perspective, the largest capitalist entities—agricultural, manufacturing, banking, and financial institutions—dominate the U.S. economy and, in so doing, direct the political agenda as well. This view of the state accords politics and politicians less weight in choosing policies. Historical change in the long run is driven by economic imperatives with little latitude for political influence independent of economics in general.

A third view, critical of the two earlier approaches, holds that the previous theories are useful but incomplete. On the one hand, imperialism certainly cannot be limited to the subjective choices made by political leaders without understanding how economic forces drive politics in most societies. To paraphrase Marx, people make their own history but not entirely as they please, and this applies to both heads of state and captains of industry. Because the U.S. economy is based on monopoly capitalism, it is inconceivable that an American president could make key policy choices that were fundamentally opposed by the corporate elite for an extended period, even if the electorate supported them. Such a scenario would quickly expose the limits of democracy.

Proponents of this third perspective also see limitations in the second approach that argues that imperialism expresses the interests of the largest capitalist entities, multi-national corporations (MNCs), and banks that set parameters for political action and therefore the agendas of political leaders acting as intermediaries rather than as policy makers. Taken to its logical conclusion, this suggests that the state is nothing more than an executive committee of the bourgeoisie and the politicians are the tools of capitalists; imperialism is not a choice and is an imperative to action to maintain the control over resources, cheap labor, and trade.

In such a context, the war against Iraq secures petroleum reserves and denies them to others. The North American Free Trade Agreement (NAFTA) and the Free Trade of the Americas Agreement expand investment opportunities and promote cheap labor while keeping European and Japanese capital out of the area. The third perspective emphasizes the need to recognize that capitalists, by their very nature, have a very difficult time agreeing about what is in their collective interest. As a result, while huge oil companies and defense firms may push for one Middle East imperialist policy, MNCs that sell consumer goods to Europe and international banks capitalized by Saudi sheiks may favor different strategies (Block, 1977). Despite their differences, all three perspectives maintain that the nation–state has not lost its previous interventionist role and continues as the main instrument for implementing imperialist objectives. States remain key players to advance the interests of capital.

Whatever the theoretical distinctions, there is unanimity that imperialism operating as neo-liberal globalization is a veritable festival of speculation for financial capitalists. Fast-moving financial capital retains no loyalty to any nation except possibly its home base, with drastic consequences for receiving nations. Throughout the 1990s, much of the finance capital that flowed into emerging economies later dried up after generating huge profits via currency speculation, extraction of cheap labor, and legal pillage of natural resources. This pattern precipitated financial crises in Argentina, Brazil, Mexico, and, most dramatically, several East Asian countries in the late 1990s. The results were increased poverty and inequality, record levels of unemployment, declines in basic quality-of-life indicators, rising infant mortality, etc. Given a continuing worldwide economic recession in subsequent years, we have little reason to expect that the widespread ruin and havoc experienced by many underdeveloped nations will soon be reversed. The global casino dynamics of contemporary capitalism based on short-term profits, if not sheer speculation, is clearly immensely profitable for high rollers and big-time players. However, it seems to offer little impetus to genuine economic growth at the peripheries or centers of today's imperial capitalism.

Imperialism and the Working Class

The human costs of today's neo-liberal globalization are felt within the core of the empire, the U.S. Since 1979, 5 million manufacturing jobs disappeared overseas—a condition disastrous for labor (Friedman, 2003). NAFTA alone reportedly relocated 766,000 jobs, primarily in manufacturing, to assembly plants in Mexico, Central America, and the Caribbean (Scott, 2001). In the U.S., the service industry absorbed the slack, and since 1989 almost 99% of new jobs in the U.S. appeared in the service sector, which on average pays wages nearly 25% below those of manufacturing (Mishel, Bernstein, and Schmidt, 2001). Concurrently, the class divides widened. The annual incomes of the top 400 wealthiest taxpayers quadrupled between 1992 and 2000, from $46.8 million to $174 million, while their taxes declined from 26.4 to 22.3%. Federal Reserve Board data show that 75% of new wealth created between

1989 and 1998 went to the top 10% of the nation's households. The income of the top 5% of households climbed nearly three times faster than the incomes of the remaining 95% (Browning, 2003; Friedman, 2003).

Those at the top do well even through scandal and business failure. Corporate bankruptcies, some caused by massive corruption and malfeasance like the famous Enron scandal of 2001, barely affect the wealthy. Indeed, more than 2 years after that wave of corporate fraud, few CEOs have been prosecuted. The costs of these scandals and bankruptcies were enormous for ordinary laboring people: 35,000 people lost their jobs because of the corruption, $1 billion in pension funds went up in smoke, and shareholders and workers claimed $29 billion in losses (Rovella, 2003). Compounding the grim outcomes (never presaged by the globalization gurus), the stock market stepped onto the proverbial slippery slope. Inevitably, unemployment rose above 6% and remains at that level. What makes this recession so unusual, however, is that nearly 20% of the unemployed are of the professional sector, the heart of the fabled American Dream, the middle class.

California provides an excellent example of the effects of globalization on the average U.S. worker. Since the mid-1980s the state's manufacturing jobs declined from 2 million to 1.8 million and service industry jobs doubled from 2.3 million to 4.6 million. Wages dropped accordingly. The average manufacturing job paid $55,000 annually. The average for service work stands at $30,000 (Skelton, 2003). Further manufacturing-job losses and service-industry growth in California and across the country are guaranteed if the proposed Free Trade Agreement of the Americas is implemented.

The *export* of jobs, sometimes given the bloodless label of *capital flight*, depends on efficient transportation. Products formerly produced in the U.S. and now made at far lower cost overseas must still find their ways to relatively affluent consumers in places like the U.S. In Chapters 1 and 2 of this volume, George Lipsitz and Thomas Reifer describe how technological developments— like supertankers that cross the Pacific in a few days, containerization of shipping, and computerized inventory control and logistics—affect California's economic geography, employment prospects at the ports and inland, and opportunities for labor organizing. Lipsitz offers a compendium of changes attendant on the global reorganization of production, including large new streams of labor migration, inequality in the U.S. and elsewhere, radical changes in the marketing of consumer goods, and new transnational identities and social movements. His coverage of a range of impacts of global neoliberalism and the new forms of imperialism makes his work an ideal introductory chapter. Reifer's essay provides a finer-grained analysis of the emerging logistic sector in the U.S., with special focus on the massive Long Beach–Los Angeles port complex, the Alameda transportation corridor, and the rise of a huge concentration of distribution warehouses in the "Inland Empire" of southern California.

One lesson that emerges through this analysis is the value of developing labor-organizing strategies that directly interrogate and challenge the expansive but locality-specific processes of globalization. Reifer contends that transnational production, supply, and distribution networks create potential arenas for alliances for the workers who dominate such industries, including people of color, immigrants, and women. Analyzing the Mexico–China–Southern California triangle, he points out that ports such as those in Los Angeles and Long Beach and warehouses in Ontario could be strategic places for workers to exercise these options and become "a potential Achilles Heel of the giant retail firms and the global production networks of which they are an integral part."

Identifying new alliances and possibilities produced from globalization can take place in more localized arenas as well. Lipsitz's discussion of the organization by the Labor/Community Strategy Center (LCSC) of the Bus Riders' Union in Los Angeles identifies a strategic local space for organizing and building broad coalitions. He notes that the LCSC identified bus riding as a pivotal organizing situation for developing a multi-national membership that both crossed and connected different experiences. This group understood "that its members were also valuable 'witnesses to empire' and veterans of trade union and anti-imperialist struggles around the world," enabling workers to use their transnational networks to mobilize.

William Robinson and James Petras contribute chapters that illustrate the larger structural dynamics of contemporary imperialism in terms of their impacts on Latin America. Robinson describes the massive changes in the global arena in the latter half of the 20th century. He claims that the crises of the 1970s "led to a new mode of global capital accumulation now known as neoliberalism," resulting in a fundamental economic restructuring of Latin America through transnational processes. This transnational activity profoundly reorganized political relations and hierarchies beyond individual nation–states and promoted the transfers of capital and products within one consolidated world arena.

Integration in the global economy during this period, however, resulted not in growth but in stagnation in many parts of the world, with Latin America becoming more dependent on commodity exports and global capital markets. The accompanying national debts accumulated by Latin American countries only deepened their relationships to unequal transnational networks while promoting the rise of an "emergent transnational power bloc in the region."

Similarly, James Petras identifies neo-colonialism of Latin America led by the U.S, MNCs, and banks and supported by political leaders like George W. Bush. Petras discusses the deleterious effects on labor in this region through military rule, privatization, massive debt, and trade agreements favoring outside countries.

Neo-liberal pressure to delegitimize states and governments around the globe undermines gains made over decades by "welfare states" and removes crucial political levers exercised in the past by workers, unions, and even middle-class citizens.

Petras argues, "Empire building is essentially a form of *class warfare from above*." The unfulfilled promise of so-called free trade has meant the loss of jobs, the elimination of social support systems, the gradual demise of small agriculturalists, the increasing inequality between the top income tier and the working peoples, and descent from the heralded middle class. The price for this progress, as William Robinson comments regarding Latin America, is paid by the poor and the working class whose exploited cheap labor becomes an asset for attracting outside investment. He notes succinctly, "The poor have to run faster just to remain in the same place."

Processes of globalization are far reaching, not only dramatically transforming the economic policies that bind nations and economies, but also reconfiguring social and political dynamics in other arenas, even in areas typically considered private and intimate, such as sexuality. Useche and Cabezas argue that issues as seemingly diverse as international tourism, the pharmaceutical industry, and the spread of HIV/AIDs have all become stages for the unequal relations produced by and consolidated through neo-liberal economic policies. One common consequence of these larger policies is that men and women who need work turn to employment in the international sex trade. Witness, for instance, the Mexican women who are unable to cross the border into the U.S. and find sex work as a primary labor option in border cities like Tijuana where the industry is mainly frequented by U.S. tourists.

Imperialism, Migration, and Citizenship

Supporters of free-trade reforms argue that the reforms will bring an end to underdevelopment; however, the reforms worsened the conditions of poverty and drove people from their homes and communities. For example, the free entry of agricultural products from the First World into Third World markets has a devastating impact on small farmers and producers. After the imports saturate the marketplaces in less-developed countries, prices for the commodities fall, causing a decrease in the demand for domestic products and driving small producers and farmers out of business. In other cases, multinational agribusinesses take advantage of neo-liberal policies by buying large swaths of the countryside, then convert peasant plots that once raised subsistence crops into large-scale plantations for export crops. Victor Quintana's Chapter 16 explains how this process worked in Mexico over the past two decades and its devastating impacts on the agricultural sector and rural populations.

Ironically, while the rise of large-scale corporate monoproduction of crops like coffee for western markets may make economic sense (and profits) in a neo-liberal world economy, the dramatic reduction in small-holder subsistence agriculture frequently worsens food shortages and leads to more hunger in poor countries. Small peasant farmers are driven from the land, and once thriving countryside communities become deserted villages. Older generations are left behind and younger generations are uprooted. Many seek employment in urban areas where they face inadequate housing, lack of basic public health facilities, and fierce competition for employment. Some find seasonal work as street vendors or in the service, construction, manufacturing, and tourism industries (Smith, 1996).

Swelling cities of the Indian subcontinent are frequently offered as quintessential examples of Third World squalor, deprivation, and desperation. Leela Fernandes's chapter on class, space, and the state in India zeroes in on Mumbai (Bombay). This sprawling metropolis is largely the product of massive cityward migration of the rural poor who often end up as members of an urban underclass of squatters, beggars, hawkers, and vendors. Recent neo-liberal reforms also created a new Indian middle class that is more affluent and oriented toward western-style consumerism. Economic liberalization programs (and the dismantling of vestiges of state socialism) led to a collaboration of the state and the private sectors, producing exclusionary forms of citizenship based on neo-colonial hierarchies of class, ethnicity, and religion. The result is further segregation of the working classes and the emerging middle class in the workplace, in consumption patterns, and in the privatization of public space.

Concurrent with such segregation is a rise in racialized and exclusionary Hindu nationalist political activities targeting Muslim immigrant workers. Fernandes reminds us that the dynamics of empire are far reaching, extending beyond countries at the center of global capitalism and those leading the war on terrorism. The economic and military–political dimensions of empire building are extremely salient. Liberalization policies do not weaken the role of the militarized state; rather, they reorganize and strengthen it, often under cover of the war on terror.

This free entry of finance capital and surplus commodities creates an internal migratory process and fosters conditions for immigration to other countries and continents. Hoping to find more promising economic opportunities, the displaced citizens immigrate as documented and undocumented workers to Australia, the U.S., Canada, and Europe—countries that have demands for cheap labor. The laborers face immense pressures because they are expected to support families left behind in the villages who depend on them for survival.

Thus, in this era of neo-liberal models of economic restructuring, immigration is not an act of free choice but is constrained by powerful market forces that regulate labor costs in rich and poor countries *vis-à-vis* state-to-state agreements between sending and receiving countries. This international marketplace of cheap and flexible labor is geared to exporting labor in the service of MNCs and nation–states.

Active state policies produce an international gender division of labor, for example, with preferences for men in agricultural and construction work and women in domestic or factory work. In some cases, both sexes are recruited to provide segmented labor needs, with the assumption that the presence of family members will pacify the male workforce. Women are recruited to fill positions as domestics, nannies, nurses, and home-care workers abroad. A vast inexpensive female labor pool from the Third World services the needs of the young and old in the First World.

Rhacel Parreñas's Chapter 7 analyzes the predicaments of domestic workers who relocate from underdeveloped countries to richer nations and focuses on women from the Philippines. State policies in the wealthy countries limit the incorporation of these temporary or guest workers, forbid them from bringing family members with them, and grant them only partial citizenship rights. These restrictions disrupt family life and force relatives and friends left behind in the sending communities to care for the children of these transnational laborers. An enormous emotional cost is also paid by members of these transnational families. Their cheap labor benefits employers and the economies of the receiving states that do not have to pay family reproduction costs. Furthermore, the states are free to deport the workers when their labor is no longer in demand.

Neo-liberal policies have also forced women to turn to the informal labor sector by doing sex work in tourist enclaves or militarized zones to escape rural poverty and support themselves and their families. Although coercive trafficking of women who are brutally kidnapped, sold, or lured into sexual slavery certainly occurs, other situations are more complex (Kempadoo and Doezema, 1998). In many cases, women may have much greater agency and control over their sexual labor.

In Chapter 5, Amalia Cabezas examines the impact of globalization on the informal economy of sex tourism in Cuba and the Dominican Republic and contends that the economy is not automatically exploitative. She argues that although a racial hierarchy exists, the boundaries between labor practices and romantic relationships are blurred because some women see sex work as a way to augment their meager wages and spend leisure time. Some even expect to find love, friendship, and even marriage with foreigners. Although some women choose to participate in these intimate relations to improve their socioeconomic status, others and even children are coerced into lives of sexual exploitation. It is not a coincidence that many of the women and men who are sexualized in these situations come from developing countries in Asia and Latin America, and it is not accidental that minority women are especially vulnerable in those countries.

A connection exists between imperialism and immigration patterns, particularly the subordination of a racialized labor force. Displaced persons migrate from Asia, Africa, the Caribbean, Latin America, and, to a lesser extent, Eastern Europe and the Middle East. Immigrants and refugees who go to wealthy countries are accused of undermining wages, misappropriating services, increasing crime rates, and weakening national cultural values. High immigration rates and economic instability correlate with heightened levels of anti-immigrant sentiments and racial violence.

Kitty Calavita, in Chapter 9, describes the marginalization of immigrant laborers in Italy and Spain, most of whom are from the underdeveloped world, most notably northern Africa. Although the European states promote a discourse of tolerance, they practice a policy of economic marginalization of immigrants. They systematically and legally exclude immigrants, denying them opportunities for full integration into civil society. Calavita's study strengthens the concerns of critics who argue that global inequalities and post colonial relations reproduce empires *within* nations, particularly where pre-Fordist and post-Fordist systems of production exist. Destabilization brought on by global neo-liberalism, including policies of structural adjustment in poor countries and dismantling of welfare states and antilabor policies in rich ones, continues to produce massive global labor migrations.

The billions of dollars in remittances global workers send home support their families. The funds also subsidize the economies of the sending states and help them resolve balance-of-payment issues and reduce their national debts. Third World governments, encouraged by international lenders, actively persuade migrants to funnel remittances into government-sponsored projects supposedly aimed at helping develop the villages. Ironically, these types of programs created the crises that originally forced people off their lands and out of their homelands. These policies amount to little more than the privatization of welfare programs—having the poor subsidize the poor in the face of increasing cutbacks in social services and government farm subsidies. Again, the division between labor-supplying nations and labor-utilizing nations replicates a colonial pattern embedded within global neo-liberal policies.

Although migration from Third World nations is restricted, foreign investors, assembly-plant managers, retirees, tourists, and others enter such countries freely. Miguel Tinker Salas, in Chapter 10, analyzes the social and cultural impact of multi-national petroleum companies in Venezuela. He is interested not only in the effects on workers in the oil camps (*campos petroleros*), but also how MNCs transformed Venezuelan society as a whole. Promoting the notion of corporate citizenship through the work culture, they restructured family arrangements, female labor participation, relations with foreigners, and class mobility. The big oil firms represented themselves as agents of modernization to be emulated; however, Venezuela is now experiencing a major economic crisis that created social havoc as a result of the struggle to control oil revenues.

Salas's work speaks to conditions facing developing nations that desire to attract foreign capital to boost national economies. These nations adopt contradictory economic policies of privatization and state control, often leading to internal power struggles, mismanagement, and corruption. Old power relationships are difficult to change, and former neo-colonial masters and corporate power structures retain a great deal of control. This can lead to a loss of national sovereignty—in some cases through foreign intervention and even occupation.

Resistance to Global Imperialism

The predicament that laborers face in the contemporary period parallels the conditions they faced over a century ago. On a global scale, at one level, the gap is between the First and the Third World nations; however, we cannot ignore the widening disparities between the wealthy and the poor within national boundaries. Work conditions are deteriorating not only for manufacturing and service-industry jobs, but also for those in the high-paying technology and biotechnology industries.

First World countries that formerly hired domestic workers and imported highly skilled workers from the Third World on temporary or even permanent visas can now, with technological advances, hire workers who remain overseas at a fraction of the wages. This practice is known as global sourcing. Increasingly footloose capital demands flexible workers and flexible production locations. Global sourcing improves competitiveness but is detrimental for workers worldwide. The conditions facing laborers counter the arguments by neo-liberal advocates that unencumbered movement of capital, goods, and services is advantageous for all.

Broad coalitions of different types of workers in various parts of the world are beginning to resist. This is evident in the large-scale antiglobalization protests (reactions against what we described as imperialism), particularly against the WTO and massive mobilizations against state policies that attack unions, deteriorate working conditions, and eliminate employment opportunities. Laborers, even those with the most precarious immigration and citizenship status, have challenged state and multi-national corporate power, using their social agency to mobilize for improved and humane working and living conditions.

Although financial and other corporate entities use their powerful national states to act as advance guards, agents, and negotiators for their interests, opposition from within to those same polities is rising around the globe. As William Robinson notes in Chapter 3, instabilities in Latin America provide openings for further resistance against and challenges to political structures, even if increased oppression is another result. This reveals the potential of massive movements that transcends nation–state and regional boundaries.

Indeed, since the epochal "Battle for Seattle" in 1999, rallies, large and small, have dared to protest globalization policies sponsored by the dominant nations and administered by their governments. Popular movements demand, among other things, that their respective states rescind deleterious economic policies, particularly privatization and austerity measures, and that governments serve their nations and place national sovereignty above foreign interests.

Consequently, there is a great deal of contestation over nation–states in the underdeveloped world.

The Third World state has become something of a sanctuary of last resort for workers and peasants to resist the devastation wrought by policies designed at the headquarters of MNCs. Workers in Argentina and peasants in Mexico, for example, protest that the state does not serve the people and propose the state create alternative policies at odds with the international lenders and MNCs. On the other hand, lenders and MNCs search for ways to weaken the poor countries to guarantee business as usual. It is evident from the articles in this volume that the struggles by opponents of neo-liberalism use the state as a means of defense against free-trade agreements and policies of similar ilk. The state is a sort of "disputed territory," not merely among the peoples of various nations but between the peoples of nations, foreign governments, and the corporations they serve.

How has recent global imperialism changed the way scholars, labor organizations, and other activists think about resistance; about who is likely to protest; what forms this protest will take; and what kind of leadership is emerging? Issues motivating protest involve racist, sexist, homophobic, and anti-immigrant public policy; the exploitation of children in foreign assembly plants; the wanton murders of nearly 400 young women maquila workers in Juarez, Mexico; the liberal importation of products that compete with small producers; the curtailing of pensions; privatization of water supplies; raising university fees; and, of course, mortgaging entire economies to international lending agencies.

Resistance covers many activities and is broadly defined, ranging from consumer boycotts of products; student takeovers of university buildings; united front marches; worker factory occupations; community-wide shutdowns; street vendor demonstrations; peasant marches on national capitals; teachers shutting down main thoroughfares; imported domestics organizing unions; and open rebellion against U.S. military presence in Korea, Afghanistan, and Iraq.

In the 21st century, women, immigrants, sexual minorities, rural people, and other marginalized groups are increasingly moving to the forefront of global struggles. Combating racial, gender, and heterosexist privilege and anti-immigrant attitudes and promoting an analysis of imperialism that engages everyday experiences are critical challenges facing the emerging global anti-imperialist movements.

Debates among neo-Marxist and postmodern scholars often center on the place of the proletariat in these struggles. Wai Kit Choi's Chapter 11 reflects on Hardt and Negri's (2000) argument that the current regime of flexible production ushers in a period in which workers are highly differentiated and their stratification makes identification with one another unlikely. Choi's case study of Shanghai labor uprisings in the 1920s shows that historical proletarian-based struggles were much more contingent than is generally thought; that the workers constituted a heterogeneous group; and that only through left leadership did a diverse coalition of workers, gangsters, bourgeoisie, and assorted nationalists sustain a unified general strike.

Choi's emphasis on the importance of the ability of the communist organizers in early 20th century Shanghai to overcome the obstacles faced by the stratified groups of protesters suggests that organized resistance to 21st century global capitalism uniting varied types of workers and ordinary citizens may be more feasible than many think. This raises questions about the prospects of transnational coalitions in the current phase of fragmented production. Will workers be likely to support one another across national boundaries or even across racial groups, especially if the dominant thinking places blame on workers who accept lower wages and conditions?

Ideology and leadership are critical elements in the forging of solidarity and transnational coalitions, and a number of chapters in this volume comment on transnational and interethnic labor organizations. Mark Le Vine's Chapter 12 is also an historical case study, examining the significance of interactions of Zionist and Palestinian workers during the mandate period. His evidence suggests that the two groups cooperated sufficiently on occasion, to the extent that elites considered their labor solidarity a threat until the dominating influence of settler colonialism overshadowed attempts to create class unity.

The Zionist colonization project brought Jewish workers to Palestine and marshaled them to the cause of taking over Arab territory. Arab workers, on the other hand, were employed to meet nascent Israeli society's labor needs, then displaced by immigrant workers recruited from Asia, Africa, and Europe. Israel, like other newly industrialized countries and like Europe and the U.S., has become a magnet for labor migration. People from poorer countries, impoverished by structural adjustment, rural displacement, and other globalizing forces come to such countries to work for very low pay.

Labor movements and anti-imperialist organizations increasingly face the problem of how to campaign against the "race to the bottom" dynamic—a problem not restricted to rich industrialized countries. In Chapter 13, Stephen Chiu and Alvin So recount the "boom and bust" nature of the rise of flexible production in Hong Kong. Workers initially reaped the benefits of flexible work arrangements, and many women held jobs with small and medium-sized manufacturers. In what workers called the golden years of the late 1970s, pay and benefits were liberal and businesses vigorously competed for workers despite lack of strong union organizing and strong state–business links. However, rapid growth of export-oriented manufacturing led to labor shortages; by the mid-1990s, economic restructuring shifted manufacturing facilities to nearby provinces in the People's Republic of China (PRC). After the formal handover of the colony to China in 1997, economic situation rapidly deteriorated for most working people, with particularly devastating impacts on women workers who were reduced to the status of itinerant casual workers.

Undocumented immigrants from Southeast Asia flooded in to fill low-wage domestic and service-sector jobs. Chiu and So argue that the vitality of the labor movement may shift to Thai, Nepalese, and Filipina women service workers who are mobilizing to protest the free-market policies that undermined the positions of all workers in Hong Kong. Massive demonstrations against the neo-liberal policies of the PRC-appointed Hong Kong government spark hopes of a new labor insurgency, but signs also indicate that worker frustrations may be displaced by conflicts within the working classes. Immigrant and gender issues are the most divisive, producing chauvinistic responses, particularly from the old-line male-dominated labor movement. Bridging the gender divides and schisms between native and new immigrant labor is crucial to successful challenges to global neo-liberalism.

Immigrant-worker activism has also brought a resurgence of energy to the labor movements in the U.S. and Canada. The Justice for Janitors' actions, the homecare workers' massive union victory, the hotel workers' innovative strategies, the Immigrant Workers' Freedom Ride, and the emergence of cross-ethnic coalitions offer visions of a re-invigorated labor movement (Milkman, 2000; Wong 2001). Many immigrants are in the informal sector or are governed by complex webs of contractors and employers; their struggles are unconventional and their triumphs may be short lived.

Workers in the informal sector in many parts of the Third World are using creative means to improve their status. Learning more about how female construction workers in India, for example, are challenging gender hierarchies while engaging in a common struggle with their male counterparts for transformation of exploitative conditions can be useful for imagining new ways of struggle (Ramakrishnan, 1996). Chang's Chapter 14 looks at the way racism, structural adjustment, and privatization of health care support the continued exploitation of Filipina caregivers in the U.S. and Canada and the forms by which nurses and domestic workers are resisting. In addition to documenting the insidious exploitation of these migrant women in North American care work and exposing the complicity of state policies in both countries, Chang highlights a participatory action project for Filipina nurses in Canada.

Chang also discusses the work of an interethnic coalition of Domestic Workers United and Andolan, a South Asian group that is pushing for legislation and organizing demonstrations in New York City. This group organizes to help domestic workers overcome their isolation and fight the abuse and exploitation they regularly encounter by raising public awareness of their plight, offering social support, and putting political pressure on city government to pass ordinances to regulate employer conduct.

The main labor organizations in the U.S. and Canada recently committed resources and energy to organizing immigrants and communities of color, and they have made other progressive moves such as creating constituency groups for major ethnic groups and for gays and lesbians (Pride at Work). Yet, the history of organized labor, particularly in the U.S., makes it difficult for the movement to change from the old "bread and butter unionism" linked to unwavering support for the Democratic party and acceptance of the American myth of a social contract between labor and business that creates equal treatment for all. This means that U.S. workers uncritically internalized chauvinistic support for inequality on many fronts, including gender and racial privilege and support of imperialism wars.

Bill Fletcher's Chapter 15 explores this history and what must be done by the working class movement in the U.S. to embrace an anti-imperialist, antiracist ideology and participate in a true international labor solidarity movement. He argues that left leadership must develop and convince workers to organize on the principle that it is in their material interest to fight for a democratic U.S. foreign policy, for massive social and economic transformations, including reparations for slavery, assistance to the Global AIDS Fund, and global wealth redistribution. He also contends that an anti-imperialist movement must disengage strategies for security from military ones that create states of permanent war and fear. Additionally, the billions spent on military domination were diverted from resolving domestic social and economic issues, and the results were shut-downs of hospitals and schools. Protesters in Okinawa and East Asia already point the way toward this vision, holding international delegations, art festivals, and using popular and institutional methods to spread counter-hegemonic ideas about what real security means (Fukomura and Matsuoka, 2002).

Certainly, opponents of neo-liberalism have reason to rebel. The so-called industrialization of the Third World has not led to genuine national development. If anything, the establishment of foreign-owned assembly plants is nothing more than a reflection of a country's cheap wages and does nothing to stimulate local economic growth and dynamism. Under present conditions, the underdeveloped world receives only assembly plants and increased poverty.

Mexico and the Philippines are prime examples of massive construction of export factories that employ millions. The factories are ringed by appalling shantytowns and squatter settlements that often lack basic services. In Mexico, for example, the 3000 or so maquiladoras are the nation's largest employers of labor, numbering over a million, for the production of goods consumed in the U.S.; however, the workers, the majority of them women, are guaranteed poverty and places among the 60% of the Mexican population that lives below the poverty line by Mexico's standards (McConnell, 1991; Kraul, 2000; Warnock, 2001).

The record is replete with widespread opposition to neo-liberal free-trade policies—the imperialism of the late 20th century that drives the politics of the 21st Century. Workers have had to develop new strategies and organizations such as more use of direct-action tactics. Chapter 4 by James Petras discusses the changing locus of organizing from the workplace to the neighborhood in Latin America and growing movements in the countryside to protest U.S. imperialism. The widening gap between rich and poor countries portends increasing discontent, protest, and rebellion.[1] Internal contradictions and rivalry among the imperial nations are accompanied by threats from below. Fractures among the imperial countries dominate the globalization agenda from Seattle to Doha to the recent meeting in Cancun.

Trade relations between the European Union (EU) and the U.S., often in the form of charges and counter-charges of unfair trade policies, are marked on both sides by protectionist tariffs trumping lowered trade barriers. Simmering tensions in the WTO underscored in the confrontation at the United Nations between "Old Europe" and the "coalition of the willing" over the Iraq invasion and occupation reveal increasing open hostility among traditional allies. It comes as no surprise that the economic reconstruction program designed by the Bush administration for Iraq is nothing more than a repeat of classic global imperialist schemes of the past; in fact, officials have spoken of a free-trade agreement with Iraq.[2] In doing so, the EU, Russia, and China are effectively kept at bay and out of their once-busy trading relationships with Iraq.[3]

Imperial hostility, however, is often at its strongest in controlling lucrative Third World markets and free-trade agreements serve that purpose. The Free Trade Agreement of the Americas, for example, championed by the current Bush administration (and earlier by the Clinton administration), has little to do with trade and more to do with keeping the door open to finance capital, the utilization of cheap labor, and export of subsidized agricultural goods from the U.S. Meanwhile, foreign competitors are kept out of the huge U.S. market under rules of origin at the heart of free-trade agreements that prevent competitive assembly-plant development. In Chapter 16, Victor Quintana documents the impoverishment of Mexican peasants in the name of development and the displacement of millions of rural people.

Rural Mexico provided the basis for Mexico's rapid economic growth, writes Quintana, until government policies undermined prices of agricultural products and reduced agricultural subsidies that were then further diminished by NAFTA in the name of free trade.[4] The same economic measures that promote poverty also propel internal and international migrations. Nonetheless, while macroeconomic structures and policies drive this mass uprooting, the peasantry is not passive in the face of exploitation and poverty. Quintana's chapter captures movements such as *El Campo no Aguanta Mas* (the countryside cannot take it any more), *El Barzón* (representing indebted peasants), the *Confederacion Nacional Campesina*, and the *Consejo Agrario Permanente*. These organizations mobilized in response to the policies that continue to impoverish the peasantry and drive their migration to Mexican cities and to the U.S. They are examples of the ways in which rural communities and indigenous people are forging effective movements against imperialism.

Over the long term, imperialism is unsustainable. In the face of greater competition by the imperial nations for profitable ventures and cheap labor, the Third World will be eventually drained of its resources and the neo-liberal adversaries will be forced to turn against each other and inward to plunder rival nations and peoples as well as their own. Inevitably, the cost of empire weighs increasingly upon workers far beyond the Third World to include inhabitants of the imperial nations. If history teaches any lesson, it is that as living and working conditions for people around the world worsen, discontent and oppositional politics will advance proportionately. Ultimately, labor and all those opposed to imperial domination will shape the politics and societies of the coming century.

Bibliography

Arrighi, G., "Globalization, State Sovereignty, and the 'Endless' Accumulation of Capital," In Smith, D.A., D.J. Solinger, and S.C. Topik, Eds., *States and Sovereignty in the Global Economy*, Routledge, London, 1999, p. 53.

Block, F., "The Ruling Class Does Not Rule: Notes on a Marxist Theory of the State," *Socialist Revolution* 33: 6, 1977.

Boot, M., "The Case for the American Empire," *Weekly Standard*, October 15, 2001.

Browning, L., "U.S. Income Gap Widening, Study Says," *New York Times*, September 25, 2003.

Cox, R., "A Perspective on Globalization," In Mittelman, J., Ed., *Globalization: Critical Reflections*, Lynne Rienner Publishers, Boulder, CO, 1996, p. 21.

Eakins, E., "It Takes an Empire, Say Several U.S. thinkers," *New York Times*, April 2, 2003.

Escobar, A., *Encountering Development: The Making and Unmaking of the Third World*, Princeton University Press, Princeton, NJ, 1995.

Finnegan, W., "The Economics of Empire: Notes on the Washington Consensus," *Harper's Magazine*, May 2003.

Friedman, D., "White Collar Blues," *Los Angeles Times*, August 3, 2003.

Fukomura, Y. and M. Matsuoka, "Redefining Security: Okinawa Women's Resistance to U.S. Militarism," In Naples, N. and M. Desai, Eds., *Women's Activism and Globalization: Linking Local Struggles and Transnational Politics*, Routledge, New York, 2002, p. 239.

Gosselin, P.O., "Middle, Lower Classes Feel Pinch," *Los Angeles Times*, September 23, 2003.

Johnston, D.C., "Wealthiest See Share of All U.S. Income Grow," *Orange County Register*, June 26, 2003.

Kaplan, A., "'Left Alone With America': The Absence of Empire in the Study of American Culture," in Amy Kaplan and Donald Pease, Eds., Cultures of United States Imperialism, Durham, NC: Duke University Press, 1993.

Kaplan, R.D., "Supremacy by Stealth: Ten Rules for Managing the World," *Atlantic Monthly*, July–August 2003.

Kempadoo, K. and J. Doezema, Eds., *Global Sex Workers: Rights, Resistance, and Redefinition*, Routledge, New York, 1998.

Kraul, C., "Growing Troubles in Mexico," *Los Angeles Times*, January 17, 2000.

Gill, S., "Globalization, Democratization, and the Politics of Indifference," In Mittelman, J., Ed., *Globalization: Critical Reflections*, Lynne Reinner Publishers, Boulder, CO, 1996, p. 205.

Hardt, M. and A. Negri, *Empire*, Harvard University Press, Cambridge, MA, 2000.

Krauthammer, C., "Who Needs Gold Medals," *Washington Post*, February 20, 2002.

Lenin, V., *Imperialism: The Highest Stage of Capitalism*, Moscow Foreign Language Press, 1970.

McConnell, P., "Maquilas Offer Work But Not Prosperity," *Los Angeles Times*, June 17, 1991.

Marx, K. and F. Engels, *The Communist Manifesto*, McLellen, D., Ed., Oxford University Press, New York, 1998.

Milkman, R., *Organizing Immigrants: The Challenges for Unions in Contemporary California*, ILR Press, Ithaca, NY, 2000.

Mishel, L., J. Bernstein, and J. Schmidt, *State of Working America: 2000–2001*, ILR Press, Ithaca, NY, 2001, p. 169.

Mittelman, J.H., *Globalization: Critical Reflections*, Lynne Reinner Publishers, Boulder, CO, 1996.

Moore, S.W., *The Critique of Capitalist Democracy: An Introduction to the Theory of the State in Marx, Engels, and Lenin*, A. Kelley, New York, 1979.

Ramakrishnan, G., "A Struggle Within A Struggle: The Unionization of Women in the Informal Sector in Tamil Nadu," In Carr, M., M. Chen, and R. Jhabyala, Eds., *Speaking Out: Women's Economic Empowerment in South Asia*, IT Publications, London, 1996, p. 167.

Rovella, D., "Three in Charge Not Charged," *Orange County Register*, August 14, 2003.

Scott, R.E., "NAFTA's Hidden Costs," Economic Policy Institute, Washington, D.C., 2001.

Shulman, B., "Four Myths, Thirty Million Potential Voters," *Alameda Times–Star*, August 24, 2003.

Skelton, G., "Squeeze on Business Puts Strain on State's Declining Middle Class," *Los Angeles Times*, April 14, 2003.

Smith, D.A., *Third World Cities in Global Perspective*, Westview, Boulder, CO, 1996.

Smith, DA., D.J. Solinger, and S.C. Topik, *States and Sovereignty in the Global Economy*, Routledge, New York, 1999.

Soros, G., "The Capitalist Threat," *The Atlantic Monthly*, 279: 45, 1997.

U.S. Census Bureau, http://www.census.gov/hhes/www/poverty.html. 2000.

Wade, R. and F. Veneroso, "The Gathering World Slump and the Battle over Capital Controls," *New Left Review*, 231: 13, 1998.

Warnock, J.W., "Who Benefits from the Free Trade Agreement," *Regina Leader Post*, April 18, 2001.

Wong, K., *Voices for Justice, Asian Pacific American Organizers and the New Labor Movement*, Center for Labor Research, University of California, Los Angeles, 2001.

---

[1] *1999 Human Development Report*, United Nations Development Programme. See also Ramonet, I., "The Politics of Hunger," *Le Monde Diplomatique*, November 1998.

[2] Andrews, E.L., "Import Invaders Besiege Iraqi Businesses," *New York Times*, June 1, 2003. Andrews noted that Iraq "suddenly faces the full fury of globalization and international competition," and that U.S. officials "speak grandly about a free-trade agreement between Iraq and the United States."

[3] See Sanders, L., "Reaping the Spoils of War: Ousting Saddam Could Put U.S. Oil Giants in 'Driver's Seat,'" CBS.MarketWatch.com, January 31, 2003; Crutsinger, M., "Billions Pledged to Rebuild Iraq," *Orange County Register*, April 11, 2003. Crutsinger writes, "IMF and World Bank first plan to study an economy buried for decades," intending to "help provide billions of dollars to rebuild Iraq."

[4] Arturo Escobar (1995) and others note that sustainable development is a term usurped by international financial institutions; the goal of ecologically informed economies that benefit indigenous and rural people remains an integral demand of an anti-imperialist movement.

I
Empire: Global Capitalism and Domination

1

New Times and New Identities: Solidarities of Sameness and Dynamics of Difference

GEORGE LIPSITZ

We live in a time of tremendous transformation and change. New patterns and practices permeate virtually every aspect of production and politics, technology and trade, communication and consumption. New social institutions and new social relations radically reconfigure economic activities, changing the scale and scope of production, the significance of time and place, and the salience of longstanding social identities. Containerization in shipping, computer-generated automation, outsourcing of production, Internet commerce, fiberoptic telecommunications, and satellite technologies seem to have terminated the isomorphism (the congruence or one-to-one relationship) between culture and place. Traditional social movement strategies to secure concessions from capital seem confounded by these new realities. It seems more and more difficult to "trap" capital in any one place long enough to regulate its practices or tax its profits, much less bargain collectively with it on an equal footing. In the process of losing dominion over place, ordinary workers, consumers, and citizens seem to lose the leverage they need to exert influence on the key decisions that affect their lives.

The new realities of our time have enacted a fundamental rupture in the relationships linking place, politics, and culture. For example, one of the most important container ports on the west coast today is not actually on the west coast at all. It sits 4400 feet above sea level in the high desert country of northern Nevada, some 233 miles from the Pacific Ocean. No ocean-going ships ever dock in the "port" of Sparks and Reno, but cargo from ocean-going ships is unloaded, stored, assembled, and dispatched from there every day. Shoreside cranes in Tacoma, Oakland, San Pedro, and other west-coast ports unload huge containers from ships and place them on road and rail conveyances that take them to distribution centers inland.

The container revolution of the 1950s made it possible for high desert railroad switching centers like Sparks to become ocean ports. The use of automated cranes and interchangeable containers by the shipping industry created a totally integrated freight transport system built upon transfers from ships to trucks and trains. Metal boxes 40 feet long, 8 feet high, and 8 feet wide quickly became the universal mechanisms for cargo shipments. The interchangeability and flexibility that they facilitated bolstered the profits of manufacturers and shipping lines alike, but they also transformed dramatically the practices and processes of production, distribution, and consumption for people all over the globe.

Before the advent of containerization, longshore workers assembled at places like Pier 39 in San Francisco to unload bulk products like coffee. Today, longshore workers no longer gather at Pier 39. The pier has been turned into a "festival mall," a renovated historic site with a splendid view of the San Francisco harbor. Pier 39 houses 11 full-service restaurants with ocean views and hosts more than 100 specialty stores that sell products to tourists and upscale consumers. Workers no longer handle bulk containers of coffee at the pier, but crowds of tourists and downtown office workers stream to coffeehouses there every day to purchase elaborate concoctions at premium prices.

The transformation of a high desert city into a busy ocean port and the evolution of a coffee loading dock into a coffeehouse provide vivid examples of the ways in which new technologies, business practices, and social relations are transforming the spaces we inhabit as workers and consumers. The same technologies and business practices that produce new sites for the production and distribution of products also produce new physical spaces devoted to consumption. Festival malls like Pier 39 turn abandoned factories, train stations, and waterfronts into upscale shopping centers. Gigantic super stores rely on new technologies to bring standardized low-cost products to previously under-served and isolated rural locations. Digital capitalists develop new forms of marketing and new points of sale for traditional products on the Internet while at the same time generating needs for completely new products like Internet modems, servers, and security systems.

The new spatial and social relations we encounter through new forms of production and consumption help mold us into new kinds of social subjects. Disturbances in work practices and consumption patterns change our relationships to other people, to public and private space. Containerization is an automated technology primarily designed to give management control over production and productivity in the longshore industry. Yet once it was implemented on a large scale, it became clear that containerization also entailed a larger cultural logic about the integration and interlocking of products, consumers, and communities.

A product of the era of Fordist mass production, containerization has become the core concept guiding commodity production and distribution in the present post industrial post-Fordist era. The linkage of production to modular forms of distribution achieved during the late industrial period provides the basic model for the full integration of consumption through linked modular units. In the emerging era of digital capitalism, integrated computer networks make it possible to rationalize and maximize the profitability of consumption in much the same way that containerization transformed the social relations of production, distribution, and reception in the previous era. Sometimes it seems as if production and consumption have changed places—and that the real work of society is consuming rather than producing.

The leverage lost by labor with the implementation of flexible accumulation and "on time" production has been disastrous for society. Deprived of the power to paralyze production, unable to trap capital long enough to bargain with it successfully, and no longer able to rely on commitments to locality and nation that capital assumed in the era when fixed investments in plant and equipment gave it a stake in social peace, the labor movement has been unable to stop declines in real wages, the evisceration of the welfare state, and the disintegration of the social fabric that flows from pervasive inequality and injustice.

The commercial culture of containerization and digital capitalism follows the well-worn pattern produced in previous periods of capitalist growth and technological transformation. Confronted with declining rates of profit and resistance at the point of production by workers, business leaders seek access to new markets and new ways of reducing labor costs. They pressure governments to develop new technologies to be appropriated for private purposes. Containerization and digital capitalism enable entrepreneurs to transcend political, cultural, and commercial boundaries, secure new markets, create new points of sale, turn previously noncommercial social activities into for-profit transactions, and force others to pay the social costs and suffer the social consequences of the disruptions caused by the new economy.[1]

New financial network technologies produce capital flows with sufficient speed and volume to overwhelm the monetary policy mechanisms of even the most powerful nation states.[2] As a result, a few dozen corporations hold approximately one third of private sector assets in the world. Corporations now surpass entire countries in riches and power. Wal-Mart is wealthier than Greece; the assets of Philip Morris exceed the gross national product of Chile. The Chrysler Corporation's holdings equal the economy of Pakistan, and the Hungarian economy is the same size as the holdings of Nestle.[3] The money that Domino's derives from the sale of pizzas every year exceeds the annual collective expenditures of the governments of Senegal, Uganda, Bolivia, and Iceland.[4] Around the globe, more than 30,000 children under 5 years of age die every day from starvation or completely curable diseases—some 10 million a year or a child every 3 seconds.[5] The percentage of global income earned by the poorest fifth of the world's population has been cut in half since 1960. The poorest fifth accesses less than 1% of the world's wealth whereas the richest fifth controls more than 85%.[6] In Mexico, the 24 wealthiest families have more money than the 24 million poorest Mexicans.[7]

Inequalities within and across national boundaries compel workers to migrate from low-wage to high-wage countries. The subsistence wage for full-time workers in the U.S. in 1980 was four times the wage that prevailed in the Dominican Republic. It grew to six times the Dominican wage by 1987 and thirteen times higher by 1991.[8] More than 125 million people live outside their countries of birth or citizenship, and another 2 million to 4 million join their ranks every year.[9] Remittances sent home by overseas workers have become crucial components of the national economies of many countries in Asia, Africa, and Latin America. The exploitation and indignities suffered by immigrant low-wage workers in Europe and North America subsidize the standards of living enjoyed by educated urban professionals on those continents by providing them with low-cost goods and personal services. The remittances immigrant workers send home then subsidize the interests of transnational corporations by softening the impact of the devastation engendered by the low wages and low taxes that those firms enjoy in Asia, Africa, and Latin America.

Ten percent of the population of the Dominican Republic lives in the U.S. and an equal number of Dominicans live in Europe. Eighty percent of the merchant seamen in the world are Filipinos. New York City is the largest Caribbean city, even though it is not located on the Caribbean. Its immigrant population from that region exceeds the combined populations of Kingston, San Juan, and Port of Spain.[10] Forty-five percent of Los Angeles County residents speak a language other than English at home, and students who attend classes in the Los Angeles Unified School District include native speakers of more than 120 different languages and dialects.[11] Remittances sent home by overseas workers contribute more to the economies of the Dominican Republic and the Philippines than any single other export item.

Although some people find themselves forced to move, others discover that their immobility creates profit-making opportunities for transnational corporations. Because the Dominican Republic became the chief apparel-exporting nation in the Caribbean by 1990, real hourly wages fell to only 62.3% of what they had been in 1984.[12] Sixty percent of the 4.4 billion people in the poorest countries in Africa, Asia, and Latin America lack basic sanitation facilities. One billion do not have access to safe and uncontaminated water and 828 million people throughout the world are chronically undernourished. Nearly a third of them will die before their fortieth birthdays[13] Meanwhile, African countries spend four times as much on debt payments to financial institutions in Europe and North America than they spend on the health and education needs of Africans.[14]

The rising pattern of inequality in the world affects rich nations as well as poor nations. Since 1980, the wealthiest fifth of the U.S. population has enjoyed a 21% growth in its income whereas those in the poorest three fifths have seen their wages, working conditions, and living standards stagnate or fall.[15] Nearly 85% of the $3 trillion increase in stock market valuation between 1989 and

1997 went to the richest 10% of U.S. families.[16] Nearly half of the nation's income now goes to the wealthiest fifth of households.[17] The wealthiest 10% of families in the U.S. own 94% of the business assets, 90% of the bonds, 89% of the corporate stock, and 78% of the nation's real estate.[18] U.S. consumers enjoy lower prices because of the exploitation of workers in the rest of the world.

The export of production to low-wage countries overseas has a decided impact on wages and working conditions in the U.S. as well. Structural adjustment policies imposed on people in Asia, Africa, and Latin America by the International Monetary Fund and the World Bank exacerbate inequalities on those continents and provoke people to migrate to higher-wage countries like the U.S. Asian American women, many of them recent immigrants, make up more than 50% of the entire labor force in the U.S. textile and apparel industries. They work for low wages in largely unregulated small shops and contract respiratory illnesses at high rates because of repeated exposure to fiber particles, dyes, formaldehydes, and arsenic. On the assembly lines in California's Silicon Valley, the production of high-tech computers depends on the low-wage labor of Latin and Asian American workers. Forty-three percent of these workers are Asian Americans. Asian and Latina women who work on high-tech production lines experience illness approximately three times as often as workers in general manufacturing—illnesses that often entail damage to reproductive and central nervous systems.[19]

Economic, political, technological, and social changes extend beyond the conditions and rewards of work. They bring us a new sense of time as well. Corporate researchers study ways to make perfectly serviceable old products obsolete while imbuing new ones with the purely symbolic value that comes from fashion and novelty. Thirty percent of the Toshiba products sold in 1987 had been introduced within the previous 3 years. Managers at the Gillette Corporation seek to secure 40% of sales from products less than 5 years old. Manufacturers introduced 17,572 new products to consumers in 1993.[20]

These new times require new strategies, new tactics, new ideas, and identities, although our old identities have not disappeared. We still speak about race, class, gender, nation, and sexuality, but in different ways. Identities never exist in isolation; they are always intersectional, relational, and mutually constitutive. New times do not so much create new identities as much as they give new accents to old intersections, resulting in new associations, affinities, and equations of power. In our age of containerization and flexible accumulation, new social movements have emerged to reposition old identity categories. Class becomes resignified away from work sites and outside the parameters of labor–management agreements, and gender takes on new import outside the family, away from the job, and outside the purview of mass media. Purely place-based local and national forms of labor solidarity no longer suffice as ways to secure significant concessions from capital. Anticolonialist struggles for national liberation created new nations, but none of them can resist the imperatives of the World Bank, the International Monetary Fund, or the World Trade Organization in isolation. Race-based movements for social justice continue to serve as sites of organic solidarity, yet the global economy's ability to create seemingly endless new forms of difference and differentiation between, among, and within identity groups requires a more fluid and flexible formulation of identity as a basis for oppositional activity and struggle.

Nothing from the past ever disappears completely; the present is ghosted, shadowed, and shaped by the accumulated legacies of past events, ideas, and actions. However, nothing from the past stays the same. The many parts of the past that permeate the present become reaccented, rearticulated, and reworked every day. Within social movements, solidarities still stem from unified subjectivities, from the consensual illusions of sameness that social movements nurture and sustain. Yet any invocation of sameness immediately exposes the dynamics of difference. There is never one way to be a worker or a woman, a raced subject or a citizen, a consumer or community member. Moreover, the very sense of sameness that succeeds in building organic solidarity can cut off aggrieved groups from one another, occlude the systemic origins of their problems, and pit them against one another by connecting inclusion for some to exclusion of others. New social movements today navigate the dialectical tensions between the solidarities of sameness and the dynamics of difference by fashioning collective identities that are recombinant and reticulated, flexible and fluid.

New meanings of race that might form the basis for a new social warrant are emerging from social movement struggles that do not at first glance seem to be about race at all. Campaigns for affordable dwellings or against environmental pollution, for improvements in the lives of immigrants, or for saving lives threatened by AIDS find themselves forced to confront the racial dimensions of these problems and the racial divisions within the movements' own ranks. Mobilizations against police brutality, against violence against women, against the growth of prison systems, and against the consequences of educational reforms such as high stakes testing and vouchers reflect the particularly damaging effects of those policies on communities of color. Because those effects are uneven and nonequivocal, they cannot be confronted from any one static or fixed racial subjectivity or standpoint.

Contemporary movements for environmental justice in the U.S. represent one site where a battle is being waged for a new social warrant and for rethinking of the meaning of race. Environmental injuries in the U.S. are almost always racial injuries as well because they exert a disproportionate impact on communities of color. As a result, race-based movements for social justice have emerged as some of the most militant and active participants in the fight against environmental pollution.[21]

Although mainstream environmental advocacy groups still number few people of color among their members and although they acknowledge only infrequently the disparate racial effects of environmental degradation on communities of color, grassroots activists from aggrieved populations have played important roles in exposing and contesting public and private policies that poison air, water, and food, locate toxic waste dumps near residential populations, and permeate workplaces with pollutants that damage the lives and well-being of workers. They do so as a matter of self-defense, out of the recognition that race has both spatial and environmental dimensions. They see that any universal struggle to save the environment and support sustainable development must acknowledge the particular problem that environmental racism poses for working class communities of color.

At the same time, environmental justice activists recognize that the solutions to the particular problems confronting people of color must entail systemic changes in relations among different groups of humans and between humans and the environment. One important part of this struggle is to recontextualize the meaning of race, to give it an expressly political identity through the organizational learning that accompanies collective mobilization. These movements attempt to do for race what the 1934 west-coast waterfront strike did for class, i.e., win a new social warrant that transforms social relations and social identities. They recognize the importance of embodied identities without succumbing to essentialist exclusions; they build affiliations, affinities, and alliances that bring together people with different embodied identities into a unified struggle against racism without losing sight of the unique optics and epistemologies that emerge from embodied experience. Perhaps most important, by devising unexpected links of racism, environmental destruction, and capitalism, they reveal the structures, practices, and institutions behind identities often understood as purely cultural.

Struggles for clean air and water, health, housing, transportation, and education generally aim to win concrete material improvements in people's lives at the expense of entrenched and powerful state institutions and private corporations. They fight for better health and health care; cleaner and safer air, water, and food; and efficient and nonpolluting forms of public transportation; but these pragmatic, material, and local goals are parts of a bigger process. As organizations led by people of color and calling attention to the expressly racialized dimensions of environmental pollution, they are overtly and emphatically antiracist. As mass movements insisting on popular participation in decisions about planning, production, and profits, they are doggedly democratic. As popular mobilizations rooted in open challenges to decisions made by trained technical experts, they resist the social division of labor and power that deploys specialized knowledge as a form of exclusionary power.

New social movements produce communities of struggle that contest the terms of existing social identities. As Michel Foucault argues in his unconventional analysis of new social movements, the question of "Who are we?" does not have to be an atomized inquiry into identity isolated from considerations of social structure, power, and history. He explains how self-activity intrinsic to the assertion of new identities often challenges the abstract identities imposed on people by economic, political, cultural, and scientific institutions. "They are an opposition to the effects of power," Foucault writes, "which are linked with knowledge, competence, and qualification: struggles against the privileges of knowledge. But they are also an opposition against secrecy, deformation, and mystifying representations imposed on people."[22]

These movements help unite members within and across different aggrieved racial groups by focusing attention on some of the concrete ways in which race takes on significance in daily life—residential segregation, neighborhood exposure to pollutants, and occupational safety hazards. The movement goes beyond discourses of exclusion rooted in liberal individualism and challenging isolated acts of discrimination aimed at individuals to expose the collective practices and patterns that produce inequality and that keep whole collectivities subordinate to others. In this way, the environmental justice movement switches attention away from minority victimization and toward white privilege, revealing members of aggrieved minority groups to be not so much disadvantaged as taken advantage of by white supremacy.

The Labor Community Strategy Center (LCSC) in Los Angeles encourages the cultivation of fluid, flexible, multiple, and shifting identities. It presents a class-based analysis of social inequalities but does not organize at the point of production. It opposes imperialism, militarism, and neo-liberalism all over the world but does so from a distinctly local perspective. It is an expressly antiracist organization but does not admit or organize members on the basis of their individual embodied identities. It makes demands on the state but not from the standpoint of citizenship. It fights for clean air but not from a conservationist perspective. Perhaps most important, the LCSC involves its diverse membership in deliberative talk, face-to-face decision making, and direct action protests that enact the social relations and social processes that they envision.

The LCSC combines grass roots organization and mobilization with farsighted proposals for sustainable development. It specializes in campaigns that bring together workers, environmentalists, and members of aggrieved racialized communities to pursue goals that advance all their interests. In this way it anticipates and precludes the usual divide-and-conquer strategy used by those in power by telling the groups that they can make gains only at the expense of each other.

The center started as an extra-union rank-and-file caucus within the United Auto Workers' Union, organized to fight against the proposed (and eventually successful) shutdown of the General Motors plant in Van Nuys. With no point of production on which to focus, the group then concentrated on neighborhood-based anticorporate environmental justice campaigns against major polluters in heavily black and Latino sections of Los Angeles. After the rebellion of 1992, the center issued a comprehensive plan for rebuilding the city on the basis of socially responsible growth that would produce jobs for minority workers and protect the environment by emphasizing the production of safe and nonpolluting trains, automobiles, and buses.[23]

The neighborhood-based anticorporate environment of LCSC led to the formation of the Bus Riders' Union. Recognizing that the new economy of Los Angeles involved a great increase in service jobs and a decrease in industrial employment, the center reasoned that places where large masses of workers could be found were on buses. They might be traveling to many different jobs where they worked side by side with only a few others, but the cumulative total of janitors, maids, child care personnel, food service workers, clerks, secretaries, and day laborers riding the buses of Los Angeles on any given day was enormous. The center also noted that although inner-city bus riders provided the metropolitan transit system with its largest profits, they received the worst service—the oldest and most poorly maintained buses and worst-kept schedules. At the same time, although revenues from suburban train riders provided the district with constant deficits, suburban routes received the best vehicles and best services.

The center mobilized around these issues under the slogan "fight transit racism." Organizers maintained that inner-city bus riders received poor service because they were people of color or because they were white people who suffered from the neighborhood race effects of the poor services to minority communities. They argued that the fight against racism required lower bus fares, better services, and the adoption of nonpolluting vehicles. At the same time, they insisted that the city could not have cleaner air or better bus services unless it came to grips with the role of racism in legitimizing an unclean, unsafe, and inefficient transportation system.

The Bus Riders' Union struggled for lower fares, better service, and capital investment in "clean" compressed natural gas-fueled buses. They galvanized a mass constituency of low-income, transit-dependent workers (50% of whom were Latino, 25% black, 20% white, and 5% Asian). The center recognized that the segmentation of the labor market and the stratification of bus service in Los Angeles gave new meanings to race and racism, creating a multi-racial bus ridership with common grievances despite their racial, national, linguistic, and gender differences. The Bus Riders' Union claims 35,000 self-identified followers, 500 dues-paying members, and a core group of 85 extremely active member activists.[24]

Organizers for the Bus Riders' Union used the slow pace of the buses through Los Angeles to their advantage by turning the buses into moving seminars on transit racism and sites for reaching, convincing, and signing up new members. Their efforts drew a dynamic group of working class leaders whose dazzling multilingual and intercultural skills reflected the diversity of the community brought together through membership in the union. Through mass action and a civil rights suit in federal court, the bus union secured tremendous victories: a fare reduction that saved riders $25 million per year, a commitment to reduce crowding on inner-city bus routes by increasing service, and a pledge by city officials to purchase 233 compressed natural-gas buses immediately and exercise options for an additional 55 more—an expenditure of $89 million. The LCSC stressed that its victory meant more than better air and transportation; it entailed a transfer of wealth and resources from rich to poor, from middle-management suburban commuters to inner-city low-wage workers, and from subsidies for private auto dealers and suburban rail contractors to direct expenditures for safe, efficient, and ecologically sound services for office workers, janitors, teacher's aides, and other unskilled workers.[25]

Although members of every racial group participated in the Bus Riders' Union, the slogan of fighting transit racism and the politics behind it meant that more than identity was at stake. The union's victory showed that direct appeals to redress racial injuries can play a central role in community struggles while winning victories for a coalitional constituency. By presenting antiracism as a project involving fairness and better public services and by winning a victory that actually improved people's daily lives, the LCSC demonstrated how the organic solidarity that comes from race-based appeals need not inhibit the development of connecting ideologies required for transformative social change.

Perhaps most important, the LCSC enacts what it envisions. Pamphlets printed in English, Spanish, and Korean demonstrate a commitment to inclusiveness that is very conspicuous in a divided city like Los Angeles. When passengers on a bus see black and Anglo organizers who speak Spanish or Latino organizers who can speak Korean, the group makes a powerful statement about what life in Los Angeles could be. The organizers who emerged from the rank and file of the Bus Riders' Union may be low-wage workers performing menial tasks, people who are belittled and patronized at work; however, at union meetings, press conferences, city government hearings, and demonstrations, the things they have learned as workers, immigrants, and community members come into sharp relief as they design effective strategies in a shared struggle for resources, opportunities, and human dignity. The organizational learning that takes place in the course of struggle in an interethnic antiracist group like the Bus Riders' Union not only advances the present struggle, but also prepares participants for the future.

As protests against the World Trade Organization became focal points for grass roots challenges to neo-liberalism, the LCSC drew on the expertise of its multi-national membership to craft positions on global issues. The organization sent delegates to the World Congress against Racism in South Africa and embraced the demands made there by diasporic Africans for reckoning with slavery as a historical crime that requires contrition, repentance, and restitution before true reconciliation can occur. After September 11, 2001, the group engaged in intensive discussions about hate crimes at home and the costs of militarism around the world.

Bus Riders' Union members may look like dispossessed and desperate immigrants from the Third World to some, but the LCSC recognized that its members were also valuable "witnesses to empire" and veterans of trade union and anti-imperialist struggles around the world. At a time when all too many U.S. organizations and institutions across the political spectrum continue to view the world from narrow, parochial, and provincial national and (often) nationalist perspectives, the LCSC recognized that it was composed of people whose economic, social, and political survival depended on transnational networks rooted in understandings of globalism from below. LCSC members come from different countries and classes and represent diverse interests and identity groups. They do not shed their differences when they join the organization, but rather they make productive use of them to generate multiple epistemologies and ontologies rooted in complex and sometimes contradictory experiences, archives, and imaginaries. The LCSC provides a rare space for political discussions that are not shaped by the national chauvinism of an exclusive focus on the U.S.

For centuries, emancipatory projects have revolved around concepts like universality, equivalence, interchangeability, and equality. From this perspective, difference is a problem to be overcome. Yet capital does not do its work by making people more and more alike, as Marx predicted. Instead, contemporary capital exercises hegemony by creating endless new forms of difference, inequality, and incommensurability. The very system that produces so many differences and fragmentations confines us to a political language built on simple binary oppositions and appeals to interchangeability and equivalence as the only possible form of justice.

Confronted with systems of centralized power that generate seemingly endless streams of new forms of difference, social movements grounded in differential consciousness have the potential to produce a new democratic and egalitarian social warrant. This is a dangerous and difficult process in which it is sometimes difficult to distinguish symptoms of dominant power from critiques of it. Effective oppositional movements under these conditions can neither evade nor embrace ostensibly "essentialist" identities. They cannot confine themselves to purely local, national, or global terrains and must move strategically in and out of each level to produce new and perhaps unexpected affiliations, alliances, and identifications. The renegotiation of relations among individuals and groups must at some point also aspire to radical transformations in existing social structures and power relations.

Differential consciousness constitutes a crucial weapon in this struggle. Chela Sandoval identifies differential consciousness as a product of social movement struggles by contemporary women-of-color feminists. The differential mode in her formulation develops and mobilizes oppositional identities as tactical consensual illusions that entail oscillation among diverse subject positions. Instead of seeking one overarching universal ideology or identity, differential consciousness relies on multiple and competing perspectives and practices, epistemologies, and ontologies. Within this model, the sense of sameness that generates organic solidarity among workers performing the same job or among social subjects of the same racial identity gives way to a dynamics of difference, aimed at making the most of an available inventory of fluid, flexible, diverse, and dynamic subject positions.[26]

Since the successful strike in 1992 by undocumented immigrant drywall workers in southern California, low-wage immigrants in service jobs, small workshops, and even factories around the country have been fighting ferocious battles for recognition, dignity, freedom, liberty, and justice. Immigrant labor has lowered the costs of goods and services for consumers while allowing exploitative employers to violate minimum-wage laws, health and safety restrictions, and their obligations to pay social security and mandatory overtime. Wages in drywall work in Southern California went from $.09 per square foot to $0.45 per square foot when drywall work was performed almost exclusively by immigrants. In some cases, the workers did not even receive their wages. They were taunted by employers who confidently dared them to sue for nonpayment, knowing that many of them lacked documentation and risked deportation if they complained to authorities.

The drywall workers drew upon old and new forms of struggle from militant roving picket lines and mutual self-help to intervention by allies connected to the social justice agencies of the Catholic Church. As undocumented immigrants unaffiliated with any recognized union, the drywall workers were unable to obtain protection from the National Labor Relations Board and other U.S. government agencies. As expatriates, they could not secure aid from the Mexican government, either. Employers and the press harped on the workers' illegal status and portrayed them as greedy interlopers, not as hard workers who created sources of value and profit for citizen consumers and entrepreneurs.

When the balance of power, physical repression, and legal advantages of citizen employers over noncitizen workers threatened to defeat their movement, the drywall workers and their allies from the Catholic Church devised a new strategy—they asked employers to open their books and prove that they had obeyed the laws covering minimum wage, overtime, social security, and worker health and safety. Confronted with demands by "illegal aliens" that would expose construction firms as "illegals" in their own right, the firms settled with the workers and handed them a great victory.

For the past decade, immigrant workers in the U.S. have waged struggles similar to the drywall strike, struggles that require the creation of new identities and the forging of unexpected affiliations and alliances. When the largely Latino workforce at the Los Angeles New Otani Hotel sought union representation from their employer, the Japanese-owned Kajima Corporation, activists from the Asian American movement supported their efforts strongly. They recruited support in Korea from workers with long-standing grudges against the corporation for its role in benefiting from the coerced labor of Koreans during the Japanese occupation between 1910 and 1945. The prominence of Asian Americans and Koreans among the supporters of Latino workers prevented the New Otani strike from being seen as an anti-Asian battle and frustrated the assumptions of the Kajima Corporation that it could exploit Latino workers in the U.S. with impunity.

The activists even brought taiko drums to the picket lines in a brilliant move that enabled them to celebrate their ethnic heritages and traditions of struggle while supporting the class-based struggle for justice by Latino workers. The activists drew upon the organic solidarity that comes from a common ethnic background and also built links to allies in other communities in pursuit of common aims. Their struggle did not ignore race. It could not do so based on the racial polarization of labor and management, but it built solidarity on the bases of culture and commitments rather than on color. The New Otani campaign and many others like it encouraged participants to draw their identities from their politics instead of basing their politics on their identities. More recently, Korean Immigrant Worker Advocates in Los Angeles waged a successful organizing campaign in Korean-owned restaurants by building a workers' center that joins Latino dishwashers, janitors, and table clearers from the restaurants into a coalition with Korean and Korean American waiters and waitresses to wage a common fight against their immigrant employers.[27]

The new social movements of today echo the ideas that Aime Cesaire articulated in a letter to a friend in the 1940s. "I am not for a disembodied universalism," he wrote, but neither could he support a parochial particularism. Instead, Cesaire called for a universalism one that entailed the autonomy and co-existence of all and the supremacy of none. The new social movements rearticulating the meanings of race in our time fight ceaselessly for vitally needed services and real security for themselves and others. Their victories save lives and preserve hope for entire communities. In the long run, however, their greatest achievement may lie in their success in reconfiguring ideas about the solidarities of sameness and the dynamics of difference in such a way as to make Cesaire's utopian vision a practical reality.

Notes

1. Williams, R., *The Politics of Modernism: Against the New Conformists*, Verso, London, 1999, p. 122.
2. Schiller, D., *Digital Capitalism: Networking the Global Market System*, MIT Press, Cambridge, MA, 2000, p. 14.
3. Brodkin, K., Global Capitalism: "What's Race Got to Do with It?" *American Ethnologist*, 27, 237, 2000.
4. Barber, B., *Jihad vs. McWorld*, Ballantine, New York, 1995, p. 24.
5. Millen, J.V., A. Irwin, and J.Y. Kim, "Introduction: What is Growing? Who is Dying?" in *Dying for Growth: Global Inequality and the Health of the Poor*, Kim, J.Y. et al., Eds., Common Courage Press, Monroe, ME, 2000, p. 5.
6. Gershman, J. and A. Irwin, "Getting a Grip on the Global Economy," in *Dying for Growth: Global Inequality and the Health of the Poor*, Kim, J.Y. et al., Eds., Common Courage Press, Monroe, ME, 2000, p. 5.

7. Fuentes, C., *A New Time for Mexico*, University of California Press, Berkeley, 1997, p. xiii.
8. Pessar, P., *A Visa for a Dream: Dominicans in the United States*, Allyn & Bacon, Boston, 1995, p. 5.
9. Martin, P. and J. Widgren, "International Migration: A Global Challenge," *Population Bulletin*, 51, 2, 1996.
10. James, W. "Migration, Racism, and Identity: The Caribbean Experience in Britain," *New Left Review*, 193, 36, 1992.
11. Lopez, D.E., "Language: Diversity and Assimilation," in *Ethnic Los Angeles*, Waldinger, R. and M. Bozorgmehr, Eds., Russell Sage Foundation, New York, 1996, p. 42.
12. Safa, H.I., "Export Manufacturing, State Policy, and Women Workers in the Dominican Republic," in Bonacich, E. et al., Eds., *Global Production: The Apparel Industry in the Pacific Rim*, Temple University Press, Philadelphia, 1994, p. 225.
13. Schoepf, B.G., C. Schoepf, and J.V. Millen, "Theoretical Therapies, Remote Remedies: SAPs and the Political Ecology of Poverty and Health in Africa," in *Dying for Growth: Global Inequality and the Health of the Poor*, Kim, J.Y. et al., Eds., Common Courage Press, Monroe, ME, 2000, p. 120.
14. Gershman, J. and A. Irwin, "Getting a Grip on the Global Economy," in *Dying for Growth: Global Inequality and the Health of the Poor*, Kim, J.Y. et al., Eds., Common Courage Press, Monroe, ME, 2000, pp. 13, 14, 25.
15. Tabb, W.K., *The Amoral Elephant: Globalization and the Struggle for Social Justice in the Twenty-First Century*, Monthly Review Press, New York, 2001, p. 21.
16. Tabb, W.K., *The Amoral Elephant: Globalization and the Struggle for Social Justice in the Twenty-First Century*, Monthly Review Press, New York, 2001, p. 21.
17. Miller, J., "Economy Sets Records for Longevity and Inequality," *Dollars and Sense*, 229, 17, 18, 2000.
18. Plotkin, S. and W.E. Scheurman, *Private Interests, Public Spending: Balanced Budget Conservatism and the Fiscal Crisis*, South End Press, Boston, 1994, p. 29.
19. Sze, J., "Expanding Environmental Justice: Asian American Feminists' Contribution," in Shah, S., Ed., *Dragon Ladies: Asian American Feminists Breathe Fire*, South End Press, Boston, 1997, pp. 92.
20. Schiller, D., *Digital Capitalism: Networking the Global Market System*, MIT Press, Cambridge, MA, 2000, pp. 123, 124.
21. Bullard, R.L., *Confronting Environmental Racism: Voices from the Grassroots*, South End Press, Boston, 1993.
22. Foucault, M., "Afterword: The Subject and Power," in Dreyfus, H.L. and P. Rabinow, Eds., *Michel Foucault: Beyond Structuralism and Hermeneutics*, University of Chicago Press, Chicago, 1983, p. 212. For an analysis that blends the work of Foucault with the theories of Claus Offe, see Plotke, D., "What's So New about Social Movements?" in Lyman, S., Ed., *Social Movements: Critiques, Concepts, Case Studies*, New York University Press, New York, 1995, p. 113.
23. Mann, E., *L.A.'s Lethal Air: New Strategies for Policy, Organizing and Action*, Labor Community Strategy Center, Los Angeles, 1991.
24. Labor Community Strategy Center, Los Angeles, News Analysis, October 19, 1997, p. 1.
25. Rabin, J.L. and R. Simon, "Court Order Spurs Plan to Buy 278 Buses," *Los Angeles Times*, September 26, 1997.
26. Sandoval, C., *Methodology of the Oppressed*, University of Minnesota Press, Minneapolis, 2000, pp. 41, 144.
27. Cesaire, A. *Letter to Maurice Thorez* (Paris: Présence Africaine, 1957), pp. 14–15. Quoted in Kelley, R. "A Poetics of Anticolonialism" Introduction to Cesaire, A. *Discourse on Colonialism*, Monthly Review Press, New York, 2000 (pp. 25–26).

2

Labor, Race, and Empire: Transport Workers and Transnational Empires of Trade, Production, and Finance

THOMAS EHRLICH REIFER[1]

Introduction

The logistics sector—ports, railways, trucking, and warehousing—long a critical area for global capital and labor, is an increasingly strategic component of globalized flexible production and distribution networks. A key obstacle to the ability of labor to meet the structural challenges posed by the new flexibility is the racial segmentation of U.S. workers closely tied with the history of militarized U.S. state–corporate overseas expansion through formal and informal empires. Historically, radical class conflict in the U.S., including in transportation, was curbed through the crushing of militant union struggles. Simultaneously, elites sought to incorporate select groups of primarily white workers as junior partners in overseas expansion, both to minimize the radical potential of struggles for social reform at home and to secure access to lucrative resources and dispose of surplus goods and capital abroad (Davis, 1986; Mink, 1986; Forbath, 1991; Bergquist, 1996; Stepan-Norris and Zeitlin, 2003).

Today, low-wage workers of color who constitute an increasing number of largely unorganized employees in transportation and in labor as a whole may serve as a fertile social base for a new wave of unionism. The changing demographics of labor in the transportation sector and the U.S. and global economy as a whole may be creating structural opportunities for inter-racial alliances across lines of race and ethnicity critical to a labor upsurge, similar to conditions during the 1930s. Transportation networks are important here as they form a key nexus of transnational networks of states and corporations, with their empires of global trade and production crucial to working class formation and related forms of racial, ethnic, national, and gender identities (Saxton, 1971; Kanter, 1977; Rosswurm, 1992; Schneer, 1999, chap. 3; Nelson, 2001; Silver, 2003).

In recent decades, rising global trade and flexible production networks developing in tandem with the ascent of the Pacific Rim saw this region sweep past the North Atlantic as the principal U.S. trading partner—an epochal shift becoming increasingly obvious today (Davis, 1986, p. 251). In sharp contrast to the Fordist-based transatlantic economy where increases in military spending and wages stimulated aggregate demand, the transpacific one is based on huge inflows of foreign capital recycled into the U.S., which serves as a consumer of last resort (Wal-Mart is the single largest importer), as evidenced by massive U.S. trade and current account deficits (Davis, 1986, chap. 6; Davis and Sawhney, 2002; *Journal of Commerce*, April 29, 2002).[2]

The logistics sector of the Pacific Rim is an increasingly important strategic site for global capital and labor, linking up overseas production from China, Mexico, and other locations to the huge markets of Southern California, the Sunbelt, and the entire U.S. Changes in the structure of investment, production, distribution, and consumption in the Pacific Rim triangle of Mexico, China, and Southern California represent a microcosm of the changing landscape of U.S.-led neo-liberal globalization today.

Mexico and China have become leading recipients of foreign direct investment and major centers of global manufacturing via arm's length flexible contracting relationships (UNCTAD, 2002, chap. 5). Under the North American Free Trade Agreement, U.S. transnational firms use Mexico to counter growing Asian production. Now, with China's accession into the World Trade Organization, a new global pool of cheap sweatshop labor is promoting a worldwide race to the bottom, with capital from the U.S., Asia, and Europe flowing into China.

In 2002, the manufacturing powerhouses of Mexico and China were the second and third biggest suppliers of U.S. imports and the fourth and second biggest suppliers of U.S. *manufactured* imports, each exporting well over $100 billion annually into this market. Indeed, increasingly, Mexico and a host of other global investment and production centers are losing out to China.[3] Mexican exports are now growing at a slower pace than China's, yet wages are falling in both countries (Ross and Chan, 2002; U.S. Government Accounting Office, 2003, p. 26; Figure 2.1). Moreover, the recycling of China's financial surpluses to finance U.S. consumption is helping sustain the Chinese boom even after the end of the U.S. boom that came with the burst of the Wall Street bubble (*Wall Street Journal*, August 5, 2003, p. 15; *New York Times*, August 28, 2003, p. C6). Between 2000 and 2003, China doubled its holdings of U.S. Treasury securities to some $122 billion, second only to Japan's $429 billion. China now has the largest trade surplus with the U.S.—$44 billion—topping even that of Japan (*Wall Street Journal*, August 5, 2003, p. 15). This new empire of high finance is crucial to U.S. power in the global system and the current configuration of transnational empires of trade and production.

China and Mexico have strong links to Southern California, a port of entry—indeed, a gateway—to the U.S. market. Moreover, increasing inflows of immigrant

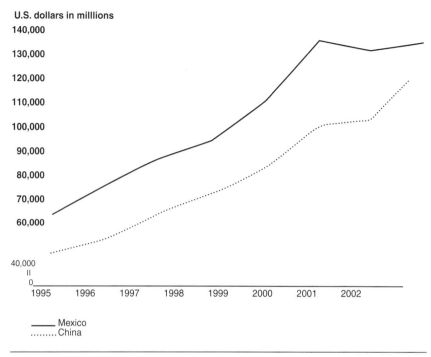

U.S. dollars in milllions

———— Mexico
········· China

Source: U.S. International Trade Commission; GAO, 2003

workers from Mexico and China into Southern California (not to mention investment flows from China) compete with and at times complement the import regime (Sassen, 1988a and b). A sizeable number of U.S. exports to these areas are inputs for goods that are reprocessed and returned to the U.S. (Kramer and Coral, 2003).

The labor forces from all three countries are thus increasingly intertwined, and developments within and between them will likely reverberate throughout global labor. Given the increasing centrality of logistics in the Pacific Rim triangle and the global economy, transborder organizing among workers here, despite serious obstacles, offers great potential. Although these low-wage workers provide global capital with great flexibility, global restructuring is forcing labor to look toward new alliances and strategies at home and abroad, even as older practices of nationalistic business unionism retain their traditional appeal (Arrighi, 1990; Silver and Arrighi, 2000; Bacon, 2004).

Producer Services: Transnational Empires of Trade, Production, and Finance and the New Landscape of Corporate Power

Much is made of sweatshops in the garment and other industries (Bonacich and Appelbaum, 2000) but few are addressing the dramatic changes in the landscape of transnational corporate power, in which retail firms with their massive logistics empires and flexible production networks hold increasing sway. These changes are embodied by the rise of giant multinational retailers such as Wal-Mart, the largest employer in 21 U.S. states, the U.S., and the world as a whole. Wal-Mart employs 1 of every 123 U.S. workers and is now the top firm in the Fortune 500 (*USA Today*, January 29, 2003; *Fortune Magazine*, March 3, 2003 and April 14, 2003).

In 2002, Wal-Mart accounted for 2.3% of the U.S. economy in a growth trajectory that will soon eclipse U.S. Steel's record 2.8% in 1917 (*Fortune Magazine*, March 3, 2003 and April 14, 2003). Given the centrality of logistics in the success of discount retailers such as Wal-Mart in global production and trade, it is no wonder that major cost-cutting initiatives have been implemented against labor in transportation. Deregulation, related offensives against workers, and the rationalization of production in logistics and transportation have substantially reduced overall unit costs for business at great cost to labor (Peoples, 1998; Belzer, 2000).

From 1981 to 2002, logistics and transportation costs fell from some 16.2% to 8.7% of GDP (Wall Street Journal, July 25, 2003, pp. A1, 16). From a record high of $1,003 billion in 2000, costs dropped by $93 billion in 2002 (Wilson and Delaney, 2003).

Logistics is, in fact, the invisible heart of the new geography of power in the global economy. Saskia Sassen (2001) underscores the importance of global cities as command, control, and communication centers for transnational empires of trade, production, and speculative high finance and highlights the rising importance of producer services. These "services are produced for organizations, whether private sector firms or governmental entities, rather than for final consumers" (Sassen, 2001, p. 91). Sassen (1988a and b; 2001) also maps the new class geography of salaried professionals and immigrant workers at the cores of global cities as part of the new global mobility of capital and labor; the emergence of postindustrial production sites; and the concomitant rise of producer services in finance, business law, and accounting.

The growth of specialized logistics firms in the transportation sector must be recognized as a critical aspect of this rise of producer services so integral to the burgeoning transnational empires of trade, production, and finance headquartered in global cities. A focus on these logistics firms and corporate discount retail firms such as Wal-Mart that specialize in what today is called supply chain management adds a previously unexplored and important new dimension to Sassen's work (Bowersox, Closs, and Stank, 1999; Bowersox, Closs, and Cooper, 2002; Armstrong & Associates, 2003).

The increased importance of logistics comes from connecting world supply and demand in the global market, the critical nexus of which is the Pacific Rim, as cheap commodities flow into the U.S. market, primarily through west-coast ports. With the rise of export-oriented industrialization and world trade promoted by U.S.-dominated institutions such as the World Bank,

International Monetary Funds, and transnational firms, labor and capital are confronted with new challenges and opportunities (Broad, 1988). Analysis of recent trends in the reorganization of global production and logistics (including transportation and warehousing) connecting China, the U.S. (especially Southern California), and Mexico paints a revealing picture.

Individually, the ports of Los Angeles and Long Beach are by far the largest entry points for goods entering the U.S., primarily from Asia. Together they constitute the third largest container port in the world, following only Singapore and Hong Kong. In the vast upsurge of imports into the U.S. that occurred in the 1970s, the predominance of U.S.-based multi-nationals, especially giant discount retailers, is evident (*Journal of Commerce*, April 29, 2002 and July 8, 2002). U.S. waterborne foreign trade transported via container ships in 2000 totalled more than 142 million metric tons, over 50% of which came from the Far East and Southeast Asia. Nearly 50% of all waterborne foreign trade enters the U.S. through west-coast ports while the percentage that comes from the Far East and Southeast Asia stands at nearly 80% (Mongelluzzo, 2002; U.S. Department of Transportation, 2002).

Accompanying these commodity flows into west-coast ports are the influx of goods via trucks from Mexico, particularly into California and Texas supplemented by railway shipments (Kramer and Coral, 2003). The contemporary dominance of the west coast, especially Southern California, as a node for the flow of Asian commodities into the U.S. makes workers in the logistics sector potential Achilles' heels of giant U.S. retail firms and the global empires of production and trade of which they are integral parts. Without continuous distribution of commodities to consumers, global production and trade would stop. Moreover, labor struggles of logistics groups link different industries and locales in the global economy and are thus strategic sites for global unionism and transborder labor organizing.

Transport Workers and Transnational Empires of Trade and Production

Efforts to spread trade unionism in transport and other sectors were crushed during the rise of informal and formal overseas empires of the U.S. that began in the late 19th century. The defeats created long-standing practices of business unionism—notably the top–down union strategies of class collaboration at home and support for U.S. militarized state–corporate expansion abroad—that remain structurally difficult for even the most progressive elements of the labor movement to break out of today.

The experiences of workers in the railroad industry were particularly critical. Railroad workers (a million strong by 1900) led the Great Rebellion of 1877 and Eugene V. Debs' Pullman Rebellion of 1894. Before mass production led to massive concentrations of labor, railway workers alone had the numbers and organic ability for national coordination (Davis, 1986, p. 30). The failure of whites to seize the opportunity to ally with their black brethren during Reconstruction and thereafter helped ensure the defeat of railroad workers in the Great Rebellion of 1877, the Pullman revolt of 1894, and other attempts to organize across lines of race, class, and gender by the Knights of Labor and the Wobblies (Du Bois, 1935; Arnesen, 2001, chap. 1). This greatly contributed to the formation of the American Federation of Labor (AFL) by old-stock immigrants whose bargaining power as skilled workers led them to form exclusivist male-dominated white racist craft unions and eschew social legislation (Mink, 1986; Forbath, 1991; Voss, 1993). This development ultimately sped the turn to overseas expansion by elites seeking to escape class struggles at home, including by incorporating conservative, white male–dominated business unions as junior partners in militarized state–corporate expansion abroad (Du Bois, 1935; Mink, 1986; Bergquist, 1996, chap. 2; Goldfield, 1997, chap. 4; Buhle, 1999; Arnesen, 2001, chap. 1).

A close connection then existed between the struggles for open shops at home and the open doors for U.S. state–corporate expansions abroad (Reifer, 2002, p. 6). The drive to impose Taylorism[4] and open shops through epic battles like Homestead in 1892, when Andrew Carnegie successfully destroyed the iron-and-steel workers' union, eliminated what Big Bill Haywood called the "manager's brain under the workman's cap" whereby craft workers threatened management control over production processes (Aitken, 1985; Montgomery, 1987; Krause, 1992; Misa, 1995). In the late 19th and early 20th centuries, the power of massive U.S. transnational firms that allowed them to crush union opposition and manipulate race, class, and gender divisions among workers were "both consequence and cause of the imperial condition," the dominance of the conservative U.S. labor bureaucracy, and corporate managerial strata thereafter "without doubt connected to the creation of empire" (Gordon, Edwards, and Reich, 1982; Bergquist, 1996; Gordon, 1996; Buhle, 1999, p. 15).

In this developing system of U.S. militarized state–corporate capitalism, there was a close connection between the transportation webs of U.S. transnational firms and the demands of military logistics underlying the expansion of the U.S. formal and informal empires. In World War I, Julius Rosenwald, the CEO of Sears, Roebuck, the largest U.S. retailer for most of the American Century (sales later represented 1 to 2% of the U.S. gross national product for almost 50 years after World War II) headed logistics supply operations for the War Industries Board. Rosenwald also helped found the Universal Military Training League as part of the corporate and upper class–led war preparedness movement. Participants and contributors included luminaries from numerous corporate firms such as Procter & Gamble, Standard Oil, the house of Morgan, and a veritable *Who's Who* of U.S. state–corporate power elites (Wood, 1913–1918; Chandler, 1977, p. 224 and 455; Chambers, 1987, p. 127).

AFL President Samuel Gompers (1917) joined the war preparedness group, the National Security League, composed of state–corporate power elites instrumental in the Open Shop drives at home and the pursuit of Open Door policies abroad. Gompers also joined the National War Labor Board, as the AFL became a junior partner in the war effort (Buhle, 1999, p. 73; Reifer, 2002).

Just as activities in the corporate sector were transferred to the military, so did the military-led rationalization of industrial production reshape corporations and the working class. The military supported Taylorist and Fordist transformations of the labor process that undermined the bargaining power of labor ironically provided for its renewal on newly enlarged social foundations with the birth of industrial unionism and the Congress of Industrial Organizations (CIO), based on the power of second-generation immigrant workers (Hounshell, 1984; Aitken, 1985; Smith, 1985; Davis, 1986; Montgomery, 1987; Misa, 1995). 1934 was a key year in this mass upsurge, as a series of successful strikes in Toledo, Minneapolis, and San Francisco rocked the country. In Minneapolis and San Francisco, the Teamsters and the International Longshoremen's and Warehousemen's Union (ILWU) played decisive roles in establishing strong bases of class power among transport and port workers for half a century or more (Preis, 1964, chap. 4).

Yet the postwar ejection of left-led unions from the CIO and labor's incorporation as a junior partner in U.S. overseas expansion during the Cold War doomed domestic and international labor solidarity. It also reinforced sexism, racism, narrow nationalism, and related forms of craft exclusivism and labor market segmentation (Davis, 1986; Rosswurm, 1992; Zeitlin and Weyer, 2001; Stepan-Norris and Zeitlin, 2003). Despite these massive defeats of labor unity that set definite limits on the postwar potential, organized labor in transport and the U.S. as a whole nevertheless managed for a time to win impressive gains. Progressive longshore workers were particularly successful, as were truckers—some 60% of whom were unionized by 1980—with wages among the highest in manufacturing (Belzer, 2000, p. 21 and 26).

Transnational Empires of Flexible Just-in-Time (JIT) Production and Warfare

This social power of labor expressed in the rising gains of transport workers and labor worldwide in the mid-20th century is being undermined through flexible production and distribution systems that are critical aspects of contemporary globalization (Harvey, 1989; Sassen, 2001, p. 32). Increased capital mobility intersects with the historic segmentation of workers to undermine labor's bargaining power in the U.S. and other advanced capitalist states while capital turns toward cheap, largely unorganized women, persons of color, and immigrants at home. The result is the decline of the social power of organized labor in the case and the rising influence of these growing sectors of the workforce in the U.S. and abroad (Davis, 1986; Arrighi, 1990).

Fundamental to all this is a revolution in the way goods are produced and distributed, from standardized mass production and consumption to more flexible and differentiated modes. Here it is important to underscore the centrality of the U.S. military and innovations in high technology coming from the militarized sector of the U.S. economy. They are changing the strategies and structures of global corporate capital and dramatically shaping the terrain for labor. Military-related technological developments and associated institutional innovations in corporate networks are crucially important in the decentralization of production networks and moves to small batch production responsive to increasingly differentiated consumer tastes. These developments are undermining the historic power of concentrated mass-production workers (Harvey, 1989, chap. 9).[5] Thus, understanding these changes is critical for analyzing the possibilities for transnational class organization.

A crucial example of military-stimulated organizational change is the role of the U.S. Army during the occupation of Japan. The U.S. trained Japanese workers and engineers in standardization and interchangeability of parts, continuous improvement, intensified time-motion studies, and quality control to meet U.S. specifications and inventory requirements (Spencer, 1967, p. 33, 40). These techniques were later diffused through the global economy. Japanese wartime innovations, revived and refined through offshore U.S. military procurements for the Korean War, combined the advantages of larger firms with a host of dependent subcontractors and subsidiaries. These "just in time" (JIT) production and delivery systems reduced overhead costs and served as the basis for the organization revolution in the strategies and structures of world capitalism sweeping the globe today (Reifer, 1995, Parts III and IV).

Crucial factors in this organizational revolution are control over and access to information necessary to monitor geographically dispersed production and logistics empires of flexible specialization (Harvey, 1989, p. 159; Bonacich, 2003, p. 42). At the heart of these transformations marking the passage from Fordism to flexible specialization and JIT production are computer, satellite, and telecommunications networks made possible through the system of industrial planning developed by the Pentagon (Alberts, Garstka, and Stein, 1999, p. 27; Reifer, 2004).[6] Information technology is used now to collect point-of-sale information about customer purchases and instantly relay it through electronic networks (satellites, etc.) to provide almost instantaneous replenishment of stocks through JIT production and distribution. With a computer network rivaling that of the Pentagon, Wal-Mart now claims ownership of the largest private satellite communications network in the U.S. (*USA Today*, January 29, 2003).

Integral to Wal-Mart's competitive superiority is its radical reduction of distribution costs—some 3% of sales versus the 4½ to 5% for its competitors—including inventory and overhead. With the emergence of the very small aperture terminal industry and the installation of a 2500-site network in 1987, Wal-Mart point-of-sale scanners collect information on an average 90 million transactions a week. The information is shared directly with suppliers (who can tap into company computers to track sales) and stored in data warehouses using "sophisticated data mining algorithms to extract trend data" (Fike, 1998,

p. 3; Alberts, Garstka, and Stein, 1999, p. 46; *USA Today,* January 29, 2003). The system puts a premium on JIT production and distribution through dependent suppliers and their contingent workforces of flexible labor, all competing against each other for access to markets monopolized by core firms (Cerna, Marshall, and Valdez, 2003, p. 38).

Another key aspect of this logistics revolution at the heart of contemporary globalization and offshore production networks is containerization. In essence, containers are trucks without wheels that can be stacked on ships by the thousands, double stacked on railroad cars, and then converted into trucks by adding wheels and a chassis. Such technical innovations allow goods to be moved interchangeably through a variety of transportation modes from production—road, rail, sea—to final destination without unloading between transport modes. The process is known as *intermodalism*. A landmark in the development of intermodalism was the "Mechanization and Modernization Plan" agreed upon by the Pacific Maritime Association and the ILWU in 1960. The Pentagon worked with industry to increase efficiencies in cargo handling to improve logistical support for the projection of U.S. military power overseas and underseas. The military and industry pushed containerization ahead in a transition speeded up by "the demands of the Vietnam War" (Noble, 1985, p. 338). Again, the dynamics driving forward U.S.-led state–corporate globalization lay at the intersection of military and corporate interests.

Today, sped along by transport deregulation and the associated wave of competition and consolidation facilitating intermodalism, containers account for 60% of global trade, and this figure is expected to increase to 70% by 2010. A single dockworker can now do what it took an army to accomplish in the past (Coulter, 2002, p. 134). Steamship companies that now use "flags of convenience" to register in countries with minimum standards play important roles by selling their ship transport services to exporters and importers. These firms often employ trucking and railroad firms in the process, with devastating consequences for seafaring unions, today almost entirely composed of men of color who are largely from the South (Bonacich, 2003, p. 43).

During the period of trucking deregulation, while the number of workers in this sector dramatically increased from 1,111,000 to 1,907,000 between 1978 and 1996, an equally dramatic offensive against labor occurred. The number of unionized workers decreased from about 60% in 1980 to under 25% at present. Wages plummeted about 30% from 1977 to 1995; trucks have become what Belzer (2000, p. 21) calls sweatshops on wheels.

"Here, the near destruction of the National Master Freight Agreement is perhaps most significant since it provided wage leadership for a constellation of distributive, processing, and wholesale industries linked to truck transport. Moreover, the decline of the Teamsters' ability to control the movement of highway-transported goods weakened the strike powers of myriad other spatially localized unions" (Davis, 1986, p. 137; Belzer, 2000, p. 110).

Although the Teamsters remain strong in small-package transport firms such as United Parcel Service (UPS), membership was virtually eliminated among west-coast port truckers. The new nonunionized port truck drivers in the Los Angeles and Long Beach area are largely immigrants from Mexico and Central America. Whereas firms formerly paid for gas, pensions, and health insurance benefits, immigrant workers are now considered by employers and the National Labor Relations Board to be independent owner-operators, akin to contingent workers.

Working in terrible conditions at bare minimum wages, these workers are legally barred from unionizing. An antitrust law that makes organizing illegal grants limited antitrust immunity to large steamship firms (Early, 1998, p. 95; Bonacich, 2003, p. 45). Despite such obstacles, workers in the Los Angeles and Long Beach area staged numerous work stoppages and massive protests in 1984, 1988, 1993, and 1996. This upsurge has been likened to the great wave of immigration and labor organization in the U.S. in the late 19th and early 20th centuries that culminated in the rise of industrial unionism and the CIO (Early, 1998, p. 95; Davis, 2000, chap. 15). As trucking firms forced the Teamsters to accept two-tiered settlements, with much better benefits for mostly senior white workers, the growing numbers of workers of color risk being locked into permanent low-wage jobs institutionalized with racism in union contracts (Hill, 1977, chap.9).[7]

Railroads present a different picture. Although the number of rail workers plummeted from 587,000 to 282,000 between 1973 and 1996 and unionization decreased, weekly wages dropped only from 79 to 74% ($491 to $470, with a 1983 high of $507 measured in 1983/1984 dollars) during the wave of deregulation from 1978 through 1996 (Peoples, 1998, p. 112). Although the share of freight shipped by rail made small gains in the 1980s, the greater flexibility of trucking allowed it to garner 73% of the $423 billion worth of intercity freight shipments in 2002, compared with only 8.7% handled by the railroad industry (*Wall Street Journal*, July 25, 2003, p. A16).

Other integral parts of the global logistics supply chain are warehouses or distribution centers (DCs). With the rise of retail discount merchandising, firms such as Wal-Mart sought to overcome the difficulties serving their primarily rural markets by inventing the DC in 1970. The system allowed them to buy goods in bulk while using information technology to track consumer purchases and transmit the information to DCs and suppliers (Cerna, Marshall, and Valdez, 2003, p. 4). One key area for DCs is east of Los Angeles, in Southern California's Inland Empire (Riverside and San Bernardino Counties) centered around Ontario. The population of roughly 3.2 million people in 2000 is predicted to exceed 6 million by 2025 (Bonacich, 2003, p. 46; Davis, 2003a; Figure 2.2). While the national workforce of the wholesale industry consists primarily of young white males between 18 and 40, the Southern California workforce consists primarily of temporary workers and appears to be staffed

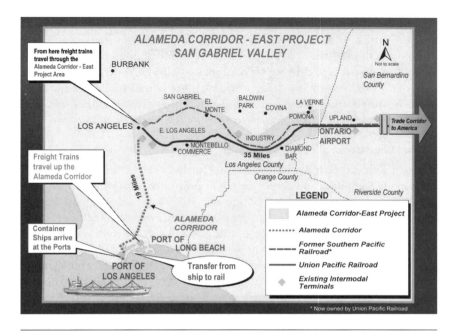

Figure 2.2. This map shows the Alameda Corrodor-East Project San Gabriel Valley. Copyright©
ACE Construction Authority, 2001.

largely by young workers of color, especially Latinos (Bonacich, 2003, p. 46; cf.
Cerna, Marshall, and Valdez, 2003, p. 22).

The primarily white, black, and Chicano west-coast Longshore workers
(whose numbers fell from 28,000 to 10,500 between 1960 and 2003) are faced
with an offensive from employers, as evidenced by the lockout of the ILWU on
the west coast starting in September 2002. The Pacific Maritime Association
(PMA), an association of employers that negotiates contracts with Longshore
workers, and the West Coast Waterfront Coalition (WCWC), an organization
of PMA's largest customers (notably giant retailing firms such as Wal-Mart,
Home Depot, and Payless Shoes), geared up for a confrontation and imposed
the lockout after accusing the ILWU of a slowdown. The employer strategy was
to have the WCWC (renamed the Waterfront Coalition) demand "injunctive
relief against the lockout and then press for severe economic and criminal
sanctions against the ILWU under the provisions of the 80-day cooling off
period" prescribed under the Taft–Hartley Act. President George W. Bush
enjoined the lockout, opened the ports, and refused to move against the ILWU
for violating the injunction, thus paving the way for a settlement. Longshore
workers, less amenable to the rise of nonunion competitors as in trucking,
have thus maintained a strong bargaining position, yet it is likely to be
undermined unless workers organize throughout the cargo supply chain
(Olney, 2003).

Another development in the transportation field is the rise of third party logistics firms. These firms are specialized intermediaries that move goods from point of production to place of distribution. Ranging from warehousing operations to package delivery services such as UPS or Federal Express these firms and their mostly low-wage workforces are bound to change the landscape of supply chain management today and provide possibilities for a new union upsurge in the 21st century (Armstrong & Associates, 2003).

Global Logistics in a "Sole Superpower" World

The late 20th and early 21st centuries offer further evidence of the intersection between U.S. military and corporate power projection capabilities in logistics. In 1993, Gus Pagonis (1994), a three-star U.S. Army general who masterminded the logistics of the U.S. Gulf War victory, was recruited as executive vice president of logistics for Sears, Roebuck and Co., where he continues to head all logistics operations. Just as flexible JIT production and logistics are at the heart of the transformations in the global corporate structure today, an integral part of the revolution in military affairs (RMA) discussed by those in charge of the Pentagon is network centric warfare (NCW) inspired by the corporate revolution in supply chain management.

These new revolutionaries, in comparing the Pentagon to firms of the old corporate economy, see Wal-Mart as the model for the transformation of U.S. global military power (Davis, 2003b). A group of military intellectuals centered around the legendary Andrew Marshall and his Office of Net Assessment in the Pentagon see

> "Wal-Mart as the essence of a 'self-synchronized distribution network with real-time transactional awareness'... through 'horizontal' networks rather than through a traditional head office hierarchy. We're trying to do the equivalent in the military," wrote the authors of *Network Centric Warfare*, the 1998 manifesto of the RMA/NCW camp that footnotes Wal-Mart annual reports in its bibliography. In 'battlespace,' mobile military actors (ranging from computer hackers to stealth-bomber pilots) would serve as the counterparts of Wal-Mart's intelligent salespoints" (Davis, 2003b).

Although claims that such innovations will overcome the fog of war leading to total battlespace dominance are rightly criticized, there is a clear turn to what is called flexible or JIT warfare by RMA/NCW enthusiasts. Just as the decentralization of global corporate networks is seen as undermining the strength of concentrated workers, so Pentagon officials hope that JIT warfare and superior power projection capability through logistics will help overcome opposition to permanent U.S. military bases and intervention worldwide, most recently expressed in the unprecedented global mobilization against the Anglo-American invasion of Iraq (Hazlett, 1995).

The centrality of logistics in U.S. postwar hegemony reflects the unique form of the supranational expansion of U.S. transnational capital and state power, in radical contrast to the old formal territorial empires of the European past. U.S.-led state–corporate globalization is largely based on expanding informal empires, through neo-colonial relationships, networks of global alliances, proxy or client states, and transnational firms. A key aspect of U.S. hegemony and the related dynamics of contemporary U.S.-led globalization is the way the U.S. provides for both the expansion of its own multinational firms and also, in select areas, for the firms of its key regional allies in Europe and Asia, who are also, of course, politico–economic competitors. Superior politico–economic and military power ensure the continuous innovations in logistics that today are arguably key sources of competitive advantage in the war for global supremacy on the military and corporate battlefields, as the rising power of Wal-Mart in the global corporate power structure and the U.S. in the global military power structure reveals. Indeed, as *Fortune Magazine* (March 3, 2003) argues:

> "Wal-Mart in 2003 is, in short, a lot like America in 2003: a sole superpower . . . . As with Uncle Sam, everyone's position in the world will largely be defined in relation to Mr. Sam. Is your company a 'strategic competitor' like China or 'a partner like Britain'? Is it a client state like Israel or a supplier to the opposition? . . . Hegemony, it would seem, doesn't get any more complete."

Flexible Specialization and the Challenges Facing Labor and the Global Peace and Social Justice Movements

The move toward flexible systems of production, distribution, and warfare today ensures that the logistics connecting labor and global production are of growing importance as strategic sites for labor and capital—and the global peace and social justice movements. Additionally, the shift of production toward women, persons of color, and immigrants in the advanced capitalist states along with its movement into the South potentially increases the social power of these rising sectors of labor, raising new challenges and opportunities to build more inclusive forms of national and international labor solidarity (Arrighi, 1990; Silver and Arrighi, 2000; Silver, 2003).

As Edna Bonacich (2003, p. 46) argues, today ports, most especially Long Beach and Los Angeles, "are vital nodes in the system of production/distribution, dependent on JIT deliveries and the cutting back of inventory." The westcoast port lockout revealed that if the logistics systems that are "choke-points" for global commodity flows "are shut down, the result can be chaotic for capital" (Bonacich, 2003, p. 46). This gives port truckers, rail workers, or those in the Ontario DCs potential strategic leverage (Leyshorn, 2000; Bonacich, 2003, 47). Logistics workers are crucial local factors in global production and delivery systems that form integral parts of transnational empires of trade, production, and finance; they "cannot be moved offshore" (Bonacich, 2003). Moreover, the growing racial and ethnic diversity of low-wage logistic workers provides the combination of oppression by class and race and ethnicity that historically led to more inclusive democratic visions of militant social movement unionism.

Today, the demographics of California, the U.S., and global labor as a whole are rapidly changing. Women, persons of color, and immigrants now make up the bulk of the U.S. working class. Furthermore, increasing numbers of commodities produced by low-wage workers in Asia, China, and Mexico are imported into the U.S. through Southern California. As these work forces becoming increasingly intertwined, initiatives for more militant and inclusive forms of labor solidarity within and across borders could gain growing support, providing new strategic openings for labor and the global peace and social justice movements to organize across racial, ethnic, gender, and national divides (Davis, 1990, 1993, and 2000).

Production and transportation workers in Asia, Latin America, and North America are all parts of a single global system. Organizing throughout the global logistics supply chain, linking workers in transportation, production, and retail, could be a source of strategic power, paving the way for a new global unionism in coordination with the global peace and social justice movements. Yet in the U.S. today, transportation, the public sector, and good-producing industries are weakly represented by unions, whereas the retail, service, and related white-collar sectors are largely open shops (Davis, 1986, p. 146). Although there has been a focus on global sweatshops, the same cannot be said of global logistics, even though it seems ready made for alliances across industries, national borders, and lines of race, ethnicity, class, and nationality.

The changing demographic composition of labor is of crucial importance. Today, Latinos are rapidly growing in the rank and file and leadership of the U.S. trade union movement, notably in Los Angeles, where the Mexican and Central American working class boasts some 1.5 million service workers and 500,000 factory workers (Davis, 2000, p. 144). These developments undoubtedly helped the AFL–CIO pass a landmark resolution calling for amnesty for undocumented workers—a crucial item for a labor–Latino alliance. Despite their stated desire to organize workers of color and immigrants, unions representing and headed by Latinos often remain trapped in the practices of business unionism, particularly through reliance on a right-moving Democratic Party. Even the historically progressive ILWU, as Peter Olney (2003) argues, risks becoming a declining craft union unless it can organize growing numbers of low-wage workers, often of color, throughout the cargo supply chain.

The strait jacket of business unionism is the product of a long history of intense class conflict in the U.S., in which labor was corralled into small- to medium-sized islands of organized labor in a growing ocean of unorganized workers (Davis, 1986, p. 210; Mink, 1986; Forbath, 1991; Voss, 1993). Starting in the late 19th century, continuing throughout the heyday of the Cold War, and right up to the present, the incorporation of crucial parts of the U.S. labor movement as junior partners in U.S. overseas expansion and the related military–corporate complex played a major role in limiting the transformative potential of the labor movement (Davis, 1986; Fraser, 1991; Lichtenstein, 1995; Bergquist, 1996). Only through a confrontation with the historical legacies shaping these institutional logics of business unionism from above and below is there a chance of a new upsurge of labor in the 21st century.

Consider the possibilities of a broad-based social movement with roots in labor supporting union drives at Wal-Mart (where women comprise over 72% of workers and only 33% of managers)—with the backlog of cases against it for violation of labor law in various organizing attempts (*New York Times*, November 8, 2002, p. A28; Public Broadcasting Service, November 8, 2002; Cerna, Marshall, and Valdez, 2003, p. 3). The movement could be combined with complementary transnational efforts to organize throughout the global supply chain, focusing on inter-racial alliances uniting workers of color with white workers in more progressive and inclusive visions of social movement unionism. Such multi-pronged initiatives could strengthen the mass movement around the global sweatshop (Bonancich and Appelbaum, 2000).

Recent strikes reveal the power of labor in the age of flexible specialization. In 1996, a 17-day strike at a United Auto Workers' brake plant in Ohio shut down nearly all of General Motors. A mass strike at UPS took on the air of a social movement (Coulter, 2002, p. 136). Recent port strikes and solidarity actions in support of the strikes across the globe also demonstrate the potential vulnerability of capital to the organization of labor in the global supply chain (Lipsitz, 2001, p. 262).

Labor must forge an increasingly militant social movement unionism across lines of race, gender, and nationality if it is to capitalize on changes in the composition of world labor and the changing geography and organization of labor and capital in the global economy. The centrality of logistics and labor in the Pacific Rim triangle presents a major opportunity, given the racial and ethnic diversity of the workforce and the organic relationship of workers in this area with overseas trade, production, transportation, and retail distribution. Ironically, even as we move into the 21st century, the growing deconcentration of labor in much of the core (though not necessarily in places like China) increases the centrality of logistics labor (see Silver, 2003: 97–103). Scholars and activists would do well to take account of this key development, as it signals a potential vulnerable area in the structure of global state–corporate capitalism today. This weakness could be capitalized on by organizing in strategic fashion, with an eye toward a new generation of labor struggles that are more inclusive, internationalist, and radical in vision and organization. Ultimately, such struggles, in the face of a U.S. superpower being reconstituted on increasingly narrow and militarized social foundations, could target the logistical heart of U.S. and global corporate and military power as a key strategic site for the labor movement and the larger struggle for global peace and social justice of which it is an integral part.

Bibliography

Aitken, H.G.J., *Scientific Management in Action: Taylorism at Watertown Arsenal, 1908–1915*, Princeton University Press, Princeton, NJ, 1985 (originally published in 1960).

Alberts, D.S., J.J. Garstka, and F.P. Stein, *Network Centric Warfare: Developing and Leveraging Information Superiority*, 2nd ed., rev., Cooperative Research Program, U.S. Department of Defense, Washington, DC, 2000.

Armstrong & Associates, *Who's Who in Logistics? Armstrong's Guide to Global Supply Chain Management*, 11th ed., Stoughton, WI, 2003.

Arnesen, E., *Brotherhoods of Color: Black Railroad Workers and the Struggle for Equality*, Harvard University Press, Cambridge, MA, 2001.

Arrighi, G., "Marxist Century, American Century: The Making and Remaking of the World Labour Movement," *New Left Review*, January/February 1990, p. 29–64.

Bacon, D., *The Children of NAFTA: Labor War on the U.S./Mexico Border*, University of California Press, Berkeley, 2004.

Belzer, M.H., *Sweatshops on Wheels: Winners and Losers in Trucking Deregulation*, Oxford University Press, New York, 2000.

Bergquist, C., *Labor and the Course of American Democracy: U.S. History in Latin American Perspective*, Verso, New York, 1996.

Bonacich, E., "Pulling the Plug: Labor and the Global Supply Chain," *New Labor Forum* 12, 2003, 41–48.

Bonacich, E. and R. Appelbaum, *Behind the Label: Inequality in the Los Angeles Apparel Industry*, University of California Press, Berkeley, 2000.

Bowersox, D.J., D.J. Closs, and M.B. Cooper, *Supply Chain Logistics Management*, McGraw Hill, Boston, 2002.

Bowersox, D.J., D.J. Closs, and T.P. Stank, *21st Century Logistics: Making Supply Chain Integration a Reality*, Council of Logistics Management, Oak Brook, IL 1999.

Broad, R., *Unequal Alliance: The World Bank, the International Monetary Fund, and the Philippines*, University of California Press, Berkeley, 1988.

Buhle, P., *Taking Care of Business: Samuel Gompers, George Meany, Lane Kirkland, and the Tragedy of American Labor*, Monthly Review Press, New York, 1999.

Cebrowski, A.K., and J.J. Garska, *Network Centric Warfare: Its Origins and Future*, 1998, http://www.usni.org/Proceedings/Articles98/PROcebrowski.htm.

Cerna, A., J. Marshall, and R. Valdez, *The Growing Role of Distribution Centers and Warehouses in the Retail Supply Chain*, University of California School of Public Policy and Social Research, Los Angeles, 2003.

Chambers, J.W., II, *To Raise An Army: The Draft Comes to Modern America*, Free Press, New York, 1987.

Chandler, AD., Jr., *The Visible Hand: The Managerial Revolution in American Business*, Belknap Press, Cambridge, MA, 1977.

Cohen, L, *A Consumers' Republic: The Politics of Mass Consumption in Postwar America*, Alfred A. Knopf, New York, 2003.

Coulter, D.Y., "Globalization of Maritime Commerce: The Rise of Hub Ports," in Tangred, S.J., Ed., *Globalization and Maritime Power*, National Defense University Press, Washington, DC, 2002, p. 133.

Davis, M., *Prisoners of the American Dream: Politics and Economy in the History of the US Working Class*, Verso, New York, 1986.

Davis, M., *City of Quartz: Excavating the Future in Los Angeles*, Verso, New York, 1990.

Davis, M., "Who Killed LA: The War Against the Cities," *Crossroads*, June 1993, p. 2.

Davis, M., *Magical Urbanism: Latinos Reinvent the U.S. Big City*, Verso, New York, 2000.

Davis, M., "Inland Empire," *The Nation*, April 7, 2003a, p. 15.

Davis, M., "Slouching toward Baghdad," February 28, 2003b, http://www.tjm.org/articles/msg00037.html.

Davis, M. and D.N. Sawhney, "*Sanbhashana*," in Sawhney, D.N., Ed., *Unmasking L.A.: Third World and the City*, Palgrave, New York, 2002, p. 21.

Du Bois, W.E.B., *Black Reconstruction in America: An Essay toward a History of the Part Which Black Folk Played in the Attempt to Reconstruct Democracy in America, 1860–1880*, Atheneum, New York, 1969 (originally published in 1935).

Early, S., "Membership-Based Organizing," in Mantsios, G., Ed., *A New Labor Movement for the New Century*, Monthly Review Press, New York, 1998, p. 82–103.

Fajnzylber, F., *Unavoidable Industrial Restructuring in Latin America*, Duke University Press, Durham, NC, 1990a.

Fajnzylber, F., "The United States and Japan as Models of Industrialization," in Gereffi, G. and D.L. Wyman, Eds., *Manufacturing Miracles: Paths of Industrialization in Latin America and East Asia*, Princeton University Press, Princeton, NJ, 1990b, p. 323–352.

Fike, B., "VSATs: Industry Changes and Growth from 1988 though 1998," http://ucsu.colorado.edu/~fikeb/prof/vsat.PDF.

Forbath, W.E., *Law and the Shaping of the American Labor Movement*, Harvard University Press, Cambridge, MA, 1991.

Fortune Magazine, "One Nation Under Wal-Mart," March 3, 2003, p. 65–78.

Fortune Magazine, "America's Largest Corporations," April 14, 2003.

Fraser, S., *Labor Will Rule: Sidney Hillman and the Rise of American Labor*, Cornell University Press, Ithaca, NY, 1991.

Goldfield, M., *The Color of Politics: Race and the Mainsprings of American Politics*, New Press, New York, 1997.

Gompers, Samuel, address to National Security League, Chicago, September 14, 1917.

Gordon, D.M., *Fat and Mean: The Corporate Squeeze of Working Americans and the Myth of Managerial "Downsizing,"* Free Press, New York, 1996.

Gordon, D.M., R. Edwards, and M. Reich, *Segmented Work, Divided Workers: The Historical Transformation of Labor in the United States*, Cambridge University Press, Cambridge, England, 1982.

Harvey, D., *The Condition of Postmodernity*, Blackwell, Cambridge, MA, 1989.

Hazlett, J., "Just-in-Time Warfare," in Johnson, S.E. and Libicki, M.C., Eds., *Dominant Battlespace Knowledge: The Winning Edge*, National Defense University Press, Washington, DC, 1995, p. 133–148.

Hill, H., *Black Labor and the American Legal System: Race, Work, and the Law*, Bureau of National Affairs, Washington, DC, 1977.

Hounshell, D.A., *From the American System to Mass Production, 1800–1932: The Development of Manufacturing Technology in the United States*, Johns Hopkins University Press, Baltimore, 1984.

Journal of Commerce, various issues.

Kanter, R.M., *Men and Women of the Corporation*, Basic Books, New York, 1977.

Kramer, W. and L. Coral, *Cross Border Trucking: U.S.–Mexico Logistics Chain*, University of California Labor Center, Los Angeles, 2003.

Krause, P., *The Battle for Homestead, 1880–1892: Politics, Culture, and Steel*, Pittsburgh: University of Pittsburgh Press, 1992.

Leyshon, H., *Port Drivers Organizing*, unpublished manuscript, 2000.

Lichtenstein, N., *The Most Dangerous Man in Detroit: Walter Reuther and the Fate of American Labor*, Basic Books, New York, 1995.

Lipsitz, G., *American Studies in a Moment of Danger*, University of Minnesota Press, Minneapolis, 2001.

Mink, G., *Old Labor and New Immigrants in American Political Development: Union, Party, and State, 1875–1920*, Cornell University Press, Ithaca, NY, 1986.

Misa, T., *A Nation of Steel: The Making of Modern America, 1865–1925*, Johns Hopkins University Press, Baltimore, 1995.

Mongelluzzo, B., "Hasbro Bolts to S. California: Move Underscores Long Term Shift in Handling of Asian Imports," *Journal of Commerce*, June 17, 2002, p. 28–30.

Montgomery, D., *The Fall of the House of Labor: The Workplace, the State, and American Labor Activism, 1865–1925*, Cambridge University Press, Cambridge, England, 1987.

Nelson, B., *Divided We Stand: American Workers and the Struggle for Black Equality*, Princeton University Press, Princeton, NJ, 2001.

New York Times, "Trying to Overcome Embarrassment, Labor Launches Drive to Organize Wal-Mart," November 8, 2002, p. A28.

New York Times, "China's Growth Creates a Boom for Cargo Ships," August 28, 2003, p. A1, C6.

Noble, D.F., "Command Performance: A Perspective on Military Enterprise and Technological Change," in Smith, M.R., Ed., *Military Enterprise and Technological Change: Perspectives on the American Experience*, MIT Press, Cambridge, MA, 1985, p. 329–346.

Olney, P., "On the Waterfront: Analysis of ILWU Lockout," *New Labor Forum*, Summer 2003, p. 33–40.

Pagonis, G., *Moving Mountains: Lessons in Leadership and Logistics from the Gulf War*, Harvard Business School Press, Cambridge, MA, 1994.

Peoples, J., "Deregulation and the Labor Market," *Journal of Economic Perspectives*, Vol. 12, Summer 1998, p. 111–130.

Preis, A., *Labor's Giant Step: Twenty Years of the CIO*, Pioneer, New York, 1964.

Public Broadcasting Service, *Now With Bill Moyers*, November 8, 2002. http://www.pbs.org/now/transcript/transcript142_full.html.

Reifer, T., "The Japanese Phoenix and the Transformation of East Asia: World-Economy, Geopolitics, and Asian Regionalism in the Long Twentieth Century," presented at the 36th annual meeting of the International Studies Association, Chicago, February 21–25, 1995.

Reifer, T., "Globalization and the National Security State Corporate Complex (NSSCC) in the Long Twentieth Century," in Grosfoguel, R. and M. Rodriguez, Eds., *The Modern/Colonial/Capitalist World System in the Twentieth Century*, Greenwood Press, Westport, CT, 2002, p. 3–70.

Reifer, T., "Satellites," in Carlisle, R.B., Ed., *Encyclopedia of Intelligence and Counterintelligence*, M.E. Sharpe, in press, 2004.

Ross, R.J.S. and A. Chan, "From North-South to South-South: The True Face of Global Competition," *Foreign Affairs*, September/October 2002, p. 8–13.

Rosswurm, S., Ed., *The CIO's Left-Led Unions*, Rutgers University Press, New Brunswick, NJ, 1992.

Sassen, S., *The Mobility of Labor and Capital: A Study in International Investment and Labor Flow*, Cambridge University Press, New York, 1988a.

Sassen, S., "Capital Mobility and Labor Migration," in Cherry, R. et al., Eds., *The Imperiled Economy, Book II*, Union for Radical Political Economics, New York, 1988b, p. 57–68.

Sassen, S., *The Global City: New York, London, Tokyo*, 2nd ed., rev., Princeton University Press, Princeton, NJ., 2001.

Saxton, A., *The Indispensable Enemy: Labor and the Anti-Chinese Movement in California*, University of California Press, Berkeley, 1971.

Schneer, J., *London 1900: The Imperial Metropolis*, Yale University Press, New Haven, CT, 1999.

Silver, B.J. and G. Arrighi, "Workers North & South," in Panitch, L. and C. Leys, Eds., *Socialist Register, 2001*, Merlin Press, London, 2000, p. 53–76.

Silver, B.J., *Forces of Labor: Workers' Movements and Globalization since 1870*, Cambridge University Press, New York, 2003.

Smith, M.R., Ed., *Military Enterprise and Technological Change: Perspectives on the American Experience*, MIT Press, Cambridge, MA, 1985.

Spencer, D.L., *Military Transfer: International Techno-Economic Transfers via Military By-Products and Initiative Based on Cases from Japan and Other Pacific Countries*, Defense Technical Information Center, Defense Logistics Agency, Washington, DC, AD660537, March 1967.

Stepan-Norris, J. and M. Zeitlin, *Left Out: Reds and America's Industrial Unions*, Cambridge University Press, New York, 2003.

United Nations Conference on Trade and Development (UNCTAD), *World Investment Report*, various issues. New York and Geneva, 2002.

U.S. Department of Transportation, *Maritime Trade & Transportation, 2002*, p. 11, http://www.bts.gov/products/maritime_trade_and_transportation/2002/pdf/entire.pdf.

U.S. Government Accounting Office, *International Trade: Mexico's Maquiladora Decline Affects U.S.-Mexico Border Communities and Trade*, Washington, DC, July 2003.

USA Today, "Wal-Mart's Influence Grows," January 29, 2003, http://www.usatoday.com/money/industries/retail/2003-01-28-walmartnation_x.htm.

Voss, K., *The Making of American Exceptionalism: The Knights of Labor and Class Formation in the Nineteenth Century*, Cornell University Press, Ithaca, NY, 1993.

Wall Street Journal, "China's Overcapacity Crimps Neighbors: Glut Swamps Southeast Asia's Exports, Roiling Currency," July 14, 1997, p. A10.

Wall Street Journal, "Battling Trucks, Trains Gain Steam By Watching Clock," July 25, 2003, p. A1, A14.

Wall Street Journal, "Despite U.S. Bond Selloff, Asia Keeps Buying," August 5, 2003, p. C1, C15.

Wilson, R. and R.V. Delaney, *14th Annual "State of Logistics Report," The Case for Reconfiguration*, 2003 . jttp://www.cassinfo.com/state_of_logsitics_2003_final.PDF.

Wood, L., *Diaries, 1913–1918*, Library of Congress Archives, Washington, DC.

Zeitlin, M. and L.F. Weyer, "Black and White, Unite and Fight: Interracial Working-Class Solidarity and Racial Employment Equality," *American Journal of Sociology*, Vol. 107, September 2001, p. 430–467.

Notes

1. I especially want to thank Edna Bonacich and Christopher Chase-Dunn for their critical comments, insights, and critiques that were instrumental in the writing of this chapter, which is part of a larger study funded by the Institute for Labor and Employment of the University of California. Thanks also to Dave Smith for editorial assistance.

2. For the contrast between models of production and consumption in the U.S., Latin America, and East Asia, see Fajnzylber, 1990a and b; Cohen, 2003.

3. The tremendous rise of cheap Chinese exports was implicated in the East Asian crisis because it hurt the exports of rival producers and thereby helped make their currencies vulnerable to speculation—a fact with potentially ominous implications for the future (*Wall Street Journal*, July 14, 1997, p. A10).

4. Although rarely mentioned, Frederick Taylor did much of his key work in the naval shipyards of the military–corporate complex, producing battleships for the expansion of the U.S. formal and informal empires abroad (Smith, 1985; Misa, 1995).

5. The social-spatial shift to small industrial factors in the more union-free Sunbelt and rural Midwest areas of the U.S. was a critical mechanism of exit from New Deal social relations (Davis, 1986, p. 121).

6. For information on the development of satellites via the Pentagon system of industrial planning and the origins of a commercial satellite sector via the privatization of publicly created technologies, see Reifer, in press, 2004.

7. Talks with Teamsters officials, Labor Notes Conference, September 2003.

3

Latin America and
the Empire of Global Capital

WILLIAM I. ROBINSON

Introduction: Globalization, Crisis, and the Restructuring
of World Capitalism

The downturn in the world economy that began in the closing years of the
20th century heralded a crisis that, in my view, was more than merely cyclical.
The turn-of-century turmoil may turn out to be the opening scenes to Act II
of a deeper restructuring crisis that began nearly three decades earlier.
Mainstream business-cycle theories are keen to identify periodic swings from
expansion to recession in the market economy, but world-system and other
Marxist-inspired theories have long pointed to deeper cycles of expansion
and contraction in world capitalism. Cyclical crises eventually usher in periods
of restructuring. These restructuring crises, as scholars from the French regulation, the U.S. social structure of accumulation, the world-system, and critical
Marxist schools have shown, result in novel forms that replace historical
patterns of capital accumulation and the institutional arrangements that
facilitated them.[1]

The post-World War II expansion—the so-called Golden Age of Capitalism—
experienced a crisis in the 1970s that precipitated a period of restructuring
and transformation that led to a new mode of global capital accumulation
now known as neo-liberalism. The Reagan and Thatcher regimes of the 1980s
catapulted neo-liberalism to the center stage of world capitalism and the international financial institutes imposed the model on much of the Third World
in the 1980s and 1990s through structural adjustment programs in what came
to be known as the "Washington consensus."[2]

I have been researching and writing about globalization and crisis since the
early 1990s. The conclusions of my earlier work can be summarized as follows:
The crisis that began in the 1970s could not have been resolved within the
framework of the post-World War II Keynesian social structure of accumulation. Capital responded to the constraints on accumulation imposed by this
earlier model of nation-state redistributional projects by "going global." What
had been international capital in the preceding epoch metamorphosed
into transnational capital that became the hegemonic fraction of capital on a

world scale in the 1980s. Transnationalized fractions of capitalist classes and bureaucratic elites captured state power in most countries during the 1980s and 1990s and utilized that power to undertake a massive neo-liberal restructuring.

Free-trade policies, integration processes, and neo-liberal reforms (including the gamut of deregulation, privatization, and fiscal, monetary and austerity measures) opened the world in new ways to transnational capital. For instance, deregulation made available new zones to resource exploitation; privatization opened public and community spheres ranging from health care and education to police and prison systems to profit making. New information technology and novel forms of organization also contributed to renewed accumulation. The correlation of social forces worldwide changed in the 1980s and early 1990s against popular classes and in favor of transnational capital.

The latter used the newfound structural leverage that global mobility and financial control provided to impose a new capital–labor relation based on diverse categories of "contingent" or deregulated employment (casualized and informalized labor). Income shifted from working and poor people to capital and to new high-consumption middle, professional, and bureaucratic strata that provided a global market segment fueling growth in new areas. All this reversed—temporarily—the crisis of stagnation and declining profits of the 1970s.

The restructuring crisis that began in the 1970s signaled the transition to a new transnational stage of world capitalism. Globalization as a new epoch in world capitalism is marked by a number of fundamental shifts in the capitalist system. One of these is *the rise of truly transnational capital*. National circuits of accumulation have increasingly been reorganized and integrated into new transnational circuits. The concepts of flexible accumulation and network structure capture the organizational form of these globalized circuits. Another feature of global capitalism is *the rise of a transnational capitalist class* (TCC), a fraction grounded in global markets and circuits of accumulation over national markets and circuits.[3]

Transnational class formation also entails the rise of a global proletariat. Capital and labor increasingly confront each other as global classes. A third feature is a *transnational state* apparatus—a loose but increasingly coherent network composed of supranational political and economic institutions and national state apparatuses that have been penetrated and transformed by transnational forces. In contrast to the predominant story line of a resurgent U.S. empire, I suggest that we are witnesses to the rising hegemony of a global capitalist bloc. There is an underlying class relation between the TCC and the U.S. national state. This ascendant empire of global capital is headquartered in Washington, but the beneficiaries of U.S. military action around the world are transnational, not U.S. capitalist groups.

This empire of global capital has barely emerged and already faces twin structural and subjective crises: one of overaccumulation and the other of legitimacy. Globalization resolved some problems for capital, but the underlying laws of capitalism remain in place and continually assert themselves. The breakdown of nation-state based redistributive projects may have restored growth and profitability, but it also aggravated the tendencies inherent in capitalism toward overaccumulation by further polarizing income and heightening inequalities worldwide. Overcapacity underpinned the Asian crisis of 1997 to 1998, and overaccumulation caused the world recession of the early 21st century. The neo-liberal model barely triumphed in the 1980s and 1990s when it began to appear moribund. I suggest here that neo-liberalism may prove to be a parenthesis between old nation-state accumulation models and a new global social structure of accumulation whose contours are not yet clear.

These propositions are broadly discussed and debated in my previous work on globalization and more generally in the interdisciplinary literature on the global political economy.[4] The ambition of this chapter is to examine the experience of one particular region, Latin America, in the crisis and restructuring of world capitalism in the late 20th and early 21st centuries. The empirical and analytical core of the essay examines Latin America's experience in the world capitalist crisis, with particular emphasis on the neo-liberal model, turn-of-century social conflicts that engulfed the region, and the rise of a new resistance politics. I will return, by way of conclusion, to the broader issues of crisis and restructuring in world capitalism raised above.

Latin America Faces a Global Crisis

Latin America has been deeply implicated in the restructuring crisis of world capitalism. The mass movements, revolutionary struggles, and nationalist and populist projects of the 1960s and 1970s were beaten back by local and international elites in the last decades of the 20th century in the face of the global economic downturn, the debt crisis, state repression, U.S. intervention, the collapse of a socialist alternative, and the rise of the neo-liberal model. The diverse popular projects and movements had their own internal contradictions as well. Economically, Latin American countries experienced a thorough restructuring and integration into the global economy under the neo-liberal model. Politically, the fragile polyarchic systems installed through the so-called transitions to democracy of the 1980s were increasingly unable to contain the social conflicts and political tensions generated by the polarizing and pauperizing effects of the neo-liberal model.

The restructuring of world capitalism, its new transnational logic and institutionality; the polarization of the rich and the poor; and the escalation of inequalities, marginalization, and deprivation taking place under globalization have profoundly changed the terrain under which social struggle and change will take place in Latin American in the 21st century.

Neo-liberalism and Stagnation in Latin America

As transnational capital integrates the world into new globalized circuits of accumulation, it has broken down national and regional autonomies, including the earlier preglobalization models of capitalist development and the social forces that sustained these models. Local productive apparatuses and social structures in each region have been transformed, and different regions acquired new profiles in the emerging global division of labor. Economic integration processes and neo-liberal structural adjustment programs are driven by transnational capital's campaign to open every country to its activities, tear down all barriers to the movement of goods and capital, and create a single unified field in which global capital can operate unhindered across all national borders.[5]

In Latin America, the preglobalization model of accumulation based on domestic market expansion, populism, and import substitution industrialization corresponded to the earlier nation–state phase of capitalism. Surpluses were appropriated by national elites and transnational corporations and redistributed through diverse populist programs ranging from packets of social wages (social service spending, subsidized consumption, etc.) to expanding employment opportunities and rising real wages. The model became exhausted, and its breakdown starting in the late 1970s paved the way for the neo-liberal model based on liberalization and integration to the global economy, a *laissez faire* state, and what the current development discourse terms *export-led development*.[6] Table 3.1 provides one indicator of this process of increasing outward orientation of Latin American countries in the final decade of the 20th century.

The dismantling of the preglobalization model and its replacement by the neo-liberal model threw Latin American popular classes into a social crisis

Table 3.1 Trade in Goods as Percentage of Gross Domestic Product for Select Countries in Latin America and Caribbean

	1989	1999
Latin America and Caribbean	10.2	18.2
Argentina	5.1	10.9
Brazil	6.3	8.4
Chile	24.0	23.7
Colombia	6.7	9.3
Costa Rica	19.9	40.6
Dominican Republic	21.4	29.0
Ecuador	15.5	20.1
Guatemala	11.5	16.6
Honduras	18.4	26.9
Mexico	14.1	35.6
Peru	7.5	12.2
Venezuela	22.6	26.6

Source: World Bank , *World Development Indicators 2001*, p. 322.

that hit hard in the 1980s, Latin America's "lost decade," and continues in the 21st century. During the 1980s, other regions, particularly East Asia, North America, and Europe, became the most attractive outlets for accumulated capital stocks. Latin America stagnated in absolute terms and experienced backward movement when seen in relation to other regions in the world economy. The region experienced a contraction of income and economic activity. Its share of world trade dropped by half (from about 6% to about 3%) between 1980 and 1990.[7] In the 1980s, Latin America became the region with the slowest growth in per capita income, behind other Third World regions and behind the world as a whole, indicating its troubled integration into the emergent global economy.

What accounted for this *apparent* stagnation and marginalization? In fact, the data indicate that Latin America did not stop producing wealth for the world capitalist system as it integrated into the global economy. To the contrary, the volume of Latin American exports to the world increased significantly throughout the 1980s and 1990s. As Table 3.2 shows, the volume of the region's exports *rose* by an annual average of 15.1% whereas the value of these same exports actually *decreased* by an annual average of 0.1% between 1983 and 2000. In other words, Latin Americans worked harder and harder to increase the wealth they produced for the global economy while the income they received from that work decreased as they became more impoverished and exploited.

This steady deterioration of the terms of trade is a consequence of Latin America's continued overall dependence on commodity exports. Venezuela and Ecuador depend almost entirely on oil exports, Chile remains dependent on copper, Brazil and Argentina on a variety of low-tech and basic agricultural

Table 3.2 Volumes and Units of Value of Latin American Exports (Average Annual Percent Growth in Batch Years)

	Volume	Unit Value
1983–1985	16.2	−9.9
1986–1988	17.7	−5.9
1989–1991	13.7	5.2
1992–1994	22.3	3.3
1995–1997	11.5	8.4
1998–2000	8.9	−0.7
1983–2000[a]	15.1	0.1

[a]Average annual change.

Source: Economic Commission for Latin America and the Caribbean (ECLAC), Economic Survey of Latin America and the Caribbean, 1983–1999, United Nations, Santiago, Chile.

exports, Peru on its mining sector, Central America on traditional agro-exports, and so on. This situation has been aggravated by neo-liberal adjustment that shifted resources toward the external sector linked to the global economy and by the region's extreme dependence on global capital markets to sustain economic growth.

This continued dependence on commodity exports is a structural asymmetry that underscores a worsening of the development (or social) crisis for the poor majorities in Latin America and should not be confused with the region's contribution to global capital accumulation. The region has remained a net exporter of capital to the world market, a supplier of surplus for the world, and an engine of growth of the global economy. Table 3.3 shows that Latin America was a net exporter of $219 billion in capital surplus to the world economy during the "lost decade" from 1982 to 1990, then became a net importer from 1991 through 1998. In 1999, the region once again became an exporter of capital.

What transpired was a massive influx of transnational capital into the region in the 1990s. This, combined with the renewal of growth for much of the decade, led transnational functionaries from the supranational economic planning agencies (World Bank, International Monetary Fund [IMF], etc.) and local elites to argue that Latin America's development crisis came to an end. However, the vast majority of the inflow of capital was a consequence not of direct investment in new productive infrastructure as much as it arose from diverse portfolio and financial ventures such as new loans, the purchases of stock in privatized companies, and speculative investments in financial services such as equities, mutual funds, pensions, and insurance.

Table 3.3 Net Capital Flows, Net Payment on Profits and Interest, and Net Resource Transfer (Billions of Dollars)

Net Capital Flows	Net Payments Profit/Interest	Net Transfer
1982–1990	99/318	−219
1991–1995	266/174	92
1996	65/43	22
1997	81/48	33
1998	78/51	27
1999	47/52	−5
2000	53/53	0
2001	50/55	−5
2002	13/53	−40

Source: Economic Commission for Latin America and the Caribbean (ECLAC), Preliminary Overview of the Economies of Latin America and the Caribbean, 2000, p. 104; Economic Survey for Latin America and the Caribbean, 200–2001, p. 80; Preliminary Overview of the Economies of Latin America and the Caribbean, 2002, p. 122.

This type of foreign capital penetration resulted in the transnationalization of the production and service infrastructure built through the previous development model. It reflected the hegemony of transnational finance capital in the age of globalization and its frenzied "casino capitalism" activity in recent years and gave an illusion of "recovery" in Latin America—an illusion shattered by the Argentine crisis that exploded in December 2001. Before the Argentine upheaval, the transnational elite believed it had resolved the debt crisis in the 1980s by making the debt serviceable and removing the issue from the political agenda. However, the continued hemorrhage of wealth from the region, combined with liberalization and deeper external integration, meant the external debt had in fact continued to grow throughout the late 1980s and 1990s from $230 billion in 1980 to $533 billion in 1994, more than $714 billion in 1997, and almost $800 billion in 1999, and its rate of growth again increased in the 1990s.[8]

Amortization of the debt exacted an ever-rising tribute from Latin American popular classes to transnational capital. However, when debt-repayment pressures reach the point where default becomes a possibility or a government can no longer meet even minimal social obligations, the spiral of crisis begins. Local states are caught between the withdrawal of transnational investors and the mounting unrest from poor majorities who can no longer bear further austerity.

The slide into crisis began at the turn of the century when the net outflow of resources once again came to surpass the net inflow. In Argentina, among other countries, the government could keep the economy buoyed so long as it had state assets to sell off. Once no quick money can be made, capital flight can—and has—plunged countries into overnight recession. As Table 3.4 indicates, Latin America began a downturn in 1998. Although th e region as a whole showed positive growth in 2000, this is accounted for by high growth rates in a handful of countries although most of them stagnated and experienced negative growth.

Most notable about Table 3.4 is that GDP per capita declined in the lost decade by 0.9% from 1980 to 1990, then barely recovered in the growth years of the 1990s, growing by 1.5% from 1991 through 2000. If we separate 1998 through 2000 from the rest of the 1990s, we find that many countries experienced renewed declines in GDP per capita over the 3-year period from 1998 to 2000. It *dropped* in aggregate by 3.3% in Argentina, 6.2% in Colombia, 10.5% in Ecuador, 3.3% in Honduras, 6.1% in Paraguay, 0.1% in Peru, 8.1% in Uruguay, and 8.3% in Venezuela. In other countries, aggregate growth in GDP per capita for this period slowed to a negligible amount, such as 0.9% in Brazil.[9]

This debt produced deleterious effects on the living conditions of popular classes and placed Latin America in ever-increasing "hock" to transnational finance capital. Argentina's debt climbed from $27 billion in 1980 to $63 billion in 1990 and moved steadily upward to $144 billion by 1998. In the same

Table 3.4 Latin America: Annual Growth Rates, GDP, and GDP per Capita by Region and Selected Countries

	GDP	Per Capita GDP
Latin America		
1980–1990	1.2	−0.9
1991–2000	3.3	1.5
Argentina		
1981–1990	−0.7	−2.1
1991–2000	4.2	2.9
1998–2000	0.2	−1.1
Brazil		
1981–1990	1.6	−0.4
1991–2000	2.6	1.2
1998–2000	1.7	0.4
Colombia		
1981–1990	3.7	1.6
1991–2000	2.6	0.6
1998–2000	−0.3	−2.1
Ecuador		
1981–1990	1.7	0.9
1991–2000	1.7	−0.4
1998–2000	−1.6	−3.5
Mexico		
1981–1990	1.9	−0.2
1991–2000	3.5	1.7
1998–2000	5.2	3.6
Venezuela		
1981–1990	−0.7	−3.2
1991–2000	2.0	−0.2
1998–2000	−0.8	−2.8

Source: Economic Commission for Latin America and the Caribbean, *Preliminary Overview of the Economies of Latin America and the Caribbean,* 2000, p. 85.

period, Brazil's debt climbed from $71 billion to $232 billion, and Mexico's increased from $57 billion to $160 billion. Colombia, Ecuador, Peru, Venezuela, and the Central American republics were also heavily indebted relative to their economic size. For Argentina, payment *on the interest alone* ate up 35.4% of export earnings in 1998. For Brazil, the figure was 26.7%; for Colombia, 19.7%; for Ecuador, 21.2%; for Nicaragua, 19.3%; for Peru, 23.7%; and for Venezuela, 15.3%.[10]

The debt also facilitated internal adjustment and a deeper integration into the global economy and cemented the power of the emergent transnational power bloc in the region. As Table 3.3 shows, Latin America continued to export annually between 1992 and 2002 an average of $30 billion in profits and interests. "Growth," therefore, simply represents the continued and increased creation of tribute to transnational finance capital.

In the wake of the Asian meltdown of 1997 and 1998, Latin American countries began the slide toward renewed stagnation. This continuous drainage of surplus from Latin America helps explain the region's stagnation, declining income, and plummeting living standards. The poor have to run faster just to remain in the same place. The social crisis in Latin America thus is not as much a crisis of production as it is of distribution. Inequality is a social relation of unequal power between the dominant and the subordinate, we should recall and, more specifically, the power of the rich locally and globally to dispose of the social product.

Globalization eliminated the domestic market as a factor strategic to accumulation strategies. This has important implications for class relations and social movements. By removing the domestic market and popular class consumption from the accumulation imperative, restructuring involves the demise of the populist class alliances between broad majorities and nationally based ruling classes that characterized the preglobalization model of accumulation. Globalization involves a change in the correlation of class forces worldwide away from nationally organized popular classes and toward the transnational capitalist class and local economic and political elites tied to transnational capital. As the logic of national accumulation is subordinated to that of global accumulation, transnationalized fractions of local dominant groups in Latin America gained control over states and capitalist institutions in their respective countries. These groups, in-country agents of global capitalism, become integrated organically as local contingents into the transnational elite. This is part of the broader process under globalization of transnational class formation.

Neo-liberal states sought to create the best internal conditions to attract mobile transnational capital, including the provision of cheap labor, depressed and lax working conditions, the elimination of state regulations such as environmental controls, little or no taxation, no insistence on transnational corporate accountability or responsibility to local populations, and so on. In the logic of global capitalism, the cheapening of labor and its social disenfranchisement by the neo-liberal state became conditions for development. The very drive by local elites to create conditions to attract transnational capital is what thrusts Latin American majorities into poverty and inequality. A new capital–labor relation is born out of the very logic of regional accumulation based on the provision to the global economy of cheap labor as the region's comparative advantage. In the new capital–labor relation in Latin America (and worldwide), capital abandons reciprocal obligations to labor in the employment contract at the same time as states, with their transmutation from developmentalist to neo-liberal, all but abandon public obligations to poor and working majorities.

New Dimensions of Inequality

Globalization brought about a dramatic sharpening of social inequalities, increased polarization, and the persistence of widespread poverty in Latin America, reflecting the broader pattern of global social polarization. Between 1980 and 1990, average per capital income dropped by an unprecedented 11%, so that most of the region's inhabitants found that their incomes had reverted to 1976 levels by 1990.[11] Poverty levels also increased throughout the 1980s and 1990s. Between 1980 and 1992, some 60 million new people joined the ranks of the poor. The number of people living in poverty went from 136 million in 1980, to 196 million in 1992, and then to 230 million in 1995—an increase from 41% to 44%, then to 48%, respectively, of the total population.[12]

There has been an explosion in Latin America of the informal sector that has been the only avenue of survival for millions of people thrown out of work by contraction of formal sector employment, austerity, the revising of labor laws directed at making labor "flexible," and the uprooting of remaining peasant communities by the incursion of capitalist agriculture. Informalization of work, moreover, is part of the transition from Fordist to flexible employment relations, whereby subcontracted and outsourced labor is organized informally and constitutes an increasing portion of the workforce.[13] National and international data-collection agencies report those in the informal sector as "employed," despite the highly irregular and unregulated nature of the informal sector characterized by low levels of productivity, below-poverty (and below legal minimum wage) earnings, and instability, usually amounting to underemployment. Four of every five new jobs in Latin America are in the informal sector.[14]

Inequality in Latin America, although high historically, increased throughout the 1980s and 1990s, as Table 3.5 shows. World Bank data for 18 Latin American countries indicates that the Gini coefficient measuring income inequality (0 = perfect equality; 1 = perfect inequality) rose from 0.45 in 1980 to 0.50 in 1989.[11] However, income inequality is only one dimension, and often not the most important, of social inequality. Added to income polarization in the 1980s and 1990s is the dramatic deterioration in social conditions as a result of austerity measures that drastically reduced and privatized health, education, and other social programs. Popular classes whose social reproduction is dependent on a social wage (public sector) face a social crisis, whereas privileged middle and upper classes become exclusive consumers of social services channeled through private networks.

The escalation of deprivation indicators in Brazil and Mexico, which together account for over half of Latin America's 465 million inhabitants, reveals the process of immiseration that most Latin Americans have experienced

Table 3.5 Per Capita Household Income Distribution in Selected Countries

	1980		1989	
	20% Bottom	**20% Top**	**20% Bottom**	**20% Top**
Argentina	5.3	46.6	4.1	52.6
Brazil	2.6	64.0	2.1	67.5
Chile	—	—	3.7	62.9
Colombia	2.5	63.0	3.4	58.3
Guatemala (1987)	2.7	62.0 (1989)	2.1	63.0
Mexico (1984)	4.1	55.9	3.2	59.3
Peru (1986)	6.2	49.7	5.6	50.4
Venezuela (1981)	5.0	47.3	4.8	49.5

Source: World Bank, Poverty and Income Distribution in Latin America: The Story of the 1980s, Washington, DC, 1997.

under global capitalism. Between 1985 and 1990, the rate of child malnutrition in Brazil, where nearly 48% of the country's 160 million people lived in poverty in 1990,[15] increased from 12.7% to 30.7% of all children.[16]

In Mexico, where over 50% of the country's 90 million people were in poverty, the purchasing power of the minimum wage dropped 66% between 1982 and 1991. In the mid-1990s it took 4.8 minimum wages for a family of four to meet essential needs, yet 80% of households earned 2.5 minimum wages or less. As a result, malnutrition spread among the urban and rural poor.[17]

In Argentina, meanwhile, unemployment rose steadily in the 1980s and 1990s from 3% in 1980 to 20% in 2001, the number of people in extreme poverty escalated from 200,000 to 5 million, and the number in poverty increased from 1 million to 14 million. Illiteracy increased from 2% to 12% and functional illiteracy from 5% to 32% during this period.[18] In fact, the United Nations Development Program's Human Development Index an aggregate measure of well-being based on life expectancy at birth, educational attainment, and GDP per capita, actually *decreased* for many Latin American countries in the 1990s.[19]

From Social Explosions to Institutional Crises: The Fragility of Polyarchy

By the late 1970s, authoritarianism as the predominant mode of social control in Latin America faced an intractable crisis.[20] On the one hand, authoritarian regimes were besieged by mass popular movements for democracy, human rights, and social justice that threatened to bring down the whole elite-based social order along with the dictatorships, which happened in Nicaragua in 1979. This threat from below, combined with the inability of the authoritarian regimes to manage the dislocations and adjustments of globalization, generated intraelite conflicts that unravelled the ruling power blocs. This crisis of elite rule was resolved through transitions to *polyarchy* that took place in almost every country in the region during the 1980s and early 1990s.

Polyarchy is a system in which a small group actually rules on behalf of capital, and participation in decision making by the majority is confined to choosing among competing elites in tightly controlled electoral processes. Emergent transnationalized fractions of local elites in Latin America, with the structural power of the global economy behind them, as well as the direct political and military intervention of the U.S., were able to gain hegemony over democratization movements and steer the breakup of authoritarianism into polyarchic outcomes.

It is not at all clear in the early 21st century whether these fragile polyarchic political systems will be able to absorb the tensions of economic and social crisis without collapsing. Most Latin American countries experienced waves of spontaneous uprisings generally triggered by austerity measures, the formation in the shantytowns of urban poor movements of political protest, and a resurgence of peasant movements and land invasions, all outside the formal institutions of the political system and generally involving violent clashes of states, paramilitary forces, and protesters.[21]

The social and economic crisis has given way to expanding institutional quandaries, the breakdown of social control mechanisms, and transnational political–military conflict. The revolt in Argentina; the struggle of the landless in Brazil; peasant insurrections in Bolivia; indigenous uprisings in Ecuador; spreading civil war in Colombia; attempted coups d'état in Haiti; and aborted coups, business strikes, and street conflict in Venezuela—such incidents became the orders of the day in the first few years of the 21st century.[22]

The region seems poised for a new round of U.S. political and military intervention under the guise of wars on terrorism and drugs. U.S. hostility to the populist government of Hugo Chavez in Venezuela and the political alliance between Washington and the displaced business class promoting his ouster are of particular significance, because Chavez may well represent a new brand of populism that could take hold as desperate elites attempt to regain legitimacy.

Remilitarization under heavy U.S. sponsorship was already well underway by the turn of the century, from the $2 billion Plan Colombia to the sale by Washington of advanced fighter jets to Chile's military, the installation of a U.S. military base in Ecuador, the large-scale provision of arms, counterinsurgency equipment, and antiterrorism training programs to Mexico, new multilateral intervention mechanisms, and a new round throughout the hemisphere of joint U.S.–Latin American military exercises and training programs.[23]

It is worth noting that one or another of the hemisphere's governments have labeled as terrorists the Landless Workers' Movement of Brazil, the Zapatistas of Mexico, the FARC and the ELN guerrilla movements of Colombia, the indigenous movement in Ecuador, the Farabundo Marti National Liberation Front in

El Salvador, the Sandinistas in Nicaragua, and other legitimate resistance movements. The U.S. Central Intelligence Agency identified in 2002 as "a new challenge to internal security" the indigenous movement that, 510 years after the Conquest began, spread throughout the hemisphere and has often been at the forefront of popular mobilization.[23] Colombia may be the most likely epicenter of direct U.S. intervention and a region wide counterinsurgency war in South America.

This panorama suggests that the state structures that are set up (and continuously modified) to protect dominant interests are now decomposing, possibly beyond repair. A long period of political decay and institutional instability is likely. We should not lose sight of the structural underpinnings of expanding institutional crises and should recall the fundamental incompatibility of democracy and global capitalism.

The model of capitalist development by insertion into new global circuits of accumulation does not require an inclusionary social base. Socioeconomic exclusion is immanent to the model because accumulation does not depend on a domestic market or internal social reproduction. A structural contradiction between the globalization model of accumulation and the effort to maintain polyarchic political systems requires the hegemonic incorporation of a social base. The neo-liberal model generates social conditions and political tensions—inequality, polarization, impoverishment, and marginality—conducive to a breakdown of polyarchy. This constitutes a fundamental contradiction between the class function of the neo-liberal states and their legitimation function.

Resistance to Globalization in Latin America

As old corporatist structures crack, new oppositional forces and forms of resistance have spread—social movements of workers, women, environmentalists, students, peasants, indigenous, racial and ethnic minorities, and community associations of the urban poor. These popular forces helped protagonize a new progressive electoral politics in the early 21st century, including the election of Luis Ignacio da Silva (Lula) and the Workers Party (PT) in Brazil (2002); Lucio Gutierrez in Ecuador (2003) with the backing of that country's indigenous movement; the near victory at the polls of Evo Morales, an indigenous leader and socialist in Bolivia (2002); and the resilience in office in the face of elite destabilization campaigns of the government of Hugo Chavez, elected in 1999 in Venezuela. These developments suggest that new political space has opened up in Latin America and that the neo-liberal elite has lost legitimacy.

These popular electoral victories symbolized the end of the reigning neo-liberal order and also the limits of parliamentary changes in the era of global capitalism. The case of Brazil is indicative. Lula, denied the presidency in three previous electoral contests and victorious in 2002, took the vote only after his wing of the PT moved sharply toward the political center. He forged a social base among middle class voters and won over centrist and even conservative political forces that did not endorse a left-wing program but were unwilling to tolerate further neo-liberal fallout.

The real power here was that of transnational finance capital. Lula promised not to default on the country's foreign debt and to maintain the previous government's adjustment policies. His 2003 budget slashed health and educational programs in order to comply with IMF dictates that the government maintain a fiscal surplus.[24] What may have been emerging was an elected left populist bloc in the region committed to mild redistributive programs respectful of prevailing property relations and unwilling to challenge the global capitalist order. Many leftist parties, even when they sustain an anti–neoliberal discourse, have in their practice abdicated earlier programs of fundamental structural change in the social order.

If transnational capital is able to emasculate radical programs through structural pressures exerted by the global economy, the popular electoral victories involved as well the mobilization of new collective subjects and mass social movements, will be unlikely to be cowed by the transnational elite. The demise of neo-liberal hegemony unleashes social forces that neither the established order nor left electoral regimes can contain.

Events in Venezuela from Chavez's election in 1999 through 2003 may presage a pattern in which the electoral victories of popular candidates spark heightened political mobilization and social struggles that may move events in unforeseen directions. The question might not be how much local populism can accomplish in the age of globalization but how local populism may be converted into transborder globalization from below.

The dominant groups in Latin America reconstituted and consolidated their control over *political society* in the late 20th century, but the new round of popular class mobilization in the 1990s and early 21st century, pointed to their inability to sustain hegemony in *civil society*. The renewal of protagonism demonstrated by subordinate groups at the grassroots level has been outside state structures and largely independent of organized left parties. Grassroots social movements have flourished in civil society at a time when the organized left operating in political society has been unable to articulate a counter-hegemonic alternative despite its continued vitality. The failure of the left to protagonize a process of structural change from political society helps shift the locus of conflict more fully to civil society.

Latin America seemed to move in the 1990s to a "war of position" between contending social forces in light of subordinate groups' failure to win a "war of maneuver" through revolutionary upheaval and the limits to power from above. As crises of legitimacy, perpetual instability, and the impending breakdown of state institutions spread rapidly throughout Latin America in the early 21st century, conditions seemed to be opening up for a renovated war of maneuver under the novel circumstances of the global economy and society.

Conclusion: Whither the Empire of Global Capital?

Globalization acted at first as a centripetal force for transnationally oriented elites and as a centrifugal force for popular classes around the world. Working classes were fragmented by restructuring. Intense competition forced on these classes in each nation debilitated collective action. Subprocesses such as transnational migration and the diffusion of consumer culture provided escape valves that relieved pressure on the system. The mass social dislocation, evaporating social protection measures, declining real opportunities, and spiraling poverty that neo-liberalism generated sparked widespread yet often spontaneous and unorganized resistance in the 1980s and 1990s, as epitomized in 'IMF food riots'.[25] Table 3.6 shows the steep rise in global inequalities in the neo-liberal age.

Organized resistance movements arose everywhere, ranging from the Zapatistas in Mexico to the Assembly of the Poor in Thailand, Brazil's Landless People's Movement, India's National Alliance of People's Movements, the Korean Confederation of Trade Unions, and the National Confederation of Indigenous Organizations of Ecuador. At a certain point in the 1990s, popular resistance forces formed a critical mass, coalescing around an agenda for social justice or antiglobalization. By the turn of the century, the transnational elite had been placed on the defensive and a crisis of the system's legitimacy began to develop, as symbolized by the creation of the World Social Forum in Porto Alegre, Brazil, under the banner "Another world is possible."

From the viewpoint of capital, neo-liberalism resolved a series of problems in the accumulation process that built up in the epoch of Keynesian capitalism but fueled new crises of overaccumulation and legitimacy. The model is not sustainable socially or politically. Its coming demise may well turn out to be the end of Act I and the opening of Act II in the restructuring crisis that began in the 1970s. As in all historic processes, this act is unscripted. The next step may be a reassertion of productive over financial capital in the global economy and a global redistributive project, just as it may be the rise of a global fascism founded on

Table 3.6 Shares of World Income 1965–1990

Population	Percentage of Total World Income			
	1965	1970	1980	1990
Poorest 20%	2.3	2.2	1.7	1.4
Second 20%	2.9	2.8	2.2	1.8
Third 20%	4.2	3.9	3.5	2.1
Fourth 20%	21.2	21.3	18.3	11.3
Richest 20%	69.5	70.0	75.4	83.4

Source: Korzeniewicz, R.P. and T.P. Moran, "World Economic Trends in Distribution of Income, 1965–1992," *American Journal of Sociology*, Vol. 102, January 1997.

military spending and wars to contain the downtrodden and the unrepentant. Historical outcomes are always open ended, subject to contingencies and to being pushed in new and unforeseen directions. The crisis in no way guarantees, the ascendancy of popular oppositional forces. It would be foolish to predict with any conviction the outcome of the looming crisis of global capitalism.

The Washington consensus, it is broadly recognized, had cracked by the turn of the century.[26] What may replace the neo-liberal order in Latin America and in global society depends on the struggle to *oppose* the neo-liberal order and also, inseparable from the struggle, on developing a viable alternative and *imposing* that alternative. Precisely because the neo-liberal phase of global capitalism may be coming to a close, resistance must move beyond the critique of neoliberalism. The problem of the particular neo-liberal model is in the end symptomatic of the *systemic* problem of global capitalism. It is not clear, however, how effective national alternatives can be in transforming social structures, given the ability of transnational capital to utilize its structural power to impose its project even over states that are captured by forces adverse to that project. Neither 'Socialism in one country' nor 'Keynesianism in one country' can any longer be sustained. The rise of a global justice movement is the clearest example that popular and oppositional forces began to transnationalize in the 1990s, moving to create alliances, networks, and organizations that transcend national and even regional borders. The prospects for counter-hegemonic social change in the age of globalization is a globalization-from-below movement that seeks to challenge the power of the global elite by accumulating counter-hegemonic forces beyond national and regional borders.

Notes

1. See *inter alia* Aglietta, M., "A Theory of Capitalist Regulation," in Kotz, D.M., T.M. McDonough, and M. Reich, Eds., *Social Structures of Accumulation: The Political Economy of Growth and Crisis*, Cambridge University Press, Cambridge, England 1994; Arrighi, G., *The Long Twentieth Century*, Verso, London, 1994; Harvey, D., *The Limits to Capital*, University of Chicago Press, Chicago, 1982.
2. See Williamson, J., "Democracy and the 'Washington Consensus'," *World Development*, Vol. 21, 1993, p. 1329; Williamson, J., Ed., *Latin American Adjustment: How Much Has Happened?* Institute for International Economics, Washington, DC, 1990.
3. The notion of a TCC is certainly not new nor exclusively my own. See Sklair, L., *The Transnational Capitalist Class*, Blackwell, London, 2002. See Robinson, W.I., *A Theory of Global Capitalism: Transnational Production, Transnational Classes, and the Rise of a Transnational State*, Johns Hopkins University Press, Baltimore, 2004, chap. 2 for a review of the literature on the transnationalization of capitalists.
4. The literature on globalization and global political economy is too vast to reference here. For a collection surveying recent theoretical directions, see Palan, R., Ed., *Global Political Economy: Contemporary Theories*, Routledge, London, 2000. On my theoretical propositions and empirical studies on globalization, see *inter alia* Robinson, W.I., *A Theory of Global Capitalism: Production, Class, and State in a Transnational World*, Johns Hopkins University Press, , Baltimore, 2004; *Transnational Conflicts: Central America, Social Change and Globalization*, Verson, London, 2004; *Promoting Polyarchy: Globalization, U.S. Intervention, and Hegemony*, Cambridge University Press, Cambridge, England 1996; "Globalisation: Nine Theses of Our Epoch," *Race and Class*, Vol. 18, 1996, p. 13; "Social Theory and Globalization: The Rise of a Transnational State," *Theory and Society*, Vol. 30, 2001, p. 157;

"The Transnational Capitalist Class and the Transnational State," in Dunaway, W.A., Ed., *New Theoretical Directions for the 21st Century World System*, Greenwood Press, Portsmouth, NH, 2003.

5. Neo-liberalism is the specific mechanism that adjusts national and regional economies to the global economy by creating the conditions, including an appropriate macroeconomic and policy environment, the legal framework, and so on, for internal productive reorganization and insertion into the global economy. These themes are analyzed in Robinson, W.I., "Social Theory and Globalization: The Rise of a Transnational State," *Theory and* Society, Vol. 30, 2001, p. 157; and Robinson, W.I., *A Theory of Global Capitalism: Production, Class, and State in a Transnational World*, Johns Hopkins University Press, Baltimore, 2004. For analysis of neo-liberal adjustment in Latin America, see also Green, D., *Silent Revolutions: The Rise of Market Economics in Latin America*, Cassell, London, 1995. See also Chossudovsky, M., *The Globalization of Poverty: Impacts of IMF and World Bank Reforms*, Zed, London, 1997.

6. See Green, *Silent Revolutions*; Robinson, W.I., "Latin America in the Age of Inequality: Confronting the New Utopia," *International Studies Review*, Vol. 1, 1999, p. 41.

7. See Wilkie, J.A., Ed., *Statistical Abstracts for Latin America* (SALA), Vol. 31, University of California, Los Angeles, 1995.

8. World Bank, Country Tables, 1998–2000, p. 36; Economic Commission for Latin America and the Caribbean (ECLAC), reports, 1985 and 1994–1995.

9. Economic Commission for Latin America and the Caribbean (ECLAC), *Economic Survey of Latin America and the Caribbean*, 1998–1999, p. 114.

10. World Bank, *Poverty and Income Distribution in Latin America: The Story of the 1980s*, Washington, DC, 1997.

11. See various reports of the Comision Economica para America Latina (CEPAL), Panorama Social de America Latina, Santiago, Chile.

12   Ibid.

13. For detailed discussion of the informalization of work in Central America, see Robinson, W.I., *Transnational Conflicts: Central America, Social Change and Globalization*.

14. "Great Reforms, Nice Growth, but Where Are the Jobs?" *The Economist*, 21, March 1998, p. 37.

15. World Bank, *Poverty and Income Distribution in Latin America: The Story of the 1980s*, Washington, DC, 1997.

16. United Nations Development Program (UNDP*), Human Development Report 1995*, Oxford University Press, New York, 1995.

17. See Barkin, D., I. Ortiz, and F. Rosen, "Globalization and Resistance: The Remaking of Mexico," *NACLA Report on the Americas*, Vol. XXX, January/February 1997, p. 14.

18. See Gabetta, C., "Argentina: IMF Show State Revolts," *Le Monde Diplomatique*, January 12, 2002, www.mondediplo.com/2002/01/12argentina.

19. See United Nations Development Program (UNDP*), Human Development Report 1995*, Oxford University Press, New York, 1995, p. 7.

20. For detailed discussion of the issues raised in this section, see Robinson, W.I., *Promoting Polyarchy: Globalization, U.S. Intervention, and Hegemony*; Cambridge University Press, Cambridge, England 1996; Robinson, W.I., "Promoting Capitalist Polyarchy: The Case of Latin America," in Cox, M., G.J. Ikenberry, and T. Inoguchi, Eds., *American Democracy Promotion: Impulses, Strategies, and Impacts*, Oxford University Press, New York, 2000.

21. See Green, *Silent Revolutions*; Robinson, W.I., "Latin America in the Age of Inequality: Confronting the New Utopia," *International Studies Review*, Vol. 1, 1999, p. 41.; Walton, J. and D. Seddon, *Free Markets and Food Riots: The Politics of Global Adjustment*, Blackwell, Oxford, 1994.

22. See *inter alia* various contributions in *NACLA Report on the Americas*, Vol. XXXVI, July/August 2002.

23. For discussion, see Habel, J. "U.S. Demands a Secure, Compliant Hemisphere," *Le Monde Diplomatique*, January 16, 2002, english@monde-diplomatique.fr.

24. See "Make or Break: A Survey of Brazil," *The Economist*, February 22, 2003, special section following p. 54.

25. Walton, J. and D. Seddon, *Free Markets and Food Riots: The Politics of Global Adjustment*, Blackwell, Oxford, 1994.

26. See, e.g., Broad, R. and R. Cavanagh, "The Death of the Washington Consensus?" in Broad, R., Ed., *Global Backlash: Citizen Initiatives for a Just World Economy*, Rowman & Littlefield, Lanham MD, 2003.

4
Empire and Labor: U.S. and Latin America

JAMES PETRAS

Introduction

Different kinds of empire building exert different impacts on the labor force, class politics, and anti-imperialist movements. A corollary to this is that the diverse structures of labor and their socio-political expressions have significantly different impacts on the process of empire building.

Labor formation in diverse regions cannot be deduced from abstract global economic categories, even less so can the diverse forms of social and political action. This paper will focus on the "new imperialism" emerging from the U.S. in the post-Vietnam, post-Soviet period and its evolving class composition, modus operandi, and impact on labor both in the U.S. and in Latin America. Secondly we will examine the changing nature of the labor force in Latin America and the *new* forms of social organization emerging to challenge the new imperialism.

The New Imperialism

Imperialism in its various expressions and configurations has been with us for a long time. In recent times, at least since World War II, imperialism has been associated with the U.S. drive to undermine the previous European colonial system and to replace it with a new set of regimes that are "formally independent" but are actually client states of Washington. This imperial system has been described as neo-colonialism because the local leaders are seen as administering their states at the service of U.S. multi-national corporations (MNCs) and banks.

The U.S. informal empire was built and sustained by a number of inter-related pillars: (1) wars and military interventions, (2) covert intelligence operations, (3) market forces, and (4) the financial clout of multilateral financial institutions (International Monetary Fund, World Bank) and the economic agencies of the imperial state (Department of the Treasury, Department of Commerce, Export-Import Bank, etc.). The driving forces of U.S. empire building from 1950 through 1973 were its MNCs and its military. From the early 1970s to the early 1980s, U.S. imperial expansion was largely fueled by MNCs; banks; surrogate military forces in Nicaragua, Afghanistan, Angola, Guinea Bissau, and Mozambique; and the military regimes throughout Latin America. More significantly, important political collaborators in the U.S.S.R. and Eastern Europe, nurtured and financed by state and private agencies, converted the former collectivist economies into U.S. vassal states, integrated and subordinated to the North Atlantic Treaty Organization and run by predator regimes closely linked to international crime syndicates allied with the U.S. empire.

The collapse of the collectivist regimes in the Eastern Europe and Central Asia and their subsequent conquest via collaborative predators gave a big boost to U.S. imperial drive, widening its scope to the world conquest envisioned by George H. Bush's "New World Order" after the Gulf War, the colonization of Iraqi airspace, and division of its territory.

The empire received further impetus from Bill Clinton's Balkan Wars, his nuclear brinkmanship with North Korea, and the worldwide spread of the neo-liberal doctrine. Yeltsin's Russia became a quasidependency of the U.S. and an arc of client associates from the Baltic Sea area (Lithuania, Latvia, Estonia), Central Europe (Czech Republic, Poland, Hungary), the Balkans (Macedonia, Montenegro, Kosovo, Albania), and Central Asia (Georgia) defined the new frontiers of Clinton's empire.

A new imperialism took shape around U.S. military outposts; Wall Street's financial speculators; client predator capitalists in the "host countries"; and neo-liberal collaborators in Latin America, Africa, and Asia. The end of the Cold War served as the beginning of a new virulent strain of imperialism built around a sense of impunity—a unipolar power configuration in which Washington saw itself as the center of the universe.

The public policy of the new empire operates through economic directives to the client states, political blackmail, economic threats to European and Asian allies, and military and covert actions against recalcitrant independent states. The "new imperialism" took a different form and substance with the ascendancy of the George W. Bush Administration and demise of Wall Street's speculative bubble. The driving forces backing the imperial presidency shifted from Wall Street investment bankers to the energy–petroleum and military–industrial complexes. A cabinet dominated by ultraright militarist ideologues replaced the conservative free marketeers of the Clinton imperial era. Empire building through the economic components of the imperial state were replaced by the ideologues of permanent war, military conquests, and colony-(nation-) building.

The new imperialist became self-consciously imperialist. Some spokespeople and publicists openly embraced the designation of imperial power, even as they continued to attribute to it a humanitarian mission. The new imperialism in its militarist variant looks toward strategies of war, military logistics, the elaboration of a vast military and security apparatus, and major increases in military spending. Economic costs and deteriorating economic conditions are given short shrift. The domestic and Euro–Japanese economic recessions are ignored. Only war and terrorism matter. A sequence of planned imperial wars targeted Afghanistan, Iraq, and other countries—the imperially designated "axes of evil" largely composed of states independent of the U.S.

The relative autonomy of the military component of the imperial state in relation to the capitalist class, particularly its industrial and financial sectors, exerts significant impact on the labor forces in the U.S. and elsewhere. The Bush regime is primarily linked to the petroleum–energy and military–industrial sectors of the economy and secures the support of most of the rest of the capitalist class via bailouts, subsidies, massive tax reductions, and interventions on behalf of business in labor disputes.

The cohesive bloc of capitalists around the Bush regime's militarist–imperialist agenda is strengthened by big-business support for the neo-liberal policies promoted overseas. These policies provide unhindered access to markets; buy-outs of lucrative privatized mines, industries; and banks; and favorable labor legislation that decreases social costs and raises profits. However, just as German business prospered at the start of Nazi imperial expansion only to run a cropper through its overextended military operations and declining economic base, U.S. imperialism has also accumulated trade imbalances, ballooning budget deficits, and a stagnant domestic industrial base heavily dependent on protection, subsidies, and quotas on imports. The empire grows but the republic declines, and with it, the social conditions of salaried and wage-earning labor.

Imperialism and Class War in Latin America

Warfare takes many political forms, and policymakers frequently combine them. In Latin America, the U.S. empire was built through surrogate military generals, one-party authoritarians, and international financial institutions. From the mid-1970s onward, a series of military coups physically annihilated anti-imperialist, independent regimes, and class forces and put in place the military clients and socio-economic institutions that allowed imperial banks and MNCs to conquer the Latin American economies. After the initial military regimes and the takeover of strategic economic positions by public and private collaborators, the empire supported the transition to civilian client regimes that deepened and extended the process of indirect empire building.

Empire building has a major negative impact on labor: Military rule was sustained through state terror and led to the physical elimination of all autonomous trade unions; mental and physical trauma; and the exiles of hundreds of thousands of skilled technical, professional, and research workers. This eliminated autonomous sources of research and development and guaranteed the imperial monopoly of these strategic areas of the economy. Privatization led to the weakening or disappearance of trade unions, massive displacement of skilled and unskilled workers, creation of ghost towns, and the pillage and asset stripping of many privatized firms. Workers lost many social benefits via corporate restructuring that included the proliferation of short-term labor contracts and a rotating labor force. The results were massive growth of structural unemployment, declines in living standards, and the weakening of labor unions and contracts. The new private—foreign and domestic—owners were able to take advantage of new business-friendly labor legislation to further weaken trade unions and increase the income polarization between executives and foreign shareholders on the one hand and salaried and wage workers on the other. Workers lost as producers (wages, job security, social benefits) and as consumers (higher public utility, transport, health, education, and pension costs).

Extortionate debt payments led to mass transfer of public resources upward and out of the country, depleting the state of public capital for financing infrastructures, public works, improved economic competitiveness, research, and social welfare. The result was that employment in construction declined, shares of world markets shrank, and the productive economy became subordinated to the financial sector that thrived under the new deregulated economy.

Trade liberalization based on indiscriminant and nonreciprocal trade agreements eliminated trade barriers in Latin America, which led to the invasion of subsidized imports form the U.S. and the European Union, the loss of markets by domestic producers, and large-scale bankruptcies of peasant and small and medium agricultural producers. In the urban sector, small- and medium-sized industries failed, leading to the growth of a burgeoning informal sector and unregulated sweatshops.

The virtual collapse of the neo-liberal model led to massive unemployment, the disintegration of the industrial and productive fabric of the provinces, widespread malnutrition, the expansion of urban slums, and emigration overseas to low-paying dirty jobs in the U.S. and Western Europe. Empire building inverts the income pyramid: Massive transfers of income and wealth move upward to the top 5% while the lowest 80% below suffer significant losses of income.

Empire building is essentially a form of class warfare from above. Military dictatorships and neo-liberal regimes are the principle vehicles for enhancing the benefits for empire-based MNCs, banks, and powerful local financial groups. The social groups physically excluded from decision making and suffering the greatest socio-economic losses are the working class, peasantry, unemployed, salaried employees, women, indigenous peoples, and the young.

Pillage and Exploitation

Traditional theories of imperialism describe several stages in which initial pillage is followed by mercantilist trade, then by an unequal international division of labor between finished-goods producers and raw-material exporters.

The final stage consists of exchanges between low-end countries with cheap manufacturing industries and the high-tech service economies of the imperial states. This schema is basically flawed. To understand the nature of U.S. empire building, certain essential dimensions not taken into account by the traditional stage theory must be considered:

1. The transfer of tens of billions of dollars of ill-gotten funds from Latin America through U.S. banks to the U.S. is a form of plunder reminiscent of the first stage of empire building and plays a vital role in sustaining the otherwise unsustainable U.S. trade deficit, the strength of the dollar, and, in the final analysis, the U.S. economy. The transfer of billions of dollars of illegally secured fortunes is accomplished through U.S., Canadian, and European banks (and in many cases by Euro–North American banks). The scope and depth of financial fraud and the appropriation of funds from millions of middle-class savers are of systemic proportions.

   In Mexico from the early 1990s to the end of the decade, over $100 billion in state loans to private firms were "unaccountable" (pilfered). The government intervened to bail out the banks at the taxpayers' expense and at the cost of social expenditures. In the same period, Ecuador experienced a $40 billion dollar financial swindle that led to massive losses for savers and again a state bailout of the banks. A $60 billion dollar banking swindle in Argentina impoverished millions of middle- and lower-middle-class depositors through losses of their savings and pensions.

   These cases of massive fraud and transfer of funds had a profound impact on the financial system, state budgets, and class formation. In the larger financial setting, the prime losers are the markets because retail investors lost confidence in the system and small-scale borrowers were squeezed out of the credit market by new high interest rates designed to entice overseas speculators. The state bailouts led to a restructuring of the budget, eliminating vital social programs and reducing financing for productive sectors.

   Most significantly, fraud led to the mass impoverishment of the middle class in a direct and visible manner. The effect was the proletarianization of social and living conditions of the middle class, reducing its size and radicalizing its outlook. The middle class turned to militant public protest and social alliances with the poor. This is most graphically illustrated in Argentina where neighborhood assemblies of the middle class and pensioners have joined with unemployed picketers in mass protests and a popular uprising.

2. The neo-liberal strategy of empire building has deindustrialized a significant number of countries in Latin America and led them

toward greater dependence on a limited array of agro-mineral products. The reversion to an earlier international division of labor in some countries created an immense pool of unemployed former industrial workers who subsist at the margins of the productive economy. The new export enclaves have introduced new labor-saving technologies that facilitate greater integration via subordination to the imperial, commercial, and financial circuits. Theoretically this reversion to an earlier form of the international division of labor calls into question linear concepts of history that exclude the role of class relations and class struggle.

3. The U.S.'s increase in subsidies for agricultural exports and protective tariffs on agricultural and industrial products while pursuing free trade in Latin America suggests that the inter-American trading regime more closely resembles a mercantilist rather than a free-trade empire—in other words, a reversion to stage two of the traditional schema. The U.S. empire's electoral politics requires political and social stability at home in order to recruit imperial soldiers, mobilize political support, and divert resources to conquest. This requires that noncompetitive sectors of the economy that include constituents influential in national or regional politics (cotton, sugar, and citrus farmers; textile, steel, and other manufacturers) be satisfied. Hence, the new imperialism combines free trade that benefits its competitive sectors with protectionism for its noncompetitive but politically important economic sectors. The net result ties sectors of the U.S. trade unions to the imperial state (in pursuit of protectionism) and weakens trade unions in Latin America via unemployment or alliances with export elites that demand greater access to U.S. markets.

4. Washington's drive to impose the Latin American Area of Free Trade (ALCA is the Spanish acronym) involves the establishment of a trade and investment commission to oversee compliance with the treaty. This commission will be dominated and, most likely, located in the U.S. (Miami?), thus eliminating Latin American sovereignty.

Neo-liberal policies have created a core group of supporters in Latin America for ALCA-style recolonization. The high-profile role of International Financial Institutions in Latin American economic decision making has already laid the groundwork and promoted the core leaders for implementing ALCA. The key theoretical point is that ALCA provides the *de jure* as well as *de facto* setting for the effective recolonization of Latin America, reversing the process of the last three stages of imperialism.

The recolonization process means that labor struggles are increasingly politicized and directed against ALCA as an instrument of domination. Massive peasants' and workers' demonstrations against ALCA are visible and are the best indicators of the rise of labor-based anti-imperialism. ALCA is understood by many labor and peasant activists as an extension and deepening of the neo-liberal policies that produced catastrophic impacts on living standards and working conditions.

These heterodox features of U.S. empire building in Latin America require a rethinking of historical processes and a more nuanced understanding of the complexities of the relation of empire building to class structure and the labor force in Latin America.

Combined and Uneven Development

Despite these historical structural reversions in form and substance of contemporary empire building, the retrograde relations are combined with the introduction of modern forms of production and social relations. High-tech industries—extremely deflated and in some cases marginalized—coexist or interpenetrate with the growth of a huge barter economy among the impoverished millions.

Landless workers and bankrupt subsistence peasants serve as temporary laborers on agro-export corporate farms that apply the latest in genetically modified seeds and computerized marketing. The most modern stylish clothing retailers import goods from subcontractors that employ young women workers in sweatshops and pay them poverty wages. Organized international crime gangs who reinvest in modern real estate, treasury notes, and shopping malls in the U.S., Europe, and Latin America exploit sex slaves, including children.

The highly privatized economies continue in tension and warfare with powerful enclaves of state enterprises defended by militant trade unions operating in a sea of nonunionized labor. Strategic economic sectors in electricity (Mexico, Ecuador) and petroleum (Mexico, Brazil, Ecuador, Venezuela) remain mostly public in a sea of privatized corporations.

Uneven and combined development also is evident in the class alliances and class relations among the labor force. Workers employed in some countries in strategic, highly productive, and high-profit economic enclaves have allied themselves with mass rural movements, particularly indigenous groups.

In Mexico, highly paid unionized electrical workers support the Zapatistas, and petroleum workers in Ecuador ally with militant Indians and unemployed workers' movements. In contrast, Venezuelan sectors of the petrol workers have joined forces with the U.S.-supported right-wing business elite seeking to overthrow an elected nationalist, populist regime. In Argentina, impoverished or unemployed middle-class sectors have joined with the unemployed, and the traditional trade union confederation of metal and manufacturing workers is allied with the neo-liberal regime.

The combined and uneven development of the economy is evident in the over-developed high-tech financial-speculative sectors and the deindustrialized and impoverished productive economy, modern shopping malls and vast barter economy systems, the computerized high-tech elite and the barrio residents living in poverty, the super-rich, and the indigent. U.S. empire building in Latin America combines the modern and retrograde in deeply class-polarized societies.

The increasingly heterogeneous nature of labor is a product of the uneven and combined development resulting from contemporary empire building. The new imperialism does not create a growing modern industrial proletariat and its subjects are not uniform in ethnic, racial, or gender composition. What does unite the disparate sectors of labor are declining living standards, physical and occupational displacement, downward mobility, the political intervention of new social leaders, new organizational structures, and increasing reliance on direct-action tactics. The older established trade unions (manufacturing in Argentina and petroleum in Venezuela) that persist in defending their narrow, relatively privileged positions have come into direct conflict with the new socio-political labor movements.

Impact of Combined and Uneven Development on Class Formation

Understanding socio-economic processes is crucial to interpreting class formation under the U.S. empire. These include massive downward mobility, large-scale long-term out migration, class conversion across the social spectrum, and, most importantly the emergence of an extremely polarized class structure in which the upper 0.1% of multibillionaires control assets that exceed those of the lowest 50%.

The key to solving the problems of poverty or extreme poverty is elimination of extreme wealth and the transfer of financial resources upward and outward through international financial circuits and networks of correspondent banks of the top ten banks in the U.S. Neo-liberal policies; state intervention; U.S. military missions; and new regulatory regimes composed of U.S.-trained economists, local financial representatives, and officials of U.S. banks, The World Bank, and the International Monetary Fund created a new class structure in Latin America and set in motion the social dynamics within the structure.

The New Ruling Class

At the top of the class structure are the billionaire owners of a diversified array of big enterprises, banks, and trading companies that represent, at most, 1% of the population. Their ascendancy was not attained through the normal operation of market forces. Most had their business beginnings as recipients of government contracts—usually via political connections. The second step in upward mobility was accomplished under the military dictatorships and the subsequent neo-liberal privatization process. Once again, through close working relations with the military ties to the neo-liberal economic and financial ministries, the billionaires were able to secure monopolistic control over lucrative public enterprises.

The third step usually involved entry into the speculative–pension fund–banking and financial fraud circuits. Billions were made via overseas borrowing and currency speculation, differential interest rates (between overseas and domestic lending), the privatization of pension funds (where management fees almost always ran to double digits), and billion-dollar bank frauds.

The key to the ascendancy of this new ruling class was deregulation of the economy and its dual linkages—the ease with which it moves capital in and out of a country and in and out of economic sectors. State power is central to the ascendancy and consolidation of this new ruling class, and the class is assured that it will retain its position by having its representatives hold key government positions, for example, in the central bank and the ministries of economy and finance. The new ruling class constitutes a hybrid of owners and directors of foreign-owned enterprises as well nationals. Both groups govern through local political (the presidency) and international financial institutions (IFI, the World Bank, and the International Monetary Fund). The formation of the new ruling class is a result of the economic opportunities opened by political institutional power. Members of the ruling class are not self-made and the ascents were not the results of market forces.

What is theoretically important for class formation is the process of class conversion. At the level of the ruling class, the conversion is from entrepreneurial to financial and speculative activity resulting in large-scale overseas transfers. This change in class configuration led to dramatic changes affecting the rest of the class structure. Equally significant, this change led to the establishment of a core group favoring ALCA and the recolonization of Latin America.

The Middle Class: The New Divisions

The upwardly mobile middle classes include elite groups of politicians, consultants, economists, stock brokers, investment bankers, publicists, and political go-betweens who serve the ruling class directly. They are accompanied by private service providers such as doctors, corporate and labor lawyers, private security agencies, politicians, generals, police chiefs, procurers, high-end prostitutes, and others who tend to the economic interests, security, welfare, and whims of the ruling class. This upwardly mobile segment of the middle class grew wealthy through the privatization process. Its members constitute a visible, accessible, and noisy stratum that attracts the attention of political scientists studying "democratic politics."

The bulk of the middle class is made up of public- and private-sector employees, including medical and educational professionals, medium- and small-business people, farmers, and manufacturers. This sector of the middle class has suffered from three simultaneously negative processes: downward social mobility (both in status and income), loss of employment, and lack of representation in the political process.

The result has been a new process of forced class conversion from middle class to unemployed and from underemployed to working class. Throughout

Latin America, the middle class has shrunk; its quality of life has sharply deteriorated; and it has become active in the streets and ballot box by allying itself with diametrically opposing political movements, depending on the country.

In Argentina, the middle class was swindled out of billions of dollars in savings under the Menem and de la Rua regimes. Between the recession in 1999 and the depression and devaluation of 2001 through 2002, middle-class living standards plunged 60%, unemployment rose to over 25%, and the bulk of the middle class became impoverished. They worked as self-employed street vendors, middle-aged prostitutes, and taxi drivers and engaged in the barter economy. The Argentine experience is important because it raises important questions about the impact of neo-liberal politics on the middle class. Before 1998, the biggest and most affluent middle class in Latin America was found in Argentina—the country that went furthest in applying neo-liberal prescriptions.

The regressive impact of the neo-liberal policies on the vast majority of the middle class gives lie to the claims of pro-empire ideologues and economists that free-market policies lead to increasing prosperity and a larger and more affluent middle class. The mass impoverishment and downward mobility of the majority of the middle class has been a determining factor in their turn toward anti-ALCA and anti-imperialist politics.

The internal polarization of the middle class is highly skewed, with the close-knit minority clamoring in favor of ALCA whereas the impoverished majority opposes it.

The responses of the disenchanted and downwardly mobile middle class in Latin America are extremely varied. In Argentina, the middle class, especially the public employee and pensioner sectors, turned to the left by organizing in popular neighborhood assemblies, participating in the overthrow of the de la Rua regime, joining the unemployed workers in marches and road blocks, and providing support to workers who occupy factories. In Brazil, most activists, cadres, and delegates to the Workers' Party congresses are public employees, although the bulk of voters are workers and the urban and rural poor. The moderate reformist promises of the Lula presidency reflect the changing composition of the party and its leadership—its becoming a *de facto* party of the middle class. In Bolivia and Ecuador, support for leftist Evo Morales and populist Lucio Gutierrez came from sectors of the downwardly mobile middle class.

In contrast, in Venezuela and Mexico, the middle class turned toward the right. The downwardly mobile middle class in Venezuela aligned itself with the pro-coup U.S.-backed far right, engaging in sustained street demonstrations, blaming the regime for the loss of purchasing power, and deeply resenting the rising influence of the predominantly poor black Chavez supporters. The case of Mexico is more complex as the downward mobility of the middle class first led to a move to the left in the late 1980s and early 1990s and then a shift to the free-market right supporting President Fox in 2000. Downward mobility, class conversion, and loss of social status of the middle classes in Latin America led to divergent political expression, depending on the political context, based on who is in power and who can be identified as the source of their malaise. There is no intrinsic factor predisposing the downwardly mobile middle class in one direction or another.

Working Class and Empire

Empire building based on neo-liberal policies and military intervention has had a profoundly negative effect on the working class, labor legislation, and trade union organization. First and foremost, the economic policies implemented by client regimes led to the massive conversion of workers into unemployed, underemployed, and low-paid self-employed street vendors and itinerant laborers. In Argentina, where more than 35% of the labor force was employed in manufacturing 30 years ago, manufacturing labor represents only 17% of the work force. The unemployment rate hovers around 20% to 25% and exceeds 50% in working class neighborhoods.

Bolivia has experienced massive losses of manufacturing and mining jobs and the growth of an informal sector that constitutes about 80% of the labor force. Similar patterns occurred in Peru, Ecuador, and Colombia. In Brazil, unemployment and underemployment total over 40% of the labor force, and the informal sector is growing. The maquiladora sector in Mexico is declining as many assembly plants move to China, resulting in the loss of hundreds of thousands of poorly paid jobs.

The social consequences include the fragmentation and dispersion of employment, declines in trade union membership, and radical changes in labor legislation. What employers and orthodox economists call *labor reform* legislation provides employers with greater power to fire workers at lower costs in terms of severance pay and gives them greater control over workplaces and working conditions. The result for workers frequently is longer hours without overtime pay. Equally important, employers evade payments to social insurance programs and pension plans and increasingly delay wage payments. Many employers have withheld wage payments for several months and then closed their factories, removing the machinery and refusing to compensate workers; wages have been arbitrarily reduced frequently.

The negative impact of empire building covers most but not all sectors of the working class. Highly organized workers in strategic sectors in some countries have been able to resist the general employer offensive and the empire's push to privatize strategic sectors. In Ecuador and Mexico, electrical and petroleum workers have successfully defended their living standards via militant action and disciplined organization. In some countries, these militant well-paid sectors have developed ties with other popular urban movements to resist neo-liberal measures and regimes, for example, in Ecuador. In other countries, trade union officials have become closely allied with privileged, corrupt senior executives and have taken action against positive legislation favoring the urban poor, as is the case of petroleum workers in Venezuela.

In Argentina, after privatization, many petroleum-processing centers were closed, leading to massive unemployment and the organization of militant unemployed workers' movements, such as in Neuquen Province.

In Colombia, U.S. military intervention via Plan Colombia led to murderous assaults, killings, and torture of hundreds of trade union leaders, activists, and members. In some cases employers contracted with paramilitary groups to eliminate labor leaders—as was the case in the Coca Cola plant.

The process of empire building includes the direct appropriation of strategic industries, the elimination of trade barriers, and the dismantling of labor legislation, all which increase the rates of profit for MNCs. The effects on the working class include a profound decline in organization and living and working conditions. As a consequence, factory workers and miners in many parts of Latin America have lost the central role in the popular struggles for social transformation and reform. Trade unions have been able to protect living and working conditions only through alliances with more-dynamic urban and rural groups.

In Argentina, unionized public employees were able to force the resignation of the de la Rua regime after he imposed a 13% wage cut. The popular assemblies of the middle class and the road blockages of the unemployed workers toppled his regime through mass protest.

In Bolivia, pensioners and urban workers' salary requirements were included in a list of ten demands put forth by the militant coca farmers' confederations that organized major highway blockages which overthrew the Sanchez de Losada regime. The peasant confederations are the most effective mass-opposition political organizations. The theoretical point is that new sectors of the peasantry, working class, and impoverished salary workers have emerged to provide leadership, organization, and spirit to the class as a whole.

The unemployed workers' movement in Argentina has been at the forefront of mass road blockages accompanied by demands for jobs, food, and housing. Urban neighborhood assemblies of downwardly mobile middle class citizens have joined militant urban protests and road blockages in Argentina, Peru, and Bolivia. Urban coalitions involving a broad array of urban social forces have been at the forefront of general strikes in Cochabamba, Bolivia (protesting the privatization of public utilities and water); Arequipa Peru; Quito, Ecuador; Santo Domingo; and Bogota, Colombia.

The organization of movements has shifted from the workplace to the neighborhood. Tactics have shifted from factory-based strikes to blockages of transportation networks. In many cases, urban workers' movements have been successful in defeating the implementation of privatization measures and in securing immediate concessions.

Theoretically, what is significant is the capacity of unemployed industrial workers to organize cohesive movements outside the factories—in neighborhoods—and bring to bear new tactics affecting the circulation of commodities and the realization of profits. The declines of trade unionism and factory employment have been offset by the growth of mass urban movements peopled by the downwardly mobile working and middle classes that have been displaced, exploited, and impoverished.

Rural Labor

Probably the most devastating impact of empire building has been on the rural labor force, particularly peasants, small farmers, subsistence farmers, rural laborers, and indigenous communities. The massive entrée of subsidized agricultural products from the U.S. and European Union has ruined small producers and bankrupted rural cooperatives. In Mexico, over 2 million peasant families—mostly small farmers and Indians—have been forced off the land since the North America Free Trade Agreement was implemented. In Brazil, under President Cardoso's neo-liberal regime (1995 through 2002), over 1.5 million peasant and family farmers were forced off the land. About a third of small farmers and peasants in Ecuador, the majority of whom are Indians, have been forced off the land in the past decade.

The neo-liberal regimes have financed agro-export sectors, starved small-scale food producers of credit and technical assistance, and opened the floodgates to cheap subsidized food imports. The results are fourfold: (1) large-scale out migration to urban slums, swelling the unemployed and informal labor sectors and emigration overseas; (2) the growth of alternative crops such as coca that provide livable incomes (Bolivia, Colombia, Peru); (3) the growth of a rural landless labor force; and (4) the re-emergence of radical peasant–Indian socio-political movements.

The conversion of peasants to urban informal activity is a result of the deindustrializing effects of neo-liberal policies. Industry cannot absorb rural migrants. To defuse the potential for urban uprising, the World Bank financed more than 10,000 nongovernment organizations (NGOs) to establish so-called local empowerment activities such as antipoverty and self-help projects to prevent the emergence of mass socio-political movements challenging the empire and its client state. In Ecuador, Bolivia, and Peru, NGO-based organizations have attached themselves to communities and in some cases to Indian movements, turning them in more-conservative directions. A few poorly funded NGOs have attempted to defend the human rights of social movement activists subject to torture, imprisonment, and state and paramilitary violence.

Rural-to-urban migration is no longer a vehicle for upward mobility because the migrants must compete with the growing number of urban unemployed for the poorest-paying temporary jobs. In some cases, the rural migrants have become active in burgeoning urban movements.

The subjective response of peasant and rural workers is resorting to rudimentary exchanges to sustain a subsistence existence based on traditional reciprocal relations. The extended family and community ties help pool scarce resources for survival. These survival strategies, however, are perceived to be inadequate. Not infrequently, family resources allow family members to emigrate overseas to find employment and then remit portions of their income to sustain their impoverished rural families.

More fundamentally, powerful rural movements based on economic and ethnic demands have emerged throughout Latin America. The most significant include the Landless Workers' Movement (MST) in Brazil; CONAIE, FENOCIN, and other groups in Ecuador; the Cocaleros of Chapare and several other peasant federations in Bolivia; and the National Peasant Federation in Paraguay. These movements have had major impacts on changing land tenure. The MST has occupied land and settled 350,000 families in less than 20 years. In Ecuador, the peasant–Indian movements overthrew two corrupt neo-liberal regimes. Throughout Latin America, such movements have become major forces in the anti-ALCA and anti-imperialist movements.

The conversion of peasants into landless or subsistence farmers produced a radicalizing impact throughout Latin America. In Bolivia, the closing of the tin mines and the conversion of miners into coca farmers has radicalized the rural movements. The displacement and appropriation of peasant lands in Colombia by military and narco-paramilitary forces increased the ranks of the two guerrilla movements in Colombia.

The result of conversion and social organization is that the principal radical opposition to U.S. empire building in many Latin American countries has moved to the countryside. This is clearly the case with the Zapatista Movement in Mexico that launched its uprising in Chiapas on January 1, 1994, the day NAFTA was inaugurated. In 2003, the major opposition to the full implementation of NAFTA has been a nationwide rural protest that included blocking major highways, hunger strikes, and threats to destabilize commercial traffic between the U.S. and Mexico. Important urban trade unions pledged support to peasant-led demands for NAFTA revision. No other social force in Mexico demonstrates the same capacity as rural labor to mobilize and take direct action to confront empire-building commercial treaties.

Uneven and combined development in Latin America is rooted in the concentration of investment, control, and extraction of wealth in the imperial financial, agro-mineral, and labor-intensive assembly enclaves. This has resulted in the regression and impoverishment of the rural sector. The imperial offensive and take-over of export earnings and budget surpluses as debt payments has led to the abandonment of the countryside. The result is that the geography of the empire is built around enclaves of wealth (urban banks, mining and energy installations, ports, agro-businesses, plantations, transport and commercial networks, and assembly plants) and military and police apparatuses that repress the surrounding populations and excluded classes.

Conclusion

The particular nature of U.S. empire—the relative strength of the military, petroleum, and energy sectors—and the impact of neo-liberal policies have led to a radical transformation of the Latin American labor force. New labor activists, tactics, and strategies have emerged to combat the empire. The weakest links in the empire are found precisely among its principal collaborators: the client neo-liberal states. The weakness of the client states arises from their draconian economic measures that have destroyed the livelihoods of millions across the social spectrum.

The empire has not developed or expanded the industrial, service, and commercial economies of Latin America. It has created pockets or enclaves of export growth and affluence in a sea of empty factories, abandoned fields, and crowded slums. It has devastated and reversed a half century of social and economic development and produced class, racial, and gender casualties. In the process of constructing a neo-mercantilist empire of free trade and protectionism, Washington has transformed a stable urban working class into an impoverished army of unemployed and underemployed masses. The empire has uprooted and displaced millions of peasants through unequal trade, state violence, and agro-business expansion.

The first consequence of the heterogeneous nature of the empire's victims was social fragmentation leading to sporadic localized struggles and organization. Overseas ideologues with no knowledge of movement dynamics concocted theories of "anti-power." They argued that the emergence of local struggles and limited demands were substitutes for taking state power. Today, as the struggles intensify, a rich mosaic of organized socio-political labor movements is challenging the client collaborators of the U.S. empire.

Each movement develops a particular base of organization. Ethnically based movements are rooted in Indian communities, unemployed workers based in the barrios are organizing, factory-based movements are linked to the occupation of bankrupt firms, and unionized workers in strategic industries are resisting privatization. The key to the advance of these movements is their resort to direct mass action, blocking the transport of goods and services and paralyzing government activities. Insofar as the movements have been deflected into electoral politics as the primary political vehicle for action, they have have lost momentum and political direction.

Anti-imperialist ideology is rapidly gaining adherents within these new labor–peasant movements replacing the antiglobalization rhetoric of the NGOs and their academic advocates. In 2003, anti-imperialism entered into the programmatic struggles against ALCA, Plan Colombia, the U.S. effort to overthrow the Chavez government, and the day-to-day struggles of farmers in Mexico to defeat NAFTA.

The weakness of the empire is found in the loss of hegemony of its neo-mercantilist economic strategy of pillage, deindustrialization, and export specialization. The U.S. empire does not exercise hegemony outside government circles and among social liberal intellectual elites. Among the activist, anti-imperialist movements identified with opposition to U.S. plunder, the U.S. is resorting to military interventions, covert actions, and economic reprisals.

The clash between the empire and the Latin American working class, unemployed masses, displaced rural classes, and downwardly mobile middle classes is visible throughout Latin America. In socially polarized Venezuela, in the mass-agrarian anti-NAFTA movement in Mexico, in the civil war in Colombia, in the struggles of the Bolivian cocaleros, among the mass unemployed workers and popular assemblies of the middle class in Argentina, the left is striking back. When the excluded cry out "Que se vayan todos!" (politician, get out!), they include U.S. generals, bankers, and coup makers.

5
Sexuality in the Marketplace

BERNARDO USECHE AND AMALIA CABEZAS

Introduction

The volume of research and number of publications on human sexuality have expanded considerably during the past decades. This renewed academic interest in sexuality springs from the present social problems associated with sexuality, of which AIDS is the most visible and dramatic issue, and from the social movements since the 1960s that have sought to strengthen the visibility, empowerment, and rights of sexual minorities. Sexuality debates are today more complicated and controversial than ever because of the complex role that sexual reproduction and eroticism play in our contemporary market society, where sexuality is not only another commodity to trade but also the arena of decisive ideological struggles.

Sexological knowledge has advanced as a result of studies done from different theoretical perspectives and disciplines. However, most studies focus primarily on sexual behavior, the physiological or psychosocial aspects of sexuality, and postmodern discourses that exclude or limit the analysis of the socioeconomic context of sexuality to a few local factors. Although some researchers limit themselves to studying basic or isolated aspects of human sexuality, other scientists, scholars, and activists investigate and engage in the field of sexual politics. These pioneers are contributing to a basic understanding of the relationship between sexuality and political economy in this era of globalization.

This chapter integrates some of the contributions of these studies with the view that neo-liberalism constitutes a macro social context of sexuality. We argue that global sexual trends are directly connected to the socioeconomic conditions created by the application of neo-liberal policies. After briefly discussing the concepts of neo-liberalism and sexuality, we maintain that the expansion of old and new forms of the commercialization of sex, the medicalization of sexual pleasure, and the globalization of the HIV/AIDS epidemic cannot be fully understood without an analysis of the social context created by the application of neo-liberal economic principles. We conclude by suggesting that students of empire need to examine the centrality of gender and sexuality to political economy and empire building.

Sex in the Neo-liberal World: Free Trade?

Neo-liberalism is the current conception and practice of monopolistic capitalism. Monopoly capital needs global expansion and control of world markets to survive. After the collapse of the Soviet empire, a new reorganization of world politics has emerged, with a First World circumscribed by the U.S.; a Second World consisting of Europe and other highly industrialized countries including China, Japan, and Russia; and an extremely poor Third World.[1] Neo-liberalism expresses corporate interests and supports the global reign of a market economy where everything is subject to a supposedly "free trade" that benefits the U.S.

Based on neo-classical economic thought, neo-liberalism proposes that the state should be "leaner and meaner," thus reducing civil service jobs and also state services and support in the areas of health, education, nutrition, and housing. Since the 1970s, the political agenda of the U.S., its donor agencies, and international regulatory institutions such as the World Bank and the International Monetary Fund have pushed economic policies that posit the market as the universal remedy for all social problems.

Neo-liberal ideology found its perfect application in the structural adjustment programs that devastated Latin America, Africa, Asia, and the Caribbean during the past two decades. Characterized by privatization, fiscal austerity, deregulation, trade liberalization, and government retrenchment, these programs increased unemployment and poverty and gave rise to labor migrations, informal labor arrangements, and extreme polarization of income throughout the world.

The U.S. and Europe have not been spared the neo-liberal revolution. Beginning with Margaret Thatcher and Ronald Reagan, the market has been made the focal point for economic and social policy in the developed world as well. With its emphasis on individual competition and market-oriented responses to issues plaguing the populations and failing economies of postindustrial cities in the global North, collective solutions to public concerns and redistributive justice have taken a secondary role in economic and social development.

The change from an economy based on industrial manufacturing and a strong welfare state to an economy based on the interests of monopoly capital and financial speculation has been fueled by technology, information, automation, and a large service sector of poorly paid temporary workers. The change has exerted devastating effects on poor people all over the world. For example, during the past 30 years, U.S. workers have experienced higher rates of unemployment, declining real wages, higher costs of living, and longer work weeks. The erosion of labor market security, although taking different forms in different countries, can be found across all European Union countries, Japan, and the U.S. (Standing, 1999).

The neo-liberal economy has diversified, expanded, and consolidated a multi-billion dollar sex industry that profits from the bodies of millions of people who are pushed out of the labor force, must supplement their low wages with extra earnings, and are attracted by the promise of higher wages and flexible schedules.[2] In this context, sexual pleasure is a commodity subject to the laws of the free-market economy.[3] The commercialization of sex has never been so extensive and diverse and never been as integrated into the political economy as it is in the current historical period.[4]

Technological advances have made possible the permeation of sexual commerce into previously private spaces such as the home and workplace. No longer relegated to the seedy side of town, red-light district, or regulated zone for prostitution, the sex industry has penetrated the strip malls of middle-class suburbs under the disguise of the new "gentlemen's club." It is not happenstance that *Playboy* and *Playgirl* magazines featured women and men who were laid off by Enron in 2002 (*Playboy*, 2002; Zipp and Derasmo, 2002). Their pictorials exemplify the values of the marketplace: if you are jobless, you still have your body to sell and a corporation can still profit from it.

Commercial sexual transactions have divergent social meanings, depending on the historical and cultural specificity of the exchange. Certainly, the Burmese and Nepali girls sold into prostitution in Southeast Asia or the desperate women who cross the border between Mexico and the U.S. daily to engage in prostitution because they do not find jobs in the maquilas are not the equivalents of the Greek hetaerae. The commercialization of sex is not new, but global economic polices that favor multinational corporations, weaken national economies in the Third World, and increase the Third World debt burden condemn a significant percentage of poor men and women to trading sex in order to survive or advance economically. Although men are increasingly engaged in performing sexual services for pay, women are still the predominant providers in global sexual commerce.

Sex Tourism in the Global Economy

The World Bank and other international agencies have spent decades promoting tourism as an alternative strategy for economic development in the Third World (Truong, 1990; Bishop and Robinson, 1998; Cabezas, 1999). The emphasis on such a development approach for impoverished countries will persist as long as the World Bank's structural adjustment programs and the current free-trade agreements promoted by the U.S. continue ruining the national agriculture, industry, and commerce of countries everywhere (Sparr, 1994).

Sex is marketed subliminally or openly by multi-national conglomerates promoting an industry that ultimately benefits airlines, hotels, casinos, and other multi-national corporations. This phenomenon occurs with its particularities all around the world, including Southeast Asia (Truong, 1990), the Caribbean (Cabezas, 1999; Kempadoo, 1999), and Latin America (Schifter, 2001). The connection between market politics and prostitution is epitomized in the sexual markets and trafficking in women conducted in the former countries of the Soviet Bloc (Aral et al., 2003).

Bishop and Robinson (1998), in their study of the Thai sex industry, show that sexuality is not, as many scholars believe, only a cultural or superstructural issue. In these neo-liberal times, sex tourism is one way in which sexuality is incorporated into the economic bases of Third World societies and represents a tacit strategy of the international agencies to replace real national economic growth. As Bishop and Robinson ironically point out, "Thailand's miracle economic recovery was built on the backs of women working on their backs" (1998, p. 251).

When traveling for pleasure involves visitors with disposable income and extremely poor hosts with little to sell except their bodies, new and old forms of prostitution flourish. As a segment of the tourism market (segmentation is one of the favorite neo-liberal marketing strategies), the sex tourism business offers to calm the alienated and unsatisfied erotic needs of male and female citizens of developed countries with leases of cheap bodies, erotic adventure, and companionship. The young people, primarily women, who migrate to tourist resorts to fulfill the demand for sexual services are routinely harassed, criminalized, and incarcerated by the police (Cabezas, 2002). It is a win–win proposition for multi-national conglomerates in the tourism business—now the largest global industry—because it profits from the low wages of tourism workers and from the many enticements that Third World states create to attract foreign investments, for example, tax holidays, repatriation of profits, and infrastructure development. Third World states, along with local and in-ternational businesses, middlemen, and entertainment establishments, all profit directly or indirectly from the sale of sex.

Sex tourism also sustains the economies of major global cities (Wonders and Michalowski, 2001). In the developed world, sex tourism plays a primary role as an attraction of the entertainment centers of cities such as Amsterdam, Barcelona, Frankfurt, Las Vegas, New York, Rome, San Francisco, and Tokyo. In many of these destinations, sex workers are migrants from Asia, Africa, Latin America, the Caribbean, and Eastern Europe.

Immigration is another factor contributing to the expansion and diversifi-cation of sex commerce. Ayala, Carrier, and Magaña (1996) have described the particular modalities of sex work performed by many Latinas who migrate to the U.S. from the rural zones of Mexico and Central America, areas devastated by the North American Free Trade Agreement (Lara and Rich, 1993). After crossing the border aided by "coyotes" (brokers who help undocumented immigrants evade immigration check points), their only opportunity to work is often in cantinas (beer joints). Because of the militarization of the U.S.–Mexican border, many women who migrate from the interior of Mexico and fail to cross the border end up as sex workers in the border cities of Juárez, Nuevo Laredo, and Tijuana, serving a clientele of tourists predominantly from the U.S. (Valdez et al., 2001).

Women from Africa, Eastern Europe, Latin America and the Caribbean, and Southeast Asia also travel to Western Europe and the U.S. to work in the sex trade. A study conducted by the European Network for HIV/STD Prevention in Prostitution estimates that between 40% and 80% of the female sex workers in Western Europe are from these regions (as quoted in Bernstein, 2001). Some studies indicate that most women are well informed about the kind of work available to them before they start on their journeys. However, they are unprepared for the unfavorable working conditions of the sex and entertainment establishments and the xenophobic policies of the receiving countries (Wijers, 1998).

Many women are deceived, coerced, forced, and enslaved in brothels and other sex-industry businesses. Some enter into the marriage trade— and contract paper marriages that give them access to work and residency permits, rendering them vulnerable to sexual, psychological, and economic exploitation because their immigration status is dependent on their marriage. For these women, leaving an abusive marriage means foregoing legal residency and facing immediate deportation. The legislation of receiving countries criminalizes women who are victims of trafficking and deports them, rendering them more vulnerable and dependent on pimps and traffickers (König, 1996, p. 117).

The internationalization of the sex industry, as manifested in sex tourism, is also related to the globalization of sexually transmissible infections, as has been documented in the case of Haiti. Contrary to the common belief that Haiti was one of the original point sources and exporters of AIDS to the U.S., epidemiological research demonstrates that gay-sex tourism originating in North America and Haiti's rampant poverty were factors responsible for the initial spread of AIDS in the country (Farmer, 1992; Hertzman, 2001).

Although males take part in the sex trade, women are particularly vulnerable to exploitation. Extreme economic inequality, poverty, unemployment, elimination of social welfare, and war are consequences of the present neo-liberal globalization, and all these reinforce gender and sexual discrimination. On the basis of the premise that women bring to the marketplace natural talents that differentiate them from men, Fischer (1999) optimistically predicts a splendid future for women in the neo-liberal world. However, along with scholars such as Jagger (2001) and Chang (2000), we argue that globalization exacerbates inequality for Third World women by undercutting social forms of subsistence and support and providing limited prospects for earning income outside domestic work, export processing, and sex work. Women's financial independence and sexual agency are severely truncated in the landscape of neo-liberal culture.

The commercialization of sexuality that is titillated by the anonymity and adventure implied in tourist marketing is only one of the areas where capital benefits from the excitement of erotic desire. Another is the medicalization of sexuality—the creation of sexual dysfunction and the promise of pharmaceuticals to heal the pathologies that they have defined as such.

Medicalization of Sexuality: The Case of Female Sexual Dysfunction

The regulation of pleasurable sex has been a constant in class societies and a major component of governing ideology since antiquity, when the Roman Empire finally conquered the Christians through a combination of military campaigns and the preaching of a new sexual morality founded on Augustine's reinterpretation of the book of Genesis (Pagels, 1989). Augustine contended that the only normal sexual behavior was heterosexual coitus intended for procreation between spouses and that sexual desire was an evil force. Thomas Aquinas later developed this concept during the Middle Ages to strengthen the forms of endogamy that supported the feudal economy, and the philosophers of the French Revolution reinterpreted it in the context of the emergent bourgeoisie.

In the 18th century, Rousseau conceived the state as a great family that, in order to "maintain itself," demands the submission of women to their husbands as the only way "to preserve and increase the patrimony of the father," ascertain paternity, and guarantee the family government. Although the family and the state are different institutions and use different methods of control, men concentrate on governing their families and state governors concentrate on ruling society; both fathers and governors, as well as families and states work "to secure individual property" through male dominance (cited in Agonito, 1977, p. 118).

Rousseau, Voltaire, Diderot, and the other French encyclopedists opened the door to the modern medicalization of sexuality. Controlling masturbation became a necessity because this behavior could endanger marriages and threaten the families and social interactions the new bourgeois economy required. Capitalism is based on individualism, but the solitary act of masturbation is perceived as an extreme and, by the same token, dangerous behavior that could put the individual beyond the reach of the state (Laqueur, 1990 and 2003).

At a time when the consolidation of monopoly capital was taking place in Europe and the U.S., medicine became responsible for redefining sexual pleasure as pathological. Krafft-Ebing, Freud, and other medical doctors rejected eroticism as a normal expression of sexuality (Zwang, 1994). Krafft-Ebing (1965, p. 1) phrased this eloquently in his masterwork *Psychopathia Sexualis*: "Man puts himself at once on a level with the beast if he seeks to gratify lust alone." The creator of psychoanalysis, Sigmund Freud, while studying "hysteric" women, recognized the harmful psychological effects of sexual repression and considered perverse every sexual activity that differed from the vaginal coitus intended for procreation. He justified women's sexual inferiority by the lack of a penis and argued for the necessity of abandoning the pursuit of orgasms by clitoral stimulation in order for women to reach "sexual maturity."

Freud, unable to accept the erotic as a healthy human realm, proposed sublimating the libido instead of satisfying sexual desire. He claimed that men and women must channel erotic energy to socially accepted activities such as work, religion, or the arts. This explains why, after the initial furious rejection of his theories, Freud received the joyous support of the European and American bourgeoisie. Freudian doctrine facilitated the classification of common and healthy erotic expressions as pathological. Masturbation, women's expression of sexual desire (nymphomania), and homosexuality were medically stigmatized, and psychoanalysis was added to the list of treatments for these illnesses. Sublimation provided monopoly capital with a psychological theory that justified the substitution of sexual desire by the desire to consume in a market economy.

In sum, and as Foucault (1979) argued in his *History of Sexuality*, the psychiatrization of eroticism—the control of the sexual body—was a way of using specific knowledge about sexuality to exercise power and regulate the individual. It is in this way that the *medicalization* term is currently understood. For Riessman (1983), for example, medicalization was the definition of a condition or behavior as an illness in order to control or suppress it.

The current stage of globalization implies a drastic change in clinical sexology and sex therapy. The contemporary medicalization of sexuality maintains the hetero-normative emphasis on "normal" sexuality based on vaginal intercourse. At the same time, however, it is favorably inclined toward the erotic as a commodity which makes it vulnerable to the voracity of pharmaceutical corporations.

The novel aspect of the medicalization of sexuality in this neo-liberal era consists of the pathologization of the erotic to create an immense lucrative market of sexual dysfunction and profit-making from selling cures. Whereas members of the old bourgeoisie were to be punished, repressed, or sublimated for erections, vaginal secretions, and orgasms, and perverts (everyone according to the Freudian definition) who could afford to do so were to lie down on psychiatric divans, the solutions for neo-liberal entrepreneurs are very expensive pills, gels, and medical procedures.[5]

Male phallocratic sexuality was easily conquered by the pharmaceutical industry with the launch of Viagra in May 1998. Millions of men everywhere (those who can afford it) take the blue pills. Many of them take Viagra as a recreational drug to enhance the excitatory and orgasmic experience (Kim, Kent, and Klausner, 2002). Its enormous commercial success has motivated drug companies to seek equivalent mega blockbuster medications, procedures, and devices aimed at enhancing sexual experiences for women.

Reproductive sexuality is already under the control of the business world in consonance with the privatization of health research and services. Today it is possible to talk about the contraceptive business, the fertility and birth delivery business, and the menopause business along with the reproductive technology and the cloning businesses!

A similar and equally serious issue is the medicalization of eroticism as promoted by the commercial interests of private corporations. It is undeniable that sexual problems do exist and that any and all components of the pleasurable function of sexuality can be affected: libido, the relationship of sexual partners, stimulation, arousal, and orgasm. What is important is to determine whether such problems can be solved with sex education, counseling, and therapy or must be treated medically.[6] The answer depends, of course, on whether the causes of those sexual problems or dysfunctions are physiological, sociocultural, psychological, or mixed and whether the dysfunction is due to a medical condition or a relational problem with a sex partner. As Alzate (1987) notes, most sexual problems are minor or pseudoproblems generated by sexual ignorance, erotophobia, relational conflicts, poor conditions of life, lack of experience, or lack of sexual opportunity. Only a minority of sexual complaints are major problems that require specialized sex therapy or medical intervention.

Tiefer (2000), who has closely chronicled the medicalization of women's sexuality, stated that the recent deregulation of the pharmaceutical industry, favorable marketing opportunities, and an auspicious political environment have facilitated conditions for a campaign to create a new market for the commercial exploitation of women's erotic lives. Tiefer is critical of the sexologists who, in a Faustian bargain, collaborate with medical corporations seeking to expand their commercial ventures. In the middle of the debate concerning the role of pharmaceutical companies in the medicalization of sexual problems (Moynihan, 2003), some scientists have defended the rationale that little basic sexual research can be done without money from drug corporations (Basson and Leiblum, 2003). This view implies an unfortunate acceptance of the state's disavowal of historical responsibility in the funding of biomedical research and an affirmative endorsement of the notion of science for profit.

Following the neo-liberal recipe of creating norms that pave the road for business, the drug companies financially supported several academic meetings that ended with a conference of experts producing a report defining and classifying female sexual dysfunction (Basson et al., 2001). The report focuses on a few modifications of the existent classification of female sexual disorders included in the *Diagnostic and Statistical Manual of Mental Disorders* of the American Psychiatric Association (2000) and emphasizes the inclusion of sexual dysfunctions that originate in biological and physiological problems that can be medically treated. It also outlines the research needs and priorities for the field and describes the steps in the clinical trials required for federal approval of medical products. Hall (2001, p. 150) elucidates the financial and political stakes: "I can only hope that some women suffering from desire disorders are also Pfizer stockholders. That is the only way they will benefit from this report."

According to Tiefer (2000), once companies obtain approvals for their products, they can advertise directly to the public and popularize their medications, devices, and treatments that will be used to cure the diseases they invented. This access to the population through the media also implies ideological manipulation because sexual problems are presented in isolation from their socioeconomic context and without identifying the social causes of dysfunction. For this reason, Tiefer and a group of scholars have started working on an alternative model for sex therapy founded on a socio-cultural approach (Tiefer, 2001; Kaschak and Tiefer, 2002).[6]

Medical science and technology are certainly helpful in treating some cases of major sexual problems, but Tiefer suggests that, through their marketing strategy, drug corporations are putting new labels on old discriminatory conceptions of women's sexuality. In the neo-liberal context, female sexual dysfunction— presently afflicting 43% of American women according to its promoters (Laumann, Paik, and Rosen, 1999)—means that almost one of two women suffers a contemporary version of frigidity. This is merely a sophisticated version of the Freudian aphorism that "anatomy is destiny" intended to recycle the idea that women are erotically inferior to men. The difference in this case is that the victims of "penis envy" must pay in cash to remedy their problems.

Research conducted by John Bancroft (2002) shows that, given the participation of brain centers and neuromechanisms during sexual excitation, it is perfectly possible that factors such as marked tiredness, stress, or a partner's negative behavior invoke sexual inhibition in women. These kinds of adaptive responses and the sexual politics that privilege male sexual pleasure can explain many of the female orgasmic and arousal problems but "should not be regarded as a dysfunction" (p. 455).[7] Specific sex information, counseling, and erotic exploration generally solve these problems. However, the urge for profit does not allow sex-business entrepreneurs to promote this approach.

AIDS, the World Bank, and the Bush Administration

Sexuality and neo-liberal globalization converge in the AIDS epidemic, intensifying systems of disparity connected with race, class, and gender. HIV/AIDS is considered a sexually transmitted infection,[7] and unprotected anal and vaginal intercourse are regarded as high-risk sexual behaviors (Ross and Nilsson-Schonneson, 2000.) The Bush administration and other conservative groups have made sexual abstinence and strict monogamy the core strategies for combatting the pandemic worldwide.

The United Nations and The World Health Organization calculate that around 40 million people were living with HIV/AIDS at the end of 2003. According to the most recent studies, AIDS primarily affects the poorest nations of the world and the marginalized populations of industrial countries (UNAIDS/ World Health Organization, 2003). These studies support previous findings showing that the distribution of HIV/AIDS infection is in concordance with the present world socioeconomic order and that the expectancies of better health are higher in countries with relatively low income inequality.

Even in the developed world, health indicators such as life expectancy at birth are superior in Sweden, where income inequality is lower, than in the U.S., where inequity in income is higher (Hertzman, 2001) and 46 million citizens lack health insurance. Health expectancies are associated with income levels and especially with social inequity. Good health status is linked to quality of life, including environment, water, nutrition, housing, education, work, and psycho-social conditions. Favorable psycho-social conditions for health are unique products of social progress and more egalitarian societies. Social well-being and less stressful environments facilitate human development throughout life (Hertzman, 2001). During the past two decades, the extreme socio-economic polarization among countries and social classes has created a social context in which HIV/AIDS is spreading primarily among the planet's poor.

Famine and AIDS go together in Africa. Steven Lewis, a United Nations envoy, explained the situation: "Everybody now understands that when the body has no food to consume, the virus consumes the body. And what, of course, is happening is that in the absence of food the immune systems are weakening, the progression of the disease is so much more rapid, and people are dying sooner" (National Public Radio, 2003a). In several African countries, more than 30% of the adult population is infected with HIV (UNAIDS/World Health Organization, 2002). In Zimbabwe, 2500 people die of AIDS weekly; in the 20 years since AIDS emerged, life expectancy there dropped from 55 to 38 years.

Confronted with a health crisis of such dramatic proportions, the White House and the World Bank designed their own strategy to combat the AIDS epidemic. Not surprisingly, the bank and the U.S. government emphasize AIDS as a cause of poverty rather than the other way around. "It is still not clear whether poverty increases the likelihood of HIV infection. However, there is strong evidence that HIV/AIDS causes and worsens poverty" (World Bank, 2003a). U.S. Secretary of Health Thompson (HRSA Press Office, 2003, p. 1) states, "Poverty, unfortunately, is a common symptom of AIDS." Nevertheless, the fact is that more than 95% of people with HIV/AIDS live in developing countries, most of them nations that suffered the structural adjustments ordered by the World Bank and the International Monetary Fund.

A central component of responses by the World Bank and the Bush administration is a program of AIDS antiretroviral medications. President Bush announced his plan in the 2003 State of the Union speech. He stated that the objective was to "provide antiretroviral drugs for 2 million HIV-infected people" in twelve African and two Caribbean countries, Haiti and Guyana. At first glance this appears to be a generous humanitarian gesture. However, such a strategy is a response to the obstacles encountered by drug companies when they attempted to sell anti-AIDS treatments at exorbitant rates—a measure intended to alleviate the pressure from the rising global protests organized by AIDS activists and a deliberate intent to use the projected assistance as an instrument to promote U.S. economic and political interests in countries most affected by the epidemic.

In a country like South Africa, less than 1% of people who need antiretroviral therapy receive it because almost no one can afford it (National Public Radio, 2003b). In the case of AIDS medications, neo-liberalism has exacerbated the basic contradictions of a capitalist system to the maximum, creating a huge potential market with almost no buyers.

During a week-long trip through Africa in July 2003, President Bush reiterated his pledge and promoted his 5-year, $15 billion initiative to fight HIV/AIDS. The monies promised would not go to the United Nations' Global Fund, set up in 2001 as a multilateral effort to combat AIDS. Rather, they would constitute a unilateral effort run by three U.S. entities: the Agency for International Development, the State Department, and the Department of Health and Human Services (Engardio, 2003).

This explains why South African Finance Minister Trevor Manuel highlighted the risks posed by the proposed fund. Expressing fears that the money would go directly to the bank accounts of the AIDS drug industry, Manuel remarked that the greater part of the $15 billion cited by Bush will end up in the coffers of U.S. pharmaceutical companies (World Bank, 2003b).

Indeed, the Bush AIDS initiative is a sort of subsidy for the pharmeceutical industry that allows the federal government to buy drugs that the companies cannot sell directly to the impoverished African and Caribbean countries. Pharmaceutical giants such as Bristol-Myers Squibb and Abbott Laboratories, seeking to promote their AIDS medications to African nations with the help of the Bush administration, are competing to promote their products and win a slice of the $15 billion fund. Encouraged by the Bush administration, pharmaceutical companies and other multi-national corporations such as General Electric, Coca Cola, and Texaco joined Republican lobbying efforts to pass Bush's AIDS initiative in Congress, having paid as much as $40,000 each to lobbying groups in an effort to win congressional backing for the initiative (VandeHei, 2003).

It is clear that in the neo-liberal epoch, the state does not disappear as the radical advocates of the free-market system proclaim. The state simply serves the economic interests of monopoly capital. In the case of AIDS medications, in addition to buying billions of dollars worth of drugs, the state provides financial support to the biomedical companies by entitling them to acquire at rebate prices the patents for medications developed through research conducted in state-funded laboratories and universities.

Since 1995, the costs of medications have basically depended on the trade-related aspects of intellectual property rights (TRIPS) established by the World Trade Organization (Velasquez and Boulet, 1999). TRIPS are the instruments through which patents guarantee pharmaceutical corporations the monopoly of the market and permit them to maintain high prices. As usual in the imposition of market rules intended to introduce overpriced products, World Trade Organization policy makers initially allowed certain regulations that give member countries the rights to produce generic drugs for a number of years. Countries like South Africa, Brazil, and India took advantage of this policy and produced generic versions of AIDS drugs, thus demonstrating that government-run industries can reduce or eliminate prices, make a profit, save health service costs, and prolong lives.

Drug companies and the U.S. government soon started to push for total international acceptance of patent monopolies. In 2000, 39 drug companies took the South African government to court to challenge the legislation (Velasquez, 2003). Mass public protests took place in South Africa, and similar public outcries occurred during the XIV International AIDS Conference in Barcelona 2002 where Secretary Thompson was confronted by the protesters. In a preventative move intended to appease the protests of African and other Third World countries during meetings scheduled by the World Trade Organization in September 2003 in Cancun, Mexico, the Bush administration and the pharmaceutical industry agreed on August 30, 2003, to allow poor countries to continue buying generic drugs temporarily. However, the agreement established the commitment of all countries to buy patented brand-name medications from pharmaceutical corporations in the near future.

At the same time that it promotes its commercial interests through the World Trade Organization, the U.S. continues to negotiate bilateral and regional agreements that impede the production and importation of generic drugs (Love, 2003). This is one reason why, nearly 10 years after antiretroviral medicines were made available, they have not yet reached the most AIDS-plagued populations of the world.

Finally, the White House-proposed AIDS plan would allow the Bush administration to better control the spending and "make it easier to steer funds to favored African governments, such as those backing the U.S. war on terrorism, and to accommodate domestic interests such as the pharmaceutical industry and 'faith-based' groups pushing sexual abstinence (rather than distribution of condoms) as the best way to prevent AIDS transmission" (Engardio, 2003, p.1). It is not a coincidence that Bush named Randall Tobias, a major contributor to the Republican political party and former chief executive officer of Eli Lilly, a leading pharmaceutical firm, to head the U.S. effort in Africa. The appointment raised concerns because Tobias lacks experience working in Africa and with AIDS organizations and is seen as vulnerable to conflicts of interest.

The AIDS actions undertaken by the White House are not free of ideological content. They pretend to universalize HIV/AIDS prevention plans that address sexual abstinence and monogamy-only messages already at the core of sex education in the United States. Cogan (2003), an HIV/AIDS educator who has taught healthcare workers in 11 African countries, criticized the fact that abstinence programs will receive one third of the money appropriated by the

Bush administration to fight the epidemic in Africa and the Caribbean. She states, "It is not appropriate for the United States to attempt to set the standards by which the entire world should live. Shouldn't other countries, cultures, and societies have their own standards, rules, mores, taboos, and lifestyles?"

The emphasis on chastity persists despite innumerable studies indicating that celibate or monogamous relationships are difficult to maintain and that anal intercourse is a common practice even in large segments of the heterosexual population (Rodríguez, 2003). HIV/AIDS prevention programs that promote sexual abstinence are not very effective among adolescents. "The weight of the evidence indicates that these abstinence programs do not delay the onset of intercourse" (Kirby, 2000, p. 87). In addition, this moralistic approach reinforces discrimination toward people because of their sexual orientations or erotic preferences and justifies a new crusade that complements the recolonization of the globe.[8]

Conclusion

Current global sexual changes emanate from socio-economic conditions created by the application of predominant neo-liberal policies. The expansion of old and new forms of sexual commercialization, the medicalization of sexual pleasure, and the globalization of the HIV/AIDS epidemic cannot be fully understood without an analysis of the social context originating in the application of neo-liberal economic principles. Although sexuality is not "the primary motivating factor in the course of human history," as Hugh Hefner believes (Petersen, 1999), eroticism and human sexual reproduction are so central to people's lives that the state early in history learned the utility of regulating sex to exercise its power. The control of sexuality continues to be instrumental for the consolidation and functioning of the state.

References

Agonito, R., *History of Ideas on Women*, Perigee Books, New York, 1977.
Álzate, H., "Vaginal Erogeneity and Female Orgasm: A Current Appraisal," *Journal of Sex and Marital Therapy*, 11, 271, 1985.
Álzate, H., *Sexualidad Humana*, 2nd ed., Temis, Bogotá, Columbia, 1987.
Álzate, H., "Travaux recents sur l'orgasme femenin," communicatin présentée au XXVe séminaire de perfectionnement en sexology clinique, Toulouse, France, March 17 and 18, 1995.
Álzate, H., B. Useche, and M. Villegas, "Heart Rate Change as Evidence for Vaginally Elicited Orgasm and Intensity," *Annals of Sexual Research*, 2, 345, 1989.
American Psychiatric Association, *Diagnostic and Statistical Manual of Mental Disorders*, 4th ed., Washington, DC, 2000.
Aral S.O., St. Lawrence, J.S., Tikhonova, L., Safarova, E., Parker, K.A., Shakarishvili, A., Ryan, C.A. The social organization of commercial sex work in Moscow, Russia. *Sex Transm Dis.* 2003 Jan; 30(1): 39–45.
Ayala, A., J. Carrier, et al. (1996). The underground world of Latina sex workers in cantinas. In: Mishra Sl, Conner RF and Magana JR (Eds.) *AIDS Crossing Borders: The Spread of HIV Among Migrant Latinos.* New York, Westview Press: 95–112.
Ayala, A., J. Carrier, and R. Magaña, "The Underground World of Latina Sex Workers in Cantinas," in *AIDS Crossing Borders: The Spread of HIV among Migrant Latinos*, Westview Press, Boulder, CO, 1996, p. 95.
Bancroft, J., "The Medicalization of Female Sexual Dysfunction: The Need for Caution," *Archives of Sexual Behavior*, 31, 451, 2002.

Basson, R., and Leiblum, S. Without funding little new research will be possible. *BMJ* 2003; 326:658 22 March.

Basson, R. et al., "Report of the International Consensus Development Conference on Female Sexual Dysfunction: Definitions and Classification," *Journal of Sex and Marital Therapy*, 27, 83, 2001.

Bernstein, E., *Economies of Desire: Sexual Commerce and Post-Industrial Culture*, Ph.D. dissertation, University of California, Berkeley, 2001.

Bishop, R. and L. Robinson, *Night Market: Sexual Cultures and the Thai Economic Miracle*, Routledge, New York, 1998.

Cabezas, A.L., "Women's Work is Never Done, Sex Tourism in Sosúa, the Dominican Republic," in Kempadoo, K., Ed., *Sun, Sex and Gold: Tourism and Sex Work in the Caribbean*, Rowman & Littlefield, Boulder, CO, 1999.

Cabezas, A.L., "Globalization, Sex Work and Women's Rights," in *Globalization and Human Rights: Transnational Problems, Transnational Solutions*, Brush, A., Ed., University of California, Press, Berkeley, 2002.

Chang, G., *Disposable Domestics: Immigrant Women Workers in the Global Economy*, South End Press, Cambridge, MA, 2000.

Cogan, L., "Let Experts Decide Usafe in HIV/AIDS Funding Fight," *Houston Chronicle*, May 10, 2003, p. 41A.

Duesberg, P., C. Koehnlein, and D. Rasnick, "The Chemical Bases of the Various AIDS Epidemics: Recreational Drugs, Anti-Viral Chemotherapy and Malnutrition," *Journal of Bioscience*, 28, 412, 2003.

Duesberg, P.H., *Inventing the AIDS Virus*, Regnery Publishing, Washington, DC, 1996.

Engardio, P., "Who Should Lead the War on AIDS?" *Business Week*, July 15, 2003. http://www.businessweek.com/bwdaily/dnflash/jul2003/nf20030715 7728 db039.htm.

Epstein, S., *Impure Science: AIDS, Activism, and the Politics of Knowledge*, University of California Press, Berkeley, 1996.

Farmer, P., *AIDS and Accusation: Haiti and the Geography of Blame*, University of California Press, Berkeley, 1992.

Fischer, H., *The First Sex: The Natural Talents of Women and How They Are Changing the World*, Random House, New York, 1999.

Foucault, M., *The History of Sexuality*, Vol. 1, Allen Lane, London, 1979.

Gorney, C., "Designing Women: Scientists and Capitalists Dream of Finding a Drug that Could Boost Female Sexuality," *Washington Post*, June 30, 2002, p. W08.

Hall, M., Small Print and Conspicuous Omissions: Commentary on the 'FSD' Classification Report," *Journal of Sex and Marital Therapy*, 27, 149, 2001.

Hertzman, C., "Health and Human Society," *American Scientist*, 89, November–December 2001.

HRSA Press Office, "HHS Awards $1 Billion to Help States Provide Health Care, Services and Prescription Drugs for People with HIV/AIDS," Washington, DC, April 10, 2003.

Jagger, A., "Is Globalization Good for Women?" *Comparative Literature*, 53, 298, 2000.

Kaschak, E. and L. Tiefer, Eds., *A New View of Women's Sexual Problems*, Haworth Press, Binghamton, NY, 2002.

Kempadoo, K., "Continuities and Change: Five Centuries of Prostitution in the Caribbean," in Kempadoo, K., Ed., *Sun, Sex, and Gold: Tourism and Sex Work in the Caribbean*, Rowman & Littlefield, Boulder, Co., 1999.

Kim, A., C. Kent, and J. Klausner, "Increased risk of HIV and sexually transmitted disease transmission among gay or bisexual men who use Viagra, San Francisco 2000–2001," *AIDS*. 2002 Jul 5; 16(10): 1425–8.

Kirby, D., "School-Based Interventions to Prevent Unprotected Sex and HIV among Adolescents," in *Handbook of HIV Prevention*, Peterson, J. and R. DiClemente, Eds. Kluwer Academic/Plenum, New York, 2000.

König, I., Ed., *Traffic in Women*, Lateinamerikanische Emigrierte Frauen in Österreich, Vienna, Austria,1996.

Kraft-Ebing, R., *Psychopathia Sexualis*, Arcade Publishing, New York, 1965.

Laqueur, T., *Making Sex: Body and Gender from the Greeks to Freud*, Harvard University Press, Cambridge, MA, 1990.

Laqueur, T., *Solitary Sex: A Cultural History of Masturbation*, Zone Books, New York, 2003.

Laumann, E., A. Paik, and R. Rosen, "Sexual Dysfunction in the United States: Prevalence and Predictors," *Journal of the American Medical Association*, 281, 537, 1999.

Levin, R., "The Physiology of Sexual Arousal in the Human Female: A Recreational and Procreational Synthesis," *Archives of Sexual Behavior*, 31, 405, 2002.

Love, J. Prescription for pain WTO reneges on drugs patents. Le Monde Diplomatique. March 2003. http://mondediplo.com/2003/03/12 generio.

National Public Radio, "Profile: Malnutrition Accelerating AIDS Epidemic in Zimbabwe," February 19, 2003a.

National Public Radio, "Commentary: Getting Medicines to South Africa for HIV and AIDS Patients," February 19, 2003b.

Pagels, E., *Adam, Eve, and the Serpent.* New York: Random House. 1989.

Petersen, J., Ed., *The Century of Sex: Playboy's History of the Sexual Revolution, 1900–1999*, Grove Press, New York, 1999.

Playboy Magazine, "Women of Enron," August 2002, p. 119.

Riessman, C., "Women and Medicalization: A New Perspective," *Social Policy*, 14, 4, 1983.

Rodriguez, J., *Queer Latinidad: Identity, Practices, Discursive Spaces*, New York University Press, New York, 2003.

Ross, M. and L. Nilsson-Schonneson, "HIV/AIDS and Sexuality," in Szuchman, L. and F. Muscarella, Eds., *Psychological Perspectives on Human Sexuality*, John Wiley & Sons, New York, 2000.

Schifter, J., *Latino Truck Driver Sex: Sex and HIV in Central America*, Haworth, New York, 2001.

Sparr, P., *Mortgaging Women's Lives: Feminist Critiques of Structural Adjustment*, Zed, London, 1994.

Standing, G., *Global Labour Flexibility*, St. Martin's Press, New York, 1999.

Tiefer, L., "Sexology and the Pharmaceutical Industry: the Threat of Co-Optation," *Journal of Sex Research*, 37, 273, 2000.

Tiefer, L., "A New View of Women's Sexual Problems: Why New? Why Now?" *Journal of Sex Research*, 38, 89, 2001.

Tiefer, L., "Beyond the Medical Model of Women's Sexual Problems: A Campaign to Resist the Promotion of 'Female Sexual Dysfunction'," *Sexual and Relationship Therapy,* 17, 127, 2002.

Truong, T.D., *Sex, Money, and Morality: Tourism in South East Asia*, Zed, London, 1990.

UNAIDS/WHO 2003. Joint United Nations Programme on HIV/AIDS (UNAIDS) and World Health Organization (WHO). Aids Epidemic Update December 2003. http://www.unaids.org/Unaids/EN/Resources/Publications/Corporate+publications/AIDS+epidemic+update+-+December+2003.asp

Useche, B., "El Exámen Sexológico en las Disfunciones Excitatorias y Orgásmicas Femeninas: Revista Terapia Sexual," *Clinica Pesquisa e Aspects Psicossociais*, 4, 115, 2001.

Valdez et al., "Sex Work, High-Risk Sexual Behavior and Injecting Drug Use on the U.S.–Mexico Border: Nuevo Laredo, Tamaulipas," Center for Drug and Social Policy Research, University of Texas, San Antonio, 2001.

VandeHei, J., "Drug Firms Boost Bush's AIDS Plan: GOP Lobbying for Support of Africa Initiative," *Washington Post*, May 1, 2003, p. A25.

Velazquez, G., "Unhealthy Profiles: Drugs Should Be a Common Good," *Le Monde Diplomatique*, July 2003, http://mondediplo.com/2003/07/10velasquez.

Velasquez, G. and P. Boulet, *Globalization and Access to Drugs: Perspectives on the WTO/TRIPS Agreement*, World Health Organization, Geneva, 1999.

Wax, E., "Ugandans Say Facts, Not Abstinence, Will Win AIDS War: Bush Likely to Hear Dissent on Policy," *Washington Post Foreign Service*, July 9, 2003, p. A18.

Wijers, M., Women, Labor, and Migration: The position of trafficked women and strategies for support in Kempadoo, K., and Doeuma J. Eds. Global Sex Workers; Rights, Resistance, and Redefinition 69–78, New York and London: Routledge 1998.

Wonders, N.A. and R. Michalowski, "Bodies, Borders, and Sex Tourism in A Globalized World: A Tale of Two Cities, Amsterdam and Havana," *Social Problems*, 48, 545, 2001.

World Bank, "HIV/AIDS at a Glance: Lessons Learned," http://wbln0018.worldbank.org/HDNet/hddocs.nsf/c840b59b982d2498525670c004def60/0560436b70e56de385256a4800524119?OpenDocument#section9, Washington, 2003a.

World Bank, "World Ban Says AIDS Worst Economic Evil: Private Sector Responds to the Epidemic," Washington, June 4, 2003b, http://web.worldbank.org/WBSITE/EXTERNAL/NEWS/0,,date:04-04-2003~menuPK:34461~pagePK:34392~piPK:34427~theSitePK:4607,00.html#Story3.

Zipp, M. and A. Derasmo, "The Rise of Enron," *Playgirl Magazine*, October 2002, p. 18.

Zwang, G., *Histoire des Peines de Sexe: Les Malheurs Érotiques, Leurs Causes et Leurs Remedes a Travers les Ages*, Editions Maloine, Paris, 1994.

Notes

1. We see this new configuration of global politics as the result of the strategy implemented by the U.S. to consolidate and expand its economic, political, and military power; the alliances generated between the empire and other industrial countries; and the extreme pauperization of the world caused by the imposition of neo-liberal reforms.

2. The expansion and diversification of the sex industry that can be found across international contexts that comprise (but are not limited to) the vast array of new and old forms of sexual commerce such as street prostitution, brothels, massage parlors, telephone and Internet sex, international sex tourism, sex clubs, escort agencies, pornography in its various manifestations, and freelance call girls and other types of sex workers.

3. Sexual pleasure or eroticism is the primary function of human sexuality. All the components of the erotic function such as sexual desire, pursuit of a sexual partner, sexual stimulation, sexual arousal, and orgasm are determined by cultural and socioeconomic factors. In the neo-liberal era, all these components have become objects of market laws as evidenced by the diverse forms of the sex trade and the medicalization of sexuality.

4. We are discussing the political economy of the present conditions of commercialization of sex, not the morality of exchanging sex for money per se.

5. The UroMetrics Corporation already markets clitoral devices such as EROS-CTD for $359, available by prescription only. Other corporations are announcing gels with testosterone to boost desire and are promoting brain implants that provide neural stimulation by remote control to the centers of the brain that trigger orgasms. In an interview with Cynthia Gorney (2000), a pharmaceutical company executive expressed his enthusiasm for a still-in-development gel from which the corporation expects to generate $837 million in 2004. "That is why we are interested in the product," he recognized.

6. There is some scientific evidence that women can have difficulty reaching excitation levels that trigger orgasm during vaginal sex simply because the stimulation provided by the male sexual organ on the vaginal walls is not strong and long enough (Álzate, 1985, 1987, and 1995, Álzate, Useche, and Villegas, 1989; Useche, 2001) and because the elevation of the vaginal wall during female sexual arousal "may reduce the frictional stimulation of the vaginal wall on the glans of the penis, leading to a loss of sensation during coital thrusting" (Levin, 2002, p. 402).

7. A small group of researchers considered dissidents by the AIDS establishment argues that AIDS is a collection of chemical epidemics caused by malnutrition and the use of recreational and anti-HIV drugs. See Duesberg, 1996; Epstein, 1996; and Duesberg, Koehnlein, and Rasnick, 2003.

8. Working to reduce the spread of the HIV virus, Uganda created national educational programs that promote abstinence *and* safer sex practices. Uganda's AIDS education program is praised for its achievements regarding AIDS/HIV infection rates that plummeted from 30% to 5% in slightly more than a decade (Wax, 2003).

II
States: Immigration and Citizenship

6

Class, Space, and the State in India: A Comparative Perspective on the Politics of Empire

LEELA FERNANDES

Introduction

In the contemporary moment, the politics of empire lies at the conjunction of two central transnational processes. In the U.S. war on terrorism, the current politics of empire is shaped by conventional dynamics of state strategies of military intervention and colonialism in ways that echo older historical patterns.[1] The most visible signs of this have been situations of overt military intervention in countries such as Afghanistan and Iraq. In the meantime, processes of economic globalization in the form of neo-liberal models of economic restructuring are reproducing and intensifying socio-economic hierarchies within nation–states.

These processes appear to place contradictory pressures on the positions and roles of modern nation–states in the contemporary world order. On the one hand, the transnational dynamics of economic globalization and the corresponding power of transnational corporations appeared to have weakened the nation–states (Appadurai, 1996; Strange, 1996; Habermas, 1998), particularly in newly liberalizing countries. On the other hand, the war on terrorism has underlined the significance of state apparatuses in line with an intensified emphasis on national security in comparative contexts. A central question that arises in the midst of these global processes is what is the role of the nation–state in the contemporary politics of empire? In this chapter, which draws on a study of contemporary politics in India, I argue that in contrast to theories of globalization that predicted the demise of the modern nation–state, the effects of empire can be better understood in terms of a restructuring of the state.[2]

India provides a case that enables an examination of the intersections of the economic and military–political dimensions of empire. In the early 1990s, the Indian government launched a program of economic liberalization that began to substantially dismantle state controls that had managed the economy since independence.[3] Meanwhile, contemporary Indian politics has also been significantly shaped by contemporary discourses on the war on terrorism since the state deployed the language of global terrorism in relation to the regional conflict in Kashmir. This deployment of the language of terrorism further coincided with Hindu nationalist discourses that portray Muslim communities in India as aliens' threat to a pure Hindu Indian nation.[4] These cross-cutting processes make India a unique case for an understanding of the complex ways in which the politics of empire interacts with and reconstitutes local and national politics beyond the boundaries of the U.S. nation–state and areas under overt U.S. intervention.

A key effect of this conjuncture between economic globalization and the war on terrorism is the restructuring of the Indian nation–state. As I will argue, this restructuring centers on the production of an exclusionary form of citizenship constituted by hierarchies of class, religion, and ethnicity.[5] I focus on the ways in which citizenship is produced through local spatial practices that involve the state, labor, and an increasingly politically assertive urban middle class. As Evelyn Nakano Glenn has argued, the "kinds of localized, often face-to-face practices . . . determine whether people have or don't have substantive as opposed to purely formal rights of citizens" (2002, p. 2).

Building on such an approach, I examine the emergence of a privatized form of citizenship, that is, a form of citizenship constructed as a private right of the urban middle classes that must be protected from the demands of subordinated groups such as workers and Muslims. I begin by analyzing the political emergence of an assertive urban middle class in the context of India's new economic policies of liberalization initiated since the early 1990s. Drawing on field research conducted in Mumbai (Bombay), I examine the ways in which this middle class has begun to produce an exclusionary form of citizenship through spatial practices that have brought it into political confrontations with workers such as street hawkers. I specifically examine the role of the state in facilitating the emergence of this form of citizenship and the ways such dynamics converge with contemporary discourses on terrorism and new state strategies that target undocumented Muslim workers from Bangladesh. Finally, I conclude with a discussion of the comparisons and connections between India and the U.S. Such a comparative perspective underlines the importance of conceptualizing the current politics of empire in relation to the subtle ways in which both economic globalization and the global war on terrorism converge with and reconstitute local and national politics in comparative contexts that may not at first seem implicated in the politics of military conflict and occupation that serve as visible markers of the U.S. empire.

Economic Liberalization and the "New" Indian Middle Class

India's new economic policies of liberalization have been accompanied by important shifts in the visible signs and symbols that embody the dominant national political culture. Such shifts have centered on the roles of the urban middle classes and images of new consumption practices and wealth generated by the liberalization of the economy. The result has been the emergence of a new discursive political category, the "new" Indian middle class. The newness of this middle class is not founded on a social change; that is, it does not signify a form of upward mobility in which segments from lower socio-economic brackets have been able to gain entry into the middle classes.[6] Rather, the newness of the middle class is an ideological construction that represents the class as the cultural and political symbol of a liberalizing Indian nation that is finally leaving behind the restrictions of state socialism.

A cornerstone of this construction is the association between the new middle class and the attitudes, lifestyles, and consumption practices associated with newly available commodities in the context of India's shift toward a liberalizing economy. Such consumption practices, in effect, signify the potential benefits of liberalization and parallel the construction of the "new rich" (Robison and Goodman, 1996; Beng-Huat, 2000) as a social group that serves as the prime beneficiary of globalization in contemporary Asia. The construction of such a category, in effect, marks the potential benefits of globalization for emerging market-oriented contexts in Asia in general and in India in particular.

Such shifts are evident in a wide array of public cultural discourses ranging from advertising images to media representations in film, television, and newspapers to public political rhetoric that has debated the social and political implications of the new Indian middle class.[7] Whereas in the early years of independence, large dams and mass-based factories were the national symbols of progress and development (Khilnani, 1997), cell phones, washing machines, and color televisions now serve as the symbols of the liberalizing Indian nation. For the urban middle classes, the availability of such commodities and new opportunities for consumer choices of brands serve as signs of the benefits of liberalization. Before liberalization, such goods were accessible only to the upper classes and individuals who had relatives living or working abroad.

Consider, for example, the symbolic politics of the automobile industry. In the initial decades of independence, the automobile industry offered consumers only one model—the Ambassador.[8] The Ambassador is continually invoked by proponents of liberalization whom I interviewed as a national symbol of the deprivation of middle-class consumers before to the 1990s. The availability of commodities such as cars has become associated with a sense of national pride, consolidating the linkages between middle-class desires for consumption and the image of the new liberalizing India. Thus, the new middle class becomes the idealized standard for this newly imagined Indian nation.

This emergence of the new Indian middle class is a discursive political phenomenon rather than a socio-economic one. The question that arises then is whether the actual economic effects of liberalization conform to the idealized images of the new Indian middle class. Although research in comparative contexts has demonstrated that policies of economic restructuring produced negative effects for the working classes and rural poor (Evans, 2002; Gills and Piper, 2002), scholars have paid less attention to the effects on the urban middle classes. In practice, liberalization has had contradictory effects for the urban middle classes.[9] On the one hand, the upper layers of this social group have benefited from expanded employment opportunities and rising salaries as Indian and multinational corporations have competed for managers with MBAs. On the other hand, large segments of the urban middle classes have faced a labor market that has been restructured in ways that have paralleled the working-class labor markets. This has been particularly the case for lower-tier white-collar private sector workers.

As with the working class labor market, the restructuring of the middle-class labor market has centered on three central trends: workplace reorganization, retrenchment, and the casualization of work. Workplace reorganization has, for instance, restructured the time, space, and movement of employees in lower-tier white-collar managerial work in ways that mirror factory-based models of discipline. An example of this process is the case of workers classified as executive assistants. They are lower-tier managerial workers who perform activities ranging from traditional secretarial duties to managerial tasks that may include contacting clients, organizing conferences, and handling public relations duties. Although these workers often perform managerial duties, their everyday work experiences include strict forms of discipline including recording their work hours on time cards, accounting for phone calls made on the job, and adhering to high levels of productivity.[10]

Such forms of employment have in many cases shifted away from permanent to contract-based temporary situations reflecting the broader economic processes of the casualization of work that have shaped economic globalization. These jobs, in fact, constitute a significant component of the expanding service sector in the major urban metropolitan cities—a "new economy" sector most visibly associated with processes of liberalization. Thus, in many ways these patterns of employment are typical characteristics of the vast segment of the new Indian middle class; they represent the work experiences of those segments of the middle class who cannot afford the costs of a professional MBA degree but aspire to the idealized image of the new Indian middle class and thus attempt to negotiate their way through the lower tiers of the private-sector labor market.

However, such parallels between the organization of middle-class and the working-class labor markets have not translated into political alliances between these social groups. The politics of the new middle classes has, in fact, centered on a politics of distinction in which the middle classes have sought to distinguish themselves from the working classes.

Public middle-class discourses construct the poor and working classes as threats to the social order. This sense of threat is compounded by a middle-class expression of anger based on a perception that the state caters to the poor and working classes at the expense of middle-class interests. Thomas Hansen describes this in terms of an emerging middle-class perception of a "plebianization of the political field" where democratization has enabled peasant and lower caste groups to gain access to political power.[11] Middle-class political identity is thus increasingly shaped by a resistance to what members perceive as a political field that caters to peasants, workers, and low caste groups.

Such middle-class resistance to the inclusionary political possibilities of democracy has provided the basis for a wider generalized perception of social order and political corruption. In particular, it has led to the emergence of a new middle-class conception of cultural citizenship that attempts to redraw the boundaries of citizenship in ways that reconstitute older social hierarchies that threaten to break down the socio-economic space between the middle classes and the poor and working classes. Thus, whereas policies of economic liberalization have restructured segments of the labor market in ways that parallel the working class labor market, the political response of the middle classes is to engage in social and political practices that seek to distinguish them from the working classes. Such practices result in the production of an exclusionary form of cultural citizenship that rests on the political emergence of a consumer identity associated with public images of the new Indian middle classes.

State Strategies, the Middle Class, and the Politics of Privatized Citizenship

Local spatial politics in metropolitan cities in India provide important arenas for an analysis of the dynamics of middle-class consumer-based forms of cultural citizenship that emerge in the context of economic liberalization. Consider, for example, the ways in which cultural practices of consumption and lifestyle are linked to broader processes of the restructuring of urban space associated with centers such as Mumbai. The production of middle-class identity in this context is linked to a politics of "spatial purification" (Sibley, 1995) that centers on middle-class claims over public spaces and a corresponding movement to cleanse such spaces of the poor and working classes.[12]

Such local spatial politics embody an exclusionary form of cultural citizenship in which the urban Indian middle classes are seen as the new consumer citizens in liberalizing India. As I will argue in this section, the politics of spatial purification reconstitutes historical hierarchies of class inequality and produces new alliances of the new Indian middle class, the state, and capital. The production of this new form of cultural citizenship is linked to the changing relationship between state and capital, and more specifically in relation to the restructuring of the state in the context of economic liberalization.

The politics of contemporary Mumbai provides a paradigmatic case for spatialized politics of citizenship. Consider some of the broader patterns involving the restructuring of urban space. At one level, such patterns echo familiar patterns of gentrification that have been analyzed in comparative contexts (Smith, 1996). Escalating real-estate prices in the South Mumbai heart of the city have pushed middle-class individuals into suburban areas. The result is the creation of new and distinctive forms of suburban cultural and social communities. In what are now considered upscale suburbs, neighborhoods in areas such as Bandra and other western suburbs[13] have witnessed the growth of upscale restaurants, shopping enterprises, and movie theaters. These spatial trends have reproduced new cultural forms of older class distinctions. For example, new upscale movie theaters in the suburbs depart from the traditional fee structures of regular theaters. Whereas regular theaters scaled prices from expensive balcony seats to cheaper seats at the bottom level, upscale theaters offer only flat high prices for all seating. The pricing system effectively keeps out poorer working class and even lower middle-class individuals. Such wealthy suburbs have also witnessed the growth of a new culture of "upmarket" clubs.[14] These developments point to the ways in which the images of the new liberalizing Indian middle classes are materialized through new forms of socio-spatial segregation.

The production of such socio-cultural spaces for the new lifestyles of the middle classes in liberalizing India rests on the production of a new urban aesthetics of class purity. Historically, in contrast to modern cities in advanced industrialized countries, metropolitan cities in India did not develop into strict class-segregated spaces. Although cities like Mumbai, Delhi, and Calcutta have certainly reproduced spatial distinctions among wealthier, middle class, and working class neighborhoods, such distinctions have historically been disrupted by the presence of squatters, pavement dwellers, and street entrepreneurs such as tailors, shoe repairmen, and hawkers (street vendors). Such street entrepreneurs and pavement dwellers located to these neighborhoods to provide services to their middle- and upper-class residents. Given the high level of poverty and the dependence of middle-class families on working class labor for household work including dhobis (laundry workers), sweepers, and cooks, the class-based management of urban space in contemporary India developed in patterns distinctive from those of advanced industrialized countries (Katznelson, 1981; Seabrook, 1996; Kaviraj, 1997).

In the context of liberalization, the invention of a new middle-class lifestyle is increasingly interwoven with the creation of an urban aesthetics based on the middle-class desire for the management of urban space based on strict class-based separation. This desire for socio-spatial segregation is not an outcome that is purely a result of policies of liberalization in the 1990s.[15] However, although notions of spatial purity were contingent on older historical processes (Kaviraj, 1997), what is significant in this context is the way in which the imposition of such spatial class-based norms have been transformed by the discourses of the new middle class in the context of liberalization in the 1990s.

A significant expression of this transformation has taken the form of beautification projects undertaken by resident associations and civic organizations in various neighborhoods in Mumbai. Such projects have begun to constitute a new civic culture for the middle classes in liberalizing India. This drive to clean up the city has been constructed around class-based discourses and, in effect, becomes inextricably linked with attempts to purge the city of the poor (Seabrook, 1996). Such practices point to the aesthetic of the civic culture of the middle classes in liberalizing India—one that attempts to manifest the image of the new Indian middle class by cleansing the urban city of any sign of the poor or poverty. The boundaries of this new civic culture thus rest on the attempt to produce a new form of class-based socio-spatial segregation.

Such spatialized practices do not merely represent the outcome of individualized middle-class desires. Rather, they are part of a broader set of strategies of state-led development in the context of liberalization. Liberalization, in other words, does not lead to the decline of state intervention as is often assumed in the neo-liberal model of economic development but to a shift in the nature of the exercise of state power and the emergence of new forms of collaboration between the state and the private sector. For instance, beautification projects have also been carried out by the local government in cities like Mumbai, often in conjunction with financial support from the corporate sector.

In Mumbai, for example, the beautification drive represents the official policy of the local government's Cultural Affairs Ministry. This drive is intended to clean up public spaces such as beaches, promenades, maidans (public grounds and open recreational areas), and other facilities. Although such plans appear to be part of a broader public drive for sanitation involving a cross section of local areas across the city,[16] they rest on the politics of class and involve driving out beggars, hutments (small huts constructed by squatters and laborers), fisherfolk, and squatters from public areas such as beaches (Sharma, 1998).

The pattern characterizes state strategies deployed in the management of urban space. The state restructures spaces in ways that cater to the wealthier segments of Mumbai and to the lifestyles of the new Indian middle classes, for example, by transforming spaces to cater to joggers. Proposed plans to restructure public parks and maidans have involved the drawing of clear social boundaries by constructing gates to control access to what were once accessible public spaces. Local residents and organizations opposed to such state-led projects of urban restructuring have often resisted such proposals. However, such proposals reveal the ways in which the lifestyle of the new Indian middle-class is not merely a symptom of the responses of individuals to advertising and media images; they signify a broader political process of class formation that involves the interests of both the state and the capital.

The convergence of such state strategies and middle-class conceptions of civic culture demonstrate the way in which citizenship is restructured in the context of economic liberalization. Middle-class conceptions are invested in creating a privatized form of citizenship, one that seeks to redraw public boundaries through the politics of class. Thus, processes of privatization associated with policies of economic liberalization also result in an attempted privatization in the political field. Privatization, in effect, represents a form of "elite revolt" (Corbridge and Harris, 2000) in the face of middle-class perceptions of the "plebianization" of democracy.

Such local dynamics point to larger implications for an understanding of the political dimensions of economic globalization. In particular, they demonstrate that the class-based politics produced by globalization do not simply reside at the point of production in more conventional sites such as factories and well-studied embodiments of global capital such as transnational corporations. A conceptual focus that limits an understanding of globalization to transnational corporations and export-processing zones misses a broader range of class conflict that shapes political responses to globalization and the significance of the role of the state in responding to such conflicts. In the Indian context, for instance, analyses that have focused only on the responses of traditional labor unions in the organized sector have tended to underestimate the significance of class politics and have identified resistance to liberalization mainly in terms of public-sector workers' resistance to privatization.

Consider one example of such class-based spatial political contestation: Middle-class claims on urban space have produced new conflicts with street vendors and led to increasing state-led crackdowns and the rise of working class protests as hawkers' unions have attempted to resist such crackdowns (Bhowmick, 2002b). As with the beautification programs, middle-class civic organizations and media discourses have largely portrayed hawkers as threats to the civic culture of the middle classes (Bhowmick, 2002a). Such discourses focused on the "hawker menace" as a threat to a wide array of middle-class interests, including inconvenience, sanitation, fears of social disorder, and threats of declining real-estate prices for residential areas marked for relocating hawkers. In the process, discourses of citizenship and public interest again converge with the interests of the middle classes. The paradox that lies at the heart of this construction is that a large segment of hawkers includes former factory workers who lost jobs in the context of economic restructuring. However, middle-class–based definitions of the service industry have served to construct hawking as a threat to the social order rather than as an integral consequence of processes of restructuring unfolding in liberalizing India.

This is most evident in the case of the textile industry, one of India's oldest manufacturing industries that had been based in Bombay. In the context of economic globalization, rising real-estate prices and the decline of traditional organized sector industries such as textiles have made it more financially lucrative for mill owners to sell land used for textile mills rather than to try to revive sick mills in the face of strong international competition.[17] Unemployed mill workers are thus often forced to turn to alternative forms of employment such as hawking in order to support themselves (Devidayal, 1998).[18]

In contrast to the hutment dwellers and beggars who were driven away from public spaces such beaches and maidans, Mumbai's hawkers have formally organized into unions and thus have been able to wield more political clout in the contest over public spaces.[19] Such political clout has placed the local state agency responsible for managing public space (Brihanmumbai Municipal Corporation, or BMC) in a conflicted position. In addition, the

BMC has used an official system of daily charges and an unofficial system of bribes for unlicensed hawking as financial sources. Thus, the local government has had to negotiate with the hawkers' union and mediate between the union and the middle-class organizations that filed legal petitions to relocate the hawkers. Such political conflicts represent structural effects of the politics of economic liberalization. In other words, the effects of liberalization unfold through the spatial reorganization of social relations (Massey, 1994). Such spatialized politics constitute a central site for the emergence of class-based resistance. Forms of resistance by groups such as the hawkers' union, in effect, disrupt the hegemonic construction of the liberalizing Indian nation through idealized images of the new Indian middle class.

I have thus far analyzed the ways in which broader processes of economic globalization reconstitute and are shaped by local and national politics. Such dynamics underline the significance of moving beyond analyses that promote deterritorialized understandings of globalization and transnationalism (Appadurai, 1996). Globalization is a deeply territorial process both in terms of the ways in which it restructures the modern nation–state and the ways it unfolds through a spatialized form of class politics. This territorialization inherent in processes of globalization distinguishes the contemporary politics of empire from older forms. In the current moment, the politics of empire unfolds in conjunction with the modern nation–state. The historical roots of this relationship between nation and empire are, of course, present in earlier imperial formations. As Benedict Anderson (1983) has noted, the European colonial powers in the 18th and 19th centuries regarded themselves as both nations and empires.

What is distinctive in the emergence of the 21st century empire is that this conjuncture between empire and nation has moved beyond the dominant colonial powers to include emerging postcolonial nation–states. The most visible instances of such processes include the rhetoric of nation building that currently constitutes U.S. military occupation in countries such as Iraq and Afghanistan. However, I am arguing that this convergence between nation and empire occurs through more subtle processes in less-visible spaces, for instance, in terms of the politics of globalization and the economic dimensions of empire. In the context of liberalizing India, the proponents of economic globalization are not simply the visible agents of global corporations; they are segments of the urban middle classes attempting to produce a vision of a new liberalizing India. The means for the production of this vision is an exclusionary form of cultural citizenship that invokes rather than undermines the power of the state. The modern nation–state and associated claims of citizenship are thus integral parts of the contemporary politics of empire.

Nation–State, Citizenship, and the Politics of Empire

Consider the ways in which the relationship of nation–state, citizenship, and empire unfolds in relation to broader political processes in contemporary

India. The production of an exclusionary form of citizenship draws on hierarchies of religion and ethnicity in addition to the politics of class. Such dynamics have centered on the rise of Hindu nationalism in recent decades. Racialized xenophobic discourses threatening "Muslim invaders" produce a form of purified Hindu citizenship that converges with the dynamics of spatial purification I have been analyzing.

Examples of such dynamics are recent political discourses on the threat from illegal immigrants who cross the border from Bangladesh. At the beginning of 2003, India's Union Home Minister, L.K. Advani, a leading figure in the Hindu nationalist Bharatiya Janata party (BJP), signaled that illegal immigration would be a central political issue for the government and party. As one news report stated, the minister "asked states to identify the estimated 15 million Bangladeshi illegal immigrants and 'throw them out'" (Chengappa, 2003, p. 41).

The announcement, in effect, consolidated the continued political significance of an issue that began to surface at a local level in the 1990s. As Sujata Ramachandran (2002) argued in her analysis of the dynamics of Operation Pushback, a 1990s government campaign designed to forcibly return alleged illegal immigrants to Bangladesh, the state characterized such immigrants, most of whom were slum dwellers in Delhi, as threatening "infiltrators" invading the Indian nation–state. Such state strategies designed to cleanse the Indian nation of unwanted immigrants from Bangladesh present striking parallels to the class-based processes of spatial purification associated with the politics of economic restructuring. Constructions of class impurity have converged with xenophobic depictions of "illegal" Muslim immigrants in the discourses of Hindu nationalist organizations.

More recently, these state strategies of purification have been intensified and transformed in light of the U.S.-declared global war on terrorism. The BJP-led government has deployed the U.S.-declared agenda in conjunction with its own Hindu nationalist project of treating Indian Muslims as alien threats to the Hindu Indian nation.[20] Consider, for instance, the ways in which state and media representations have constructed the question of Bangladeshi immigrant workers through the rhetoric of terrorism. They depict such workers as threats to national security and define immigration flows produced by poverty in terms of the threat of cross-border terrorism from Islamic nations such as Bangladesh and Pakistan. This construction is succinctly captured in the analysis of one mainstream media report:

> The fear that Pakistan Inter-Services Intelligence and Al-Qaida-linked terrorists may also be crossing India's borders along with innocuous economic refugees is all too real. Internal security concerns are now inextricably linked with the "Bangladeshi problem." According to terrorism and underworld tracker, JCP Neeraj Kumar of Delhi, "Pakistan is increasingly using Bangladesh as a base for its nefarious activities in India." The police are investigating Bangladeshi crime syndicates in the national capital. Fourteen Bangladeshi

citizens arrested in Delhi last year have confessed to a series of robberies. (Chakravarty, 2003, p. 20).

This discursive construction presents a series of associations involving Bangladeshi immigrants, the Pakistani government, Al-Qaida terrorism, and urban crime. Immigrant workers become the embodiments of both the threat of global terrorism and of internal social disorder associated with crime. Chakravarty's news report is captioned "The Immigrants: Banglo-Indians" and states, "The Bangladeshi immigrants are everywhere. They even have crime syndicates in Delhi." This association of Muslim (Pakistan sponsored) immigrants, terrorism, and crime is particularly significant as it attempts to link the external security of the nation–state with middle-class discourses on crime and social disorder.

The politicization of the Bangladeshi immigrant worker enables a convergence of three central political processes: the construction of a middle-class definition of citizenship that has been intensified in the context of liberalization, the Hindu nationalist agenda of producing a purified Hindu citizenship, and the global war on terrorism. In effect, such dynamics provide an important example of a case where the exclusionary political project of a Hindu nationalist state converges with the global economic and political dimensions of empire.[21]

The implications of this convergence are significant in shaping contemporary politics in India. At the local level, political parties have attempted to use the "threat" of Bangladeshi immigrant workers to engage in political agendas that reinforce exclusions of religion and ethnicity. In Delhi, for instance, local officials have attempted to remove Muslim voters from electoral lists by alleging that they are illegal Bangladeshi workers rather than Indian Muslims from the state of West Bengal. Because individuals from poor and working class communities often do not have official documentation proving citizenship, this tactic has enabled local Hindu nationalist officials to engage in strategies of disenfranchisement. Citizenship in this case is a category of exclusion whose boundaries rest on religious identity. Meanwhile, in another example, the Shiv Sena, the politically dominant local right-wing party in Bombay, has used the political rhetoric on Bangladeshi immigrants to further its long-term antimigrant and anti-Muslim agenda.[22] This campaign based on the racialized politics of religion and ethnicity has merged with local state strategies that target working-class squatters. Thus, the local state agency, the BMC, has now begun to deploy the rhetoric of the threat of Bangladeshi immigrants in conjunction with its project of evicting squatters from public lands.[23]

The case of contemporary politics in India demonstrates the ways in which the economic and political dimensions of empire reconstitute and intersect with local politics. I have sought to demonstrate that this intersection shows how the modern (and in the case of India, postcolonial) nation–state and the exclusionary politics of citizenship are integral to the conditions of empire. Such processes, however, are not limited or unique to the internal political

dynamics of India. Rather, this analysis can contribute to a broader comparative understanding of the politics of empire.

Comparative Reflections on the Politics of Empire

The analysis of Indian politics presented here can contribute in a number of
ways to a broader understanding of the politics of empire, particularly in relation to the U.S. nation–state—the center of empire in the 21st century. At one
level, the political dynamics in India hold a number of parallels to political
processes that have been unfolding in the U.S. For example, processes of spatial purification in the context of economic restructuring in India clearly parallel racialized and class-based processes of spatial restructuring and
gentrification in cities in the U.S. (Smith, 1996; Gilmore, 1998; Sanjek, 1998).[24]

Meanwhile, the portrayal of Muslim immigrants as potential terrorists and
stringent methods of state surveillance of Arabs and Muslims in the U.S. since
the September 11, 2001, terrorist attacks present obvious parallels to Indian
state constructions of Indian Muslims as potential terrorists and Pakistani
agents. Finally, racialized constructions of Muslims have converged with the
politics of anti-immigrant sentiment; in both India and the U.S., undocumented workers have become economic and security threats to the sanctity of
the territorial boundaries of the nation–state and are transformed into central
targets of the global war on terrorism. Citizenship is produced by everyday
social and state exclusionary practices (Glenn, 2002) that rest at the intersection of race, religion, and class. In this process, citizenship functions as a
central mechanism for the exercise of state power and consequently for the
state's political and ideological project of empire building.

At a second level, a focus on India, a site that may appear relatively removed
from the more visible areas of global conflict and U.S. intervention, points to
the significance of moving away from a bipolar center-periphery model in
an understanding of the current politics of empire.[25] Consider, for instance,
implications of the political conflicts concerning Bangladeshi immigration.
The politicization of this issue points to the deeper ways in which regional
political dynamics have been substantially transformed by U.S. discourses and
responses to global terrorism. Thus, the Indian government has been able to
invoke the new U.S. discourses on terror in its regional dealings with countries
such as Pakistan and Bangladesh and has mirrored U.S. strategies by passing
its own stringent antiterrorism legislation. In the Kashmir conflict, both the
state and the public media representations in India have sought to invoke the
U.S. war on terrorism in conjunction with the Indian war on terrorism in
Kashmir.[26] Such examples point to the ways in which regional specificities are
central to understanding the effects of the dynamics of empire, as they are played
out in the U.S.-led war on terrorism. However, such regional dynamics cannot
simply be understood as effects; they also serve as critical factors in the execution
and consolidation of empire.

In the South Asian context, this has been most visible in the Pakistan government's acquiescence to U.S. intervention in Afghanistan. However, less-visible linkages exist with increased military and political cooperation between India and the U.S., a form of cooperation supported by shared dominant national preoccupations with Islamic terrorism. In this process, the convergence of the U.S. war on Islamic terrorism and the Hindu nationalist anti-Muslim agenda in India stands to potentially serve as a critical factor in global politics in the 21st century.

Conclusion

This chapter examines the ways in which the politics of economic globalization and the U.S. war on terrorism have interacted with and reconstituted local and national politics in contemporary India. The economic, political, and military dimensions of contemporary empire converge in a set of processes that restructure both nation and state in ways that consolidate the exclusionary boundaries of citizenship. This hegemonic form of citizenship that rests at the intersection of social hierarchies of class, religion, and ethnicity thus represents a means to reproduce the dynamics of empire within the nation–state.

This calls into question the assumption that the citizenship and the nation–state represent neutral categories that can be called upon as means to resist global processes of empire. This is not to suggest that such possibilities do not exist. Subaltern groups have historically been able to subvert and deploy languages of citizenship to press for rights. Meanwhile, questions of national and state sovereignty are particularly critical in times of empire and cannot be evaded by romanticized understandings of transnationalism. My intent in this analysis has been to explore some of the dominant political processes of the current global order and to reflect on the subtle and often invisible ways in which empire works through and in relation to the postcolonial nation–state. The result is a perspective that calls attention to a politics of empire that both produces and is constituted by local, national, and regional specificities that simultaneously rest on and move us beyond the heart of empire—the contemporary U.S. nation–state.

References

Anderson, B., Imagined Communities: Reflections on the Origin and Spread of Nationalism, Verso, New York, 1983.
Appadurai, A., Modernity at Large: Cultural Dimensions of Globalization, University of Minnesota Press, Minneapolis, 1996.
Beng-Huat, C., Consumption in Asia: Lifestyles and Identities, Routledge, New York, 2000.
Bhowmick, S., "Mumbai: 'Citizens' versus the Urban Poor," In One India One People, 2002a.
Bhowmick, S., Hawkers and the Urban Informal Sector: A Study of Street Vending in Seven Cities, report prepared for National Alliance of Street Vendors in India, 2002b.
Chakravarty, S., "The Immigrants: Banglo-Indians," India Today International, February 17, 2003.
Chengappa, R., "A Neighbourhood of Trouble," India Today International, February 10, 2003.
Corbridge, S. and J. Harris, Reinventing India: Liberalization, Hindu Nationalism and Popular Democracy, Polity Press, Cambridge, U.K., 2000.
Devidayal, N., "From Handloom to Hafta," Times of India, September 26, 1998.
Dixit, R., "BMC's Anti-Hawker Drive Hinges on New Agreement," Times of India, August 24, 1998.

Evans, P., Ed., Liveable Cities: Urban Struggles for Livelihood and Sustainability, University of California Press, Berkeley, 2002.

Fernandes, L., "Nationalizing 'the Global': Media Images, Economic Reform and the Middle Class in India," Media, Culture and Society, 22, 611, 2000a.

Fernandes, L., "Restructuring the New Middle Class in Liberalizing India," Comparative Studies of South Asia, Africa and the Middle East, 20, 88, 2000b.

Fernandes, L., "Rethinking Globalization: Gender and the Nation in India," in Feminist Locations: Global/Local/Theory/Practice in the Twenty-First Century, de Koven, M., Rutgers University Press, New Brunswick, 2001.

Fernandes, L., "The Politics of Forgetting: Class Politics and The Restructuring of Urban Space in India," presented at the National University of Singapore Conference on Globalization and Forgotten Spaces, July 2002.

Gills, D.S. and N. Piper, Eds., Women and Work in Globalising Asia, Routledge, New York, 2002.

Gilmore, R.W., "Globalization and U.S. Prison Growth," Race and Class, 40, 171, 1998.

Glenn, E.N., Unequal Freedom: How Race and Gender Shaped American Citizenship and Labor, Harvard University Press, Boston, 2002.

Habermas, J., "The European Nation–State: On the Past and Future of Citizenship and Sovereignty," Public Culture, 10, 397, 1998.

Hansen, T., The Saffron Wave, Princeton University Press, Princeton, NJ, 1999.

Jenkins, R., Democratic Politics and Economic Reform in India, Cambridge University Press, Cambridge, U.K., 1999.

Katznelson, I., City Trenches: Urban Politics and the Patterning of Class in the United States, Pantheon Books, New York, 1981.

Kaviraj, S., "Filth and the Public Sphere: Concepts and Practices about Space in Calcutta," Public Culture, 10, 83, 1997.

Khilnani, S., The Idea of India, Farrar Straus & Giroux, New York, 1997.

Kothari, R., Growing Amnesia: An Essay on Poverty and Human Consciousness, Viking, New Delhi, 1993.

Massey, D., Space, Place and Gender, University of Minnesota Press, Minneapolis, 1994.

Ragunath, P., "Sena Steps up Campaign against Mumbai Migrants," Gulf News, May 6, 2003.

Ramachandran, S., "Operation Pushback: The Sangh Parivar, State, Slums and Surreptitious Bangladeshis in New Delhi," Singapore Journal of Tropical Geography, 23, 311, 2002.

Robison, R. and D. Goodman, Eds., The New Rich in Asia: Mobile Phones, McDonalds and Middle-Class Revolution, Routledge, New York, 1996.

Sanjek, R., The Future of Us All: Race and Neighborhood Politics in New York City, Cornell University Press, Ithaca, NY, 1998.

Saran, R., "Dressed to Kill," India Today International, September 11, 2000.

Seabrook, J., In the Cities of the South: Scenes from a Developing World, Verso, London, 1996.

Sharma, A., "Clean and Beautiful: That's Chowpatty," Bombay Times, October 1, 1998.

Sheth, D.L. "Secularisation of Caste and Making of New Middle Class," Economic and Political Weekly, August 21, 1999.

Sibley, D., Geographies of Exclusion: Society and Difference in the West, Routledge, New York 1995.

Smith, N., The New Urban Frontier: Gentrification and the Revanchist City, Routledge, New York, 1996.

Strange, S., The Retreat of the State: The Diffusion of Power in the World Economy, Cambridge University Press, Cambridge, U.K., 1996.

Varma, P., The Great Indian Middle Class, Viking, New Delhi, 1998.

Wallerstein, I., The Modern World System, Academic Press, New York, 1974.

Notes

1. Throughout this chapter, I refer to this dimension of empire when I speak of the global or U.S. war on terrorism; I am referring here to the ways in which state responses to the September 11, 2001, attacks have been transformed into an interventionist policy of "preemptive action."

2. Field research in India was funded by an American Council of Learned Societies/Social Science Research Council fellowship and by a Rutgers University Research Council grant. This chapter has benefitted from audiences and discussions at the workshop on "Globalization and Forgotten Places" held at the National University of Singapore and the Center for Race and Gender of the University of California at Berkeley and the workshop on "Race, Labor and Empire," University of California, Irvine.

3. See Jenkins (1999) for a discussion of the political dynamics surrounding the economic re-
    forms.

4. For a discussion of the rise of Hindu nationalism, see Hansen (1999).

5. My argument is not that this is the only major trend within contemporary Indian politics nor
    that there are no forms of democratic grassroots opposition to such exclusionary practices.
    Rather, I am concerned with analyzing one overarching dominant trend unfolding in the
    context of global processes of economic neo-liberalism and political empire.

6. For important research that deals with the question of upward mobility into the middle
    classes, see Sheth (1999).

7. For examples, see Varma (1998) and Kothari (1993). I analyze the dynamics of such cul-
    tural representations in greater depth in Fernandes (2000a and 2001).

8. In an initial limited phase of reforms, this was expanded to include a second brand, the
    Maruti, that soon became a symbol of young urban professional culture.

9. I present a detailed analysis of these findings in Fernandes (2000b).

10. These processes of restructuring also are connected to the international division of labor.
    See, for example, the "virtual" subcontracting (outsourcing) of U.S. jobs in fields such as
    the computer industry and customer services. Such jobs can be performed by middle-class
    workers in India both at lower costs and without having to open up immigration avenues
    by requiring Indian workers to migrate to the U.S.

11. Hansen, for example, discusses the ways in which middle-class politicians have been in-
    creasingly replaced by peasants and lower-caste individuals. He suggests that differences of
    "style, language, and social practices" of these new politicians are viewed by the middle
    classes as "plebian" and as corruptions of politics and democracy. See Hansen (1999), p. 56.

12. This section draws on research and analysis of the spatial dynamics of economic restruc-
    turing that I analyzed at greater length in "The Politics of Forgetting: Class Politics and the
    Restructuring of Urban Space in India" (Fernandes, 2002).

13. The western sides of the suburbs (Andheri West or Santa Cruz West) tend to be considered
    upscale whereas the eastern sides tend to house working and lower middle-class neighbor-
    hoods (Andheri East or Santa Cruz East).

14. This club culture is, of course, not new to the city and, in fact, stems back to colonial times
    when private clubs were introduced by the British. In the post independence period, these
    clubs became the preserves of upper-class and upper middle-class Indians. What is new,
    then, is not the presence of exclusive membership-based clubs for the reproduction of
    class distinction but the expansion of such social spaces and sharp increases in member-
    ship fees.

15. Such processes were foreshadowed earlier in the postcolonial period, for example, through
    events such as the coercive demolitions of squatter settlements associated with Sanjay
    Gandhi in the 1970s.

16. "BMC Gets Serious about Clean Mumbai," *Bombay Times*, September 18, 1998.

17. According to one estimate, employment in the textile industry dropped from 250,000 in
    1980 to 57,000 in 2000. See Saran (2000).

18. Note that textile production was reorganized and shifted to informal sector production
    units outside Mumbai in rural areas in Maharashtra and neighboring states.

19. Bombay Hawkers' Union is estimated to represent 120,000 workers. See Dixit (1998).

20. According to Hindu nationalist ideologies, Muslims and Christians are alien communities
    because their religions draw on traditions that emerged outside the territorial boundaries
    of the Indian nation–state. By this definition, Hinduism is associated with Indian national
    culture because it emerged within India; religions such as Sikhism, Buddhism, and
    Jainism are also defined as Indian but are classified within the rubric as offshoots of
    Hinduism.

21. This does not imply that no national conflicts of interest exist. A recent U.S. request that
    India deploy troops in Iraq was met by the Indian government's attempt to further
    its own national interests by gaining access to oil rights. The Indian government eventually
    refused the request, indicating that it needed official U.N. sponsorship of any deploy-
    ment.

22. The Shiv Sena's original agenda, when it emerged in the 1960s, focused on a nativist agenda
    that campaigned for the exclusion of migrants, particularly South Indians from Bombay. It
    later shifted toward an anti-Muslim-Hindu nationality agenda. The current attacks on
    alleged Bangladeshi immigrants join both forms of exclusion because they are based on
    both ethnicity and religion.

23. See Raghunath (2003). Although the Shiv Sena is not currently in power in the state government, it dominates the BMC and wields considerable power in local communities through grassroots political networks and via coercive methods.

24. This is not to imply that the contexts are the same. Clearly, differing positions of global power are significant; in economic terms for instance, the standard of living of a large section of middle-class Indians is comparable with working-class communities in the U.S. Moreover, such differences translate into substantial differences in the availability of basic resources and economic infrastructure. Nevertheless, it is important to examine the implications of similarities in political responses to internal social hierarchies.

25. Wallerstein (1974) discusses this in economic terms in relation to his theoretical discussion of the capitalist system by introducing the category of the semi-periphery.

26. Such invocations have also led to criticism of the U.S. alliance with Pakistan—a nation India classifies as a sponsor of terrorism.

7

Race, Labor, and the State: The Quasi-Citizenship of Migrant Filipina Domestic Workers[1]

RHACEL SALAZAR PARREÑAS

Introduction

Women are relocating across nation–states and entering the global labor market in full force. They are responding to high demands for low-wage domestic workers in richer nations. As a result of this demand, a south-to-north flow of domestic workers has caused women from Mexico and Central America to move into the households of working families in the United States (Hondagneu-Sotelo, 2001), Indonesian women to richer nations in Asia and the Middle East (Chin, 1998), Sri Lankan women to Greece and the Middle East (Gamburd, 2000), Polish women to Western Europe, and Caribbean women to the U.S. and Canada (Colen, 1995). On a much wider scale, women from the Philippines likewise respond to the demand for migrant domestic workers. Providing services in more than 187 countries and destinations, Filipino women are the domestic workers par excellence of globalization (Parreñas, 2001).

A fairly large number of Filipino women work in private households of middle- to upper-income families in Great Britain, France, the Netherlands, Italy, Spain, and Greece. In Asia, they work in the newly industrialized economies of Hong Kong, Malaysia, Singapore, and Taiwan. Additionally, they provide domestic services in the oil-rich Persian Gulf nations, including Kuwait, Saudi Arabia, and the United Arab Emirates. Finally, they can also be found in middle- and upper-income households in Canada and the United States.

The emergence of a Filipino "domestic diaspora" poses an irony in globalization: the displacement of a large group of women from their homes and simultaneous entrapment in the homes of others. Economic currents forcibly disperse Filipino women from their homeland not only to a number of

1.   This essay benefits from comments shared by David Smith. Portions of this chapter are reprinted from Rhacel Salazar Parreñas, *Servants of Globalization: Women, Migration, and Domestic Work*, Stanford University Press, 2001 Stanford, CA, and Rhacel Salazar Parreñas and Cerissa Salazar Parreñas, "Workers without Families: The Unintended Consequences" *Asian Law Journal* 10, 101, 2003.

countries, but more accurately to a multitude of domestic spheres in various geographical niches.

In this chapter, I look at the consequences of state policies for the family lives of migrant domestic workers that limit their integration into their host societies. I focus on their families to show that their displacement from their homes extends to include their forced separations from the families they must often leave behind in their country of origin. This is primarily due to their quasi-citizenship status in various host societies that often bar or deter the migration of their families.

The quasi-citizenship of migrant Filipina domestic workers and the transnational family life that results from this status remind us that nation–states do not always reward the economic contributions of migrant laborers with full membership. As guest workers, the temporary memberships of migrant Filipina domestic workers are usually contingent upon restrictive legal measures that stunt their political, civil, and social incorporation into host societies. Moreover, their status remains conditional to the sponsorship of employers. In such cases, relationships of unequal dependency between migrant domestic workers and their sponsoring employers define their integration into host societies. This leaves them more vulnerable to substandard conditions of employment. All these below-par conditions deter family migration and promote the formation of transnational families.

The imposition of quasi-citizenship on migrant domestic workers supports the growing trend of the "renationalization of politics"—increasing sentiments of nationalism in globalization. As Saskia Sassen (1996) observes, economic global restructuring encourages the macro-process of the "opposite turns of nationalism." This means globalization leads to the "denationalization of economies" as it simultaneously takes a turn toward renationalization of politics. To partially explain the renationalization at work in globalization, sudden surges of nationalism in the global cultural landscape represent the struggles of nations to assert distinct identities against the threats imposed by rapid economic transformations and a global mixture of cultural images and practices. The exclusion of those seen as culturally or racially unassimilable is one way receiving nations assert their distinctions. However, the denationalization of economies depends somewhat on the renationalization of politics because the limited integration of migrants secures a pool of low-wage workers for receiving nations.

There is now an economic bloc of receiving national states that maximizes the benefits of the low wages of migrant workers from developing nations in the global economy by limiting their membership into host polities. In globalization, receiving nations curb the integration of migrants so as to guarantee their economies a secure source of cheap labor. By containing the costs of reproduction in sending countries, wages of migrant workers can be kept to a minimum; i.e., migrants do not have the burden of having to afford the greater costs of reproducing their families in host societies. Moreover, by restricting the incorporation of migrants, receiving nations can secure a supply of low-wage workers who could easily be repatriated if the economy is depressed.

Not surprisingly, the experience of stunted integration is not exclusive to migrant Filipina domestic workers; it is part of a wider, growing trend. Addressing the rise in global diasporas, migration scholar Robin Cohen (1997) observes that contract labor-based migration is one of the rising trends in globalization as temporary settlements and intermittent stays-abroad define the incorporation of a growing number of labor migrations. Because Cohen's discussion concentrates on the increasing number of transnational professionals and businessmen in globalization, he suggests that migrants. In other words, individual and community choices and not exclusionary laws *per se* influence migrants to not exclusively adopt the citizenship of a destination country but rather to keep "a foot in two or more locations" (Cohen, 1997, p. 165).

However, it is important to note the class-based selective incorporation of migrants in globalization. Those who fill low-skill employment situations, like migrant Filipina domestic workers, for instance, are more likely to be considered undesirable and therefore unassimilable migrants. Consequently, they are more likely to confront restricted forms of citizenship. This selective inclusion of migrants reminds us of the growing split of the world based not on race or nation, but instead on skills and privilege. Indeed, as scholars Gustavo Esteva and Madhu Suri Prakash claim, the world is increasingly divided into one-third social minorities who are more likely to have the cultural, human, and social capital needed to seek more flexible citizenship and the two-thirds social majority who have fewer choices of citizenship (cited in Mohanty, 2003).

Some scholars argue that the designation of migrants as guest workers does not predictably restrict their integration into nation–states. In *Limits of Citizenship*: Migrants and Postnational Membership in Europe, Yasemin Soysal (1994) argues that guest workers are accorded: Migrants and postnational membership in Europe, on the basis of rights and protections grounded in the principles of human rights that supersedes the territorial dimensions of national citizenship. More specifically, she argues that migrants in Europe have realized their rightful membership in the host polity because of their experience of "a shared public social space; a set of abstract principles and responsibilities (such as human rights, respect for justice . . . and a 'productive life'); and the rationalized organization and routine of everyday praxis" (p. 166).

Thus, the limited national rights of guest workers are made irrelevant by the influence of universal human rights. States lose from the pressures imposed by transnational bodies. As Soysal asserts, "While states reinforce more and more strict boundaries, at the same time, transnational pressures toward a more expansive membership and individual rights penetrate the same national boundaries and profoundly transform the nature of citizenship" (1996, p. 22). Indeed, permanent residents of various host polities are entitled to full civil rights and have access to various social services, including public education, health benefits, and free access to labor markets.

To a certain extent, the arguments of Soysal hold true for various migrant workers, including Turkish guest workers who enjoy the rights and privileges of the German state. They also apply to former *bracero* agricultural workers in the U.S. whose descendants have achieved the rights to permanent membership. We should not, however, lose sight of how race, class, and gender inequalities still prevent the full incorporation of many migrants and result in the segmentation of particular groups of migrants into domestic work and other low-wage employment. Contrary to claims of the universality of the greater inclusion of migrants, I argue that continued social inequalities imposed by the state may still stunt their full membership into host societies. This is the case with migrant Filipina domestic workers.

My overview of the incorporation of migrant Filipina domestic workers illustrates their status as quasi-citizens or partial citizens because the state still determines and, more specifically, reduces their feelings of membership in various host societies. I make this point by noting the growing norm of transnational families in the domestic diaspora of Filipino workers. It is estimated that 25% of the Filipino youth population—9 million children—are growing up in transnational households. Indeed, transnational households represent a growing norm among migrant families the world over, especially among domestic workers whose occupational conditions are not conducive to child rearing.

Despite that, the growing literature on transmigration pays relatively scant attention to transnational families (Portes, 1996). This may be because of the lesser attention paid to women in the transnationalism literature, coupled with the assumption that the family is a female sphere. It is said that women identify less as transmigrants than do men because of their greater preference for permanent settlement (Hondagneu-Sotelo, 1994). As scholars of migration assert, transnationalism is a male-gendered process, and I should note that this is the perception from above and below (Smith and Guarnizo, 1998). For instance, male businessmen ("above") circle the globe with their financial transactions, and displaced male migrants ("below") reclaim their lost status through transnational activities. In other words, emasculated male migrants amend their decline in social status in the receiving community by increasing their social status in the sending community (Jones-Correa, 1998). They do this by getting involved in hometown associations and spearheading drives that raise funds to build churches, secure irrigation and water systems, ensure scholarship programs, and promote other such activities in their hometowns (Jones-Correa, 1998; Smith and Guarnizo, 1998).

The lesser attention given to transnational families may also be due to the assumption that children of migrants are unlike their parents because they keep both feet in the host society instead of keeping "a foot in two or more locations" (Orozco-Suarez and Orozco-Suarez, 2000).

As this discussion shows, studies of the children of migrants make this assertion without consideration of the "overlooked second generation"—children of immigrant workers who are unable to follow their parents in the host society.[1] Finally, the few studies on transnational families, including one I conducted on migrant Filipina domestic workers in Rome and Los Angeles, overlook the perspectives of children (Parreñas, 2001). This chapter looks at transnational families and puts emphasis on the experiences of children in order to call attention to the continued presence of exclusionary measures imposed by host societies on migrants. Indeed, transnational households, because their formation suggests that migrant parents often cannot raise their children or are deterred from doing so in the host society, represent the exclusion encountered by migrant Filipina domestic workers in various host societies.

In my discussion, I establish the partial citizenship of migrant Filipina domestic workers by explicitly defining two kinds of participants in the diaspora: permanent and transitional guest workers. Permanent guest workers are usually (but not exclusively) employed in nations with illiberal migration policies (e.g., Taiwan). Nations that prohibit the permanent membership of migrant domestic workers include countries as diverse as Singapore, Taiwan, and the Netherlands. In contrast, other countries incorporate migrant domestic workers as transitional guest workers; their permanent membership into the nation–state is usually contingent upon their completion of contractual employment with a sponsoring family. These are countries with liberal migration policies (e.g., Canada) shaped by democratic principles of citizenship. Thus, extending the discussion of Soysal, migrants in nations with liberal policies do benefit from the transnational pressures of universal human rights as they hold the advantage of eligibility for permanent membership. However, this privilege does not come without difficulties; it usually follows a period of conditional membership and vulnerability for transitional guest workers.

Partial Citizenship of Migrant Filipina Domestic Workers

Diasporas are usually contingent upon the partial citizenship of migrants. Without the imposition of partial citizenship, migrants could violate the boundaries of citizenship by developing a greater sense of entitlement in the receiving country. In other words, they would no longer be displaced from their old homeland but instead would be fully incorporated into their new one. This is true for a great number of migrants. For the most part, however, migrant Filipina domestic workers still struggle to feel welcome in the social bodies of various nation–states. Inasmuch as racial inequalities prevent their incorporation, so do state restrictions of their status as partial citizens.

The incorporation of migrant Filipina domestic workers in state regimes, as observed by Abigail Bakan and Daiva Stasiulis (1997), entails a paradoxical position of risking civil rights for the sake of economic gains. They state, "For the Third World non-citizen in search of First World citizenship, gaining access to social rights—particularly 'the right to a modicum of economic welfare and security'—commonly supersedes entry to civil and political rights." For the most part, economic gains achieved in migration entail the loss of civil and political rights, first from the nation of citizenship (in this case, the Philippines), which loses juridical–legislation rights, and second from the host nation–state, which relegates unequal rights to migrants along the lines of race, class, and gender (Lowe, 1996). The process of labor migration consequently imposes upon migrant Filipina domestic workers social and political barriers that limit their ability to develop a sense of full membership in their host societies. In other words, they are partial citizens of the host state. As I noted, this encourages the formation of transnational households in the domestic diaspora at the cost of relations between migrants and their children.

As a partial citizen, the duration of stay for migrant Filipina domestic workers is usually limited to the length of their labor contract. More often than not, such contracts bind them to stay with their sponsoring employers regardless of working conditions. In the Netherlands, for instance, domestic workers frequently enter through the *au pair* program. Under this system, a worker must be between 18 and 26 years old and can work for a maximum of 1 year. This system is similar to those in other countries that guarantee the social exclusion of migrant Filipina domestic workers by limiting the duration of their tenure. In Taiwan, domestic workers can stay for a maximum of 3 years. In Greece, foreign domestic workers must renew their work permits annually for a maximum of 5 years (Anderson, 2000).

By limiting the duration of their tenure, receiving nations deny the full incorporation of migrant domestic workers and thereby discourage them from gaining a greater sense of entitlement to their rights. Generally, labor laws do not protect migrant Filipina domestic workers from the exploitation of employers through sexual harassment and abuse, excessive work hours with no overtime pay, and substandard living conditions. For example, women who were confined in the homes of their employers are commonly found in shelters for abused migrant Filipina domestic workers in various countries in the Middle East and Asia (Parreñas, 2001). Hong Kong offers another extreme example: Domestic workers who flee abusive employers automatically face deportation proceedings because of the stringent legislation imposed against foreign domestic workers in 1987 (Constable, 1997).

Additionally, in countries where they are only temporary members, migrant Filipina domestic workers also face restrictive reproduction laws. Often, they cannot sponsor the migrations of their families, including their own children. This is the case in Middle East and Asian receiving nations that are much more stringent than other countries. State policies in Taiwan deny entry to the spouses and children of migrant workers (Lan, 1999). Singapore even prohibits migrant workers from marrying or cohabiting with native citizens (Bakan and Stasiulis, 1997). Surprisingly, this is also the case in certain European and North American countries. Domestic workers employed under the Live-In Caregivers' Program in Canada do not qualify for family reunification. Likewise, domestic workers employed under the *au pair* system in the Netherlands are ineligible to marry.

Even if migrant Filipina domestic workers were able to sponsor the migration of their families under liberal state regimes such as those of Italy or the U.S., labor conditions still discourage them from doing so. In addition to low pay, contracts of guest workers usually bind them to stay with their sponsoring employers, and this makes them incredibly vulnerable to poor labor standards. This is especially true of domestic workers because their isolation in private homes aggravates the vulnerability engendered by their legal dependency on their sponsoring employers.

Taking into account the nuances engendered by differences in domestic policies among the receiving nations of migrant Filipina domestic workers, partial citizenship comes in distinct degrees and levels of exclusion. Migrant Filipina domestic workers face different provisions of conditional membership. In some countries (e.g., Hong Kong), domestic workers do not have the flexibility to change sponsoring employers; they can do so in other countries (e.g., Italy). Moreover, some countries (e.g., Italy) allow family reunification; others (e.g., Taiwan) do not. Regardless of whether migrant domestic workers have the flexibility to choose employers or sponsor their families, full membership is still not an option. Instead, they confront racial exclusionary measures that stunt their feelings of membership in receiving countries.

Family reunification remains a challenge to many immigrants in Europe. They confront heightened anti-immigrant sentiments and political platforms from conservative parties such as the National Front in France and the Lega in Northern Italy. As a result, even if eligible to do so, most migrant Filipina workers in Europe prefer not to petition for entry of the children left behind in the Philippines (Parreñas, 2001). In Germany, children under 16 years old are required to obtain visas to visit their legally resident parents. In the United Kingdom, entry conditions for family visits have become stricter with the rising suspicion that family members intend to remain indefinitely (Koffman et al., 2000), although the presence of the second generation in some countries offers greater options for their integration into receiving societies.

One such country is Italy, despite the fact that a great number of migrants there still choose to leave their children in the Philippines. In contrast to most receiving nations in Asia and the Middle East, Italy allows guest workers to stay as long as 7 years. Short-term contracts of 2 years apply in jurisdictions such as Hong Kong. Moreover, permits to stay in Italy limit employment to domestic work but do not restrict Filipina migrants to a single sponsoring employer. Finally, temporary residents have been eligible for family reunification in Italy since 1990. Despite that, migrant Filipina domestic workers are still restricted to the status of guest workers in Italy, but because Italy has more inclusive migrant policies than do other destinations of the diaspora, it remains one of the more coveted destinations among prospective migrants from the Philippines.

However, migrants in Italy remain restricted to the status of permanent guest workers. Other nations such as Canada, Spain, and the U.S. offer migrant Filipina domestic workers the possibility of gaining full membership after a few years as guest workers. In these countries, migrant Filipina domestic workers are considered transitional guest workers. They can eventually gain full citizenship and the right to participate in the host polity, which is not the case in most other destinations of the diaspora. In Canada and Spain, migrant Filipina domestic workers are eligible for full citizenship after 2 years of legal settlement. Despite the seemingly more liberal and inclusive policies in these nations, political and social inequalities, as Bakan and Stasiulis (1997) indicate using the case of Canada, still mar the incorporation of migrant Filipina domestic workers.

The Canadian Live-In Caregivers' Program requires an initial 2 years of live-in service by foreign domestic workers before they can become eligible for landed immigrant status. During the 2 years, they are restricted to the status of temporary visitors, are denied family life, and are more prone to face abusive working conditions, including long hours and inadequate pay. Without the protection of labor laws granted to Canadian workers, migrant domestic workers—most of whom are Filipinos—have fewer rights than do full citizens.

Filipina domestic workers in the U.S. experience the same vulnerability. U.S. immigration laws have similarly produced the effects of extreme susceptibility for domestic workers who wish to legalize their stays via Alien Employment Certification. According to a handbook written for domestic workers by the Asian American Legal Defense and Education Fund and National Employment Law Project (2001), obtaining a green card via employer sponsorship in the U.S. can take as long as 10 to 15 years, during which domestic workers are unable to seek other employment and are consequently more susceptible to work under indenture-like conditions.

Without doubt, the imposition of partial citizenship on migrant domestic workers benefits employers. The guest worker status, legal dependency on the native employer, ineligibility for family reunification, and the labor market segmentation of foreign women to domestic work guarantee host societies a secure and affordable pool of care workers. At the same time these factors maximize the labor provided by these workers and constrain their abilities to care for their own families, particularly their own children. This works to the benefit of the employing family because migrant care workers can provide the best possible care when they are free of caregiving responsibilities to their own families.

The experience of partial citizenship for migrant domestic workers points to a central irony in globalization. Migrant domestic workers care for rich families in the global north while they are burdened with social, economic, and legal restrictions that deny them the rights to nurture their own families. Undeniably, the limited citizenship granted migrant Filipina domestic workers comes at high costs to their human rights and quality of family life. Thus, the elimination of these restrictive measures would at the very least grant foreign domestic workers the basic human rights of caring for their own families.

Transnational Family Life: The Painful Consequence of Partial Citizenship

Constituting one of the largest groups of migrant laborers in the new global economy, an estimated 7.38 million Filipinos work and reside in 187 countries and destinations.[2] Regardless of official status, a significant number of migrant Filipinos are parents who migrated to provide for their children economically and had to leave their children in the Philippines in the process. Their quasi-citizenship status encourages the formation of transnational families. The fact that host economies deny Filipina migrant workers the right to family reunification raises questions about the quality of family life at both ends of the migration spectrum.

Looking at the receiving end, numerous studies show the emotional difficulties and added pressures undergone by transnational mothers who raise their children from a geographic distance (Hondagneu-Sotelo and Avila, 1997; Parreñas, 2001). With limited choices in the Philippines, many women migrate to help sustain their families economically, but this often occurs at the cost of the pain of family separation. Migrant mothers who work as nannies often face the painful prospect of caring for other people's children while they are unable to tend to their own. One such mother in Rome, Rosemarie Samaniego, describes this situation:

> When the girl that I take care of calls her mother "Mama," my heart jumps all the time because my children also call me "Mama." I feel the gap caused by our physical separation especially in the morning, when I pack (her) lunch, because that's what I used to do for my children . . . . I used to do that very same thing for them. I begin thinking that at this hour I should be taking care of my very own children and not someone else's, someone who is not related to me in any way, shape, or form . . . . The work that I do here is done for my family, but the problem is they are not close to me but are far away in the Philippines. Sometimes you feel the separation and you start to cry. Some days, I just start crying while I am sweeping the floor because I am thinking about my children in the Philippines. Sometimes, when I receive a letter from my children telling me that they are sick, I look out the window and ask the Lord to look after them and make sure they get better even without me around to care after them [starts crying]. If I had wings, I would fly home to my children. Just for a moment, to see my children and take care of their needs, help them, then fly back over here to continue my work.

At the sending end of the migration spectrum, it is not easy to grow up without one's parents. Between 2000 and 2002, I spent 18 noncontinuous months in the Philippines where I conducted 69 in-depth interviews with children of migrant workers. Such children suffer incalculable losses when their parents disappear overseas, but they do understand that the limited financial options for families in the Philippines cause their losses. According to Jason Halili whose mother has worked in the U.S. as an elderly care provider for more than a decade, "[T]here are no opportunities for people unless you are filthy rich . . . . So people have no option but to go outside the country if they want to progress . . . . So it was the hardest route to take, but . . . the best route to take."

As scholars of Filipino family migration argue, children struggle with feelings of emotional insecurity including loneliness, unfamiliarity, the loss of quality time spent with their families, and abandonment (Scalabrini Migration Center, 2000; Parreñas, 2001). Denied the authority of their parents, the children also feel that they are more likely to suffer from growing up without sufficient guidance and discipline (Parreñas, 2001). Extended lengths of separation further aggravate these feelings.

Ellen Seneriches describes her loneliness related to her physical distance from her mother. It entails the constant denial of wanting to "call her, speak to her, cry to her" and the dissatisfaction of having to rely on email as their primary form of communication. Children such as Ellen, who was only 10 years old when her mother left for New York, often repress their longings to reunite with their mothers. Knowing that their families have few financial options, they are left with no choice but to put their emotional needs aside and often do so knowing that their mothers' care and attention are diverted to other children. Children of domestic workers such as Ellen often have to confront the jealousy caused by imagining the diversion of care and attention by their mothers to other children. Consequently, they experience the emotional stress of jealousy when they grow up in transnational households.

This does not suggest that migrant mothers do not attempt to sustain ties with their children. In fact they do, and their children often recognize and appreciate these efforts. Many children with whom I spoke in the Philippines actually receive a reconstituted form of the double day from their mothers across great distances. For instance, some children report that their mothers send text messages via cellular phones to check whether they ate breakfast in the morning, applied lotion before they left for school, and did their homework at night.

One such child who benefits from acts of "intensive mothering" from a distance is Ellen Seneriches (Hays, 1996). Despite the 12-year-long separation from her mother, they maintain a very close relationship because of their frequent communication. Ellen even credits her mother for her success in school. Now a second-year medical school student, Ellen graduated at the top of her classes in both high school and college. According to her, the key to her success was the open communication she maintained with her migrant mother. In fact, Ellen and her mother email one another at least two or three times a week. Moreover, Ellen could always turn to her mother about her problems and, in fact, felt more inclined to do that than seek the advice of her father.

The good fortune of having a "super-mom" is not universal, but it does raise questions about how children withstand such geographical strains, whether and how they maintain solid ties with their distant parents, and what circumstances lead some children to feel that those ties have weakened or disappeared. Generally, surrogate parental figures and frequent communication with the migrant parent, along with the knowledge of the migrant parent's income contribution to the family, ease many of the emotional insecurities that arise from transnational household arrangements. Children who lack these resources have greater difficulty adjusting. Those who feel that their parents did not provide sufficient care from a distance were more likely to feel abandoned.

This group includes Jeek Pereno, whose life has been defined by longings arising from feelings of abandonment. At 25, he is a merchandiser for a large department store in the Philippines. His mother provided for her children and managed with her meager wages, first as a domestic worker and then as a nurse's aide, to send them $200 a month. Not satisfied with his mother's financial support, Jeek wishes she offered him more guidance, concern, and emotional care.

Jeek was 8 years old when his parents relocated to New York and left him and his three brothers in the care of an aunt. Eight years later, Jeek's father passed away, and two brothers (the oldest and youngest) joined their mother in New York. Visa complications prevented Jeek and his remaining brother from going and their mother has not once returned to visit them in the Philippines. According to Jeek, she said, "It will cost too much."

Years of separation breed unfamiliarity among family members. Jeek does not have the emotional security of knowing that his mother genuinely tried to lessen that estrangement. Only a visit could shore up Jeek's security after 17 years of separation. His mother's weekly phone calls do not suffice. Because he experiences his mother's absence as indifference, he does not feel comfortable communicating with her openly about his unmet needs.

Jeek feels that his mother not only abandoned him but also failed to leave him with an adequate surrogate. His aunt had a family and children of her own, Jeek recalls, "While I do know that my aunt loves me and she took care of us to the best of her ability, I am not convinced that it was enough . . . because we were not disciplined enough. She let us do whatever we wanted to do." Jeek feels that his education suffered from this lack of discipline, and he greatly regrets not concentrating on his studies. Having completed only a 2-year vocational program in electronics, he doubts his competency to pursue a college degree. At 25, he feels his only option is turning from one low-paying job to another.

Although extended kin can provide sufficient amounts of guidance and discipline and tend to do so if not taxed by other familial responsibilities, one cannot assume that they do so openly and willingly. The uncle of Gailanie Tejada—a college student too old to qualify for immediate reunification with her parents—saw his responsibility as an unwanted burden:

> I never really chose to be anyone's guardian. Just that, you know, this responsibility had to fall on my lap because I was here most of the time. And it was like, hey, you know, they are my nieces. I just feel responsible . . . but it wasn't really my responsibility because I was not their parent . . . But being the brother of one of the parents, I felt it was my responsibility because they weren't there. And my mother was too old to deal with them.

Expressed in tears, the statement of Gailanie's uncle, Guillermo Tremaña, suggests that guardians do sometimes resent the unwanted responsibility that falls on them when parents migrate without their children. It also suggests that children left behind are susceptible to receiving inadequate care.

The case of Norbert Silvedirio, a 21-year-old college dropout whose mother and father have worked in New York City as domestic workers for more than 13 years, is no exception. Norbert also feels that his schooling suffered from the lack of guidance brought about by parental absence:

> I remember that I was in Grade 2 [when my parents left for the U.S.]. I was just left on my own. I was the one who looked after myself. [My older siblings] would just hand me my allowance and it was up to me to budget it . . . . I would go to school everyday but in high school, I would only go to class once in a while. I was always at the billiard hall. [Laughs] . . . . I think it would have been better if I grew up with them around. There was no one around to guide me. I just did what I wanted to do. I would go to school if I felt like it. My [older brother] would try to tell me to go to school, but I never really listened to him.

Without the option of following their parents to the U.S., children like Norbert, Jeek, and Gailanie have to rely on extensive efforts from kin. As in the case of Gailanie's uncle, we cannot assume that extended family members are always willing to extend their help with open arms. Similarly, migrant parents have to double their efforts of caregiving, as the monetary support that they provide from a distance cannot alone quell the emotional insecurities facing children in transnational families.

Migrant mothers such as Rosemarie Samaniego have to, in essence, work a double day from thousands of miles away to allay the insecurities of their children. They call their children frequently and perform various acts of mothering from a distance. These struggles indicate that transnational family life presents added challenges to the maintenance of strong intergenerational ties. Surely, they are challenges that would be eased by geographical proximity of the family. However, this option is not available to families in the domestic worker diaspora—families such as those of Norbert, Jeek, Ellen, and Gailanie, who, by default, also confront the stringent restrictions imposed by the quasi-citizenship status of their migrant parents in host societies.

Conclusion

This chapter addresses the quasi-citizenship confronted by migrant Filipina domestic workers in various nation–states. The relegation of their status to quasi-citizenship is not restricted to illiberal nations and includes countries in Europe and America that have liberal state regimes. The restriction of the incorporation of migrant domestic workers into the nation–state works to the benefit of receiving economies that we can picture as an economic bloc of nation–states that maximizes the labor of migrants through the imposition of partial citizenship. The partial citizenship status of guest workers—whether permanent or transitional—discourages the development of feelings of rightful membership in various host societies.

Consequently, migrant domestic workers are less inclined to demand labor rights commensurate with those of native-born citizens. In this way the wages of migrant domestic workers can be kept to a minimum. The partial citizenship status of migrant domestic workers also facilitates the formation of transnational households. This means the receiving nation–states contain the costs of reproduction of migrant workers in sending countries and consequently minimize the wage demands of the migrant workforce. The minimization of the wage demands of migrant domestic workers often comes at the cost of denying family intimacy.

As a consequence of partial citizenship, transnational households represent the flexibility of family forms in the Filipino diaspora. However, they should not be considered celebratory symbols of family diversity. Transnational families represent the continued racial exclusion of migrants in the age of globalization that emerges from the partial citizenship imposed on migrant workers. The formation of transnational families must be seen as enforcement of border control against migrant workers and their families. Transnational households signify the segregation of migrant workers from the host polities of various receiving national states through globalization. The growing number of such households in the domestic diaspora of the Philippines tells of the continued impact of the juridical and territorial boundaries imposed by nation–states on the incorporation of migrant workers in globalization.

Acknowledgments

This chapter benefits from comments shared by David Smith. Portions of this chapter are reprinted from Parreñas, R.S., *Servants of Globalization: Women, Migration, and Domestic Work*, Stanford University Press, Stanford, CA, 2001;

and Parreñas, R.S. and C.S. Parreñas, "Workers without Families: The Unintended Consequences," *Asian Law Journal*, 10, 101, 2003.

References

Anderson, B., *Doing the Dirty Work? The Global Politics of Domestic Labor*, Zed, London, 2000.

Asian American Legal Defense and Education Fund and National Employment Law Project, 2001 *Rights Begin at Home: Protecting Yourself as a Domestic Worker*, New York: Asian American Legal Defense and Education Fund and National Employment Law Project, p. 22.

Bakan, A. and D. Stasiulis, "Introduction," In *Not One of the Family: Foreign Domestic Workers in Canada*, in Bakan, A. and D. Stasiulus, Eds., University of Toronto Press, Toronto, 1997.

Chin, C., *In Service and Servitude: Foreign Female Domestic Workers and the Malaysian "Modernity" Project*, Columbia University Press, New York, 1998.

Cohen, R., *Global Diasporas: An Introduction*, University of Washington Press, Seattle, 1997.

Colen, S., "Like a Mother to Them: Stratified Reproduction and West Indian Childcare Workers and Employers in New York," in Ginsburg, F. and R. Rapp, Eds., *Conceiving the New World Order: The Global Politics of Reproduction*, University of California Press, Berkeley, 1995.

Constable, N., *Maid to Order in Hong Kong: Stories of Filipina Workers*, Cornell University Press, Ithaca, NY, 1997.

Gamburd, M., *The Kitchen Spoon's Handle*, Cornell University Press, Ithaca, NY, 2000.

Hays, S., *The Cultural Contradictions of Mothering*, Yale University Press, New Haven, CT, 1996.

Hondagneu-Sotelo, P., *Gendered Transitions: Mexican Experiences of Migration*, University of California Press, Berkeley, 1994.

Hondagneu-Sotelo, P. and E. Avila, "I'm Here But I'm There: The Meanings of Latina Transnational Motherhood," *Gender and Society*, 5, 1997.

Hondagneu-Sotelo, P., *Domestica*, University of California Press, Berkeley, 2001.

Jones-Correa, M., "Different Paths: Gender, Immigration, and Political Participation," *International Migration Review*, 32, 1998.

Koffman, E., A. Phizacklea, P. Raghuram, and R. Sales, *Gender and International Migration in Europe: Employment, Welfare and Politics*, Routledge, New York, 2000.

Lan, P.C., "Bounded Commodity in a Global Market: Migrant Workers in Taiwan," presented at the 1999 Annual Meeting of the Society for the Study of Social Problems, Chicago, August 6–8, 1999.

Lowe, L., *Immigrant Acts*, Duke University Press, Durham, NC, 1996.

Mohanty, C., *Feminism without Borders: Decolonizing Theory, Practicing Solidarity*, Duke University Press, Durham, NC, 2003.

Orozco-Suarez, M. and C. Orozco-Suarez, *The Children of Immigrants*, Harvard University Press, Cambridge, 2000.

Parreñas, R.S., *Servants of Globalization: Women, Migration, and Domestic Work*, Stanford University Press, Stanford, CA, 2001.

Parreñas, R.S. and C.S. Parreñas, "Workers without Families: The Unintended Consequences" *Asian Law Journal*, 10, 2003.

Portes, A., "Transnational Communities: Their Emergence and Significance in the Contemporary World System," in Korzeniewicz, P. and W.C. Smith, Eds., *Latin America and the World Economy*, Praeger, Westport, CT, 1996.

Portes, A. and R. Rumbaut, *Legacies: The Story of the Immigrant Second Generation*, University of California Press, Berkeley, 2001.

Sassen, S., *Losing Control? Sovereignty in an Age of Globalization*, Columbia University Press, New York, 1996.

Scalabrini Migration Center, *Impact of Labor Migration on the Children Left Behind*, Quezon City, Philippines, 2000.

Smith, M.P. and L.E. Guarnizo, Eds., *Transnationalism from Below*, Transaction Publishers, New Brunswick, NJ, 1998.

Soysal, Y., *Limits of Citizenship: Migrants and Postnational Membership in Europe*, University of Chicago Press, Chicago, 1994.

Soysal, Y., "Changing Citizenship in Europe: Remarks on Postnational Membership and the National State," in Cesarini, D. and M. Fulbrook, Eds., *Citizenship, Nationality, and Migration in Europe*, Routledge, New York, 1996.

Notes

1. My discussion of the overlooked second generation bears significance to the new direction in immigration studies as I bring attention to the children of immigrants who are not within the territorial boundaries of the U.S. A growing interest in the lives of the children of immigrants or "immigrant second generation," as they are referred to, dominates contemporary immigration studies. Researchers believe that the case of the immigrant second generation warrants focus because it would show how far-reaching are the integration and acceptance of racialized minorities in the U.S. population. See Portes and Rumbaut (2001).

2. Information obtained from meetings with officers at the Commisson for Filipinos Overseas on August 30, 2001.

8

On the Border of Love and Money: Sex and Tourism in Cuba and the Dominican Republic

AMALIA LUCIA CABEZAS

Introduction

The tourism industry is the primary economic development strategy for both Cuba and the Dominican Republic, creating local direct employment and producing a number of multiplier effects within the countries. Both tourism and remittances represent the major earnings for the state, signifying a continual reliance on former colonial powers and outside forces for economic stability (Jiménez, 1999; Mesa-Lago and Pérez-López, 1999; Wiarda, 1999; World Bank, 2001; Orozco, 2002). This chapter will examine the Cuban and Dominican sexual markets connected to the travel and tourism industry.

Drawing on field work with sex-trade participants, hospitality workers, and other informal sector workers, I examine some of the manifestations of flexible labor and sexual identities. Although these two Caribbean nations have many differences, this chapter concentrates primarily on commonalities. Nevertheless, a few comments are in order to highlight some features of both countries. Certainly the most glaring and profound differences are Cuba's adherence to a centrally planned government that espouses socialist principles and its diplomatic break with the most powerful empire in the world today.

At the beginning of the 20th century, both Cuba and the Dominican Republic were under U.S. hegemonic control characterized by periodic military intervention and occupation, loss of national autonomy, and the bolstering of brutal political regimes. In 1959, Cuba broke away and became the first socialist country in the Western Hemisphere. This challenge to U.S. capital and strategic interests was to influence the growth of the Dominican tourist industry and prompt the assassination of its "butcher" dictator Rafael Trujillo (Atkins and Wilson, 1998).[1]

The Dominican economy for the past 20 years has increasingly moved toward the implementation of neo-liberal, free-market reforms. After it was ravaged in the 1980s by the implementation of structural adjustment programs imposed by the International Monetary Fund, mismanagement, and corruption, its economy showed high rates of growth during the 1990s (Wiarda, 1999). However, most of the population continues to live in extreme poverty (World Bank, 2000). A World Bank report comments that the Dominican Republic is notable in Latin America as the country that allocates the lowest share of its public capital to education, health, and public safety (2000).[2]

At the end of the 1980s, the collapse of the Soviet Union and the socialist trading bloc obliged Cuba to move quickly from state-controlled central planning to a mixed-market economy that emphasizes social welfare. As with its neo-liberal Dominican neighbor, the Cuban state has implemented neo-classical economic reforms, including the general retrenchment of the state, a move toward export-oriented zones, implementation of incentives to attract foreign capital, privatization of utilities, and labor restructuring (Susman, 1998).

Notwithstanding these radical and contradictory changes, the state has continued to support an infrastructure that stresses social well-being and acts as a safety net for the most vulnerable segments of society. As Paul Susman asserts, "What makes the Cuban response to crisis conditions so interesting is that it appears to accept many capitalist economic practices, but with restrictions aimed at maintaining its commitment to socialism" (1998, p. 185). Despite a tightening of the U.S. embargo that has caused resource scarcities, epidemics, and shortages of food and medicine, Cuba has held fast to its health and educational programs, continuing to make them universally available, although they are continuously ravaged by scarcities.

According to the Economic Commission for Latin America and the Caribbean, "Social indicators for Cuba continue to be outstanding in comparison to the regional average, despite the economic difficulties the country has been experiencing since 1989."[3] The rapid move to a mixed-market system during the past 10 years coupled with the "dollarization" of the economy produced the emergence of new social classes, resulting in an inverted social pyramid that privileges workers in the tourist industries and those who receive remittances over professionals in all other economic sectors.

Despite these and other important differences, my aim is to demonstrate similar economic and social outcomes that stem from the adoption of international tourism—or the four Ss, as they are known in the literature: sun, sea, sand, and sex—to create economic growth. First, I argue that the link between tourism and the sex trade points to the flexible reorganization of the labor process, through the creation of seasonal work, the proliferation of informal market arrangements, and the erosion of boundaries between the formal and the informal sectors of the economy (Portes, Castells, and Benton, 1989; Portes and Schauffler, 1993; Sassen, 1998; Freeman, 2000). These changes are related not only to the reorganization of labor but also to new patterns in the social organization of personal romance. Second, I argue that workers consequently inform, shape, and challenge the labor process through their use of intimacy and sexuality and that they contest and defy uncomplicated categorizations of sex tourism as sex work. Finally, I offer some preliminary thoughts on an alternative to the prevalent paradigm that characterizes all sex tourism as sex work.

Most sex-tourism studies have focused primarily on relationships that are spatially discernable and public (Pruitt and LaFont, 1995; O'Connell-Davidson, 1996; Brennan, 1998; de Albuquerque, 1998; Cabezas, 1999; Kempadoo, 1999; Sánchez-Taylor, 2001). These encounters attract attention because they are highly public and involve participants from different racial, ethnic, and class backgrounds. Most studies have examined relations between otherwise unemployed "freelance workers" or beach boys in tourist centers (Pruitt and LaFont, 1995; de Albuquerque, 1998; Oppermann, 1999; Ryan, 2000; Herold, García, and De Moya, 2001; Sánchez-Taylor, 2001) and overlook on-the-job tourism workers as participants in the sex trade. These workers are accessible and in constant and intimate contact with tourists. Furthermore, most studies assumed they knew in advance who was a sex worker and what counted as sex work.

Although the literature has begun to challenge studies that narrowly define sex tourism as solely involving monetary exchange, the category of sex worker has remained unexamined and immutable within the field of sex tourism. If we account for spatial factors and assumptions based on race, sexuality, and class, the sex-worker category loses its stable meaning. This study proposes a more complicated approach that accounts for the provisional practices and identities that constitute sexual markets and envelops understandings of labor and sex more as matters of continua than as hard and fast definitions.

Tourism and New Patterns of Sexual Labor

The lack of viable work and the dependence on foreign exchange drive young men and women to migrate to the tourist areas to earn their livings. Sex with tourists is one of a broad spectrum of services and activities in which people engage to procure earnings.

Sex tourism is not only about sex and money; it concerns other kinds of opportunities as well. Liaisons with tourists provide the means to get by and get ahead. Such liaisons supplement low wages and also allow participants to procure opportunities for recreation, consumption, travel, migration, and marriage. Because of these opportunities, any liaison, sexual or not, is perceived as a potential boon for a local participant. Therefore, sex tourism is more than an illicit activity; it involves socially acceptable behaviors and values. It is a contingent and open-ended activity whose blurred boundaries are intertwined with elements of romance, leisure, consumption, travel, and marriage. Although many of the participants in the sexual economy trade sexual services for cash, others do not.

Patterns of flexible labor with decentralized networks of production and distribution are common within tourist economies (Poon, 1990; Mullings, 1999). Those who have no formal employment in tourist enterprises hustle at various activities connected to tourists. In Cuba, these hustlers are known as *jineteros* and *jineteras.* A *jinete,* according to the *Oxford Spanish Dictionary* (1996, p. 362), is a horseman or horsewoman and *jinetear* is to ride and break a horse.

In Cuba, *jineterismo* is a colloquial term that refers to the broad range of activities and behaviors associated with hustling, including, but not limited to, sex for cash. *Jineteros* trade in the margins of the tourist economy; they are often seen in the streets of Havana, peddling everything from cigars and rum to sexual services. They act as tourist guides, escorts, brokers of sexual services, and romantic companions.

Jineterismo is also a gendered term and is applied to both men and women, with *Jineteras* perceived as providing primarily commodified sexual services and companionship to foreigners. When applied to women, the term *jinetera* conjures images of a woman riding the tourist, alluding to the sexual and power relationship of a woman on top and in charge (Fernández, 1999).[4] The term *jinetera* emerged in the early 1990s with the sudden growth and expansion of international mass tourism after the collapse of the socialist trading bloc. Initially, little stigma was attached to the identity. Even Fidel Castro said that *jineteras* worked for pleasure and not for money. The new term signified a distance from the stigma associated with prostitution and also separated the activities of *jineteras* from the commercial practices of prostitution in Cuba before the revolution.[5]

Another sexual identity to emerge with the Cuban tourist economy in the 1990s is *pinguero,* derived from *pinga,* a slang term for penis, which is used to categorize men who provide commodified sexual practices within the tourist sector.[6] Although some *pingueros* identify themselves as straight, they tend to provide sexual services mainly to gay tourists because male-to-male sexual practices are more lucrative than straight sex.

In the Dominican Republic, men who work in the informal economy of the tourist sector are known as *sanky pankys* (a word play on *hanky panky*). *Sanky pankys* or beach boys are gigolos who cater exclusively to foreign tourists and provide sexual services and companionship to both men and women, straight and gay. The more-successful beach boys tend to be friendly and nonthreatening in their pursuit of female tourists, using heavy doses of flattery in an overall seduction plan that involves a wide array of social activities and experiences, such as sightseeing, dining, and dancing (Herold, García, and De Moya, 2001). The more-professional gigolos do not consider it appropriate to exploit women by engaging in "one night stands" (Herold, García, and De Moya, 2001). It is more productive to cultivate a relationship that could provide substantial rewards, such as the possibility of a long-lasting romance that brings return visits and perhaps even marriage and migration.

The Labor of Romance

In a tourist setting, it is difficult to discern who is a prostitute and what counts as prostitution. Instead of socialized and institutionalized spaces for sex work, as found in Southeast Asia, Western Europe, and the U.S., where forms of contract or indentured labor operate, the new patterns of sexual commerce in Cuba and the Dominican Republic are opportunistic, fluid, and ambiguous. They are different from the brothels in the Dominican Republic that cater to a domestic clientele and were prevalent in Cuba in the 1950s. A sexual economy operates within the heavily guarded resort compounds where hospitality workers provide sexual services and in the streets where young men and women seduce foreigners. The transactions that take place are difficult to recognize and categorize as a form of labor; instead, the landscape of tourism lends itself more to interpretations of adventure and romance.

As with most of the Caribbean, mass tourism in Cuba and the Dominican Republic has moved to the all-inclusive model of resort development. At an all-inclusive resort, a tourist's expenses, including airplane travel, accommodations, meals, transfers, entertainment, recreation, tips, and drinks, are paid for in the country of destination, usually with a credit card. Typified by the French conglomerate Club Med that opened in Cuba in 1996, most resorts in the Caribbean have now adopted some form of the all-inclusive model. These enclaves strive to cater to all tourists' needs, keeping them virtually locked into the confined space of the resort and segregated from the local population. Guests must wear color-coded plastic bracelets that allow "uniformed security personnel to better control their movements" (Stanley, 2000, p. 68).

The change to the all-inclusive model of tourism produced devastating effects for workers who depend on the tourism economy and affected neighboring areas. Many hospitality workers who formerly counted on gratuities to complement their meager wages and earn foreign exchange are now pushed into the sex sector to replace lost earnings. For example, hotel workers participate in the sex trade by allowing tourists to take their "dates" back to their rooms or by facilitating sexual liaisons between tourists and locals. Along with room service and extra towels, many hospitality workers also provide sexual services to guests.

Maira, a chambermaid in Varadero, Cuba's premier beach resort, recounts her initiation into providing sexual services with a Spanish tourist: "I fell in his good graces. He would always be looking at me. He always left me a gift. As he said, he was buying me. He was always looking at me, my movements, my gestures, my way of being, and things like that, until one day he approached me [about having sexual relations]." This marked the beginning of Maira's extra-docket activities at the hotel. Carefully and discreetly, she was able to earn extra cash and received two marriage proposals from hotel guests.

The transition into the sexual economy can be smooth for hospitality workers for a number of reasons. First, sex and romance, whether offered by the host or requested by the guest, constitute parts of an organizational dynamic structured by the industry. Second, hospitality workers, educated to please their guests, must contend with a clientele's high expectancy of servility. Third, the highly militarized compounds with their round-the-clock security details effectively keep the local population out and the guests in. Finally, the constant police aggravation and incarceration of women in the neighboring areas make hotel workers easy targets for sexual propositions and harassment.

Hotel guests turn to resort workers who are often more than eager to procure extra earnings while on the job. Therefore, sex tourism operates within the tourist enclaves to subsidize the low wages of formal sector workers and redistributes the wealth of tourists more directly to hospitality workers. A tourism worker in Varadero sums up this new contingency: "*Camareras* [chambermaids] are the legitimate and official *jineteras*."

From tourism advertising and marketing to the organizational structure of the workforce, travel for pleasure and leisure to Third World countries is exceedingly dependent on gendered and racialized sexual constructions. Most hotel workers in Varadero are trained at the local tourism training center, the José Smith Comas Institute of Hotel and Tourism Services. The school has strict regulations covering physical appearance and imposes weight, age, and height requirements. Trainees must be young, attractive, and in good physical shape. Not only are youth and aesthetics premium considerations, but so is race. The training and distribution of work are organized according to racial, sexual, and gender considerations, resulting in occupational segregation. Whereas most of the front desk workers are lighter skinned Cubans, entertainment workers and back-kitchen help are mainly black.

Entertainment workers, also known as *animadores* (animators), are young, scantly clad, dark-skinned young men and women who instruct the guests in dancing, games, and other forms of recreation. Their work is mainly physical and sensual and often involves suggestive and sexualized contact with guests. Black performers are also predominantly employed in hotels that feature live shows. The organization of work is, therefore, a circuitous interplay of international tourism's rigidly formalistic prescription of inclusion and exclusion of workers based on racial and sexual occupational categories.

The racial and sexual ordering reflects the consequences and legacy of colonialism as they play out on this current stage of global capitalism. Writing about the representation of the *mulata* body in Cuban touristic culture, critic Alicia Arrizón notes that the racialized performativity encompasses "all the complexities and unstable processes about how race, gender, and sexuality enact the power relations within colonial, neocolonial, and postcolonial discourses" (2002, p. 137).

Studies conducted in the Dominican Republic also revealed the prevalence of sexual relations between tourists and workers in food and beverage services, maintenance, administration, entertainment, and reception. One study reports that almost 20% of resort workers admitted to having had sexual relations with tourists (CEPROSH, 1997). Another study confirms that 38% of male sex workers had regular jobs in hotels as waiters, porters, and security guards (CESDEM, 1996). This was confirmed by a recent study of *sanky pankys* who regularly worked as tour guides, waiters, or bartenders or rented beach and sports equipment (Herold, García, and De Moya, 2001).

Many of these young men and women hope their liaisons with foreigners will lead to marriage and migration. Studies confirm that most *pingueros*, *jineteras/os*, and *sanky pankys* prefer to accept gifts of clothing, jewelry, and meals from tourists rather than negotiate money for sex because direct commercial transactions foreclose other possibilities. Furthermore, direct commercial transactions would identify them as prostitutes—an identification they do not desire. Self-identified *sanky pankys* in the Dominican Republic, for example, reveal that they never ask for payment directly. Some even offer to pay for drinks or admissions to discos. They use covert strategies to procure financial gains.

After establishing a more intimate connection with a tourist, a *sanky panky* will talk about being poor, having a sick relative, wanting to continue his education or start a small business, and his inability to do so because of poverty (Herold, García, and De Moya, 2001). *Sanky pankys* often maintain and continue to cultivate romantic relationships after the tourists leave the island. Letters, telephone calls, faxes, and return visits keep the fires burning. A few receive money and plane tickets for travel to Europe or Canada.

Studies also indicate that many beach boy–tourist relationships are focused on companionship and that love and sex do not enter the picture. Some liaisons are based on affection, intimacy, or friendship as opposed to sexual behavior. In both situations, the general tendency is to back away from overtly commodifying sexual relations by carefully navigating the borders of love and money. As a 21-year-old native of Havana explained, "It's better to act as if this is your first time and not to discuss the money. That way they'll think that you are not doing it just for the money, that you really love them." It is a preferable strategy for participants to distance themselves from commercial sexual exchanges in order to attain a more stable and lucrative social role such as that of a girlfriend or wife.

Women I interviewed referred to their tourist acquaintances as *amigos*, or friends, indicating an unwillingness to characterize them as customers or paying clients. This reluctance to characterize the relationships as strictly commercial endeavors allows them to create and expand on multiple possibilities for their relationships. Gifts are seen as expressions of love and not as payments for services rendered; they are used to blur the dichotomy between love and money. Emotional labor is used to break down the boundaries of commercial exchanges or at least distort the lines between intimacy and labor and preserve the dignity of the local participant. This liminal space is marked by fluidity, ambiguity, and heterogeneity and provides opportunities that direct commercial transactions cannot.

Beyond Sex and Romance

Notwithstanding all this flexibility in social and economic arrangements, some individuals become stigmatized as sex workers. Who meets the criteria? What counts as sex work under these circumstances? The social location and characteristics of the participants (more than a particular type of behavior) often determine what counts as sex work. I maintain that race, class, and gender create and delimit the playing field.

For example, a *mulata* from Santiago living in Havana, seen in the company of foreigners, is automatically categorized as a sex worker. A pale-skinned university student who dates only foreigners and eventually marries a Frenchman is not considered a sex worker. A graduate student from California who walks the streets of Havana with a black Cuban man is readily perceived as a sex tourist. An office worker in the Dominican Republic who visits a hotel casino with the hopes of attracting a foreign boyfriend is not considered a sex worker, but a Dominican woman with dark skin exiting a disco alone in a tourist area runs the risk of incarceration during a mass arrest of prostitutes.

Identity as a prostitute or sex worker applies to specific situations. It is not ambiguous and is contingent on the social location and perceived characteristics of the participants. In most situations, the permeable boundaries between leisure and labor, paid work and unpaid work, and private and public are difficult to discern, thus making it possible to resist categorization as a "worker." The category of "sex worker" has its own disciplinary functions and tends to signify the participation of a subordinate racial, gender, and class.

The sex worker concept presents an either–or view of relationships and sexual practices. It creates a dichotomy between commercial transactions devoid of affectional attributes and vilified as racial fetishism and normative relations not based on material gain and racial desire. Put another way, desire and affection are defined as "lighter" pursuits and prostitution as "darker," effectively racializing the entire process. This binary opposition presumes relations not tainted by economic dependence, speculation, motivation, and interest take place between individuals of the same racial, national, and class background.

Separating sex work and sex tourism from the homosexual and heterosexual relationships that take place in tourist-sending societies creates artificial boundaries between human relationships that cannot pass close scrutiny. To place sex tourism and sex work as something that happens "over there" avoids "the challenges and insights" into our society that such an examination can provide (Ryan, 2000, p. 36).

The concept of sex work is also difficult to apply to the new forms of flexible labor and to same-sex desire within tourist economies. Consequently, I make a case against portraying all practices and social relations within tourist economies as sex work and subsuming significantly different forms of sexuality under the category of "sex worker." The sex worker is presupposed to have a fixed identity that creates and freezes differences and subjects. The identity may be fixed where institutions like brothels or pimps control the conditions of women's sexual activities but it is not fixed in less-constrained situations.

Although "sex worker" is the prevalent term applied to participants of sex tourism in the Caribbean, I argue that the prevalent socio-labor realities underscore the need for a more complex analytical framework that accounts for the fluid arrangements and complex relationships that do not easily lend themselves to collective identification and action. Pruitt and LaFont (1995, p. 423) found with "rent-a-dreads" in Jamaica that although such a relationship may appear to outsiders to involve prostitute (the Jamaican man) and client (the European or American woman), both partners perceive the relationship as courtship. In other words, in tourism and romance, the motivations that people attribute to actions cannot be specified in advance. "Sex worker" is an empowering term only in situations where the woman or man has no substantial control over the disposition of sexual activities because it marks those activities as labor and therefore as entailing worker rights. There is no justification for imposing the sex-worker title on people who do not identify themselves as such. In this context, the term imposes an arbitrarily derogatory and racist label. If we consider other possibilities, we can just as easily understand the activity as the typically gendered, raced, and classed disciplines of romance. I propose that we closely examine sex tourism not as an either–or proposition but as a landscape for a multiplicity of gradations of erotic, affectional, and even spiritual practices and as a landscape with some institutions and practices that mark sexual activities as labor.

Gayle Rubin contends that, whereas "'good' sex acts are imbued with emotional complexity and reciprocity, sex acts 'on the bad side' of the line are considered utterly repulsive and devoid of all emotional nuance" (quoted in Hubbard, 1999, p. 44). I suggest that we examine our notions and separation of love, romance, and money. The refusal to commodify all sexual relations with foreigners, the insistence on procuring gifts instead of cash payment, and the creation of flexible identities for themselves and their tourist *amigos* challenge our notions of love devoid of economic interests and of work devoid of sexuality.

Conclusion

International mass tourism in the Caribbean has eroded the boundaries between labor practices and romantic relationships. Greater economic informality makes it difficult to clearly define all the new social and economic ventures as labor. Cubans and Dominicans challenge and shape their conditions of subordination within the global economy by eroding and confusing the lines between love and money, romance and work. They navigate the interstices of the racialized, gendered, and sexualized structures imposed by the transnational tourism industry and the state. Mass tourism offers them the possibility of escaping brutal poverty through love, friendship, companionship, or sex.

The implementation of neo-liberal reforms and promarket forces and the exigencies of globalization are some factors driving the growth of sex tourism. A broader framework than the one used to examine sex tourism is needed; it should account for the provisional practices and identities that constitute sexual markets and envelop notions of labor and sex as liminal. We need more-complicated approaches that enhance our understanding of erotic behaviors and place sexual agency and citizenship at the core of the analysis of labor.

References

Arrizón, A., "Race-ing Performativity through Transculturation, Taste, and the Mulata Body," *Theater Research International*, 27, 136, 2002.

Atkins, G.P. and L. Wilson, *The Dominican Republic and the United States: From Imperialism to Transnationalism*, University of Georgia Press, Athens, 1998.

Barry, T., B. Wood, and D. Preusch, *The Other Side of Paradise*, Grove Press, New York, 1984.

Brennan, D.E., "Everything Is for Sale Here: Sex Tourism in Sosúa, the Dominican Republic" Ph.D. dissertation, Yale University, New Haven, CT, 1998.

Cabezas, A.L., "Women's Work Is Never Done: Sex Tourism in Sosúa, the Dominican Republic," in Kempadoo, D., Ed., *Sun, Sex, and Gold: Tourism and Sex Work in the Caribbean,* Rowman & Littlefield, Boulder, CO, 1999, p. 93.

CEPROSH (Centro de Promoción y Solidaridad Humana), *Proyecto Hotelero*. Puerto Plata, 1997.

CESDEM (Centro de Estudios Sociales y Demográficos), "Encuesta sobre conocimientos, creencias, actitudes, y prácticas acerca del SIDA/ETS en trabajadoras sexuales y hombres involucrados en la industria del sexo en las localidades de Puerto Plata, Sosúa, y Monte Llano," Mimeo, Puerto Plata, COVICOSIDA, 1996.

de Albuquerque, K., "Sex, Beach Boys, and Female Tourists in the Caribbean," *Sexuality and Culture*, 2, 87, 1998.

del Olmo, R., "The Cuban Revolution and the Struggle against Prostitution," *Crime and Social Justice*, 12, 34, 1979.

Economic Commission for Latin America and the Caribbean, *Economic Survey of Latin America and the Caribbean 1998–1999*, United Nations, Santiago, Chile, 1999.

Fernández, N., "Back to the Future? Women, Race, and Tourism in Cuba," in Kempadoo, D., Ed., *Sun, Sex, and Gold: Tourism and Sex Work in the Caribbean*, Rowman & Littlefield, Boulder, CO, 1999, p. 81.

Freeman, C., *High Tech and High Heels in the Global Economy*, Duke University Press, Durham, NC, 2000.

Herold, E., R. García, and T. De Moya, "Female Tourists and Beach Boys: Romance or Sex Tourism?" *Annals of Tourism Research*, 28, 978, 2001.

Hubbard, P., Sex and the City: Geographies of Prostitution in the Urban West. Hants: Ashgate, 1999.

Hubbard, P., "Sex Zones: Intimacy, Citizenship and Public Space," *Sexualities*, 4, 51, 2001.

Jiménez, F., *El Turismo en la Economía Dominicana*, Secretaría de Estado de Turismo, Santo Domingo, Chile, 1999.

Kempadoo, K., Ed., *Sun, Sex, and Gold: Tourism and Sex Work in the Caribbean*, Rowman & Littlefield, Boulder, CO, 1999.

Lladó, J., "El Plan Nacional de Desarrollo Turístico," presented at Convención Nacional y Exposición Comercial X, Santo Domingo, Chile, September 25–28, 1996.

Mesa-Lago, C. and J. Pérez-López, "Cuba's Economy: Twilight of an Era," *Transition Newsletter*, World Bank Group, Washington, DC, 1999.

Miolán, A., *Turismo: Nuestra industria sin Chimeneas*, Editorial Letras de Quisqueya, Santo Domingo, Chile, 1994.

Mullings, B., "Globalization, Tourism, and the International Sex Trade," in Kempadoo, K., Ed., *Sun, Sex, and Gold: Tourism and Sex Work in the Caribbean*, Rowman & Littlefield, Boulder, CO, 1999.

O'Connell-Davidson, J., "Sex Tourism in Cuba," *Race and Class*, 38, 39, 1996.

Oppermann, M., "Sex Tourism," *Annals of Tourism Research*, 26, 251, 1999.

Orozco, M., "Attracting Remittances: Market, Money, and Reduced Costs," Multilateral Investment Fund of the Inter-American Development Bank, Washington, DC, January 28, 2002.

Oxford Spanish Dictionary, Oxford University Press, Oxford, U.K., 1996.

Poon, A., "Flexible Specialization and Small Size: The Case of Caribbean Tourism," *World Development*, 18, 109, 1990.

Portes, A., and R. Schauffler. 1993. "Competing Perspectives on Latin American Informal Sector." Population and Development Review 19, (1, March):33–60.

Portes, A., M. Castells, and L.A. Benton, Eds., *The Informal Economy: Studies in Advanced and Less Developed Countries*, Johns Hopkins University Press, Baltimore, 1989.

Pruitt, Deborah, and Suzanne LaFont. 1995. "Love and Money: Romance Tourism in Jamaica." Annals of Tourism Research 22(2):422–40.

Ryan, C., 2000. "Sex Tourism: Paradigms of Confusion?" in Clift, S. and S. Carter, Eds., *Tourism and Sex: Culture, Commerce, and Coercion*, Cassell, London, 2000, p. 23.

Sánchez-Taylor, J., "Dollars Are a Girl's Best Friend? Female Tourists' Sexual Behavior in the Caribbean," *Sociology*, 35, 749, 2001.

Sassen, S., *Globalization and Its Discontents*, New York University Press, New York, 1998.

Schwartz, R., *Pleasure Island: Tourism and Temptation in Cuba*, University of Nebraska Press, Lincoln, 1997.

Stanley, D., *Lonely Planet: Cuba*. Lonely Planet Publications, Sydney, Australia, 2000.

Susman, P., "Cuban Socialism in Crisis: A Neoliberal Solution?" in Klak, T., Ed., *Globalization and Neoliberalism: The Caribbean Context*, Rowman & Littlefield, Boulder, CO, 1998.

Wiarda, H., 1999. "Leading the World from the Caribbean: The Dominican Republic," *Hemisphere 2000*, 7, 4, 1999, http://www.csis.org/americas/pubs/hemvii4.html.

World Bank, *Dominican Republic Social and Structural Policy Review*, Vol. I, Report 20192, Washington, DC, March 23, 2000, http://inweb18.worldbank.org/External/lac/lac.nsf/ ebaf58f.

World Bank, *World Development Indicators*, Washington, DC, 2001.

World Tourism Organization (WTO). "International Tourism Arrivals and Tourism Receipts by Country of Destination," 2000, http://www.world-tourism.org.

Notes

1. Tourism development is seldom a "voluntary" development option; rather, it is structurally linked to the stipulations of international capital. The United Nations Educational, Scientific, and Cultural Organization, the World Bank, and the Organization of American States pressured the Dominican Republic to build its tourist infrastructure after the U.S. lost access to Cuba's tourist industry (Barry, Wood, and Preusch, 1984; Miolán, 1994; Lladó, 1996). Loans, technical guidance, and development packages were arranged for the Dominican Republic to transform the structure of its economy to capture the surplus income and investments of developed nations. The number of tourists arriving in the Dominican Republic grew from 63,000 in 1970 to 2.6 million in 1999 (World Trade Organization, 2000).

2. The World Bank notes that high levels of unemployment, illiteracy, child labor, malnutrition, and unsafe drinking water are ordinary aspects of the lives of the poorest segments of Dominican society (World Bank, 2000).

3. Approximately 52% of the national budget goes toward basic services (Economic Commission for Latin America and the Caribbean, 1999).

4. Cuba was a major tourist destination for U.S. travelers from the 1920s to the late 1950s. Billed as a pleasure-oriented playland with a vibrant nightlife of music, dancing, restaurants, world-famous nightclubs, shows, and Mafia-controlled gambling casinos, Cuba's tourism industry practically ceased to exist with the ascent of the revolutionary government. In the early 1960s, the U.S. ended diplomatic and trade relations with Cuba and forbade its citizens from traveling to Cuba (Schwartz, 1997, p. 203). Schwartz attests, however, that sex work in Cuba today has little in common with the prerevolutionary era of "institutionalized sex shows and brothels" when Havana had more than 10,000 prostitutes (p. 122). Rosa del Olmo (1979, p. 36) indicates that by 1961 Havana had 150,000 prostitutes and 3,000 pimps.

5. The connubiality of the suffix *ero* to *pinga* creates the designation *pinguero* to describe someone whose essential quality, as in activity or profession, has to do with his *pinga*, or male erotic organ.

6. Herold, García, and De Moya (2001) indicate that not all female tourists provide money at the end of their visits. In some cases, the men receive only free meals and drinks. Generally, the men reported receiving $100 to $500 from each woman, although some received more. Some of the women also bought them gifts such as motorcycles or expensive clothes. *Sanky pankys* are very successful financially and earn substantially more than typical males in the Dominican Republic. For example, some reported earning about $1,000 a month or more. In comparison, the average wage is $60 a month.

9

Work, Immigrant Marginality, and 'Integration' in New Countries of Immigration: Déjà Vu All Over Again?

KITTY CALAVITA

Introduction

On February 5, 2000, a group of men in the southern Spain province of Almería set up barricades across the roads leading into the town of El Ejido. They then stormed into the neighborhoods of North African farm workers, burned tires, turned over cars, and ransacked a Muslim butcher shop. The rampage continued for several days, as locals armed with knives, crowbars, and baseball bats set fire to immigrants' homes and stores and went on what they called a "caza del moro" (Arab hunt). More than 70 people were badly injured and hundreds were left homeless (Foro Civico Europeo, 2000; S.O.S. Racismo, 2001). A year later, in the southern Italian town of Salandra, angry locals attacked an orphanage where 31 Albanian children were staying. Crying "Lynch the Albanians!" and carrying rocks and clubs, the mob of 500 people became outraged because Albanian boys "had looked at" local girls during a neighborhood get-together (Bisso, 2000, p. 16).

I begin with these two episodes not because they are particularly unique or represent the attitudes of most Spaniards and Italians. They serve as emblems of something both more subtle and more consequential—the real and perceived status of immigrants as marginalized and different "others." Ghassan Hage (2000, p. 15) introduces his book about racialization in Australia with the insight that there is a "structural affinity . . . between what is characterized as 'racist' and the discourse of the dominant culture," even when that discourse calls for tolerance.

These outbursts of anti-immigrant racism in Spain and Italy are the violent cousins of more civilized folk like "suspicion," "economic marginalization," and even "tolerance." The affinity is "structural" because underlying both are the common perceptions of immigrants as different and the structural location of immigrants as Third World laborers in First World economies that, in fact, make them different.

Immigration from so-called Third World countries[1] to Spain and Italy has increased dramatically in the past 10 to 15 years. In the face of this influx, immigration policies, even those of the right-wing Aznar and Berlusconi governments currently in power, ostensibly place a priority on immigrant integration. In fact, integration has become a mantra on the lips of government officials, opposition party members, and immigrant advocates alike. Despite all the rhetoric and policies aimed at facilitating integration, immigrants remain a class of pariahs, vulnerable to the kinds of attacks I just described and vulnerable, too, to the everyday experiences of exclusion that derive from and signify their marginality.

This chapter is part of a larger project that explores what that marginality and exclusion consist of and how they are constructed and reconstructed in daily practices in the operating procedures of local institutions, through the economy, and through the law. That project also tries to make sense of the paradox that although the law and the rhetoric of policy makers stress the urgency of immigrant integration, not only are they obviously failing in this endeavor, but the law plays an important role in that failure. For purposes of this chapter, I will address briefly the legal and economic sources of immigrant marginality and then touch on the similarities and differences between immigrant exclusion in today's post-Fordist and global economy and exclusion of immigrants to the U.S. in the industrializing era. It will help first to fill in the contexts of the new immigration to Italy and Spain.

Overview of New European Immigration

Spain and Italy have long been countries of labor emigration, sending millions of working men, women, and children to virtually every corner of the globe beginning in the late 1800s. In the decades after World War II, Spaniards and Italians found labor opportunities closer to home, shuttling back and forth to north and central Europe where they supplied the backbone of the industrial labor force for the postwar economic boom (King and Rybaczuk, 1993).

By the late 1970s and early 1980s, this migrant stream began to reverse. Many emigrants returned home, and Spain and Italy attracted large numbers of immigrants. The initial influx occurred at precisely the moment when northern European countries were closing their doors to Third World workers. To some extent, Spain and Italy became the "back doors" for immigrants intent on reaching the rest of Europe; they also became alternative destinations.

Italy experienced its own economic miracle in the post–World War II decades, and by the mid-1970s the gap between Italy and its northern European neighbors had narrowed. The increased employment opportunities and higher wage levels associated with this transformation attracted immigrants from Africa, Asia, and Latin America, much as in earlier years Italians migrated north to better jobs. By 2001, approximately 1.7 million foreigners legally resided in Italy. The vast majority came from countries outside the European

Union (EU), and a third of them came from Africa. The majority of non-EU immigrants work in low-wage sectors of the economy such as domestic service, tourism, construction, hotels, and agriculture (Ambrosini, 1999; Caputo, 2000; Gruppo Abele, 2001).

Spain's economy traversed quite a different course and has been shaped by a unique set of historical circumstances, most notably the Francoist regime. Since Franco's death in 1975, the economy has grown by spurts and starts, undergoing unprecedented levels of expansion from 1986 to 1990, when over 2 million new jobs were created—more than in any other European country (Maxwell and Spiegel, 1994, p. 89).

Spain's economy has continued to expand, with the number of jobs growing 24.2% from 1996 to 2001 (*El País*, July 16, 2002, p. 7). Although still lagging slightly behind Italy in terms of real wages and standard of living, Spain, too, has gone far in narrowing the gap with the rest of the EU. As in Italy, Spain's social protections have expanded rapidly, and its welfare state is now almost comparable with those of other western European democracies.

Since the mid-1980s, Spain has experienced net immigration for the first time in modern history. By 2002, over 1.2 million foreigners legally resided in Spain. Two thirds came from countries outside the EU, and most of them came from the Third World (Ministerio del Interior, cited in Generalitat de Catalunya, 2002).

Even more concentrated in certain niches than in Italy and less likely to be found in manufacturing, most immigrants in Spain work in agriculture, domestic service, tourism, construction, and other low-paying and underground sectors of the economy (Colectivo IOÉ, 1999, p. 70; Ministerio de Trabajo y Asuntos Sociales, 2002). As in Italy, immigrant labor is lauded for the flexibility it provides the economy. The former Director General of Migration pointed out that a high unemployment rate and the need for immigrant workers are not mutually contradictory, noting that the Spanish labor market "contains certain rigidities" that Third World labor helps counteract (quoted in *Mercado*, February 24, 1992, p. 27).

Despite much talk of coordinating policies at the EU level, most European immigration laws remain localized within the nation–states. Borders between EU countries have come down, summits have been held, and pacts determining how to manage external migration have been signed. Nonetheless, by the time of the European Council summit in Seville, Spain, in June 2002, virtually none of the many policy proposals for common immigration and refugee laws had been ratified. Despite considerable posturing by the new president of the European Council, Spanish Prime Minister José María Aznar, the Seville summit produced mostly squabbling and dissension, with the conservative Spanish and Italian governments "locking horns" with more progressive states, notably France and Sweden (Papitto, 2002, p. 2).

Spain and Italy passed their first comprehensive immigration laws in 1985 and 1986, respectively, and subsequently enacted amendments, revisions, and regulatory changes with dizzying frequency. Despite what seems like constant tinkering, several themes continue to characterize these laws. Above all, they are oriented toward immigration as a labor supply and contain few provisions for permanent legal residency or naturalization. Regularization or legalization programs are implemented every few years, with applications reaching several hundred thousand individuals (Borrás, 1995; Izquierdo, 1996; Pugliese, 2000). Those who are legalized, however, generally attain only temporary legal status and must demonstrate continued formal employment and navigate a maze of government bureaucracies to renew their permits.

Along with their emphasis on immigrants as workers, these policies stress the importance of immigrant integration. I use this admittedly vague term deliberately, as it is used by policy makers and in the laws. Judging from the rhetoric and the programs devised in its name, the integration term refers generally to social and cultural inclusion and is contrasted to segregation, exclusion, and rejection. The vagueness of the term is compounded by the varied strategies devised to enhance it, ranging from language courses and socialization classes designed to assimilate, to—conversely—tolerance campaigns that pitch the benefits of cultural difference and multiculturalism.

The Construction of Marginality

Despite these efforts at integration, immigrants continue to be marginalized economically, working in jobs and under conditions that locals shun. Hothouse agriculture around El Ejido, where the riots described above took place, is a good example. The arid and sparsely populated province of Almería began developing its signature hothouse agriculture (bajo plástico, or "under plastic") in the late 1960s. Four decades later, Almería, with a population of only 500,000, generated $1.5 billion from this labor-intensive industry.

Much of this growth began in the early 1990s when a massive increase in the intensification of cultivation occurred and Moroccan workers began to arrive in large numbers to work *bajo plástico*. Almería now officially has one of the largest ratios of foreigners to local residents in Spain. The legal immigrant population more than doubled in 5 years, from 11,255 in 1995 to over 25,000 in 1999. Most of the increase in legal immigration came through the quota worker program. Indeed, the Spanish government favors this region in its allotments of quota workers (*contingentes*). The small province of Almería received 9% of Spain's total annual contingent of foreign workers. If the estimated 70% of undocumented immigrant workers in Almería are included, the total size of the immigrant population approaches 100,000 (Foro Civico Europeo, 2000; S.O.S. Racismo, 2001).

The town of El Ejido emerged only recently. It is a creature of the new hothouse industry and was officially incorporated in 1987. Boasting some of the highest productivity levels in hothouse agriculture, the El Ejido area contains over 6500 hothouse farms—one for every six inhabitants. The vast immigrant workforce is almost entirely Moroccan, most of whom are undocumented. According to the report released by S.O.S. Racismo after the riots of February 2000, immigrant workers have become "one of the prerequisites of the hothouse production system that requires the ability to enhance substantially the size of the available workforce at a moment's notice during periods of intense activity" (2001, p. 16). Contrary to what might be assumed about agricultural production in southern Spain, it is not based on age-old techniques but "is a paradigmatic example of the workings of late capitalism" (S.O.S. Racismo, 2001, p. 19).

It is the agricultural equivalent of post-Fordist manufacturing in northeastern Italy. The farms are small-scale production units with intense levels of productivity and heavy investments in technology and equipment. As described by S.O.S. Racismo (2001), this sector:

> is inserted into a globalized economy. Product prices are fixed in Perpignan, France. The speed at which crops mature can be artificially increased by modifying temperatures and ventilation in the hothouses and this requires that a supplemental labor force be permanently available—that of illegal immigrant workers. Intense [global and local] competition requires a reduction in labor costs, especially wages, with a cheap and docile workforce, and increases in the pace of production (p. 19).

Much of the work is irregular. Three harvests a year are forced from the overworked soil, each requiring 40,000 workers for 1 to 3 weeks at a time. With only 12,000 jobs officially registered, the remaining laborers work underground, or *sumergido*. Seemingly immune to labor inspections from the federal government, these hothouses depend on itinerant undocumented workers to provide the supplemental workforce, the temporary status of which is a fixture of this system of production.

The typical workday lasts 10 hours. Temperatures can reach 113°F with 90% humidity inside the hothouses. In some cases, workers sleep under the plastic structures or in nearby shacks and are expected to provide round-the-clock security, a role that effectively extends their workdays to 24 hours. Owners often deduct money from workers' wages to pay for these hot, humid accommodations where air is heavy with toxic pesticides. A 45-year-old Moroccan farmworker in El Ejido described living conditions this way: "We live eight in one room without running water or electricity. We live together, eat together, cook together. But, at the moment only two of us are working, the others either aren't working or work only one or two days a week" (Chattou, 2000, p. 216). What contracts exist are oral. Wages even for legal immigrants, at about $18 to $24 a day, are lower than those established for agricultural work in this region (which has the lowest wage rates in Spain). Undocumented immigrants who are often hired for short periods of time follow the harvest from town to town and earn even less. In this context, notes the S.O.S. Racismo report (2001, p. 22), "[L]ack of protection against exploitation is absolute."

These workers across Spain and Italy are the "new untouchables" (Harris, 1995)—a class of outcasts whose utility is precisely their marginality, whose exclusion is their passport. It has long been recognized that vulnerable immigrants "work scared and hard" (Marshall, 1978, p. 169). Ari Zolberg (1987) and others (Ambrosini, 2001) have already exposed the contradictions, if not the hypocrisy, of policies that ostensibly embrace integration for immigrants whose primary virtue is their otherness. But marginality is not simply a characteristic that immigrants bring with them like a Third World passport that gains them admission and ushers them onto the fringes of the economy, nor is it solely constructed through legal systems that deny them permanent legal residence and work permits.

Legal and economic marginality are mutually constituted—with the fragility of legal status in Spain and Italy contributing to immigrants' disempowerment vis-à-vis employers, and their concentration in the underground economy jeopardizing their ability to legalize, which is usually dependent on a legal work contract. We can take this one step further because the immigrants' locations in the host economy reproduce their otherness, as their economic marginalization as an underclass of workers earning substandard wages sets them apart from the local population. This marginality effectively closes access to housing, health care, and education, impedes full membership in the national community, and invites backlash of the sort seen in El Ejido. In other words, it is not just that long-standing global inequalities among nations produce postcolonial subjects who provide cheap labor to First World powers; those inequalities—and those postcolonial subjects—are reproduced from *within*.

We might ask, is there anything new here, or is history simply repeating itself? The conditions in El Ejido agriculture sound like the conditions that braceros in the southwestern U.S. encountered 50 years ago (Calavita, 1992), that Chinese and Japanese farm workers endured over a century ago (Chu, 1963; Lyman, 1977; Chan, 1991), and that European immigrants to New York and Boston experienced in their urban form (Higham, 1955).

U.S. Immigration in the Industrial Era: "Men, like Cows ..."

In the 1880s, Andrew Carnegie (1886, p. 34) referred to immigrants as "that golden stream that flows into the country each year" and valued each immigrant at $1500 because "in former days an efficient slave sold for that sum." A few years later, the *New York Journal of Commerce* (1892, p. 2) declared, "Men, like cows, are expensive to raise and a gift of either should be gladly received. And a man can be put to more valuable use than a cow." The U.S. Congress (1901, p. 313) praised the combined effects of mechanization and immigrant labor: "The fact that machinery and the division of labor open up a place for the unskilled immigrants makes it possible not only to get the advantages of machinery, but also to get the advantages of cheap labor."

These immigrants did not simply contribute labor power to the industrialization of the U.S.; they provided the cheap labor power unique to marginal populations. In the 1890s, the marginalization was racially explicit. An ad for workers in a New York newspaper in 1895 (quoted in Gambino, 1975, p. 77) included the following daily wage rates:

Common labor, white: $1.30 to $1.50
Common labor, colored: $1.25 to $1.40
Common labor, Italian: $1.15 to $1.25

It was within this context that "Americanization" programs were launched. The Americanization movement gathered momentum in the early years of the 20th century as the new immigrants from southern and eastern Europe were declared racially inferior. Frederick Taylor (quoted in Roberts, 1912, p. 73) once advised employers that "the best kind of man to do certain kinds of work should be [sic] so stupid and so phlegmatic that he more nearly resembles the ox than any other type—a type to whom you can talk as you would not dare talk to white men." Education of a certain type was thought beneficial. Classes in English, civics, loyalty, and industrial techniques were taught by local governments and by employers. Henry Ford's English School was a pioneer. The first words taught were "I am a good American." Higham (1955, p. 248) describes the later stages of Ford's program:

The students acted out a pantomime which . . . symbolized the spirit of the enterprise. In this performance a great melting pot (labeled as such) occupied the middle of the stage. A long column of immigrant students descended into the pot from backstage, clad in outlandish garb and flaunting signs proclaiming their fatherlands. Simultaneously from either side of the pot another stream of men emerged, each prosperously dressed in identical suits of clothes and each carrying a little American flag.

The emphasis on cultural assimilation in these Americanization programs bears some resemblance to the integration efforts underway in Italy and Spain today, although the earlier programs were more oriented toward patriotic loyalty and anti-communism, particularly in the post–World War I period. More importantly, however, these current and former efforts at assimilation have collided head-on with economic realities that both produce and benefit from marginality.

Doing Empire from Within

The marginalization of immigrants in the new global economy is at the same time more subtle and more pronounced than the marginalization experienced in industrializing America. It is more subtle because we no longer explicitly categorize workers according to race. But, marginalization is also more pronounced. If we look carefully at policies and practices in new countries of immigration, we see a couple of patterns that should give us pause. Both patterns are related to this era of global post-Fordism and the empire-building practices associated with it that I call "doing empire from within."

One such practice is embedded in the immigration laws of Spain and Italy where legal status is almost always temporary and contingent. As a result, a category of vulnerable, differentiated, "disintegrated" workers is built into the legal system. The other pattern is revealed in the fact that immigration began to increase in these countries at the same time their economies *slowed down* after the post–World War II "economic miracle." In the industrial era, immigration flows to America always slowed during downturns in the economy, and net migration was sometimes even negative as immigrants returned home. Instead, the new immigration to Italy and Spain continues despite unemployment rates in the double digits.

Italian sociologist Maurizio Ambrosini (2001, p. 58) claims that no real contradiction exists between high unemployment rates and high rates of immigrant employment. Both conditions are parts of the same phenomenon of a late capitalism consisting of pre-Fordist and post-Fordist work and little in between. The three most significant areas of immigrant employment are small- and medium-sized manufacturing shops (especially in northern Italy), domestic service, and agriculture. Despite the obvious variations in the types of work involved, what these sectors have in common is their embeddedness in the global post-Fordist economy, the retention of essentially pre-Fordist labor relations, and rejection by local workers.

Domestic service and agriculture are in some ways pre-Fordist economic sectors that have leapfrogged the period of collective bargaining and government regula tions associated with industrial employment in the mid-20th century, and today they constitute an amalgam of pre-Fordist employment relations and post-Fordist globalization. The environments and contours of domestic service have changed dramatically, but quasi-feudal employment relations remain the norm. Agricultural employment, too—as exemplified by the El Ejido hothouses—with intense periods of productivity, short-term hiring, and global markets, price structures, and labor force, is a hybrid of pre- and post-Fordist labor relations and employment structure. The small manufacturing shops in northern Italy are similar hybrids.

The effect of this combination of pre- and post-Fordist work in modern capitalism helps explain the paradox of high local unemployment and high immigrant employment: too few good jobs and too many bad ones. As Ambrosini (2001, p. 174) points out, "From a strictly economic point of view, the best immigrant is one who has just arrived, is . . . willing to work hard, [and is] undemanding in terms of health and other social services; in other words, the immigrant who is not integrated. . . ."

Conclusion

The El Ejido and Salandra incidents described at the beginning of this chapter served a literary purpose as dramatic symbols of the failure of so-called integration efforts, but my use of them may have been misleading. This chapter is not a "look-at-the-racists freak show" (Hage, 2000, p. 20). On the contrary, it is a view of something far freakier by virtue of its ordinariness: the largely routine and systematic practices and structures that comprise exclusion and create and recreate Empire from within.

Sociologist Georg Simmel (1950), in his now-classic treatise on "the stranger," suggested that immigrants are prototypical strangers—physically present in a community but not parts of it. By virtue of their distinction literally as outsiders, immigrants and all other strangers are to varying degrees not perceived as full members in and participants of the social and cultural life of a community. Pierre Bourdieu (1991, p. 9) described the immigrant as "atopos," displaced or without place, and as a "bastard" between a citizen and a real outsider. Rogers Brubaker (1992, p. 47) talks about "the modern figure of the foreigner—not only as a legal category but as a political epithet . . . condensing around itself pure outsiderhood."

But, in the new economic and social order of 21st century globalization, the issue is more complicated than the dichotomy of immigrant–citizen or stranger–member implies. In the cases of Spain and Italy, the community has extended beyond the nation–state to include the EU. Thus, not all foreigners come from "outside the community," and not all foreigners are "strangers" or "others." As the forces of globalization have effectively brought together affluent members of First World countries into one economic club of consumers, the category of immigrant–stranger is increasingly reserved for outsiders from the so-called Third World. As I argued here, their outsider status is, in part, the product of long-standing global inequalities associated with the old colonialisms and imperialisms, but these postcolonial subjects are reproduced from within through law and the economic marginality it helps constitute.

References

Ambrosini, M., *Utili Invasori: L'inserimento degli Immigrati nel Mercato del Lavoro*, FrancoAngeli, Milan, 1999.

Ambrosini, M., *La Fatica di Integrarsi: Immigrati e Lavoro in Italia*, Il Mulino, Bologna, 2001.

Bisso, M., "Linciamo gli Albanesi," *La Repubblica*, January 14, 2000, p. 16.

Borrás, A., Ed., *Diez Años de la Ley de Extranjería: Balance y Perspectivas*, Fundación Paulino Torras Domenech, Barcelona, 1995.

Bourdieu, P., "Preface," in Abdelmalek, S., Ed., *L'immigration: Ou les Paradoxes de l'alterité*, De Boeck-Wesmeal, Brussels, 1991.

Brubaker, R., *Citizenship and Nationhood in France and Germany*, Harvard University Press, Cambridge, MA, 1992.

Calavita, K., *Inside the State: The Bracero Program, Immigration, and the I.N.S.*, Routledge, New York, 1992.

Caputo, G.O., "Salari di Fatto dei Lavoratori Immigrati in Italia," in Pugliese, E., Ed., *Rapporto Immigrazione: Lavoro, Sindacato, Società*, Ediesse, Rome, 2000, p. 88.

Carnegie, A., *Triumphant Democracy, or Fifty Years' March of the Republic*, Charles Scribner's Sons, New York, 1886.

Chan, S., Ed., *Entry Denied: Exclusion and the Chinese Community in America, 1882–1943*, Temple University Press, Philadelphia, 1991.

Chattou, Z., "Los Trabajadores Agrícolas Marroquíes de El Ejido: de la Invisibilidad a la Toma de Conciencia de Sí Mismos," *Migraciones*, 8, 203, 2000.

Chu, P., *Chinese Labor in California, 1850–1880*, State Historical Society of Wisconsin, Madison, 1963.

Colectivo IOÉ, *Inmigración y Trabajo en España*, Secretaría General de Asuntos Sociales, Madrid, 1999.

El País, "El Empleo ha Crecido en Cataluña el 22.1% en Cinco Años, por Debajo del 24.2% de la Media Española," July 16, 2002, p. 7.

Foro Civico Europeo, *El Ejido: Tierra sin Ley*, Libros Solidarios, Bale/Limans, 2000.

Gambino, R., *Blood of my Blood: The Dilemma of the Italian-American*, Doubleday, New York, 1975.

Generalitat de Catalunya, *Dades de la Immigració a Catalunya*, Generalitat de Catalunya, Barcelona, 2002.

Gruppo Abele, *Annuario Sociale 2001*, Feltrinelli, Milan, 2001.

Hage, G., *White Nation: Fantasies of White Supremacy in a Multcultural Society*, Routledge, New York, 2000.

Hardt, M. and A. Negri, *Empire*, Harvard University Press, Cambridge, MA, 2000.

Harris, N., *The New Untouchables: Immigration and the New World Worker*, St. Martin's Press, London, 1995.

Higham, J., *Strangers in the Land: Patterns of American Nativism, 1860–1925*, Rutgers University Press, New Brunswick, NJ, 1955.

Izquierdo, A., *La Inmigración Inesperada*, Editorial Trotta, Madrid, 1996.

King, R. and K. Rybaczuk, "Southern Europe and the International Division of Labour: From Emigration to Immigration," in King, R., Ed., *The New Geography of European Migrations*, Belhaven Press, London, 1993, p. 175.

Lyman, S.M., *The Asian in North America*, ABC–CLIO, Santa Barbara, CA, 1977.

Marshall, F.R., "Economic Factors Influencing the International Migration of Workers," in Ross, S., Ed., *Views Across the Border*, University of New Mexico Press, Albuquerque, 1978.

Maxwell, K. and S. Spiegel, *The New Spain: From Isolation to* Influence, Council on Foreign Relations Press, New York, 1994.

Mercado, "Miedo a lo Desconocido," February 24, 1992, p. 27.

Ministerio de Trabajo y Asuntos Sociales, *Estadistica de Empleo*, January 2002, Table 13.6, www.inem.es.

New York Journal of Commerce, December 13, 1892, p. 2.

Papitto, F., "Immigrati, Salta l'accordo UE; Lite tra Ministri, Francia e Svezia: Niente Tolleranza Zero," *La Repubblica*, June 18, 2002, p. 2.

Pugliese, E., *Rapporto Immigrazione: Lavoro, Sindacato, Societá*, Ediesse, Rome, 2000.

Roberts, P., *The New Immigration*, Macmillan, New York, 1912.

Simmel, G., *The Sociology of Georg Simmel*, translated and edited by Kurt H. Wolff, Free Press, New York, 1950.

S.O.S. Racismo, *El Ejido: Racismo y Explotación Laboral*, Icaria, Barcelona, 2001.

U.S. Congress, *Reports of the House Industrial Commission*, 57th Congress, First Session, House Document 184, Vol. 14, 1901.

Zolberg, A., "Wanted but Not Welcome: Alien Labor in Western Development," in Alonso, W.A., Ed., *Population in an Interacting World*, Harvard University Press, Cambridge, MA, 1987.

Note

1. The term "Third World countries" is awkward in this context, especially after I cited the presence of "Third World laborers in First World economies," calling attention to the interpenetration of supposedly distinct worlds. As Hardt and Negri (2000, p. xiii) said, "[T]he spatial divisions of the three worlds (First, Second, and Third) have been scrambled so that we continually find the First World in the Third, the Third in the First, and the Second almost nowhere at all." Although the world's populations may have been "scrambled," the mixing is by no means complete and in any case does not obliterate the broad-brush distinctions among the economies of this now-globalizing world.

10
Culture, Power, and Oil: The Experience of Venezuelan Oil Camps and the Construction of Citizenship

MIGUEL TINKER SALAS

Introduction

During most of the 20th century, Venezuela has been identified with its principal export, oil. Despite extensive scholarly production on the Venezuelan oil industry, the existing U.S. and Venezuelan literature fails to fully examine how this enterprise reshaped the lives of those it employed or how this process influenced social relationships and the construction of citizenship in Venezuela. The prevailing scholarship tends to ignore the cultural or power dynamics engendered by the oil industry, the contentious racial conditions that initially framed labor relations, and the ways in which this process shaped political participation.

To address this lacuna, this work begins by analyzing the roles that multinational oil companies played in promoting class aspirations, models of citizenship, and the social structures that influenced organised Venezuelan society after the discovery of oil in 1922. The study also provides the opportunity to consider Fordist and post-Fordist models of social reproduction and the debate over imperialism, globalization, and the pervasive influence it generated in Latin America. Control over oil revenues and policy and the public discourse over how citizenship is defined inform much of the current struggle between the administration of president Hugo Chávez and the opposition forces in Venezuela. Although this work predates the current crisis, it nonetheless offers a historical perspective from which to understand the class and racial polarization that has gripped the country since the election of Chávez.

The oil industry transformed the rural Venezuelan countryside, displaced older population centers, and created new communities. These new oil camps, or *campos petroleros* as they became known in Venezuela, represent the principal nexus of interaction among Venezuelans of various regions and social classes and foreigners employed in the oil industry. The camps served an important role in recasting regional differences, introducing distinct lifestyles, reformulating the use of public and private space, notions of work and time, and promoting new consumer patterns.

Aware of the dislocation that employment in the oil industry implied for an entire generation of Venezuelans, the multi-national companies sought to incorporate the family into this process while simultaneously redefining the roles of working and middle-class women. The oil enclaves and their neighboring communities constitute a social laboratory where the foreign oil companies promoted a model of citizenship and social and political participation that had long-term implications for the entire nation.

The possibility of work in the oil industry also expanded opportunities for an emerging and ambitious middle class. After the 1940s, corporate practices coincided with interests of certain middle-class political leaders who viewed the foreign oil companies as allies that could undermine the power of the old political order. This sector accepted the premise that the foreign enterprises represented agents of change that permitted Venezuela to break from its purported "backward past" and enter a new modern age.[1] The lifestyles associated with the oil camps and the social stature they conveyed became prototypes for broad segments of Venezuelan society. Over time, these sectors found common ground with the oil companies and actively cooperated in the formulation of a national social and cultural project that aligned the interests of the foreign oil companies with those of the nation.

This study breaks with the traditional schema that has characterized foreign economic enclaves in Latin America as self-contained units that interacted principally with the international economy and produced few or no repercussions on the cultural or political norms of the host countries. Admittedly, the number of people actually employed in the oil industry never accounted for a significant portion of the Venezuelan labor force. In 1941, the number of people engaged in all the oil companies represented 1.55% of labor force; by 1948, it peaked at 4.5%. This general pattern continued throughout the 1950s and the 1960s.[2] The impact generated by the oil industry therefore cannot be considered solely in relation to the number of people it employed. Instead, the Venezuelan oil industry must be measured by its strategic position in the world economy, its association with an emerging class structure, and the influence it exerted on the social and cultural norms of the country. From the perspective of the Venezuelan experience, the foreign enclaves cannot simply be considered extractive industries connected to international markets. Rather, they represent the focal points of a dramatic experimentation that, over time, recast social norms and political attitudes for a significant portion of the Venezuelan population.[3]

Most oil companies that arrived in Venezuela during the first decades of the 20th century previously operated in Mexico, where they encountered thorny labor problems and an emerging nationalism that blamed foreigners for despoiling the nation's wealth. *El Farol,* a publication of the Creole Petroleum Company, a wholly owned subsidiary of Standard Oil Company of New Jersey, summarized this experience indicating that nationalism was destructive: "We can cite the case of Mexico . . . where it produced noticeable consequences for the country, originating from the expropriation of the foreign enterprises."[4] Their experiences in Mexico, including the nationalization of oil in 1938, proved a decisive factor for U.S. petroleum interests. Avoiding "another Mexico" in Venezuela framed the policy concerns of the U.S. oil companies throughout the 1940s and 1950s.

The politics of the Cold War, characterized by an exaggerated fear of communism, became the other critical factor that influenced relations between the U.S. government, the foreign oil companies, and the Venezuelan state. By the late 1950s, the issue of avoiding another Mexico had become conflated by the obsessive fear posed by a purported communist takeover of Latin America. These broader geopolitical concerns determined the policies U.S. oil companies implemented in Venezuela. According to a U.S. business publication, their actions provided "strong insulation against communism and political instability."[5]

Confronted by political turmoil in Mexico and declining production, British and, subsequently, U.S. companies turned their attention to promising oil deposits in Venezuela.[6] The U.S. firms feared that their British competitors would emerge as dominant forces in the region. To initiate operations, the foreign enterprises needed thousands of laborers to cut down tropical growth, build ports, construct new roads, begin drilling, and eventually erect new settlements to house their employees.[7] The search for oil along the shores of Lake Maracaibo attracted thousands of formerly rural Venezuelan laborers from the nearby states of Mérida, Trujillo, Tachira, Lara, and Falcon and from the distant states of Nueva Esparta and Sucre.[8] The existence of these *campos petroleros* eroded regional barriers, creating the possibility of a new national identity and generating new forms of political organization. These settlements also set in motion profound personal exchanges between Venezuelans and foreigners from the U.S., the Caribbean, the Middle East, and Asia.[9] This dramatic movement of people produced a host of social and racial tensions that Venezuelan politicians and U.S. corporate officials manipulated to their advantage.[10]

Initially, the settlements established by the foreign companies resembled a makeshift society in which all regional groups and nationalities sought to recreate their own social norms and local cultural traditions against the backdrop of an emerging corporate culture. As oil became an important source of employment and attracted hundreds of former agricultural laborers, the industry undermined the political and economic powers of the traditional landed elite.[11] It also restructured the nature of political relations and civic participation, as the national government and myriad state and local entities attempted to negotiate different political arrangements and incorporate new political actors.[12]

During this chaotic period, the oil companies faced labor protests, disputes with local municipalities, and the increasing resentment of an established landed oligarchy. Seeking to avoid another Mexico, they gradually elaborated a vision of corporate citizenship that attempted to allay nationalist concerns over the roles of foreign corporations operating in Venezuela. As part of this approach they developed a sophisticated social project that sought to incorporate their labor forces into an all-inclusive corporate culture.

The oil camps that arose in Venezuela after 1930 represent adaptations of the Fordist model in which the foreign company organized production and also attempted to influence the social and cultural lives of its workers. The Venezuelan oil camps provided important spaces in which to analyze the ways the oil industry altered the lives of Venezuelans and foreigners it generated complex levels of cultural interaction, and, it permits us to examine the construction of a distinct model of political participation and a concept of citizenship that favored the interests of the foreign oil industry.

Los Campos Petroleros (Oil Camps)

Marked by visible social and racial distinctions, a pattern of segregated housing arrangements, its organization of public and private space, and the promotion of defined consumer patterns, the oil camps exerted significant influence over the people who resided within their boundaries.[13] Creole Petroleum's publications highlighted how the composition of the camps affected the use of public spaces and also contributed to the social organization of life for those who worked in the industry. According to *El Farol*: "When you visit our camps, the most impressive feature that you observe is the strict order that pervades in the settlement; this order permits everything to function . . . . Everything operates in concert with each other."[14] The camps embodied established housing arrangements and also represented an organizational structure—a model of class, social, racial, and occupational hierarchy the companies wanted to reproduce among their workers and their families. As a result, camp life both determined work habits and broadly influenced family, gender, and lifestyle patterns.

Consisting of a series of immediately adjacent residences of relatively uniform size, shape, and color, housing in the oil camps disarticulated the Venezuelan workers and their families from their previous agricultural activities. For those accustomed to a rural existence where different constructions of space and time prevailed, the new housing arrangements required remarkable adaptations. The living quarters and spaces they provided accentuated dramatic changes the workers and their families now experienced. The interior space of a house usually contained two small rooms: a kitchen and a living room. This arrangement tended to undermine the traditional extended-family networks that pervaded typical Venezuelan society.[15] By eroding the basis of the extended family with multiples levels of authority, it also promoted the traditional patriarchal family overseen by the male figure. Among oil workers, especially those newly employed, complaints about the size of the housing arrangement proved quite common. In some cases, employees creatively altered their living spaces whereas others opted to live in adjacent communities that formed outside the gates of the formal oil camps in order to preserve their traditional family arrangements.[16]

Life in the oil camps reconstituted familiar relations, emphasized the role of the nuclear family, and exalted the male parental figure as the primary breadwinner. Formed, in many cases, by groups of individuals with no established familial bonds, the camps forced people to develop new social contacts within environments in which the foreign oil companies exerted ever-present influence. Conscious of the fragility of these new associations, the companies promoted the notion of a broader corporate family to which the workers and their families belonged and on which they could rely for social support. Company publications announced marriages, births, baptism, graduations, and other events that transpired in the camps. These practices sought to create the sense of an extended corporate family while promoting social practices and norms the company found constructive.[17] The fact that the oil workers represented a highly mobile labor force subject to constant transfers among camps increased the need to establish broad levels of solidarity among company employees. As part of this project and to assure the diffusion of their ideals, the corporations promoted the concept of the nuclear family. According to a Creole publication:

> The spiritual level of the family determines the spiritual level of the community and the nation. When we mention spiritual we refer to a complete set of social practices, habits, beliefs and ideals that influence an individual's character. The home is the central place where these spiritual qualities take shape.[18]

In keeping with these objectives, life in the camp revolved around a daily routine involving the worker and incorporating the entire family in activities that included sports, social functions, night classes, and even religious instruction. In some cases, even priests received subsidies from oil companies.

Sports and Corporate Culture

The foreign oil corporations paid particular attention to the social lives of their workers because employees who had few or no recreational alternatives regularly frequented the bars and brothels that sprung up outside the gates of the oil camps in the initial phases of operations. To avoid practices that usually generated social disorder, companies such as Lago, Caribbean, Venezuelan Oil Concessions, and later Creole sought to integrate workers into what they considered "clean" forms of entertainment.

One 1940 publication entitled the *Muscle,* published by Sport Caripitense, pointed out that "sports is the way that individuals in modern society establish bonds of solidarity."[19] With this frame of reference, the transnational oil companies gradually established a sports directorate in every camp whose responsibility was to involve workers and their families in athletic events. These sporting activities initially developed at the local and regional levels. Eventually they evolved into a sophisticated network of intercamp rivalries that culminated in a national Olympics-style competition that pitted various production centers in Venezuela against each other. These activities involved men, women, and children.

Players who demonstrated athletic prowess received special treatment and could aspire to become members of professional teams sponsored by the companies. Some sports directors believed that they should involve workers in activities that would enforce their moral character and assure their loyalty to the company. Many workers complained that opportunities for economic advancement were tied to their participation in company-sponsored activities. One critic of the oil companies, Rodolfo Quintero, believed that the foreign oil companies sought to "create a new oil culture" in which workers and their family would be completely absorbed by company-sponsored activities.[20]

These organized sports teams also reveal the presence of a multi-national labor force. For example, in Campo Rojo, the Lagunillas cricket team composed of Trinidadian workers defeated the team from Maracaibo, and the Trinidadians were crowned champions of the Lake Maracaibo region.[21] U.S. citizens also engaged in a wide assortment of sporting activities. One of the more unusual events involving U.S. employees was "burro baseball." Players mounted the four-legged animals, batted balls, fielded, and ran bases.[21] At Tia Juana on the eastern shore of Lake Maracaibo, a game between married and single men attracted large crowds of expatriates. As one U.S. resident said, the activities were "silly things, but there was nothing else to do."[22]

Women

Corporate projects involved both men and women. Although the roles of women in the oil industry were traditionally overlooked, they proved central to understanding life in the oil camps and the social relations that this experience engendered. The companies initially hired employees without concern for their marital status but later gave preference to married individuals. The presence of women, according to the company, increased the social commitments of the male workers and, as a result, favored labor peace. In this context, the nuclear family and its associated responsibilities mitigated the problems that arose from employing single men who had no social obligations.

The oil industry redefined the role of the family, accentuating the roles that women played in the social structures of the families and in the social activities that stamped life in the camps. Class position determined the different sets of social, cultural, and familial obligations expected of women. In addition to camp committees, social clubs, and a variety of sports programs, companies such as Creole Petroleum also developed educational programs for women.[23] In 1948, to cite one example, the company established "home economics schools in Las Salinas, Lagunillas, and Tía Juana. Almost 100 wives are currently enrolled in these classes."[24] They received instruction on homemaking and social skills, fashion, and other matters considered important to life in the camps. The courses also proved important in promoting new consumer patterns and even fashion trends.

Middle-class women were entrusted with a different set of social obligations that included a host of interminable welcoming parties, retirements, birthdays, weddings, and the inevitable arrivals and departure of camp superintendents and other company officials.[25] Instead of formal classes, the semi-obligatory social events proved as important in establishing norms to which this social sector aspired. The relative isolation of some camps, their physical dimensions, the close proximity of the residences, and the small sizes of their populations invariably compelled people to attend social functions. Company publications advised women how to select the appropriate attire to suit specific activities. For example, one suggestion was that a "decorative hat and a black dress provide great decoration for cocktails and an early dinner."[26] The presence of a large U.S. population, especially considering the social hierarchy that functioned in the camps, proved to be an important factor influencing consumer patterns, fashions, and the social calendars in most camps.[27]

The oil companies recognized the new social functions that they expected women to fulfill. On more than one occasion, their publications addressed not only women's position within the family, but also the role they played in the oil industry. As early as the 1930s, the opportunity of employment in the oil companies modified traditional gender relations and recast women's employment patterns. In 1940, Creole employed only 111 women in different capacities, and by 1949 that number had increased to over 1500.[28] In most cases, women found themselves limited to traditional occupations, such as nurses, teachers, and clerical positions. As the number of women in the industry increased, the oil companies were forced to address their role in the labor force.

Since the 1930s, women's issues were discussed at various Pan-American conferences. In fact, elite Latin American women participated in conferences promoting the causes of universal suffrage and childcare at meetings held in Cuba and Mexico. This campaign was covered in the pages of publications such as the *Pan-American Union* and the *Inter-American Monthly*.[29] By the 1940s, *El Farol* joined the debate with an article titled "Lucha por la Liberación de la Mujer en Venezuela" (the struggle for the liberation of women in Venezuela), in which it promoted the idea that the "modern woman works, thinks, and struggles in peace and in war because she is just as capable as any man. That is why women in the U.S. refuse to blindly follow men."[30] Beyond its wartime context, the publication sought to link its version of women's liberation with notions of modernity and progress derived by emulating developments in the U.S.[31]

Beyond these general values and as part of a broad campaign, the oil companies promoted their version of a model female worker. In an interview, Ana Victoria, who worked in the laundry department at the Amuay refinery, said she saw "no contradiction between working in an all-male environment [sic] since she knew that the company appreciated her services." The article further affirmed that even though Ana Victoria and women like her worked, they had not forsaken their traditional tasks in the home.[32]

Thus it became clear that the multi-national corporations promoted a certain model of "women's liberation." Within this scenario, women's participation in the labor force did not undermine male patriarchy; rather, their role was framed within the discourse of modernization. In the end, women's participation accomplished the feminization of a certain sector of the labor force that would eventually be identified as women's work within the oil industry. Participation in the industry, even in this initially limited arena, nonetheless created new public spaces for women.

Office Boys, Junior Staff, and the Formation of the Middle Class

By the 1940s, Creole and Shell, the two largest oil companies operating in Venezuela, had established influential public relations departments.[33] These were new enterprises for multi-national corporations, and their creation attests to the complex social and political conditions they confronted in the postwar period. These new departments served multiple functions: Internally they sought to instill in their employees personal practices deemed useful. Outside the plants they served as the public faces of multi-national corporations in Venezuelan society. These tasks were not mutually exclusive because both Venezuelan and U.S. employees served as company "ambassadors." Through this newly formed enterprise, the oil companies promoted their own concepts of exemplary workers and model Venezuela citizens.

In its publications, Creole promoted its view of an ideal worker who arrived early every day, returned home to help with domestic duties, and participated in functions at the camp's social club or attended baseball games at night. The work ethic became a central characteristic of the model worker:

> Punctuality, loyalty, efficiency, and interest in work are at the heart of the covenant between the worker and the employer. These are the things the worker gives up for his weekly paycheck. Under these conditions work ceases to be a dull routine and becomes an ultimate goal.[34]

In addition to a set of accepted personal and social practices, the company frowned upon certain unacceptable practices, including joining unions, participating in political activities, and publicly criticizing company policies.[35]

The model employee sought to advance his career through individual initiative and sacrifice and never through collective action. According to Creole, "Individuals build themselves."[36] The promotion of U.S. individualism ("pulling yourself up by your own boot straps") served to counter all efforts at collective social action.

Creole and other companies regularly promoted individuals who relied on personal inventiveness to overcome adversity. Company policy actually encouraged individual initiative, offering employees training programs and scholarships and publicly promoting workers who succeeded in these endeavors. Under the auspices of a good investment, Creole publicized the case of an individual who, "when others dedicated themselves to baseball . . . was at home studying for his night classes at the Chávez school in Cabimas." According to the Creole publication, "at 18 years of age, Moreno had moved from the anonymous post of apprentice 'E' earning 5 bolivares a day to that of assistant and later first technician in the laboratory where he performed work that others had required years of training."[37]

Undoubtedly, this individual's efforts to improve his standing appeared admirable, but it is also clear that by promoting his achievements, the company sought to establish a prototype or model employee that would benefit it and the country. The company endorsed the concept of a social contract with its employees. By adhering to this contract, the employee achieved a level of compensation and benefits unmatched in the Venezuelan private sector. In addition, the purported social contract also involved an element of nationalism. The company repeatedly associated its role in Venezuela as an agent of modernization for the nation. Thus within this broader context, the worker, through his loyalty to the company, also contributed to the advancement of the nation.

Although Venezuelans held the majority of the entry-level positions, their presence in the hierarchy of the oil companies remained limited. During the initial phase, along with U.S. citizens, foreign oil companies recruited significant numbers of West Indians from islands such as Trinidad, still under British colonial rule, to fill administrative posts in Venezuela. By doing so, they hoped to acquire loyal employees who had experience with European customs, spoke English, and would not easily develop bonds with Venezuelan workers.[38]

The multi-national firms insisted that Venezuelans lacked the skills to perform these operations. During the first decades of operation, the employment of West Indians in positions that Venezuelans could have performed caused tensions among the foreign companies, incipient labor organizations, the nascent middle class, and the government of Andean strongman Juan Vicente Gómez (1908–1935). Confronting a wave of protest and the presence of an organized labor movement that demanded better conditions and wages, the multi-national corporations modified their policies and slowly began hiring Venezuelans into administrative posts.[39]

Beyond the entry-level laborer category, Venezuelans could aspire to two other general job categories within the social and racial hierarchies of the oil companies where U.S. and West Indian males predominated. The English language classifications of "office boy" and "junior staff" used in Venezuela underscored the asymmetry that pervaded employment in the oil industry. To a certain extent, the categories also socially and racially distinguished senior staff employees, usually white U.S. or British males at the top, white or mixed-race Venezuelans who attained employment as junior staff in the middle, and mixed-race Venezuelans who initially filled the ranks of the office boys at the bottom of the administrative hierarchy.

The relationship between senior staff and Venezuelan junior staff or office boys also embodied the distinction between foreign experts and Venezuelan neophytes expected to implement policies decided by the upper echelons of the firm. After the oil industry was nationalized in 1976, the mantle of expertise became the domain of the Venezuelan professional sector. They manipulated their newly acquired positions and constituted the only group who could supposedly address the complex issues associated with the oil industry. Common workers appeared incapable of understanding the complex issues that confronted the industry and therefore became marginalized from national debates related to oil.[40]

Distinctions between foreigners and Venezuelans also found expression in salaries, benefits, the selection of housing, and the construction of the use of public and private spaces in the oil camps. The larger oil camps had separate sectors for senior staff employees, junior staff, and other employees. The staff and junior staff usually lived in protected, gated communities surrounded by fences and watched over by guards known as *guachimanes,* or watchmen.[41] Each camp also had separate social clubs for senior and junior staff and another club for *obreros,* or laborers. This social and, even at times, racial stratification acquired importance both in the camps and also in the larger Venezuelan society where it tended to reinforce prevailing views on race.

The position of office boy, despite its paternalistic connotations, became one of the most important entry-level positions open to people with basic elementary educations. The office boy was usually assigned as a helper or secretarial assistant in a certain department. Because such entry-level or temporary positions were usually filled by younger persons in Venezuela, they became the principal sources of training and administrative employment for many adults. Creole Petroleum regularly published information about employment opportunities for office boys. The first issue of its in-house magazine titled *Nosotros* (us) publicized the case of Braulio Rodríguez, who had begun as an office boy and became "director of his department and oversaw the work of 18 other office boys."[42]

This article and a host of others promoted the belief that office boys could easily advance beyond their initial training positions and attain high rank.[43] In addition to acquiring important practical experience, the position of office boy also exposed individuals to the value system embedded in the corporate culture. One of the principal lessons many former office boys from this period recalled was the idea of *superación personal* (culture of personal improvement) the company extolled. If they expected to advance, office boys had to demonstrate inventiveness, resourcefulness, and loyalty to the enterprise. As one individual recalled, "I arrived early, left late, and sought to learn from the professional staff."[44] The position also proved important in the development of client–patron relations that became essential for the promotion of the individual office boy and were intended to endure throughout a career in the oil industry. Although the company promoted the notion of meritocracy, client–patron relations proved to critical to an individual's ascent in the company. Moreover, despite that many individuals managed to climb the social ladder, the companies simply did not have enough positions to accommodate all those aspiring to employment.

The lack of university degree programs in fields related to the oil industry limited the number of Venezuelans who could attain positions as petroleum engineers or geologists. Nonetheless, Venezuelans with university or professional titles eagerly sought general administrative or junior staff ranks within the oil companies. As noted earlier, many of these jobs were previously reserved for foreigners. One exception was in legal departments where the oil companies invariably had to hire Venezuelans because foreigners could not appear in court to argue cases on behalf of multi-national corporations, but even in these cases, the upper echelons of legal departments tended to be occupied by foreigners.

In response to pressures received, the foreign companies gradually established scholarship programs for individuals who demonstrated loyalty and particular skills within the enterprises. Again, previous experience and loyalty to the company appeared to be decisive factors in the scholarship selection process. The companies preferred to hire and promote within their own ranks, thus assuring loyalty from employees. During the 1940s and 1950s, *El Farol* regularly publicized cases of Venezuelans who, after having proven themselves at the company, received scholarships to continue postgraduate education in the U.S.[45] In addition to formal scholarship programs, the companies and the government oversaw the expansions of university departments associated with the petroleum industry.

Under relentless pressure from the emerging middle and the working classes, the oil companies began to hire more Venezuelans. They employed Venezuelans as lawyers, bookkeepers, accountants, and engineers, and the Venezuelans became powerful allies of the foreign companies and the primary interfaces between the transnational enterprises and the population at large. The success of the Venezuelan middle class depended in large measure on the maintenance of the export model promoted by the foreign oil companies.

Junior staff members seen as the professional sectors of the industry formed important social and political networks that found expression in the middle-class parties and professional associations that dominated the Venezuelan political scene before the rise of Hugo Chávez.

Among the professional sectors, the corporate culture promoted a middle-class lifestyle that paralleled its U.S. counterpart. The company model for junior staff encouraged a U.S. middle-class lifestyle that found expression in consumer patterns, housing arrangements, fashion, food, and even lifestyle choices.[46]

In addition to postgraduate scholarships for skilled employees, Creole and Shell also fostered the arts by subsidizing the works of artists, musicians, and other cultural elements most closely associated with an emerging middle-class lifestyle. An important element of this effort was the creation of consumer patterns most closely identified with an emerging middle class. Company commissaries stocked with U.S. products "functioned as modern supermarkets" in which consumer patterns would gradually take hold and eventually influence broad segments of the population.[47]

These new consumer patterns influenced the middle-class standard of living, aspirations, fashions, and recreational activities. The middle class served as an important link between the U.S. culture that functioned in the oil camps and the Venezuelan society of which they were a part. This did not require coercive actions on the parts of the companies. Rather, they encountered a convergence of interest between an emerging middle stratum and the interest of a foreign multi-national enterprise that managed to present itself as the principal agent of modernization in Venezuela.

Harvesting Oil (*Sembrando el Petróleo*)

The programs sponsored by the foreign multi-national corporations in Venezuela expanded opportunities for an emerging middle class who saw its future tied to the success of foreign oil companies. By adopting policies that favored this group, the companies addressed several interrelated issues. They amassed support among an important social group that they viewed as long-term factors in social and political stability. They also managed to establish clear connections between these sectors and their own economic objectives. Creole, in particular, often reiterated that there existed no contradictions between its objectives in Venezuela and the well-being of the nation and its various social classes. Company-sponsored publications reasoned that by the 1950s, strikes had become things of the past because work stoppages would affect the company, deprive the state of needed revenues, and negatively affect the well-being of the middle class.[48]

The publicity campaigns promoted by these multi-national corporations revolved around the idea of *sembrar el petróleo*, or harvesting the benefits of oil production. Corporate and even the state discourses presented oil as an agent of modernization, of progress, and as an essential element of civilization. Of course, progress under this scheme depended on an acceptance of the social hierarchy that developed in oil camps throughout Venezuela. Likewise, any critique of this new social order quickly became categorized as "ignorant" or worse, "retrograde," and therefore harmful to the nation. Thus, the national discourse on development and modernization was framed by acceptance of the role foreign oil companies played in the economy.

Central to the preservation of this image was the campaign associated with the notion of "sowing," or harvesting Venezuelan oil to benefit the nation. The notion of Venezuela's sowing its petroleum found expression in corporate and government publications. One such example is a report dedicated exclusively to Creole Petroleum Corporation and published by the National Planning Association with the apparent support of the company. Titled *Venezuela Sows its Petroleum*, the publication described how Creole helped modernize Venezuela. Walter Dupouy, a Creole spokesperson and often-cited news source, echoed these sentiments in 1949. He noted that just as the Spanish colony "had depended on the Guipuzcoana Company (the Caracas Company) to modernize, in our epoch the modernization of the country is the result of the stimulus of the powerful oil industry. Thanks to their efforts we have achieved or are trying to achieve the progress that stamps our century."[49] The ideal embodied in the "sow our petroleum" slogan became the point of consensus between the foreign multi-national corporations and a generation of Venezuelans who believed that oil revenues would transform their nation.

The oil companies, especially Creole, appropriated this concept and projected their role in helping Venezuela achieve this goal. In an article titled "The Company and the Nation," published in 1964, Harry Jarvis, then president of Creole, concluded that "our 45 years of experience . . . give us the hope for a future of sustained prosperity for the nation and the company."[50] The link between the progress of the nation and the multi-national corporations appeared firmly embedded not only in the politics of the Creole Petroleum Corporation, but also in the minds of middle-class Venezuelans who directly or indirectly depended on the industry for employment and social standing.

Civil Society

The oil companies did not simply concern themselves with the conditions of their employees in relatively isolated rural oil camps. Their strategy of promoting constructive social and personal practices went beyond their own employees and involved Venezuelan society at large. Increasingly, the oil camp embodied the model of personal behavior and citizenship, and the experiences gained there could be generalized throughout Venezuela society. To accomplish this task, the foreign oil companies supported an entire arsenal of modern public relations tools that sought to influence broad sectors of Venezuelan society.

The two largest companies, Creole and Shell, sponsored their own radio shows, published cultural magazines and educational literature, subsidized university departments, and staffed offices of "experts" who were regularly cited in the Venezuelan media. After 1953, they also maintained their own television shows that included "Farol TV" and a highly respected nightly news program known as the *Observador Creole* (Creole observer).[51] Every oil camp also had its own local bulletin, for example, the *Caripito Mail* and the *Amuay Pelican*.

The companies' public relations departments took the values transmitted to oil-camp residents and disseminated them throughout Venezuelan society. Central to this perspective remained the need to remake the Venezuelan character; promote Western concepts of time, labor, and management; and purge Venezuelans of purported negative traits stereotypically associated with Latin American culture. The practical issue of time was central to the companies. Western ideas of punctuality and efficiency were promoted. In 1944, a national publication Creole Petroleum promoted this ideal for all of Venezuelan society:

> "Today! This word is the paramount symbol of men who triumph in life. 'Mañana' is the word that condemns men to an existence of lamentable sterility [sic]. If we become accustomed to saying, 'Mañana I will do this; mañana I will begin this or that thing,' we will soon reach old age without having accomplished anything of importance for ourselves, or for our nation or for humanity."[52]

Besides affirming work, punctuality, efficiency, individualism, and respect for authority, the multi-nationals also promoted morality, religion, and ways of organizing politics and union activities. These themes acquired new importance after the nationalization of Mexican oil in 1938. After the Mexican nationalization, Venezuela became one of the few countries in Latin America that welcomed foreign oil companies. After 1938, the need to promote models of citizenship and political participation that favored the extraction of oil by U.S. enterprises acquired a new urgency. Increasingly, Creole Petroleum sought to associate itself with the very existence of the nation. In this setting, Creole and Venezuela represent the same set of interests. The country depended on Creole, and likewise the company depended on the goodwill of the nation.

From the perspective of the foreign oil companies, their most important policy concern in Venezuela remained the preservation of their investments in the nation's oil production. Venezuela's acceptance of the roles of foreign companies in the extraction and refining of its petroleum proved to be the cornerstone of this arrangement. Over the long term, the companies appeared less concerned with the form of government that operated in Venezuela. They proved quite adept at working with dictatorships, military strongmen, and even purported nationalist middle-class governments. Of course, they objected to any changes that might alter the revenue arrangements they established with the government. Venezuela became an important symbol in Latin American for the benefits of the free-enterprise system. In fact, according to *Fortune* Magazine, "If there had been no perfect illustration of what U.S. technical and capital resources could do for the world's 'under-developed areas,' it would have been necessary to invent the Republic of Venezuela."[53] The preservation of that system became paramount to the oil companies' relations elsewhere in the region and even in the Middle East.

El Farol served as one of the principal tools of Creole's public relations apparatus. The other large oil companies also sponsored national publications. Shell published *Revista Shell*, and Mene Grande, a subsidiary of Gulf Oil, produced *Circulo Anaranjado* (orange sphere). From its inception, *El Farol* proposed to "give preference to everything Venezuelan, to promote our traditions, our folklore whether in literature, art, science or history."[54]

The use of "our" is not coincidental because Creole purported to represent Venezuela and its culture. With a staff of highly acclaimed Venezuelan intellectuals, the political undertaking initially promoted by *El Farol* paralleled developments in other countries of the region. In Mexico, Central America, and the Caribbean, similar projects had been initiated during the 1930s and 1940s by intellectuals associated with *indigenismo* (negritude). In Venezuela, after almost 30 years of one-man rule, the state and its cultural institutions remained relatively weak. The foreign oil companies stepped into this void and portrayed themselves as promoters of national culture. To fulfill its cultural and social function, *El Farol* published articles about the indigenous presence in Venezuela, the role of Afro-Venezuelan culture, the origins of carnival, and numerous recipes for making hallacas (a Christmas dish similar to tamales) and arepas (corn cakes). They also dedicated significant coverage to the various regional manifestations of Venezuelan culture.

On the surface, it seems ironic that a publication sponsored by a subsidiary of a U.S. oil company would be instructing Venezuelans on their heritage and on how to make national dishes such as hallacas or arepas. Yet, through these and other publications, the experiences of the llaneros (cowboys), the way of life of the Andinos (Andeans), and the cultural traditions of the orientals (easterners) ceased being simply manifestations of isolated regional cultures and became central components of a broader Venezuelan national culture. This process appears closely tied to the forging of a Venezuelan identity, real or invented, whereby cultural practices, dietary patterns, fashions, and even notions of identity are homogenized. This venture developed in close association with important groups of Venezuelan intellectuals who viewed the oil companies' magazines as Venezuelan cultural enterprises.[55]

During the 1940s and 1950s, the pages of Creole's magazine created new public spaces for Venezuelan writers and essayists who, by and large, opposed the government of strongman Marcos Pérez Jiménez (1948–1958). The magazine also provided these authors access to a readership (oil workers) they normally would not have been able to reach. The presence of these intellectuals in the magazine implied a balancing act and a degree of self-regulation between their political views and their largely literary or cultural functions. They usually remained free to write about diverse topics as long as they refrained from directly addressing political issues that the company or the government may have found sensitive. As one former magazine editor acknowledged, they knew the range within which they could operate, and seldom did they violate this space.[56] Although the Venezuelan authors refrained from addressing political issues, the magazine editors faced no such limitations. The publications openly attacked the left and the roles of labor unions whereas they lauded capitalism, the free-market system, and other policies favored by the company.

The pages of *El Farol* during the 1940s and 1950s contained articles or works by notables such as Mariano Picón Salas, Arturo Uslar Pietri, Juan Pablo Sojo, Ramón Díaz Sanchez, Miguel Acosta Saignes, Armando Reverón, and Héctor Poleo.[57] The topics addressed by these writers included essays by Sojo titled "Los Abuelos de Color" (our grandparents of color) and "El Negro y la Brujeria en Venezuela" (blacks and Venezuelan magic). Saignes, a renowned anthropologist, wrote about the Timoto Cuica, an indigenous group that inhabited the Venezuelan Andes before the arrival of the Spaniards. Salas described the origins of Venezuela's national food, the arepa.[58] Even *Mene*, the highly acclaimed novel by Díaz Sanchez that criticized the exclusionary and racist actions of U.S. oilmen, found its ways in serialized fashion onto the pages of *El Farol*. Although the Venezuelan intellectuals refrained from addressing politics, their presence in this corporate publication represented a broader political project. Such a distinguished group of Venezuelan intellectuals lent a certain aura of credibility to the activities of the company in the country and facilitated its identification with the nation's economic and cultural progress.

Paramount to the multi-national corporations and their activities in Venezuela were the association with modernity and progress and the role of foreign capital in the extraction of Venezuelan oil.[59] By the 1960s, the character of the magazine changed dramatically. Gradually, its cultural and social functions became the domain of the new democratic state and various sectors of civil society. The magazine continued to be the mouthpiece of the company but lost its cultural and social elegance.

Conclusions

Beyond its economic function, oil fundamentally transformed the Venezuelan social and cultural landscape. Venezuelans employed in the industry confronted different notions of time and work, as well as new social and cultural expectations driven in large part by U.S. culture. This does not imply that they simply became passive recipients of a U.S. way of life. Venezuelans from diverse social classes responded in multiple ways, including resistance, adaptation, and even accommodation. The oil camps also provided the basis for a new level of social interaction between people of diverse social status who previously functioned primarily within discrete regions in Venezuela. They also altered the relations of power between these regions and the central government while establishing the basis for a centralized political apparatus and a national economy.

The camp experience reconfigured regional identities, introduced a new lifestyle, and recast the use of public and private spaces, time management, and the establishment of new consumer patterns. It also reformulated the role of the Venezuelan family and accentuated the positions of the nuclear family and male patriarchy. Aware of the fundamental changes underway in the oil camps, the multi-nationals incorporated families within their structures and paid attention to the role of women as agents of change in this new process of socialization. Without the participation of women, it is doubtful that this process would have succeeded.

Oil exploration increased employment opportunities for thousands of previously rural laborers. Although Venezuelans remained relegated to the lower socio-economic strata, constant pressure by labor and a nascent middle class eventually provided them access to administrative employment opportunities with oil companies. Such employment expanded the economic base of the middle class. Despite these new sources of employment, their positions in the multi-national firms continued to be marked by asymmetrical power relations that accentuated differences between Venezuelans and foreigners.

This chapter underscores the role that multi-national oil companies played in the promotion of social and citizen participation that developed in the oil camps of Venezuela. Political conditions allowed these multi-nationals to find willing allies among some middle-class political groups and intellectuals who accepted the foreign oil companies as important agents of change. The experiences acquired in the oil camps eventually found their way into various sectors of Venezuelan society. This process shaped several generations of Venezuelans who lived in the oil camps or functioned within this broader society and, after 1960, assumed the reigns of power in the country. The model of the nation they promoted remained rooted in the earlier experiences of the oil camps and the notions of citizenship and political participation that they generated.

Bibliography and Notes

1. These terms continue to influence the Venezuelan public discourse on the role of the oil industry and its role in the country.
2. Dupouy, W. "Consideraciones sobre algunos efectos económicos y sociales de la industria del petróleo en Venezuela," *El Farol*, (Julio, 1949), p. 8.
3. Other works that also follow this approach include Finn, J. *Tracing Veins, of Copper, Culture and Community from Butte to Chuquicamata*, University of California Press, Berkeley, 1988. Klubock, T.M., *Contested Communities, Class, Gender and Politics in Chile' El Teniente Copper Mine*, Duke University Press, Durham, 1998. Chomsky, A. and Santiago, A.L. *Identity, and the Struggle at the Margins of the Nation State, the Laboring people of Central America and the Hispanic Caribbean*, Duke University Press, Durham, 1998 and Putman, L. *The*

Company they Kept, Migrants and the Politics of Gender in Caribbean Costa Rica 1870–1960, University of North Carolina Press, Chapel Hill, 2002.

4. Editorial, *El Farol*, Noviembre, 1940, # 18 Año II p.1.
5. Taylor, W.C. and Lindeman J. *Venezuela Sows its Petroleum*, National Planning Association, Washington, 1955. p. 3.
6. "Biggest Oil Well Yet," *New York Times*, March 18, 1923 p. 13.
7. Salazar, P.G. *Aporte para la historia del movimiento zuliano, Maracaibo*: Autor 1982, Prieto Soto, J. *Luchas obreras por nuestro petróleo*, Litografía Lorenzo, Maracaibo, 1970 y Quintero, R. *La Cultura del Petróleo*, Universidad Central de Venezuela, Caracas, 1985. Croes, H. *El movimiento obrero venezolano*, Ediciones Movimiento Obrero, Caracas, 1972.
8. Briceño Parilli, A.J. *Las migraciones internas y los municipios petroleros*, Caracas 1947, p. 34.
9. See Tinker Salas, M. "Relaciones de poder, cultura y raza en los campos petroleros venezolanos 1920–1940," in *Asuntos*, PDVSA, (Caracas) Año 5, N. 10, Noviembre 2001, pp. 77–104.
10. See Ellner, S. *El Sindicalismo en Venezuela, en el contexto democrático*, Fondo Editorial Tropykos, Caracas, 1995, Tennassee, P.N. *Venezuela, Los Obreros Petroleros y la lucha por la democracía*, Editorial Popular, Caracas 1979, and Bergquist, C. *Labor in Latin America*, Stanford University Press, Stanford, 1986.
11. Castillo D'Imperio, O. *Los años del buldózer ideología y política 1948–1958*. Fondo Tropykos, Caracas, 1990, p. 13
12. Boletín del Archivo Histórico de Miraflores, #70 (enero/febrero, 1972) Año XVIII., Memorando, #11 Pérez Soto a Gómez. Memorial 26 Junio 1926 p. 319–346. Also Linder, P. "Coerced Labor in Venezuela, 1880–1936," *The Historian*, #57 1994, p. 43–58.
13. "El caso de los comisariatos," *El Farol*, N. 129, Año XI 1950, Also *Nosotros*, Noviembre 1947.
14. "Líneas directrices," *El Farol*, Febrero, 1945 #69 Año VI p.10.
15. *Study of Operations, Temblador district*, Petroleum Engineer Department, Standard Oil Company of Venezuela. October/November 1942.
16. Interview with José Omar Colmenares, July 2003, a former Shell employee who recalled the creative steps families took to overcome the crowded space they inhabited.
17. *El Farol*, Maracaibo, *Suplemento de Occidente*, Mayo,1943 p. 3.
18. "La responsabilidad del hogar," *El Farol* Noviembre 1944 p. 3.
19. "El Musculo" citado en *El Farol*. Enero, 1940 #8 Año II p.30 Semanario "El Musculo" publicado por Centro Deportivo Caripito, Sport Caripitense.
20. Quintero, R, *La Cultura del Petróleo*, Universidad Central de Venezuela, Caracas, 1985, p. 51.
21. *El Farol*, June 1942, p. 29
22. *The Caracas Journal*, March 24, 1954.
23. *El Farol*, Suplemento de Oriente, Caripito Febrero, 1945, p. 3
24. *El Farol*, Ano X 1949
25. "Cocktail de despedida." *Diario de Occidente*. Maracaibo, 2 Octubre 1951, p.1; also several interviews of women who lived in the oil camps.
26. "Últimos dictados de moda." *El Farol*. (Enero, 1942) #32 Año III. p. 26.
27. Venezuelans in the camps were exposed to U.S. holidays such as 4th of July, Thanksgiving and the Germanic version of Christmas.
28. "Las Mujeres en la Creole," *El Farol*, Marzo, 1949.
29. "Inter American Commission of Women," *Inter Americana Monthly*, December, 1942 p. 29.
30. "La lucha por la liberación femenina," *El Farol*, Noviembre 1945. p. 9
31. Ibid.
32. "Las mujeres en la Creole," *El Farol* Marzo 1949.
33. See "Our Legacy in Public Relations," in Coordinating Committee of the Jersey Company, Agenda for Seaview Conference Standard Oil Company of New Jersey, May 16, 1944, Seaview (NJ) Country Club.
34. *El Farol*. Febrero 1940. p. 15.
35. "En Buena Compañía" *El Farol*, Año X N. 125 1949. "Elba Porras, trabaja y Sueña, *El Farol* N. 133, Año XI 1951 y "De Ayer y Hoy," *Nosotros*, Agosto, 1955.
36. "El ingeniero que se construyo a sí mismo," *El Farol*, N. 134, Año XI, 1951.
37. "Una Buena Inversión," *El Farol*, Febrero de 1949, año 10 p. 2.
38. Tinker Salas, "Relaciones de poder, cultura y raza en los campos petroleros venezolanos 1920–1940,"
39. Ibid.

40. For a development of this perspective, see Carlos Luis Villalobos, "Las representaciones sociales de la tecnocracia petrolera y las transformaciones de la política petrolera," Presented at "La Visión de Venezuela," Sección venezolana of LASA, Maracaibo, June 13–14, 2002.

41. Bracho Montiel, G. Guachimanes, (Watchmen) Doce aguafuertes para ilustrar la novela del petróleo, Francisco Javier, Santiago, 1954.

42. Revista inicial de *Nosotros*, Año 1 Numero 1 Agosto 1946 De Office Boy a la Jefatura de la Sección

43. "De Office Boy a Secretario," *Nosotros*, (mayo, 1947) p. 12.

44. Interview, July 10, 2003, Mérida, Venezuela. José Omar Colmenares. Mr. Colmenares worked as an office boy in Mene Grande during the 1930s.

45. *El Farol*, "El ingeniero que se construyo a si mismo," #CXXXIV, 1951 p. 26. (During this period *El Farol* no longer indicated its month of publication.)

46. *El Farol*, Ano X 1949

47. *El Farol*, "El caso de las Casas de Abasto," Ano XI 1950.

48. Taylor, W.C. and Lindeman, J. *Venezuela Sows its Petroleum*, Washington: National Planning Association, 1955, p. 62.

49. Dupouy, W. "Consideraciones sobre algunos efectos económicos y sociales de la industria del petróleo en Venezuela," *El Farol*, (Julio, 1949), p. 2.

50. Jarvis, H. "Empresa y Nación," *El Farol*, (Abril, Mayo, Junio 1964.)

51. This new program continues today but is simply known as "El Observador."

52. *El Farol*, "Editorial," Febrero de 1944. p. 1.

53. *Fortune*, "It's Hot in Venezuela," (May 1949) vol. 39 p. 101.

54. *El Farol* Febrero 1946.

55. "Una empresa de Cultura Venezolana," Guillermo Meneses, *El Farol*, (abril, mayo, junio 1964.) p. 28,

56. Personal conversation with former Shell magazine editor, June 2002. Maracaibo, Venezuela.

57. Uslar Pietri A. "La Maravillosa Jornada de Alejandro Humboldt," *El Farol*, Marzo Abril 1959, y Acosta Saignes M. "Los Timoto-Cuicas, un pueblo previsivo, *El Farol*, Setiembre, Octubre 1958.

58. Sojo, J.P. "Los abuelos de color," *El Farol*, June 1946. Salas Picón M. "Pequeña historia de la arepa," *El Farol*, Abril 1953.

59. *El Farol*, "Necesitamos Capital Extranjero," mayo 1, 1942

III

Workers: Solidarity and Resistance

11

Empire, Strategies of Resistance, and the Shanghai Labor Movement, 1925–1927

WAI KIT CHOI

Introduction

Suppose that capitalism develops through different stages, and that by *empire* we mean the current stage of global capitalist expansion. How then should we conceptualize the relationship between the periodization of capitalist development and the strategies of resistance? Should we, in other words, periodize or historicize our strategies in the same way we periodize the dynamics of capitalist development so as to identify a strategy of resistance that is adequate to this particular stage of capitalist development?[1]

A large number of new social movements that promote and defend the rights of women, people of color, gays, and lesbians emerged since the 1960s. Some theorists point out that these new forms of social movements as well as the concomitant socioeconomic and cultural changes in the most advanced industrial societies reveal the limitations of traditional social theories (Lyotard, 1984, p. 11; Best and Kellner, 1991, p. ix; Laclau and Mouffe, 2001, p. 2). For example, there is skepticism about the traditional Marxist approach that sees the industrial proletariat as the agent of resistance, aiming to subvert capitalism through mobilization of the industrial working class.

A *totalizing* theory,[2] as the postmodern critics understand it, is unidimensional and tries to capture the dynamics of social change by means of a "grand narrative" that suppresses important differences among social categories (Ritzer, 1997, p. 12). A Marxist view that privileges the industrial working class is seen as an example of this problem because it is blind to the multidimensionality of social interaction. Analysts of the new social movements in the past three decades claim that multiple points of conflicts are present in capitalist societies and that all these conflicts cannot be reduced to a "fundamental" contradiction between capitalists and the proletariat.

By the mid-1990s, as Harvey notes, the tide of opinion shifted (1999, p. xvii). Theorists who previously played important roles in the upsurge of postmodern theories now argue for the continued relevance of Marx's writings (Derrida, 1995; Rorty 1997; Butler, 1998). Hardt and Negri (2000) published *Empire*, a book described as a rewriting of the *Communist Manifesto* for the era of globalization. The ensuing debates in both the academic and the wider public arenas illustrate a resurgent interest in the relevance of Marx to contemporary social and economic developments.

Although it is criticized in the writings of the postmodern theorists, the traditional Marxist strategy of resistance is likewise deemed antiquated by Neo-Marxists such as Hardt and Negri. They argued that the "internationalist proletarian subject" (by "subject" they mean an active agent) was seen as the purveyor of revolutionary change in the earlier era of capitalist accumulation (2000, pp. 52–53). That was the era of mass production when great numbers of workers were concentrated in large factories. In the current stage of global capitalist expansion referred to as the empire, the economy is dominated by flexible production (see Chiu and So, Chapter 13, this volume).

Production processes are now broken up and performed in different parts of the world; workers are no longer amassed in single locations. As a result, it is no longer fruitful to try to organize the proletariat by constructing a common language and common enemy. We should accept that resistance in the present era has become isolated and fragmented. Hardt and Negri assume that the way capitalist production is structured at present makes it impossible to organize industrial proletariat into a unified agent of resistance. Laclau and Mouffe, (2001), who modified Marxism from a postmodern perspective in the mid-1980s, make a similar argument regarding the formation of a unified revolutionary agent in colonial and advanced capitalist societies. It although their recommendation of the new strategy is different from Hardt and Negri's.

I will question both neo-Marxist and postmodern arguments in this chapter, illustrating my theoretical arguments with a case study of the labor movement in Shanghai from 1925 through 1927. I have reasons for focusing on Shanghai. It became a treaty port in the mid-1800s, and, until the Japanese occupation in 1941, it played an important role in the global capitalist system because it served as a nodal point to facilitate trade between the periphery and the empires.

By the early 20th century, Shanghai became the indisputable center of China's modern industry (Lu, 1999, p. 58), and in the 1920s the city already had a radical, mass-based, and sustainable labor movement, the culmination of which was a worker revolution in 1927. I will show that it is an oversimplification to attribute the formation of a unified proletarian revolutionary subject in an earlier era to the structural features of capitalist development that existed then. As is true today, the proletariat of the past was also composed of diverse elements, and many points of conflict existed among the different social groups participating in popular movements.

The revolutionary subject that existed in Shanghai in the 1920s was a contingent construction resulting from a fusion of different and even contradictory social groups into an *ad hoc* alliance based on political finesse. Whether this coalition would collapse or be sustained over a long period depended on changes in the external political and economic circumstance as well as the skills of the actors involved in holding it together. This revolutionary proletarian subject did not result automatically from the macro political and economic conditions of the time; its formation was not an historical necessity peculiar to that stage of capitalist development.

Although important differences between the past and the present can be noted, we should not be blind to crucial similarities. If as much diversity and heterogeneity existed among the proletariat or people in the past as exists today and it were still possible to build broad-based and sustainable movements to coalesce in the earlier period, then we should not resign ourselves to the view that these forms of resistance are impossible today.

Historical Background I: An Overview

Although China was nominally an independent republic after the overthrow of the Manchu dynasty in 1911, its vulnerability and subjugation to the military, political, and economic domination of the Western powers since the 19th century reduced the country to what many writers designated a "semi-colony." Hong Kong was ceded to Great Britain in 1842 after the Manchu empire's defeat in the Opium War (Bianco, 1971, p. 2), and Taiwan was given to Japan in the late 1800s. In certain coastal cities, the Western Powers—Great Britain, France, Italy, Belgium, Germany, Austria-Hungry, and Japan—had their own jurisdictions or concessions, their own police forces, and rights to levy taxes.

The most important concession was the International Settlement of Shanghai. It was formed in 1863 when the areas occupied by the U.S. and the British merged and created a single elected governing body, the Shanghai Municipal Council. Chinese people living in the International Settlement were required to pay municipal taxes, but unlike the Western "ratepayers," the Chinese had no right to vote. The French occupied an area south of the settlement and the French concession in Shanghai maintained its own governing structure (Honig, 1986, pp. 13–14).

Another example illustrating the loss of China's autonomy in that period was the economic domination exercised by the Western Powers and Japan. In addition to the cession of Hong Kong to Great Britain, the Nanjing Treaty of 1842 placed a 5% cap on customs duties that could be levied by the Manchu Empire. After the Taiping Rebellion (1851–1864), the Western Powers seized greater control over Chinese customs. A General Inspectorate of Customs was created and the chief inspector and other high officials were all foreigners. Indemnities were imposed on China by the Western Powers and Japan after its repeated defeats in battles against them. When the Chinese government was unable to pay its indemnities, it borrowed from these Powers and also contracted other loans to meet its general expenditures. After the overthrow of the Manchu dynasty in 1911, the Powers designed a system that required customs inspectors to transfer the revenues they collected to designated banks—the Hong Kong and Shanghai Banking Corporation (a British bank established to facilitate colonial trade, now among the world's top 10 banks), the Yokohama Specie Bank, the Banque de l'Indochine, and others—and use that revenue to pay off interest on the various loans that the Chinese government owed them. The Chinese government was allowed to keep only the remainder and only with the consent of Western diplomats in Beijing. The same system was extended to collection of the revenue from the Chinese salt tax after the government lost control of it in 1913 (Chesneaux, 1968, p. 6).

A parallel exists between the domination that the World Bank and International Monetary Fund (IMF) exert over many developing nations today and the way China ceded control of its finances to the Western Powers. The parallel suggests that the contemporary global capitalist expansion that we call *globalization* today is not an historically unprecedented phenomenon. Much of the developing world, as in the case of China, is *re-experiencing* global capitalist domination today.

When examining the impacts of global capitalist expansion in the 21st century, it would be wise to understand how global capitalism unfolded in these areas in an earlier historical period. More importantly, familiarity with the anti-imperialist movements organized by Chinese workers and revolutionaries in the 1920s should inform present discussion about the strategies of resistance against global capitalism in the 21st century. Shanghai is especially relevant in this connection. After the city became a treaty port in the 19th century, it was China's most important economic center. In 1922, the revenue collected by Shanghai customs constituted 37% of the total revenue collected for the entire country; by 1931, Shanghai's share increased to 51% (*The Maritime Customs*, 1933, p. 9). To understand Shanghai worker resistance against global capital, the period from 1925 through 1927 is crucial. In 1925, a general strike was held in support of the May Thirtieth Movement. Three general strikes were held in the city in 1927 during workers' uprisings against the warlord regime of Sun Chuanfang (*The Maritime Customs*, 1933, p. 21).

Historical Background II: The Story of Li Qihan

Li Qihan, also known as Li Sen, was among the first to join the Chinese Communist Party (CCP) immediately after it was founded in 1921 and was assigned the task of organizing the nascent Chinese urban proletariat. Although he was not a top-rank leader in the CCP, Chesneaux's classic work on the Chinese labor movement (1968) contains enough references about Li to assemble a series of snap shots of Li's life as a communist revolutionary.

Li Qihan was a student from the Hunan province, the home province of Mao Zedong. By 1921, even before the official founding of the CCP, Li had already become an ardent communist and was organizing an evening school for workers living in the cotton-mill district in Shanghai (Chesneaux, 1968, p. 171). Through a woman worker who attended his school, Li was accepted into the Green Gang, one of the two major secret societies in Shanghai. Membership in the gang allowed him to establish contacts with workers in the tobacco and silk factories located in the Pootung and Chapei districts of Shanghai.

Later that year, in July 1921, delegates from seven of the eight small existing Communist groups, along with a representative from the Comintern known as Maring, held a meeting in Shanghai and declared the founding of the CCP. Li was immediately appointed as the assistant to Zhang Guotao, the leader of the newly formed Chinese Labor Organization Secretariat of the CCP.

In January 1922, Li held a meeting commemorating the deaths of Rosa Luxemburg and Karl Liebknecht. It was held in the Labor Secretariat office at 19 Chengtu Road in the International Settlement of Shanghai. The Hong Kong seamen's strike began around the same time, and Li headed the Shanghai Labor Secretariat committee formed in support of the strike. In June 1922, Li was arrested by the British police in the International Settlement for his labor activities. He was then handed over to a Chinese warlord and remained in prison until 1924, after which he was sent to Guangdong by the CCP and again became a union activist under the name of Li Sen.

At the end of the 20th century, as Western multi-national corporations extended or re-extended their reach into different corners of the world, the global expansion of capitalism produced a global pastiche. As a result, we see monks in Tibetan Buddhist monasteries drinking Coca-Cola and Vietnamese soldiers wearing fake Nike sneakers. Although these examples may seem trite, the globalization of capitalism in the present era represents a world where McDonald's meets Jihad and where one desires both a Lexus and olive trees (Barber, 1995; Friedman, 1999).

However, it is not only the process of global capitalist expansion that is eclectic. The resistance against global capitalism also takes on a contradictory character. In this connection, Li Qihan and the early experiences of the CCP become relevant to contemporary debates on strategies of resistance against globalization. The important question that needs an answer is how was a unified proletariat constructed despite the fragmentation that existed among the Chinese urban workers at the time, fissures produced by regional linguistic differences, differences in skill levels, differences among industrial sectors, and differences in age and gender?

Theory: Hardt and Negri's Strategies of Resistance

In the writings of Hardt and Negri, contemporary globalization is seen as a rupture from the previous historical periods that involved global capitalist expansion; it is different from the era of imperialism. The term *empire* is introduced to capture the articulation of global power and economic production that is peculiar to the present juncture. Unlike the era of imperialism, global domination today is exercised by a deterritorialized supranational body composed of both nation–states and transnational organizations, not by rival colonial nations. Another difference is that economic processes are no longer dominated by manufacturing. Economic processes are dominated by service and information sectors distributed throughout the world.

On the basis of these changes, Hardt and Negri argue that the strategies of resistance used during the era of imperialism are outdated. They propose that in the earlier period, the single social group that played a central role in resistance against global capitalist expansion was the industrial proletariat. In the "previous era, the category of the proletariat centered on and was at times effectively subsumed under the industrial working class, whose paradigmatic figure was the male mass factory worker . . . [the] industrial working class was often accorded the leading role over other figures of labor (such as peasant labor and reproductive labor) in both economic analyses and political movements" (2000, pp. 52–53).

However, for these authors, the subject of resistance to the empire is no longer a unified industrial proletariat but a highly differentiated and heterogeneous class of immaterial laborers. "Traditional forms of resistance . . . lost their power . . . a new type of resistance has to be invented" (p. 308). Central to this new form of struggle against global capitalism is the idea of "immaterial labor" (pp. 53, 209, 289–294). They argue that services and information are the dominant sectors of the economy today, and that the workers in those sectors constitute immaterial labor. Unlike the industrial proletariat, immaterial labor is characterized by stratification and heterogeneity and includes workers involved in knowledge-based laboring processes such as programming and those who hold poorly paid low-skill service jobs.

This argument implies that strategies of resistance against global capitalism are dependent on periodization or labor segment. Capitalism develops over different stages and has transformed from a manufacturing-based economy to one based on services and information. The organization of production is also different throughout the distinct stages. The early stage was characterized by mass production in which workers became concentrated in a factory or industrial town. The later stage is flexible production (see Chiu and So, Chapter 13, this volume); workers involved in the production process no longer work together in the same locale. Although the unified industrial worker class characterizing the earlier stage could have carried out resistance, it cannot happen at a later stage. Resistance against capitalism in the present stage inevitably became fragmented because the proletariat is much more diversified, and the old strategy of organizing them into one big union or party will not work. A strategy adequate for resisting capitalism during one stage of capitalist development may not be adequate for a later stage.

This method of periodizing strategies of resistance is not uncommon. Laclau and Mouffe (2001) expressed a similar view in their influential *Hegemony and Socialist Strategy: Towards a Radical Democratic Politics.* In Third World countries, "imperialist exploitation and the predominance of brutal and centralized forms of domination tend from the beginning to endow the popular struggle with a centre, with a single and clearly defined enemy. Here the division of the political space into two fields is present from the outset, but the diversity of democratic struggles is more reduced" (p. 131). Thus, in these settings, we see the emergence of two clearly defined antagonistic camps in society, with the masses opposed to imperialist and capitalist domination (p. 131).

Although the contrast cited by Laclau and Mouffe is between advanced industrial and Third World countries rather than between manufacturing-based and flexible production-based capitalism, the underlying logic of their position is the same as that of Hardt and Negri. In the less advanced stage of capitalist development, whether it is a manufacturing stage or colonial capitalism, social conditions are more clearly defined, the points of conflict are less heterogeneous, and the strategy of unification is feasible because the proletariat and other social classes can come together as a unified agent or subject of resistance. In the more advanced stage, multiple points of conflict arise, more diversity exists among the proletariat and other social classes, and resistance inevitably becomes splintered.

Critique

Problems arise with the ways Laclau and Mouffe and Hardt and Negri think about the strategies of resistance. These authors oversimplify the complicated process by which a unified rebellion arose in the earlier period when they suggest that the rebellion was made possible simply by the "structural" conditions of that stage of capitalist development. What if just as much diversity and heterogeneity among the masses and just as many multiple points of conflict existed earlier? In that case, a unified subject of resistance cannot be seen as something produced by the structure of capitalism in that period. Instead, it may be the result of an arduous construction in which all the differences among a diversified populace were bridged and reconciled.

To illustrate my objections to these authors, I focus on the labor movement in Shanghai from 1925 through 1927. Numerous general strikes and other strikes occurred then. The labor movement was very large and powerful in Shanghai and constituted what we could call a unified proletariat. However, a great deal of heterogeneity and stratification was present among the Shanghai proletariat, as Perry's (1993) pioneering work on the Shanghai labor movements demonstrates. Therefore, labor unity could not simply be the result of the "structure" of colonial capitalist development.

Following Perry's lead, I will focus on those historically and socially specific features of the Chinese proletariat. Labor unity emerged because these features were overcome and manipulated; the pre-existing characteristics did not generate labor unity. The general point is that if a unified Shanghai proletariat developed, it was through a contingent process that succeeded in bridging all the differences within a heterogeneous working class. This suggests that the diversity and stratification of immaterial labor today do not automatically justify a politics of fragmentation and should not preclude organizing a unified movement against present-day imperialism.

Shanghai Labor Movement, 1925–1927

The CCP campaign to organize Shanghai workers entered a new stage in 1925 with the eruption of the May Thirtieth Movement. It began on May 15, when seven Chinese workers were shot by a Japanese foreman during a scuffle at a Japanese-owned cotton mill. One worker was killed (Shanghai Municipal Council Annual Report, 1925, pp. 61–62). On May 30, several thousand people took part in a demonstration to condemn the killing. As the protesters marched along Nanjing Road in the International Settlement, British police, attempting to disperse the crowd, arrested students who were distributing leaflets. Some of the protesters, however, followed the police and the arrested students to the Louza Police Station (*Minguo Ribao*, May 31, 1925).

Edward William Everson, the British Police Inspector in charge, gave an order to shoot the protesters outside the station (*North China Daily News*, July 3, 1925). Four protesters died at the scene, and at least 12 were seriously wounded (*Minguo Ribao*, May 31, 1925). A mass meeting was held the next day; among the participants were representatives from the Student Federation, the CCP, and various shopkeepers' associations. An agreement was reached to conduct a general strike with participation from workers, students, and businessmen and boycott foreign banks by withdrawing money they had on deposit. On the same day, a new organization called the Shanghai General Labor Union (SGLU) was organized to oversee strikes. The SGLU was directly linked to the CCP; its top leaders, Li Lisan and Liu Shaoqi, were members of the party.

By June 4th, the movement had 74,000 strikers; it had approximately 200,000 by June 20 (*Minguo Ribao*, June 22, 1925). As Chesneaux observes, "[T]he enterprises primarily affected were the Japanese and British firms and the municipal services. The ships in the docks were immobilized and the goods left standing; the telephones ceased to function and foreign newspapers ceased publication; there was nothing but a skeleton staff left at the power station in the International Settlement, and there were even quite a number of defections among the Sikhs of the Muncipal Police" (1968, p. 264). Economic activities in the city basically came to a halt. A list of demands was presented during a demonstration on June 13. In addition to the rights to strike and organize unions, the group demanded the right to vote for Chinese ratepayers in the International Settlement, the abolition of extraterritoriality, the withdrawal of foreign troops, and other political measures aimed at eliminating the privileges of Japan and the Western Powers.

The ramifications of the May Thirtieth Movement went beyond Shanghai, as shown by the Guangdong–Hong Kong strike. On June 19, sailors, telegraphers, newspaper workers, and workers in foreign firms in Hong Kong went on strike to show solidarity with the workers in Shanghai. In nearby Guangdong, a demonstration was held on June 23. As the marchers approached Shameen where the Western concessions were located, British and French soldiers fired on the crowd, killing 52 and wounding more than 100. A general strike on the British colony immediately went into effect. By the end of June, over 50,000 workers from different sectors left Hong Kong and went to Canton, and by the end of July, over 80,000 workers departed the colony. The strike lasted 16 months, ending in October 1926. During that time, the economy of the British colony was completely immobilized (Chesneaux, 1968, pp. 291–292).

Interpreting the May Thirtieth Movement

The May Thirtieth Movement was a popular action that struck at Western and Japanese capital and at their colonial rule in China. Shanghai workers were key players in the movement, and CCP labor organizations played a central role in providing direction to the workers and dealing with the logistics of the strike. However, it would be wrong to conclude that the CCP succeeded in mobilizing the Shanghai proletariat simply because the industrial working class concentrated in large factories and that made labor organizing easier. They were not concentrated, and it is also not true that the unity and cohesion achieved during the strike resulted from the homogeneity of Shanghai proletariat.

The colonial policies of the Western Powers in Shanghai directly fomented a broad coalition of Chinese workers, students, and bourgeoisie. However, the emergence of this coalition was not inevitable, nor was it easily sustained in the long run. There were also other basic "structural" contradictions among the "people," for example, between the Chinese workers and the bourgeoisie.

The coalition was formed for a very specific purpose under very specific circumstances. The Western Powers had many options to break up the coalition, and toward the end of the movement, fissures did indeed appear. We should not assume that imperialist domination automatically leads to the formation of a popular movement. Instead, we must examine the specific political and economic circumstances under which the multiple points of conflict were put aside and also how broad coalitions can and often do collapse.

Although the strike in Shanghai lasted more than 3 months (June to mid-September) and the workers clearly constituted a "unified subject of resistance," the unity was not based on homogeneity among the workers. Rather, the Shanghai proletariat consisted of heterogeneous groups affiliated with different regional cultural traditions and organizations. The broad social coalition was composed of different classes, but it was a fragile alliance, as a more detailed analysis of the different actors involved will show.

Heterogeneity of the Shanghai Proletariat I: The Gangster Connection

Writing about the May Thirtieth Movement, Perry observed that "[g]angster support was the *sine qua non* of a large-scale strike in Shanghai" (1993, p. 82). Chen Duxiu, one of the founders of the CCP, confirmed the power of the gangs:

> What type of people are most powerful in Shanghai? A superficial look shows that major political and economic power is in the hands of the Westerners, but the internal social institution is quite different. The majority of factory laborers, all of the transport workers, and virtually all of the police are under the control of the Green Gang. The great strike at the time of last year's student movement [i.e., May 4] already revealed their authority. The commands of gang leaders are more effective than those of the Municipal Council. The only way of eliminating them is to publicly establish legal unions in each industry. Whether Shanghai unions are developed is thus not only an urgent matter for labor but is also a matter for Shanghai social order (Chen, quoted in Perry, 1993, p. 73).

To explain why the gangs had such power over Shanghai labor, we need to understand a unique feature of China proletarianization—the *pao-kung*, or contract labor system. Factory owners and capitalists did not hire workers directly; they recruited them through intermediaries. Wages and arrangements regarding working conditions were negotiated by these intermediaries, most of whom were gang members, rather than with workers directly. For example, in the cotton-mill industry, labor contractors would go to villages to recruit young girls. The contractors would pay parents about $30 for 3 years' work by a daughter. After the girl arrived in the city, the contractor kept all her wages. Her 3 years of labor were worth about $254. After deducting the costs of recruitment and room and board, a contractor could earn about $204 for one girl (Honig, 1986, pp. 111–112).

The contract labor system was used widely by British and Japanese companies to hire sailors, dockers, and coolies in the big ports and laborers in the mining industry and many other fields of transport and industry (Chesneaux, 1968, pp. 57–59). This system gave the gangsters a powerful influence over Shanghai labor. Even establishing legal unions did not end the influence of the gangsters. After the right wing of the Guomindang, as represented by Chiang Kai-shek, decimated the CCP and gained control over Shanghai, Du Yuesheng, a gang leader and opium magnate who financed Chiang's army through his operations, maintained control over Shanghai labor through "yellow unions." Such unions were approved by the government and dominated by officials with close ties to the gangs and typically included semiskilled workers such as "[m]ail carriers at the Shanghai Post Office, drivers and conductors at the French Tramway Company, and cigarette rolling machine operators at the British American Tobacco Company" (Perry, 1993, p. 102).

Gangster power explained why communist activists such as Li Qihan became involved in gang activities. The gang connection was especially crucial for his organizing efforts among workers in the cotton and tobacco industries (Perry, p. 74). Even Li Lisan, a top communist and one of the leaders of the

SGLU, was invited to become a disciple of one of the Green Gang bosses during the May Thirtieth Movement, and with the approval of the party he joined the gang (p. 81). The cooperation of the gangs in Shanghai was one of the factors accounting for CCP's success in organizing the general strike, but the gangsters were fickle allies, as events in 1927 show.

Heterogeneity of the Shanghai Proletariat II: The Right-Wing Unions

The United Front of the CCP and GMD was established in 1924 (Skocpol, 1979, pp. 243–246). After Sun Yat-Sen's death in 1925, the split between the left and the right wings of the GMD became conspicuous. The left wingers remained cooperative with the CCP whereas the right wingers were hostile and opposed the expansion of a radical labor movement. The right wingers' concern led to their direct participation in labor organizing. In 1924, the Shanghai Federation of Labor (SFL) was formed, and it brought together 32 conservative labor groups. It also maintained close ties to the right wing of GMD.

The problems they presented to the CCP-organized labor movement became obvious through the May Thirtieth Movement. By early August, 1925, the strike had continued for more than 2 months, and many workers were weary. The right-wing SFL seized the opportunity to attack the SGLU and accused its leadership of unnecessarily prolonging the strike for personal gain. On August 22, about 50 men entered the offices of SGLU, destroyed documents and office equipment, and wounded at least eight union officials (Shanghai Municipal Council Annual Report, 1925, p. 50). The SFL was quickly identified as the culprit behind the attack (Chesneaux, 1968, p. 269; Perry, 1993, p. 82).

Fragile Alliance of Workers and Capitalists

Chinese capitalists also played a role in the May Thirtieth Movement. A large fund was needed to maintain the subsistence of workers who were on strike, and the Chinese business people of Shanghai contributed a large part of the fund. Patriotism was one the factors accounting for the Chinese business circle's action. However, the changing dynamics of competition between the Chinese and the Western capitalists became an equal if not more important factor in explaining the Chinese bourgeoisie's initial alliance and eventual break with the CCP-organized labor movement.

Patriotism made economic sense for Chinese capitalists who competed with Western and Japanese business rivals on an unfair basis because of the political and economic privileges the foreigners enjoyed in China. Chinese businesses had to pay a *likin* tax imposed on the domestic circulation of goods. Western and Japanese products were exempt from this tax because of the unequal treaties signed with the Manchu Empire in the 19th century. The treaty of Nanjing stipulated that the tariff rate the Chinese government could impose on Western goods could not be more than 5%, and this made protectionist policies to nourish the growth of Chinese industries impossible.

Because of the political status of Shanghai, the Chinese bourgeoisie there experienced additional disadvantages in competition with Western capitalists. Representatives in the Shanghai Municipal Council were elected by foreign ratepayers who owned land worth at least 500 taels (about U.S. $365) and paid assessment fees or by foreigners who paid assessed rental fees. Although the Chinese paid a higher proportion of the rate, they still had no rights to vote in council elections.

In the spring of 1925, the relationship between the Shanghai Municipal Council and the Shanghai Chinese bourgeoisie further deteriorated when the council attempted to implement new fees and regulations that disadvantaged Chinese businesses (Shanghai Municipal Council Annual Report, 1925, p. 65). When the anti-imperialist May Thirtieth Movement erupted, the Chinese bourgeoisie were receptive to it, but their participation in the movement did not last long. The merchants' strike organized by the Chinese bourgeoisie terminated on June 26 (*Minguo Ribao*, June 26, 1925). This decision was made after the Western authorities agreed to the possibility of "returning the Mixed Court to the Chinese, admitting wealthy Chinese to the Municipal Council, and reopening the negotiations on customs control provided for in the Washington Treaty in 1922" (Chesneaux, 1968, p. 267). On July 2, the Electricity Department of the International Settlement issued an open letter to the public announcing that power would be discontinued unless strikes ended and normal conditions were restored (*North China Daily News*, July 2, 1925). The editor of the *North China Daily News*, the leading English newspaper in Shanghai representing British interests, pointed out that the strike targeted mainly British and Japanese businesses, and Chinese cotton-mill owners were not affected by it. However, by terminating power supplies, "not only would the Chinese mill owners lose on their produce, but they would naturally be called on to do something towards the support of their wrkpeople [sic]" (*North China Daily News*, July 2, 1925).

The Shanghai Municipal Council cut off power supplies on July 6 (Shanghai Municipal Council Annual Report, 1925, p. 72). The Chinese General Chamber of Commerce disbanded the Committee for Aid and Peace established to collect funds for the strikers shortly afterward (Chesneaux, 1968, p. 268).

Just as the unity of the Shanghai proletariat was partly based on an *ad hoc* coalition of the CCP-led unions and the Green Gang, the class alliance between the Shanghai workers and the Chinese bourgeoisie involved in the May Thirtieth Movement was no less fragile. Imperialist domination and patriotism played roles in the formation of a "unified subject of resistance," but calculation of political and economic gains peculiar to a social group or class also shaped the decisions of the Chinese bourgeoisie and the gang leaders. When external circumstances changed so that their political and economic interests no longer benefited from an alliance with the CCP-organized labor movement, the unified revolutionary group faltered, as the events of the 1927 insurrection will show.

Shanghai Insurrection of 1927

On July 7, 1926, the GMD government that was still in cooperation with the CCP announced the departure of the Northern Expedition from its base in Guangdong. The purpose of this military campaign was to unify China by eliminating the unruly warlords who controlled the northern provinces. The CCP supported this campaign despite the appointment of Chiang Kai-shek from the GMD right wing as the commander of the northern expeditionary troops.

Outside the International Settlement and the French Concession, Shanghai was under the control of a warlord named Sun Chuanfang. As the expeditionary troops won several battles and began to head toward Shanghai, the CCP-run SGLU decided to join the campaign. The first uprising involving armed workers occurred in October 1926 but was crushed by Sun's forces. In February 1927, a second uprising was launched. On February 19, the SGLU declared a general strike, demanded the overthrow of Sun, and expressed its solidarity with the northern expeditionary troops.

Workers in business firms, public transport facilities, city services, cotton mills, silk-reeling factories, and longshoremen all stopped work, and Shanghai's economy was paralyzed. About 350,000 workers were involved in the strike (Perry, 1993, p. 85). Sun immediately tried to break the strike by force. The day after the strike started, 20 strikers were publicly executed, and in the next few days, 300 workers were arrested (Chesneaux, 1968, p. 355). Only after work resumed did the SGLU give the order for an armed uprising involving several thousand workers on February 22, but it was again suppressed by Sun.

With the approval of Zhou Enlai, who had been sent to Shanghai earlier to direct the CCP struggle, a third uprising was attempted on March 21. The northern expeditionary troops of Chiang Kai-shek were at the outskirts of the city and decided not to interfere, perhaps in the hope that the CCP forces would expend themselves in a battle against Sun. A general strike and an armed uprising were launched simultaneously on March 21. The strike started at 1 p.m. (*North China Daily News*, March 22, 1927), and within 3 hours, about 800,000 workers from different industries stopped working, again immobilizing the city (*Shenbao*, March 22, 1927).

Worker militias targeted different key parts of the city—train stations, police stations, and arsenals. Numerous workers even fought bare-handed against Sun's soldiers (*Shenbao*, March 26, 1927). In a neighborhood in northern Shanghai where the heaviest battles occurred, about 1500 houses were burnt down (*North China Daily News*, March 24, 1927). After all the fighting ended on March 22, Shanghai was held by the SGLU and its allies who formed the Provisional Municipal Government of Shanghai, ruled by a committee of Chinese capitalists and representatives of the CCP.

However, just as CCP appeared to expand its control of Shanghai, the balance of power began to shift and the United Front started to falter. Although the Northern Expedition was financed in large part by Chinese capitalists, they became increasingly threatened by the growth of union activities. Workers were making demands in Chinese and foreign factories. Many members of the GMD right wing were from gentry families and were hostile to the growth of peasant unions organized by CCP (Chesneaux, 1968, p. 349).

Events in 1927 led the Chinese bourgeoisie in Shanghai to question their alliance with the popular labor movement. The British began to approach the GMD as it became obvious that the northern expeditionary troops would rout out the warlords. In January 1927, the British announced their intention to gradually abandon their privileges in Shanghai once the political chaos ended, and the Americans made a similar declaration (Chesneaux, 1968, p. 350). At the end of 1926, the colonial administration agreed to accept Chinese members into Shanghai Municipal Council, and the Mixed Court was restored to the Chinese government in January 1927. The tension between the Chinese bourgeoisie and the Western Powers was reduced by 1927—a more pressing problem for local businesses was the growing power of the workers and CCP.

Chiang Kai-shek arrived in Shanghai in March, after the formation of the CCP-backed Provisional Municipal Government of Shanghai. As early as March 24, reports circulated about Chiang's potential collaboration with a warlord to eliminate the CCP (*North China Daily News*, March 24, 1927). When he arrived, the Federation of Commerce and Industry, whose members included Chinese bankers, cotton-mill owners, compradors, etc., sent a delegation to Chiang, "who received it very cordially, and apparently they not only discussed a large loan, but actually negotiated one for the expenses of the April 12 coup" (Chesneaux, 1968, p. 363).

The gangs of Shanghai also decided to collaborate with Chiang. During the CCP's third armed uprising in1927, gang leaders such as Huang Jinrong and Du Yuesheng pledged their cooperation to the CCP in exchange for the continuation of their opium operations (Perry, 1993, p. 86). However, by the end of March 1927, Huang, Du and Zhang Xiaolin, another Green Gang leader, met with Chiang's representative. They formed an organization called the Mutual Advancement Society. A confidential report of the British police asserted that this group was designed to "oppose the Shanghai General Labor Union and radical elements among the workers. This movement has the full and energetic support of Chiang Kai-shek" (Perry, 1993, p. 91).

Early on April 12, more than 1000 armed GMD men wearing blue laborers' uniforms and arm bands decorated with the Chinese character for *labor* attacked SGLU offices in different parts of the city (*North China Daily News*, April 13, 1927). Chiang's soldiers from the 27th Army immediately arrived on the scene and, under the pretense of mediating between the two groups, demanded that the SGLU workers disarm. Chiang's troops started shooting when the workers refused to disarm, and some labor leaders, including Wang

Shouhua, the president of SGLU, were abducted (*Shenbao*, April 13, 1927). The SGLU called for a general strike and organized marches in different parts of the city to demand the return of their weapons, but soldiers from the 26th Army fired into the crowds (*Shenbao*, April 14, 1927), leaving at least 100 dead and several hundred wounded in addition to the 300 who died in the attack a day earlier (Chesneaux, 1968, p. 370). With the support of the Green Gangs, the Chinese bourgeoisie, and the Western Powers, the right wing of GMD represented by Chiang destroyed the CCP-organized labor movement. The ensuing period in Shanghai is known as the White Terror.[3]

On April 15, 1927, only 3 days after Chiang's coup in Shanghai, the right wing of GMD in Guangdong began its own bloody repression against the CCP there. Martial law was declared in the city of Guangzhou (*Guangzhou Minguo Ribao*, April 16, 1927). At least 2000 trade unionists, communists, students, and peasant leaders were arrested in Guangdong, and about 100 activists were killed. Li Qihan, who was sent there after his release from prison in Shanghai, was among the victims (Chesneaux, 1968, p. 371).

In recent major protests against the World Trade Organization, World Bank, and IMF, protesters from different or even opposed ideological camps—environmentalists, anarchists, liberal human-rights activists, communists, farmers, union members, lobbyists, etc.—came together. However, as Li Qihan's experience in the early 20th century shows, resistance against global capitalism and imperialism required the coalescence of unlikely or contradictory classes and social groups in earlier times and places. The Green Gangs, the Chinese Communist Party, Rosa Luxemburg, Karl Liebknecht, the British police, and Chinese peasants transformed into urban proletariats all ultimately played roles in Li's story. Although the Shanghai cotton mills might have exemplified modernity in the 1920s, premodern social relations also came into play via the powerful influences of the gangs and secret societies. A variety of diverse groups and influences, some seemingly diametrically opposed, converged in the truncated revolutionary career of Li Qihan, who committed his life to resisting Western and Japanese imperialism.

Conclusion

Shanghai's labor movement in the 1920s was among the most organized, popular, and revolutionary labor movements in the world then. However, my analysis shows that even in this case the revolutionary proletarian popular movement did not automatically result from the macro political and economic conditions of that time and place. The proletariat in Shanghai was composed of diverse elements, and the unity that was forged required an alliance between the CCP-led unions and the Green Gangs. The general strikes that the SGLU organized required financial support, and the Chinese bourgeoisie's conflicts with the colonial authorities played an important role in motivating it to initially fund the strikers.

The revolutionary subject and collective action that existed in the 1920s was constructed by stitching together all the heterogeneous and contradictory groups into a coalition, and as the sustained general strikes show, this coalition was able to sustain itself for a long time. This example shows the great heterogeneity among workers and socially marginalized individuals in historic Shanghai, but they organized a broad-based movement. It suggests that disparate groups of working people—fragmented and disorganized as they may be under "flexible accumulation"—may still successfully oppose empires and capitalist imperialism today. We have no need to resign ourselves to complacency because of putative structural impediments. Rather, we should develop strategies for creative alliance building in an era of enormous global inequality.

Of course, one might question whether a strategy of building popular movements by establishing coalitions of diverse social groups and classes guarantees success. In the Shanghai of the late 1920s the alliance faltered, and the radical labor movement was decimated after Chiang's coup in 1927. This illustrates a key point: There is no guarantee that this strategy will lead to success. Changes in political and economic conditions can break movements apart, and success also depends on social actors who are deft at the sorts of political maneuvers that maintain the broad alliances. Sometimes it fails, but this strategy does not always lead to disaster. In fact, even after the CCP's retreat to the countryside, building a United Front continued to be an important part of its revolutionary strategy that ultimately succeeded. The field of resistance is open and fluid. It is important not to prioritize or reject *a priori* a strategy by claiming that the structural features of current global capitalist expansion render it inappropriate or obsolete.

Primary Sources

Official Publications

The Maritime Customs, Decennial Reports, 1922–1931, Vol. II, Southern and Frontier Ports: Shanghai, Statistical Department of the Inspector General of Customs, 1933.
Shanghai Municipal Council Report for the Year 1925 and Budget for the Year 1926, F. & C. Walsh, Shanghai.
Shanghai Municipal Council Report for the Year 1928 and Budget for the Year 1929, F. & C. Walsh, Shanghai.

Newspapers

Guangzhou Minguo Ribao (Guangzhou Republican Daily News), 1927.
Minguo Ribao (Republican Daily News), 1925.
North China Daily News, 1925 and 1927.
Shenbao (Shanghai Daily), 1927.

References

Barber, B. (1995), *Jihad vs. McWorld: How Globalism and Tribalism are Reshaping the World*, Times Books, New York.
Best, S. and D. Kellner (1991), *Postmodern Theory: Critical Investigations*, Guilford Press, New York.
Bianco, L. (1971), *Origins of the Chinese Revolution, 1915–1949*, Bell, M., translator, Stanford University Press, Palo Alto, CA.

Butler, J. (1998), "Merely Cultural," *New Left Review*, 227, 33.

Chesneaux, J. (1968), *The Chinese Labor Movement 1919–1927*, Wright, H.M., translator, Stanford University Press, Palo Alto, CA.

Derrida, J. (1994), *Specters of Marx, the State of the Debt, the Work of Mourning, and the New International*, Kamuf, P., translator, Routledge, New York.

Friedman, T. (1999), *The Lexus and the Olive Tree*, Farrar, Straus, Giroux, New York.

Geras, N. (1987), "Post-Marxism?" *New Left Review*, No. 163.

Geras, N. (1988), "Ex-Marxism without Substance: Being a Real Reply to Laclau and Mouffe," *New Left Review*, No. 169.

Hardt, M. and A. Negri (2000) *Empire*, Harvard University Press, Cambridge, MA.

Harvey, D. (1999), *The Limits to Capital*, Verso Press, London.

Honig, E. (1986), *Sisters and Strangers: Women in the Shanghai Cotton Mills, 1919–1949*, Stanford University Press, Palo Alto, CA.

Jameson, F. (1991), *Postmodernism or the Cultural Logic of Late Capitalism*, Duke University Press, Durham, NC.

Laclau, E. and C. Mouffe (1987), "Post-Marxism without Apologies," *New Left Review*, No. 166.

Laclau, E. and C. Mouffe (2001), *Hegemony and Socialist Strategy: Towards a Radical Democratic Poltics*, 2nd ed., Verso, London.

Lu, H. (1999), *Beyond the Neon Lights: Everyday Shanghai in the Early Twentieth Century*, University of California Press, Berkeley.

Lyotard, J.F. (1984), *The Postmodern Condition: A Report on Knowledge*, Bennington, G. and B. Massumi, translators, University of Minnesota Press, Minneapolis.

Perry, E. (1993), *Shanghai on Strike: The Politics of Chinese Labor*, Stanford University Press, Palo Alto, CA.

Ritzer, G. (1997), *Postmodern Social Theory*, McGraw Hill, New York.

Rorty, R. (1997), "Back to Class Politics," *Dissent*, Winter, p. 31.

Skocpol, T. (1979), *States and Social Revolutions: A Comparative Analysis of France, Russia and China*, Cambridge University Press, Cambridge, U.K.

Notes

1. I must thank Raul Fernandez for suggesting my participation in the writing of this book. I also thank Gilbert Gonzalez for his patience with my delay in submitting this chapter, the editorial collective for valuable suggestions on the initial draft, and David Smith for his helpful comments on subsequent drafts of this chapter.
2. For criticisms of Laclau and Mouffe, see Geras, 1987; Laclau and Mouffe's rejoinder, 1987; and Geras's response, 1988.
3. For a description of the decline in CCP activities see Shanghai Municipal Council Annual Report, 1928, p. 59.

12

Crossing the Borders: Labor, Community, and Colonialism in the Jaffa–Tel Aviv Region during the Mandate Period

MARK LE VINE

Introduction: Land, Labor, and the Dynamics of Empire in Palestine/Israel

With the unparalleled military and economic power of the U.S. in the post–Cold War era of globalization, the relationship between imperialism and capitalism that has long been of concern to both scholars and activists has come under renewed scrutiny. Indeed, Lenin argued that imperialism was inseparably bound to capitalism and, in fact, was capitalism's highest stage, today scholars recognize imperialism as more than merely a stage of capitalism. As the contributors to a recent issue of the *Monthly Review* argue, imperialism has been inherent to the history of capitalism from the start.[1]

The dynamics of the Zionist–Palestinian conflict bear witness to relationship between capitalism and imperialism in a manner that challenges a two-directional and -dimensional calculus and points to the need to expand the relationship in two ways. The first is an examination of how European imperialism intersects with capitalism through both settler colonialism and colonial nationalism—a much more complex set of actors than Lenin imagined or most contemporary critics are engaging. A broader approach is to understand that imperialism and capitalism are two components of a larger four-fold matrix of discourses that includes modernity and nationalism as equally important factors.[2]

This chapter takes this reality as the starting point for an exploration of the role of labor in the struggles for control of the territories, resources, and larger political economies of the sister cities of Jaffa and Tel Aviv, the economic and cultural capitals of Palestinian Arab and Jewish Palestine. Specifically, it argues that an analysis of the conflict and cooperation between workers of the two communities reveals the appearance of two simultaneous phenomena. First, in attempting to create labor solidarity, workers challenged the hegemonic, exclusivist nationalist discourses of their elites; second, at the same time, however, such activities served ultimately to further the ends of the Zionist labor movement by facilitating the "conquest" of the economy and territory of the country and of the Jaffa–Tel Aviv region in particular.

This ambivalent function of labor discourses in the larger nationalist pre-1948 politics suggests that Palestine is a unique case study of the relationship of the four discourses comprising what I term the *modernity matrix*. What this matrix reveals is that we cannot examine imperialism in a direct relationship to labor. Rather, their interaction must be studied in the context of other contemporaneous discourses and nodes of power: The evidence in Palestine suggests strongly that the specific dynamics of capitalism development in the country, the militant nationalisms it helped produce, colonialism in which both were imbedded, and the modernist ideologies that supported the other three components, were all deeply implicated with imperialism in a synergistic (and thus extremely powerful) manner.

To address only the specific intersection of empire and labor is to view a three-dimensional image imposed onto a two-dimensional plane. Significant depth and motion are easily overlooked, and that hinders our ability to understand exactly how imperialism works. The research presented below argues that imperialism in Palestine worked precisely to the degree it was inflected by and inflected the discourses of nationalism, capitalism, and modernity at large. Together they produced a profound impact on the way labor evolved in the country and point to the fact that, in confronting imperialism, labor has always had to engage a more complex set of parameters than a one-to-one correspondence of workers confronting empire and its various agents.[3]

This dynamic was particularly important in Palestine because British rule was not based on typical imperial considerations. Palestine generated no real economic benefit to the home country and, in fact, constantly threatened to be a drain on the treasury (and thus British taxpayers).[4] The relative lack of economic and exploitative rationales for ruling the country meant that the British were often content to let the Zionists take the lead in setting or implementing economic policies, especially when the influx of Jewish money meant fewer British tax pounds spent on Palestine. Because of this dynamic, the British often supported Zionist policies even when they contravened Britain's stated obligation toward the "natives." Via this contradictory process, the average Palestinian or Jewish worker interfaced with the empire.

Finally, it is important to recall that Zionism was itself an imperialist and colonial discourse. The Jewish workers' conquest of Palestinian Arab jobs was part of an imperial–colonial discourse in its own right, regardless of whether an activity was sanctioned by the British. One can even say that the British were not the primary vehicles of imperialism in Palestine, but rather played more of a supporting role vis-à-vis Zionism, doing whatever was necessary to maintain the status quo and in so doing keep Egypt and India, the jewels in the British Empire's crown, secure.

The roots of imperialism in Palestine run even deeper than the interface of Zionism and British empire and date from the late Ottoman period. We need to see the 40 years from 1880 to 1920 as a transition from one great imperial system to another—a transition that witnessed continuities and changes between the Ottoman–Islamic and British legal, political, and social systems that had important consequences for workers in both communities. More specifically, by the 1880s, the Ottoman state had been modernizing economically and politically for decades; it even dreamed of joining the ranks of European imperial and colonial powers by finding new lands to conquer in Africa. Nevertheless, the empire was also gradually losing its hold over outlying districts such as Palestine. At the same time, the Jaffa region saw rapidly increasing prosperity, thanks largely to citrus exports and increased tourism and pilgrimages through its port.

Although this ambivalent situation created space for a local cosmopolitan Mediterranean modernity to emerge in Jaffa, one that largely avoided a direct conflict with imperial discourses, this system could not last after it encountered an exclusivist colonial modernity that arrived with Zionism and attained hegemony under British rule. What is important about the dynamic of this period is that Zionism, with its open allegiance to modern European imperial and capitalist discourses—even if the labor movement was ideologically socialist—was an enterprise based on the expansion of capitalism to the "slumbering East." Zionism found sympathy with an Ottoman state that increasingly had its own European-style imperial, ethno-national (Turkish), and capitalistic preoccupations.[5] This coincidence of interests, cemented by the fact that the Ottoman state desperately needed tax revenues at the very moment that Zionist land purchases could supply them, helped Zionism implant itself in the soil of Palestine, and in Jaffa specifically, even though many Zionist activities were forbidden by law.

Although Ottoman imperialism, capitalism, and nationalism helped facilitate the early development of Zionism in Palestine,[6] there can be no doubt that the ideological alignment of Zionism and British imperialism was much stronger. Both shared what I term a "discourse of development" that viewed Palestine as a backward, stagnant country whose indigenous population was essentially incapable of developing or modernizing on its own, and for which the only solution was European—that is, Zionist led, British supervised—development.[7] Thus the relationship between the Zionists and the British affected the dynamics of labor in Palestine in important ways, in most instances worsening an already difficult situation. On the one hand, the indigenous Palestinian working class, like its counterparts in European colonies (and in Europe too), was viewed as a threat to the social, political, and economic order. Their demands were incompatible with the efficient and economical administration of and profit from Palestine. This was reflected particularly in the debate over the "absorptive capacity" of the country that began in the late

186 • Mark LeVine

1920s as escalating Jewish land purchases drove poorer Palestinian Arabs off their lands, proletarianizing them at a time when the government had neither the will nor the finances to deal with the problem.[8]

To counter claims of dispossession, the Zionist leadership argued that "modern" techniques of intensive agriculture were the keys to developing the country, specifically because they greatly enhanced its absorptive capacity by allowing Palestinian peasants to produce greater yields on less land. In the Jaffa–Tel Aviv region, this discourse was reflected in the successful arguments of municipal and national Zionist leadership that claimed that the rural areas of the six surrounding Arab villages had acquired an "urban value."[9] This meant they were ripe for annexation into and urbanization through Tel Aviv. In both cases, the result was the same. Increasing numbers of Palestinians lost their lands at a time when the country's divided economy (as the British and Zionist leadership imagined it, and vis-à-vis which Palestinian society was considered by both the British and the Zionists as fundamentally separate and developing autonomously from European Jewish Zionist society) greatly limited their ability to find jobs in the cities, especially in "modern, exclusively Jewish" Tel Aviv.

On the other hand, the Jewish working class and especially the labor movement were viewed with suspicion by the British government in London and Jerusalem because of their originally Bolshevik leanings and seeming willingness (when not reined in by Zionist leaders) to put class interests, and thus solidarity with Palestinian Arab workers, ahead of national Jewish and European imperial interests.[10] Both the workers and the leaders of the Jewish labor movement in Palestine (whose factions included nonsocialist unionists and hard-core anti-Zionist communists) felt a historic sense of obligation to liberate Palestinian Arabs at the same time as Jews from the bondage of feudalism or the exploitation of the Arab and Jewish bourgeoisies. Nevertheless, the solidarity emerging from such sentiments was usually short lived; on the whole, competition over jobs between Eastern European Jewish immigrants and Palestinian Arabs helped transform the socialist Labor movement into a "militant nationalist movement" by the first decade of the 20th century, which saw the exclusion of Palestinian Arabs from (or at best their marginalized incorporation through a split labor market) an incipient Zionist Jewish economy as the only means to secure jobs for a rapidly increasing Jewish population.[11]

The means for securing such closure were found through the conquests of labor and, ultimately, land. The conquest of labor (*kibush ha-'avoda*) sought the successful entry of Jews into various occupations that had previously been largely Arab, either by lowering the standard of living of the Jewish immigrants or raising it for Palestinians. In either case, Jews would be in a better position to demand jobs from the Jewish bourgeoisie who controlled the burgeoning Zionist economy of the late 19th and early 20th centuries. When this strategy failed to produce the intended results by the end of the 1900s, the labor movement developed the conquest of land (*kibush ha-karkaʻa*) as an alternative strategy (one that correlated with the Ottoman state's need for revenue). This conquest was based on acquisition of land upon which Jewish settlements would be established, as epitomized by kibbutzes or collective farms. These exclusively Jewish spaces fostered a Jewish economy in which Palestinian Arabs were, by virtue of their absence, unable to compete for jobs.

Whereas the kibbutz is the best known symbol of this process, a similar dynamic was followed in the urban sector. The suburb-turned-metropolis of Tel Aviv founded in 1909 (the same year the first kibbutz, Degania, was established) epitomized the creation of exclusively Jewish urban spaces within which bourgeois and working class counterparts to agricultural Zionism could be accommodated. Indeed, at almost every turn, the founders and leaders of Tel Aviv attempted to control greater portions of the land, resources, and economy of the Jaffa region. Even before the town's establishment, Zionist leaders succeeded in establishing "a state within a state in Jaffa." Within 4 years of the creation of Tel Aviv, its leaders expressed the desire to "conquer Jaffa economically."[12]

Jewish and Palestinian Arab Workers in the Jaffa–Tel Aviv Region during the Mandate Period (1920–1948)

During the mandate period, (the years 1920–1948, when Great Britain ruled the country under a "mandate" of the League of Nations) league of both Jaffa and Tel Aviv developed at extraordinary rates. Jaffa almost quadrupled its population and economy, whereas Tel Aviv's increased more than 10-fold. The working classes of the two communities played crucial roles in this transformation. Although Tel Aviv was established by 60 bourgeois families from Jaffa, working class Jews and Palestinian Arabs were also important presences in the neighborhood-turned-city from the start. It could not have been otherwise because of the centrality of the Jaffa–Tel Aviv region as an export zone, port, and destination for Jewish immigrants and capital.

Although Jewish workers and their leaders sought to conquer Palestinian Arab jobs from the start of Zionist colonization, they concomitantly attempted to develop ties with Arab workers. These two contradictory tendencies point to a fundamental ambivalence in the Zionist project that reveals how hegemonic national and imperialist discourses are challenged by exigencies and requirements of everyday life and the struggle for decent working conditions and wages. Indeed, the contradictions were reflected in Zionist propaganda and policies alike.

Arabic-language newspapers published by the labor movement sought to convince Arab workers that Jews were their comrades instead of their enemies.[13] In so doing, they followed the standard Orientalist line of calling Arab workers and *fellahin* (peasants) to "awake from your slumber" of hundreds of years and work with the labor movement and Jewish Tel Aviv (and specifically not Arab Jaffa). The Arab workers constituted the only group protecting the rights of workers in the city, whereas the fellahin represented "Zionism help[ing] the East to recover its former glory."[14]

Beyond mere propaganda, the local and national Zionist leadership devoted significant energy throughout the mandate period to developing ties with Palestinian Arab workers. The records of their successes and failures provide the best, and often the only, documentation of labor conditions in Arab Jaffa. In 1921, for example, Jewish woodworkers sought, with varying degrees of success, to develop ties with Arab carpenters, bakers, government (railway, postal, and telegraph) workers, and camel drivers. The shared goal for camel drivers was to get rid of the Bedouin drivers (nicknamed the "fifth aliyah" the word used to describe Jewish immigration) and prevent their continued immigration. Normally rival communities to expand the boundaries of their competing identities to face a perceived common threat to their economic interests.[15]

Such cooperation waxed and waned. Palestinians generally sought help from the Histadrut (the national federation of Zionist trade unions in Palestine) largely when their interests were not served by their own leadership. The Histadrut's leadership felt such cooperation would make it possible to see the day when "*we* will be the rulers . . . and will be able to do great things there, both politically and economically."[16] In fact, the success of the Zionist efforts prompted the newspaper *Falastin* to issue a public call in 1934 for the creation of an Arab union, which led to the establishment of the Arab Workers' Society in Jaffa in October 1934.[17]

The vociferous resistance by Arab employers and religious and nationalist leaders to any attempt at cooperative work by the Histadrut clearly indicated that Jaffa's Palestinian Arab elite was—to say the least—suspicious of these activities. However, it is also clear that not all leaders opposed the Histadrut for reasons of solidarity with workers. Indeed, even the Histadrut's limited successes in organizing Arab workers led one Arab worker to ask, "Who is responsible for this comedy?"[18] The Arab press, specifically *Falastin, al-Difaʿ*, and *al-Jamiʿa al-Islamiyyah*, attempted to convince workers not to join the Zionist labor unions, but Palestinian Arab workers continued to approach the Histadrut until the early part of 1936—right before the outbreak of the Palestinian revolt.[19]

Indeed, Palestinian Arab trade unionists resolved to beat the Histadrut at its own game by setting up pickets against Jewish workers in Jaffa. This action mirrored the Jewish union's actions against Arab workers in Tel Aviv,[20] a tactic that clearly succeeded when all the port workers in Jaffa quickly joined the strike declared on April 19, 1936.[21] Although the outbreak of the strike and revolt in 1936 temporarily severed connections between the Histadrut and Arab workers, the latter once again contacted the Histadrut regarding even worse conditions at the port after it reopened in October of 1936.[22]

Improved relations lasted until 1948, at least in part because the Zionist union filled a void by endeavoring to fight for the rights of Palestinian Arab workers in situations where no one on the Arab side would.[23] As one worker tearfully explained in an article in *al-Difa'*, 700 of his comrades who joined the Histadrut did so because they were angry and exasperated. Unable to "escape the oppression of our bosses . . . and unable to feed our children, [the workers] entered the arms of the Histadrut because they despaired of ever getting justice from their bosses," who summered in the orchards around Jaffa or in Beirut.[24]

The Palestine Labor League (or PLL; the Arab union created by the Histadrut in 1932) even signed a labor agreement with the Jaffa municipality in 1944 to increase basic wages and provide clothing and shoes for workers. More interesting than the terms of the agreement were the comments of the Deputy Mayor of Jaffa to PLL representatives: "Why do you bother us and meddle every day in the interests of the workers?" he asked. The PLL representative replied: "Times change, there is democracy, there is freedom to organize, justly and honestly." The Deputy Mayor did not appreciate this line of reasoning, answering: "What democracy? We don't have democracy; we scorn democracy . . . . We only understand one thing: the worker that [sic] puts forth demands to us is a worker that wants to be lord over us and this we will not suffer."[25] Another official entered the room and the conversation, declaring that the PLL only wanted to "upset our order" by getting involved with workers, which would hurt the unity of the Arabs and make it harder to maintain a united front against the Zionist movement as a whole.[26]

This exchange clearly reveals the contradictory position of the PLL–Histadrut relationship within the larger arena of Palestinian Arab labor politics in Jaffa. Whatever its role in securing the overall "conquest of Hebrew labor" in Jaffa, its aims and activities were in many cases closer to the interests of Jaffa's Palestinian Arab workers than those of the national leadership that was riven by factionalism and often put its own economic interests ahead of national considerations by secretly serving as a significant source of land sales to Jews. However, as Palestinian Arab trade unions became better organized in the mid-1940s, Arab workers had less reason to turn to the PLL, and its fortunes quickly began to wane. In fact, in Jaffa we can pinpoint this turnaround to May of 1944, when protests by Palestinian Arab residents of Manshiyyeh against residents who joined the PLL, coupled with the storming of a PLL May Day celebration by Palestinian Arab workers, forced the union to move its office across the border to Tel Aviv.[27]

Palestinian Arab Labor in Tel Aviv

Although Tel Aviv was conceived of and portrayed as a purely Jewish city, the reality was that Palestinian Arab workers maintained a small but significant and visible presence in the city in the years after its establishment. Palestinian Arabs continued to work in Tel Aviv after it was granted municipal autonomy in 1921, and as the Tel Avivan economy grew, so did the "problem" of Arab labor and even residency in the town.[28]

From the beginning of the mandate period (and probably earlier), the Tel Aviv municipality hired Palestinian Arabs to work at the post office and other public institutions in the city during the Sabbath.[29] The town boasted its own club for Palestinian Arab railway workers; the club had 25 members by 1931.[30] Even during the 1936–1939 revolt, the PLL sought to bring Palestinian Arabs into Tel Aviv and tried to find Arabic-speaking Jews to give 3-month courses in Tel Aviv on such issues as the Arab Community in Eretz Israel and the question of Jewish Arab cooperation and joint organization.[31]

In addition to the officially sanctioned presence of Arabs in the Jewish city, a much larger, unofficial, and officially unwelcome presence existed. As early as 1921, a Yemenite contractor wrote a letter to *Falastin* complaining about pressure from Russian Jewish workers to fire a Palestinian Arab in his employ.[32] The situation was so tense that the governor of the Jaffa district asked Mayor Meir Dizengofff to ensure that the municipality would enforce a guarantee from the Histadrut not to interfere with Arab contractors or workers.[33] In another situation, the United Rabbinical Council of Jaffa appealed to the Tel Aviv municipality and the government to prevent the desecration of the Sabbath in Tel Aviv by non-Jewish mongers and traders.[34] Jewish shop owners similarly complained about numerous Arabs who set up shop in front of their stores daily without permission.[35]

By the mid-1920s Arabs in Tel Aviv were selling market wares at prices so low that Jewish merchants were forced to reduce their prices drastically to compete. Despite its best efforts, the municipality realized that it was "impossible to get rid of them so we have to force them to register so we can regulate them and charge taxes and control situation."[36] In essence, Palestinian Arabs could not be kept out of Tel Aviv; at best they could be regulated, like their Jewish counterparts. Even this proved difficult, as many Palestinian Arabs worked in unregistered, illegal, or unofficial factories and restaurants located in the homes and apartments of Jewish residents in Tel Aviv.[37]

By the early 1930s, the problem of Arab labor prompted renewed discussions between the local Histadrut affiliate, *Mifleget po'elei tel aviv-yafo* (MPTAY), and the Tel Aviv municipality aimed at combating the problem.[38] Ultimately, the Histadrut was forced to admit that "Arab labor has encroached upon the first Jewish city," whether in the commercial center, poorer Jewish neighborhoods, or outskirts of the city (where supervision was difficult). Hundreds and ultimately thousands of Palestinian Arab workers were employed by Jews as construction workers and porters, with a significant increase in the years preceding the 1936 revolt.[39]

In response to this situation, the Histadrut's executive committee and MPTAY decided in 1935 to take measures including the commencement of a public war to force contractors to use only Jewish labor in order to decrease the number of Palestinian Arab construction workers in Tel Aviv. The alliance renewed efforts of the Tel Aviv municipality and citizens' groups to fight for

Jewish labor.[40] Because of this increased pressure, Jewish businessmen seeking to continue the employment of cheap Palestinian Arab labor began to "smuggle factories into the Palestinian Arab village (Summel), thus freeing themselves from the obligation to employ Jewish labor."[41] This may be one reason the municipality became so interested in annexing the lands of Summel and other villages adjoining Tel Aviv in the ensuing years. It demonstrates the increasing importance of administrative borders for policing the porous national boundaries intended to separate the Arab and Jewish communities and economies in the Jaffa–Tel Aviv region.

Jewish Labor in Jaffa Port

The increasing nationalization of land in the Jaffa–Tel Aviv region during the mandate period also affected the way the two communities viewed Jaffa Port. As the "Gateway to Palestine" and the country's primary port until the Haifa Port opened in 1934, Zionists developed plans to develop Jaffa since the first days of the movement's activities. By the end of the Ottoman period, Jewish presence and influence in Jaffa Port were increasing. This led Palestinian Arabs to define the port more and more as an exclusively Arab space.[42]

By 1920, Jews were working on Jewish boats such as the *Halutz* and the *Pioneer*, and the Jewish press wrote about the importance of Jewish workers in Jaffa Port in light of increased immigration.[43] At the same time, Tel Aviv's leadership sought to build a new port in which Jews would have greater presence, influence, or even control.[44] In 1922, Mayor Dizengoff wrote to British officials to advocate the construction of a new port closer to Tel Aviv, arguing "If today it is allowed to hope that in a very near future the town of Jaffa will witness the beginning of the construction of a modern harbor, this is to be thanked solely and exclusively to the initiative and energy of Jewish citizens of Tel Aviv." This letter reflecting the shared discourse of development mentioned earlier bore fruit after violence and the closure of Jaffa Port in April 1936 presented a new opportunity to press for a new port *in* Tel Aviv.

Until such a port could be built, Jewish workers, on their own initiative and with the help of the Histadrut, periodically attempted to obtain significant levels of employment at Jaffa Port, despite the extremely difficult conditions that led to designating them "pioneers" for their efforts. One group known as the Hebrew Coachman's Group was established in 1922.[45] Although vigorous hatred (often expressed in violence) was the response of Palestinian Arab coachmen to the arrival of the Jewish pioneers, the young Jews persevered and eventually performed all levels of work in the port. The penetration of Jews into the port was, like every important conquest, the fruit of the pressure of immigration and the need to absorb immigrants. "The Arabs reconciled themselves to our presence in the port and got used to us; peace prevailed between them and us, and now there are friendships between us."[46]

A similar group was formed in 1933, as the Histadrut increasingly became interested in expanding the conquest of Hebrew labor in Jaffa Port.[47] By the 1935–1936 financial year, Jews comprised roughly 7% of the port workforce.[48] If we consider that the majority of the port's workforce was composed not of residents of Jaffa or its vicinity—who numbered only 400 or so—but rather of about 3000 Syrians and Egyptians,[49] it becomes clear that although Jews comprised only a small percentage of the overall workforce, their numbers were substantial vis-à-vis the local Palestinian Arab population.

Whatever the limited success of Jews in gaining employment at Jaffa Port, the desire to move the port closer to the area of Tel Aviv and the resistance of Palestinian Arabs to that demand remained constant. Palestinian Arab leaders argued that the Zionists wanted to move the port to Tel Aviv "in order to kill Jaffa."[50] As we have seen, conquest, as opposed to murder, is a better description of the goal of Zionist leadership. The perception that Jews wanted to build a new port rather than rebuild the old one was not inaccurate. Even when Dizengoff wrote the government to press for the establishment of a new port in Jaffa to handle the increased traffic generated by the booming citrus trade, he presented many reasons why such an enterprise would, in fact, be almost impossible at the port's then location. He suggested the mouth of the Cauja/Yarkon River, which he termed "the natural boundary of Tel Aviv and Jaffa," as a good alternative location.[51]

The government by and large supported Zionist interests, whether by allowing the creation of a Jewish port in Tel Aviv or permitting Jews to obtain the majority of the jobs at the Haifa port, the largest in the country when it was opened in 1934. The combination of a lack of will to remove low-priced foreign competition, the sometimes stringent antilabor positions of the port administration and other government facilities such as the railway system, and the ideological sympathy with the Zionist leadership in economic matters (contrasted with general hostility toward the Palestinian Arab leadership) all contributed to the ability of the Zionist movement to gain increasing control of and redirect the activities of the country's ports to its benefit.

The issue of officially sanctioned Jewish workers at Jaffa Port was threatening enough to the local Palestinian population that the high commissioner presciently asked the newly formed Jewish Lighterage Company to delay introducing Jewish workers only days before the outbreak of the 1936 revolt and strike.[52] However, the outbreak of the strike and closure of the port on April 19 rendered the debate about Jewish workers largely moot because of the creation of a port in Tel Aviv. It should be noted, however, that Yemenites continued to work as porters at Jaffa Port[53] even as labor leaders argued that the prohibition of Jewish workers was "tantamount to creating an economic pale for Jews in Palestine and placing Jaffa Port outside it."[54]

The ethnic politics of labor in the Jaffa and Tel Aviv ports reflects the larger conflict between the two national communities and the role of the British government as a mediator of that conflict. Jaffa Port became in the wake of the strike and revolt a synecdoche for the larger sentiment that Palestine was lost to the Jews; the normal state of the port was understood to be one in which the "life of the port is Arab and needs to remain Arab."[55] As the *al-Difa* newspaper noted 2 months before the revolt:

> This is a pure Arab port . . . . We here repeat and state over and over again, that this Port has been Arab since time immemorial and that it will keep its Arab feature until the end of time, and if Government continues to insist to let the Zionist hands toy with this Port, then Government alone will bear the responsibilities of the consequences of such action, consequences that the Government itself does not wish for.[56]

This sentiment was, of course, the mirror image of the Jewish vision for Tel Aviv and its hoped-for port, and the strike and closure of Jaffa's port allowed Tel Aviv's leadership to achieve its long-held goal of the creation of an independent Jewish port within its borders, one whose national significance and symbolism were matched by its importance as a source of jobs for the rapidly increasing Jewish population of the region. It is not surprising, then, that the eruption of the revolt led local and national Zionist groups and their British supporters to unite in the belief that Jaffa and its port were no longer safe for Jews and that never again could Tel Aviv and its surrounding districts be "at the mercy of the Arab lightermen" of Jaffa.[57] Thus, Jews had no choice but to build their own independent port.[58]

Perhaps the clearest description of the Zionist understanding of the role and function of Tel Aviv Port comes from an article from *Hapoʻel Hatzaʻir*, the labor newspaper. The editors asserted that:

> The conquest of the port in Tel Aviv is one of the biggest settlement activities of our movement . . . . We must see that this activity [the opening of the port] was much more than an answer to the disturbances of Jaffa. It is today one of the main links in the chain of our activities in opening up the country.[59] Tel Aviv is not mentioned in the article, but clearly its role was understood more in terms of its national than local significance.

Moreover, because of the way in which the leaders of Tel Aviv and the larger Zionist movement were able to frame the port to the British in a combination of security and development discourses, the government—unlike the local Palestinian Arab population—did not understand the larger significance of the creation of Tel Aviv's port. The article concludes that "the debate is not about sharing ports but [about] the vision of our port as a great settlement enterprise. The question is, if we go also here in the same way that we went in agricultural colonization . . . only someone who doesn't see the port as a settlement enterprise would give up on its independence." In other words, as I noted elsewhere with regard to Jaffa's Jewish neighborhoods,[60] the goal of settlement was to take spaces that were inhabited or used by both communities and transform them into exclusively Jewish territory.

The port was not the only water resource to become the site of a conflict involving workers. During the 1936 strike, workers at the Tel Aviv Port evicted licensed Palestinian Arab fishermen who attempted to moor their boats between the mouth of the Cauja/Yarkon River and the port. *al-Jami'a al-Islamiyyah* indignantly asked "Has the Cauja River become Jewish and consequently Arabs are not allowed to fish there?"[61] The Jewish port workers complained that "the foreshore was a Jewish foreshore and was not to be trodden by Arab feet," and that they "could not work any longer seeing the Arabs gradually come nearer and nearer." More interesting was the reply of the leader of the fishermen, who answered that "the strike was off, and that half of the Moslems were in Tel Aviv and half the Jews in Jaffa, and therefore he too came to fish."[62]

Spaces that were nationalized within exclusivist and bounded notions of identity during times of trouble (when boundaries are always most clearly drawn) were experienced by many Arab residents of the Jaffa–Tel Aviv region as having reverted to the more open (yet vis-à-vis the hegemonic nationalist discourses, more clandestine) reading of space "as lived by its inhabitants," as Henri Lefebvre described it. However, for the Zionist leadership and Jews committed to maintaining a rigid separation from the *galut*, or Diaspora (non-Eretz Israel) environment, once the space was nationalized there was no turning back. As a result of this incident, an official prohibition against Arabs fishing in that area was enacted,[63] and a river that served all the residents of the Jaffa–Tel Aviv region for generations took one step closer to becoming an exclusively Jewish space.

Conclusion

Evidence presented here demonstrates that however ambivalent the relations of Jewish and Palestinian Arab workers and the two labor movements, the working classes of both communities maintained enough interaction and interest in cooperation to be considered significant threats to elites on both sides. Yet on the whole, and particularly when solidarity was most needed (as in times of intercommunal strife), the four components of the modernity matrix meant that nationalist, capitalist, colonial, and modernist considerations combined to demand an exclusivist, hierarchized, and confrontational labor politics in the Jaffa–Tel Aviv region and Palestine as a whole.

The depth and political implications of this threat are clear from the words of Tel Aviv mayor Israel Rokach at a meeting with Zionist leaders to discuss the fate of several Jewish neighborhoods on the Jaffa side of the border region between the two towns:

> I will tell you what it was. This morning the new District Commissioner told me "We received confirmation for a new market in Kerem Hateimanim, the plan will be executed by Jews from Kerem Hateimanim that want to establish a modern market in their neighborhood." I said: "If I could I would blow it up with

bombs." The District Commissioner told me that the plan to establish the market was approved, and he is a *goy* [gentile], so he doesn't understand anything . . . [and] said, "Isn't this market designed for Tel Aviv[?]" [But] it's clear that it will be a cancer for Tel Aviv . . . . The clear intention is to ruin our economy . . . . Already today this part is a cancer on the Jewish economy, and what will happen if they built a big modern market? And this in the borders of Jaffa Municipality? You see that I can't stand there with a guard making sure no one goes to this new market. This is also the situation in the south [of Tel Aviv]. . . .[64]

If a working class market could generate such antipathy, it is not surprising that the Tel Aviv municipality took great pains to prevent collaboration between Jewish and Palestinian Arab fishermen and port workers after Tel Aviv's port was established in the wake of the 1936 strike and revolt. In fact, Jewish workers often initiated conflicts with Palestinian Arab workers, particularly during times of heightened conflict. Ultimately, despite the best efforts of Tel Aviv's leaders, municipal borders were never the ultimate arbiters of sovereignty or political, economic, or security control over lands in Jaffa and Tel Aviv. It took the war of 1948 and the massive dislocation it produced—what one Israeli architect watching events unfold in the neighboring village of Salama called the "erasure" of the Palestinian Arab presence in the region—to achieve the desired security and hegemony. Today, however, Israel's "world city" is home to tens of thousands of mostly illegal workers from Europe, Asia, Africa, and even surrounding Arab countries such as Egypt and Jordan. This latest unsanctioned *aliyah* is profoundly reshaping the Israeli polity despite the best efforts of the municipality and state to prevent the illegal workers from becoming a permanent presence in the city and country at large.

Although the state may have found a way, through long-term closures and destruction of the peace process, to remove the noncitizen Palestinian presence from Tel Aviv, the city's economy, like those of all global cities, demands a large, unskilled, cheap, and malleable migrant population to fill the innumerable service, construction, textile, and other menial jobs without which world cities and the globalizing discourses they represent could not function. Thus, although two generations ago Tel Aviv's leaders succeeding in conquering Palestinian jobs and land around the city, her present administration is face to face with a far more powerful and relentless force: the neo-liberal global economy.

Although Tel Aviv had to contend with Bedouins who refused to obey its respatialization of the region via a modern, stratified, and hierarchized set of discourses 100 years ago, it remains to be seen how the more-or-less permanent implantation of globalization's "Bedouin hordes" will transform the identities of Tel Aviv and of Israel as well. Although Palestinians in the West Bank and Gaza—tens of thousands of whom are "sons of Jaffa"—are now permanently barred from working in the Jaffa–Tel Aviv region (a central location for Palestinian labor after the conquest of the West Bank and Gaza in 1967),[65] the Thais, Romanians, Nigerians, Jordanians, and Egyptians who made their ways into global fortress Israel to find work made redundant by their countries' International Monetary Fund/World Trade Organization-inspired reforms are ultimately challenging the existence of both Tel Aviv and the state of Israel as exclusively Jewish entities.

Indeed, a strong argument can be made, on both the macro (national) and micro (urban) levels, that the economic dynamics of the now-dead Oslo process so crucially tied to neo-liberal globalization doomed any chances of peace. We are thus forced to consider a new landscape, one built around Israeli domination of the Palestinian market and economy, the permanent removal of Palestinians from work in Israel, their replacement by more manageable and (ostensibly) less threatening or ideologically problematic foreign workers, and new threats to a hegemonic Israeli identity presented by the new workers. It is far from certain whether the tens of thousands of Israeli Jews who suffer from the neo-liberal policies of a generation of Israeli governments—particularly Middle Eastern or Mizrahi/Sephardic Jews who tend to be associated with conservative parties such as Shas—will have more success putting class solidarity ahead of ethnic identification in this new environment. The ideologies motivating and protecting Zionism are extremely formidable. What is certain, however, is that now, as during the Ottoman and British periods, the relations of workers and capital will be at the root of the struggles for justice and peace in Israel Palestine for the foreseeable future.

Notes

1. See Amin, S. and E. Wallerstein, "Imperialism Now," *Monthly Review*, July–August 2003, Vol. 55, No. 3.
2. For a more detailed discussion of the four-fold matrix, see Levine, M., "'Overthrowing Geography,' (Mis)Reading Modernities: Jaffa, Tel Aviv and the Struggle for Palestine's History, 1880–1948," *Journal of Mediterranean Studies*, 12, 81, 2002.
3. This is a lesson with continuing relevance when we consider how contemporary American imperialism is built upon a deification-cum-glorification of the nation, coupled with an ideology of hypermodernization and market capitalism that is uncritically accepted even by liberal critics within the metropole.
4. We can describe the three reasons Britain was in Palestine as (1) the prestige and power associated with ruling the holiest sites in Christendom; (2) the geostrategic importance of Palestine vis-à-vis the Suez canal, the land and sea routes to India, and the Hejaz oil pipeline (whose terminus was Haifa Port); and (3) the promises made to Zionists during World War I when the British needed Jewish support that coalesced with Christian Zionism growing in Britain at the time.
5. This should not imply that the Ottoman state blindly imitated or followed the lead of Europe. Indeed, the modernization policies of the Porte (as the state bureaucracy was known) in many ways began earlier than in most European countries aside from France and Great Britain.
6. Not surprisingly, it strengthened the already-burgeoning Palestinian nationalist sentiments; Palestinian leaders understood that the Ottoman state was unable or unwilling to fight against Zionism.
7. For a detailed analysis of the discourse of development and the intersection of the various modernities described here, see LeVine, M., "The Discourses of Development in Mandate Palestine," *Arab Studies Quarterly*, Winter, 1995; LeVine, M., *Overthrowing Geography: Jaffa, Tel Aviv and the Struggle for Palestine*, University of California Press, Berkeley, 2004.
8. Cf. LeVine, "The Discourses of Development," op cit.
9. Tel Aviv Municipal Archive (TAMA), Minutes of Meeting, July 13, 1937, 4/2667b.

10. For a detailed discussion of the complex relationships of Jewish and Palestinian Arab workers in Palestine, see Lockman, Z., *Comrades and Enemies: Arab and Jewish Workers in Palestine, 1906– 48*, University of California Press, Berkeley, 1996.

11. Shafir, G., *Land, Labor, and the Origins of the Israeli–Palestinian Conflict, 1882– 1914*, Cambridge University Press, New York, 1989, p. 89.

12. As Tel Aviv's first mayor, Meir Dizengoff, and Zionist leader, Arthur Ruppin, respectively, described the situation. For a discussion, see LeVine, M., *Overthrowing Geography*, chaps. 1– 3.

13. Cf. Lockman, *Comrades and Enemies*, op cit.

14. *Ittihad al-'Ummal*, Inaugural Issue, April 1925, p. 1; June 19, 1925; November 10, 1925; January 2, 1926; *Haqiqat al-Amr*, May 19, 1937, p. 1.

15. Lockman, *Comrades and Enemies*, pp. 74, 129, 155.

16. Central Zionist Archive (CZA), S/25/2961, letter from Zaslani to Hoz, October 14, 1934 (emphasis in original), quoted in Lockman, *Comrades and Enemies* , p. 219.

17. *Falastin*, September 19, 1934, p. 2; September 21, 1934, p. 3; September 23, 1934, p. 7.

18. Labor Archive of the Zionist movement (LA), IV/208/1/3348a, "A General Proclamation."

19. For example, help was sought in securing promised (but undelivered) wage increases from a member of one of the most prominent nationalist families in the city, Azmi Bey Nashashibi. LA, IV/208/1/4495, Arabic list of workers with Hebrew notes.

20. Soon the "first Arab Garrison in Jaffa" was formed, whose 100 members tried to "prevent Jews from working in the middle of this Arab city," particularly on three new schools in Jaffa. The construction of the schools was originally contracted by the government to a Jewish company that did not employ Arabs. *Falastin*, February 21, 1936, p. 5; Lockman, *Comrades and Enemies*, p. 236.

21. This is in contrast to Haifa, where more pro-Zionist municipal and port leadership made it much harder for Arabs to support the strike. All the port workers quickly joined the strike in Jaffa. Lockman, *Comrades and Enemies* , p. 241.

22. LA, Oral Memoir of Eliyahu Agassi, February 22, 1972.

23. Lockman, *Comrades and Enemies*, p. 227.

24. LA, IV/104/143/30, Agassi file; clipping from *al-Difa'*, January 18, 1935.

25. LA, IV/219/239, May 23, 1944, protocol of Arab Secretariat.

26. Ibid. The harsh treatment and illegal wages received by his 160-odd workers led a group of them to contact the PLL for assistance.

27. HA, 105/205, Intelligence Report, 1944.

28. Cf. TAMA, 2/38b, February 1, 1922, letter; Shchori, 1990, p. 324. For the similar situation in Jaffa, see TAMA, 8/57, Report of the Va'ad Ha'ir Leyehudei Yafo, 1925.

29. TAMA, 2/68a, October 9, 1923, letter from Dizengoff to the Chief Rabbi of Jaffa–Tel Aviv; CZA, S25.4618, quoted from February 12, 1935, issue.

30. LA, IV/208/32a, March 31 report by the Arab Secretariat of the Histadrut.

31. LA, IV/208/1/1287, November 11, 1936, meeting of Arab Secretariat of Histadrut.

32. LA, S/EC/H, December 8, 1921 meeting.

33. TAMA, 2/38b, December 7, 1921, letter (emphasis in original).

34. Ibid., January 22, 1922, letter to Governor of Jaffa District.

35. TAMA, 4/334a, July 14, 1927, Apel, B., letter to Tel Aviv Municipality. Like the United Rabbinical Council, he, too, asked the municipality to order the Tel Aviv police to expel the Arabs.

36. TAMA, August 11, 1924, Protocol of Town Council. The Tel Aviv Council voted to revoke all permissions to traders and hand out only temporary ones.

37. Problems also arose with Arab traders who brought zifzif to the streets of Tel Aviv, where Jewish carters purchased and resold it to building sites in the city. LA, IV/250/72/1/2594, Report of the Secretariat of the MPY, 1923–1924. The MPY asked the Jewish carters to make arrangements with the Jewish Cameldrivers' Committee, and they agreed if the MPY would stop the Arab zifzif trade in the streets of Tel Aviv.

38. Including the increase in the number of guards against Arab workers at Jewish businesses and building sites. LA, IV/208/1/642, protocol of June 18, 1934, meeting of Va'ad Hapo'el of MPTAY.

39. These included many unlicensed Bedouins, Houranis from Syria, and Egyptians, who together "reined [sic] almost supreme" in the porterage, construction and zifzif trades. CZA, S25/4618, clipping from *Ha'aretz*, September 19, 1934; LA, IV/208/1/642, May 14, 1934, meeting of MPTAY and EC/H.

40. LA, IV/208/1/642, May 14, 1934, meeting of MPTAY and EC/H.
41. CZA, S25/4618, clipping from *Davar*, March 26, 1935.
42. *al-Difaʿ*, January 13, 1936, p. 4; *Falastin*, October 8, 1945, p. 3. Jaffa was an "Arab" port after its reconquest by Salahaddin's brother (who was in fact a Kurd) at the end of the 12th century.
43. HA, 40.00023, Oral History of Elchas Steinberg; *Hapoʿel Hatzaʿir*, February 13, 1920.
44. Not surprisingly, this was also when *Falastin* began warning its readers about the Jewish desire to move the port near or to Tel Aviv. TAMA, 20/20, clipping of *Ha'aretz*, October 6, 1920; *Falastin*, September 14, 1921, p. 1.
45. Ibid.
46. LA, IV/250/72/1/2468, "Hebrew Coachmen's Group in Jaffa Port," Passover Eve, 1927. Most Jewish businesses importing through the port and even some non-Jewish businesses used the the Hebrew group.
47. LA, IV/208/1/642, July 8, 1934 memo titled "A Suggestion for the Establishment of a Partnership for Work in Jaffa Port"; LA, IV/208/1/642, June 2, 1934, meeting of MPTAY.
48. CZA, S25/4618, "Employment of Casual Labor," cited 17,388 man-days of casual labor by Jews versus 244,634 by non-Jews.
49. CZA, S25/4618, Memo, Non-Jewish Immigration from Neighbouring Countries; clipping from *Davar*, January 22, 1935.
50. *Falastin*, June 20, 1924, p. 1.
51. TAMA, 3/102, Memorandum to Palmer.
52. CZA, S25/4618, April 9, 1936, letter from Chief Secretary to Jewish Agency.
53. LA, IV/250/72/1/1834, Minute Book of Yemenite Workers Club, 1936–1937, February 3, 1937, meeting.
54. CZA, S25/4618, "Evidence on the Jewish Share in Public Works, 1936," p. 6.
55. *Falastin*, October 8, 1945, p. 3.
56. *al-Difaʿ*, February 2, 1936. The Government was annoyed at the constant attempts of the Palestinian Arab press to give nationalist interpretations to petty incidents that were parts of the normal, daily quarrels between lightermen and porters. (Israel State Archive [ISA], untagged file, report dated October 2, 1936). Cf. ISA, untagged file, leaflet dated November 29, 1936, concerning Palestine Communist Party's opposition to the construction of a port in Tel Aviv.
57. Public Records Office [PRO], CO733/362/10.
58. A note in the margins by a Colonial Office official noted "Yes, but in their own interest and therefore at their own risk." PRO, CO733/362/10 (emphasis in original). Cf. PRO, CO733/298/8, July 17, 1936, telegram from High Commissioner to Secretary of State for the Colonies.
59. *Hapoʿel Hatzaʿir*, July 5, 1937, p. 9.
60. See LeVine, *Overthrowing Geography*, chap. 4.
61. *al-Jami'a al-Islamiyyah*, October 14, 1936.
62. ISA, M3C/995/1951, October 15, 1936, letter to Jaffa Port Manager.
63. Ibid.
64. CZA S25/5936, May 16, 1940, meeting, p. 15.
65. For a discussion of the geography of Palestinian labor within Israel after 1967 and especially in the Jaffa-Tel Aviv region, see Portugali, Y., *Implicate Relations: Society and Space in the Israeli–Palestinian Conflict*, Kluwer Academic, Boston, 1993.

13

Flexible Production and Industrial Restructuring in Hong Kong: From Boom to Bust?[1]

STEPHEN W.K. CHIU AND ALVIN Y. SO

There is no such thing as long-term job in this kind of work. When he (the boss) wants to dismiss you, he dismisses you.

Remark of worker cited in Chiu and Lee (1997, p.18)

Introduction

"The 1970s," as Immanuel Wallerstein (2003, p. 4) points out, "was the era when the United Nations proclaimed the decade of development. Developmentalism was the name of the game from the 1950s through the 1970s. Everybody proclaimed that countries could develop—if only a state was organized properly . . . . Development was to be achieved by some kind of control over what went on within sovereign national states."

Many states, however, have done more than simply pursue developmental goals in the post–World War II era. In Polanyian terms, some states have also strived for "re-embedding the market" in society or in the state so as to minimize the harm done by unrestrained market forces. In the global north, the "Keynesian Welfare National States" (Jessop, 2002, p. 59) promoted full employment, welfare rights, collective consumption, and antisexism and antiracism laws and developed a social contract with labor within their national boundaries. In the global south, the developmental states set up regulations to prevent the domination of their domestic markets by foreign capital.

By the 1980s, however, these state-led developmental projects were challenged by the neo-liberal globalization project in the U.S. and Great Britain. Wallerstein (2003, p. 5) argues that "globalization simply meant opening up all

1. We would like to thank the participants of the March 2003 "Labor, Race, and Empire" Conference held at University of California, Irvine, especially David Smith and Gil Gonzalez, for their useful comments and suggestions. We would also like to acknowledge financial support from the HKSAR Research Grants Council through the project on "Flexible Employment and Social Life in Hong Kong: Tracing the Impact of Globalization" (HKUST6054/02H).

the frontiers, breaking down all the barriers for: (a) the movement of goods; and more importantly (b) capital; but not (c) labor. And the United States set out to impose this on the world."

The neo-liberals accused the state-led developmental projects of erecting national barriers in production and trade, leading to inefficiency, decreasing productivity, and declining corporate profit. They argued that these national barriers must be removed so the market could be de-embedded from society and the state could regain its competitiveness in the global market.

In this respect, globalization can be taken as a neo-liberal counter-offensive against state-led developmental projects at three levels: (1) to reduce wages worldwide; (2) to reduce costs and end ecological constraints on corporations, permitting total externalization and socialization of such costs; and (3) to reduce taxation that subsidizes social welfare (that is to say it subsidizes education, health care, and lifelong guarantees of income).

To dismantle the fetters of production caused by the state-led developmental projects, the new globalization project (Jessop, 2002, p. 139) advocates:

- Deregulation: changing the regulatory framework to facilitate labor-market flexibility and mobility within national economic space
- Liberalization of foreign exchange movements with the effect of internalizing and accelerating capital flows
- De-territorialization: Modifying institutional frameworks to enhance international trade and foreign direct investment; promoting appropriate conditions for the global spread of national and regional capitalism

Through deregulation, liberalization, and deterritorialization, the globalization project has exerted a profound impact on production relations, labor markets, and working class politics, leading to the emergence of a new flexible accumulation regime by the late 1980s (Harvey, 1989). The focus of this chapter is the examination of the emergence and transformation of flexible employment in the context of Hong Kong society and economy over the past four decades.

When we look back at the 20th century, it was generally expected that full-time work would continue indefinitely and was performed at the employer's place of business under the employer's direction. This standard work arrangement was the basis of the framework within which labor law, collective bargaining, and social security systems developed. At the turn of the 20th century, however, this standard employment relationship began to unravel (Kalleberg, 2000).

In the era of globalization, flexible employment relations (part-time work, temporary employment, contract work, and home work) have become increasingly prominent ways of organizing work. Various labels, such as alternative work arrangements (Polivka, 1996), disposable work (Gordon, 1996), contingent work (Polivka and Nardone, 1989), time-based flexible manufacturing

(Alasoini, 1993), and lean production (Womack et al., 1990), are used to characterize these new forms of employment relationships.

The management literature argues that the flexible employment practices enrich both employers and employees. From a business viewpoint, *flexible* means being able to adjust quickly to changing economic conditions: expanding, contracting, or relocating labor supply as needed and improving service in order to become more competitive by increasing productivity and decreasing costs. Human resource professionals report certain positive outcomes of flexible employment: increased productivity, improved morale, and better recruitment and retention (Avery and Zabel, 2001). From the workers' viewpoint, flexibility is seen as the ability to adjust work time or work pace when personal needs are in conflict with their work current schedules. They can alter starting and quitting times occasionally; reduce paid work time for a while so they can return to school, start families, or recover from burn-out; or attend family activities (such as parent-teacher conferences and taking children to medical or dental appointments) without penalty. Management literature reports that flexibility is associated with employees' greater job satisfaction, reduced work and family stress, increased job enrichment and autonomy, reduced tardiness and absenteeism, and improved productivity (Scandura and Lankau, 1997). Hong Kong seems to be an ideal case to test the validity of this enrichment thesis because Hong Kong has been known for its flexibility in the manufacturing industry for decades.

This chapter has two aims. The first is to examine the changing patterns of flexible work in Hong Kong over the past 40 years, i.e., from the 1960s to 2000s. In particular, we will highlight the critical differences between flexible production in the boom days and those in the bust period. The second aim is to show how this changing pattern of flexible work has shaped working conditions, working lives, and labor insurgency in the contemporary era. Instead of enrichment, this paper argues that globalization and economic restructuring over the past two decades totally altered the meaning of flexible work in Hong Kong, leading to misery for the working class and new patterns of labor insurgency.

Flexible Production during Economic Expansion: The Boom Days

Flexible production was said to be the hallmark of Hong Kong's manufacturing industry and purported to have laid the foundations of Hong Kong's rapid economic development between the 1950s and the 1990s. Unlike Korea's state-led and *chaebol*-led industrialization, Hong Kong's industrialization was propelled by small and medium (S&M) firms.

Because they are smaller and less bureaucratic, S&M firms can make prompt decisions when something unforeseen occurs and respond quickly to the ever-changing nature of the global market. For example, the order-to-delivery cycle time is only 14 days for small garment firms and 17.5 days for small knitwear firms (Lee, 1997, p. 189). The S&M firms bid for as many orders as possible and then subcontract the parts that exceed their capacities. As a result, a dense subcontracting network emerged among S&M firms, forming an integrated production process to capture new market niches in the global commodity chains of the garment, knitwear, toys, and electronics industries (Gereffi et al., 1994).

In addition, Hong Kong's state–business relationships contributed to the formation and consolidation of flexible production in Hong Kong. Coming from a *laissez-faire* heritage and developing a strong alliance with big businesses, the colonial state preferred not to intervene directly in the economy but let businesses have as much freedom as they wanted. In industrial relations, the colonial state adhered to the voluntarist framework by not introducing statutes compelling employers to recognize labor unions as bargaining partners. Even if collective agreements between employers and unions were concluded, they did not carry legal significance and were, in effect, "gentlemen's agreements." Thus, the authority of business to hire and fire was unchallenged and business unilaterally determined terms of employment.

Under such state–capital hegemony, Hong Kong's labor had little power, as shown by the movement fragmentation between the pro-mainland *leftist* unions (Hong Kong Federation of Trade Unions) and the pro-Taiwan unions (Hong Kong and Kowloon Trade Union Council). Hong Kong unions were generally politically oriented, i.e., more interested in participating in Chinese mainland affairs than in local economic matters. A second factor showing the weakness of Hong Kong's labor was the low density of trade-union membership (only 16%). In order to recruit more members, Hong Kong unions tended to be welfare oriented, i.e., they focused on how to provide more welfare services by running canteens, workers' cooperatives, recreation centers, and mainland China tours.

With weak labor unions, collective bargaining was rare as a method for protecting labor interests. Bargaining at the enterprise level was typically in the form of unilateral determination of conditions of employment by the employer. Labor unions played almost no role in collective bargaining or in waging strikes and protests to protect the workers. In short, flexible production, strong state–business links, lack of collective bargaining, and weak labor unions made Hong Kong a capitalist paradise in the minds of neo-classical economists.

However, the case of Hong Kong is unique because workers could reap benefits from flexible production. Hong Kong workers' wages rose both absolutely (in terms of real wages above inflation) and relatively (compared with wages in mainland China, Taiwan, South Korea, and Singapore). During interviews with former manufacturing workers, Chiu and Lee (1997, p. 30) found that the workers were nostalgic for the days when they worked in the factories. They expressed occupational pride in their jobs and incomes. For example, female manufacturing workers remarked:

> The golden years were 1976 to 1978 . . . . Even in 1989, I was earning more than HK$300 a day . . . . This was one third more than my husband's clerical job.
>   I was earning HK$10,000 a month [in 1990]. Because we were in production, with overtime, we could double our income. If, say, we worked an extra 4 hours a day, we could have up to HK$15,000 . . . . [In the 2000s, a college graduate's starting salary was only HK$8,000 a month.]

In spite of weak labor unions and the lack of collective bargaining, Hong Kong manufacturing workers had strong bargaining power because of their peculiar market situation. During the 1960s through the 1980s, Hong Kong's economy expanded so quickly it created a labor shortage and a worker's bargaining power was his threat to quit. Because workers could easily find better jobs the next day or the next week, a very high degree of job mobility existed. In order to keep workers, small manufacturing firms competed to offer higher wages and benefits and better working conditions, for example, having a company bus transport workers to and from work, having air conditioning in the office, and offering double pay for overtime work. True to the neo-classical assertion, sheer market supply and demand—not class power and collective bargaining—drove up wages and benefits in the manufacturing sector in Hong Kong during its export boom in the 1960s through the 1980s.

However, flexible labor appeared in the S&M firms of the manufacturing sector only. To compete for workers and to retain them, large firms in the private sector (such as electric, gas, water, phone, and transportation companies) had to provide generous wage and salary packages. They tolerated joint consultation committees and were willing to work with labor on terms of employment, although these arrangements still failed to allow unions formal representation and participatory roles in collective bargaining (Levin and Chiu, 1997).

Although similar in some ways to the large private sector firms, the employment system of the Hong Kong civil service differed from the former in three aspects. First, the civil service offered permanent employment until retirement age for most staff. Second, the service had a highly structured internal labor market with well-defined points of entry, career paths, and seniority pay scales linked to occupation and rank. Unionization subsequently spread, especially among white-collar civil servants who were prompted by dissatisfaction with their occupational pay scales and promotion prospects (Levin and Chiu, 1997, p. 145). Third, the civil service saw the spread of a dense network of joint consultation bodies after the late 1970s. Civil service management was more tolerant of union representation and participation in such committees than were large private sector firms with similar bodies (Levin and Chiu, 1997).

The Transition Period: From the Mid-1980s to the Mid-1990s

Business organizations tolerated rising wages and benefits only because of the tight labor market and the rapid economic development of Hong Kong during the 1960s and 1970s. By the 1980s, Hong Kong's manufacturing industries faced a variety of problems, including rising land rent, protectionism, and keen competition from neighboring Asian countries. As a result, to find a large pool of docile, cheap labor, they quickly relocated their plants across the border in the densely populated Pearl River Delta of the People's Republic of China (PRC).

This industrial relocation started in the mid-1980s. In only 10 years, almost all the manufacturing relocated out of the territory and Hong Kong's old industrial towns were left with empty factories. The number of Hong Kong manufacturing workers was drastically reduced from 892,140 in 1980 to 375,766 in 1995—a loss of more than half a million jobs. Subsequently, the proportion of the Hong Kong labor force that worked in manufacturing dropped from 47% in 1971 to only 14% in 1996.

By the mid-1990s, this disappearance of manufacturing jobs remained largely hidden from the public because of the rapid expansion of service-sector jobs at the same time. Hong Kong's service sector grew at a yearly average of 14% from 1980 to 1999; the number of service workers expanded from 789,454 in 1980 to 2,648,600 in 1999 (Yeung, 1997, p. 251).

Also, a tight labor situation remained in place throughout this transition period. Immigration from mainland China was tightly controlled; the limit was set at 105 a day and eventually increased to 150 a day after July 1, 1995. Additionally, a massive out-migration of Hong Kong residents to the U.S., Canada, and Australia because of the political uncertainty of 1997 averaged 60,000 workers per year from the late 1980s to the mid-1990s. The estimated population of Hong Kong residents who emigrated then was around 500,000. The rapid expansion of the service sector and the massive out-migration of workers pushed the wages of professional and managerial employees to even higher levels than in the 1970s because of a shortage of such people (Ngo and Lau, 1996).

Until 1997, the year of the transfer of sovereignty, Hong Kong still had a very tight labor market. The unemployment rate was below 2%. Workers who were removed from the manufacturing sector during the process of deindustrialization were quickly absorbed by the expanding service economy. During this transition period, some labor unionists wanted to push for a bill in the legislature to establish the right to collective bargaining. The Employee's Rights to Representation, Consultation and Collective Bargaining Ordinance was passed by the Legislative Council (LegCo) on June 30, 1997, the very last day of colonial rule. Had this bill remained in effect, it would have introduced a major change to the voluntaristic system of industrial relations by providing a legal mechanism whereby trade unions represented workers in wage bargaining. It could have potentially affected 900,000 employees working in enterprises with 50 or more employees. However, the pre handover LegCo was immediately replaced by a Provisional LegCo that excluded those from the democratic camp. In a few months, the Provisional body quickly had the collective bargaining ordinance repealed (*South China Morning Post*, August 16, 1997; October 1, 1997).

Flexible Production during Economic Decline: The Bust Days

The year 1997 was a turning point of Hong Kong's history. Hong Kong ended its colonial era and became a special administration region (SAR) of the PRC in 1997. It also experienced the trauma of the Asian financial crisis that compelled Asia to follow the globalization agenda of opening some of its national economic barriers. When all its previously hidden problems suddenly came to light, Hong Kong experienced a prolonged and drastic economic decline after 1997.

Real-estate prices dropped 60%, the stock market was in a slump, the SAR state carried a serious budget deficit, and the unemployment rate hit a record of 7.8% in 2002. The number of unemployed rose drastically from 71,200 in 1997 to a record-high 275,800 in July 2002. In the garment industries, for instance, the number of factories was halved from 3,000 in 1997 to only 1,500 in 2002 (Hong Kong Catholic Commission for Labour Affairs, 2003, p. 6).

Instead of out-migration, Hong Kong experienced a massive influx of workers in the mid-1990s. Labor importation schemes brought in approximately 23,000 foreign workers to work on the construction of the massive new airport and other big infrastructure projects in 1995 (Ngo and Lau, 1996). Anticipating that they would be eligible to become Hong Kong citizens after the handover, many wives and children of Hong Kong residents arrived legally and illegally in Hong Kong around 1997. Additionally, because the handover was relatively smooth and the mainland government did not directly intervene in Hong Kong's affairs, many overseas Hong Kong residents returned to the territory to find work. The most conservative estimate of the government held that 10% to 12% of the emigrants returned to the city after they secured citizenship in Canada, Australia, and the U.S. Other estimates of return migrants range from 100,000 to 250,000 (Skeldon, 1997, p. 269; hknews@ahkcus.org, July 29, 1999).

By the late 1990s, Hong Kong also lost a large number of service jobs to the Pearl River Delta. Every weekend and during long holidays, millions of Hong Kong residents went across the border to shop, eat, and participate in recreation. Many lived across the border and commuted to work. These cross-border flows led to significant declines of Hong Kong's retail, trade, real estate, restaurant, and entertainment industries. Taxi drivers complained about

206 • Stephen W.K. Chiu and Alvin Y. So

reduced business during weekends and holidays. By the late 1990s, many Hong Kong banks, credit card companies, and airlines followed the manufacturing sector's footsteps by out-sourcing their service and office jobs across the border.

Because of these significant transformations, flexible production in the late 1990s was fundamentally different. Gone were the expanding economy and labor shortage. Instead, Hong Kong's workers faced the disappearance of manufacturing jobs, economic recession, contraction of the service sector, oversupply of workers in the labor market, and record-high unemployment. This unfavorable situation hit middle-aged female workers hardest; this group served as the backbone of the manufacturing industry in the 1960s and 1970s. These "working daughters" usually started working around age 15 or 16, without finishing their secondary education, then remained in the manufacturing sector all their working lives. By the 2000s, they had become working mothers with families to raise (Lang et al., 2001).

During this period of economic recession, a new pattern of flexible labor with certain characteristics gradually replaced the old system. Job security became a thing of the past. Workers could no longer take their jobs for granted; they constantly had to worry about the risks of losing their jobs, that their posts could be abolished, that existing contracts might not be renewed, and, most importantly, that they might not find other full-time jobs if their present ones disappeared.

A second factor was that more workers were engaged in contingent or casual jobs—defined as hire on a day-to-day basis or for a fixed period of less than 60 days. A 2001 survey (Census and Statistics Department, 2001) found 93,800 persons (3.3% of those employed) had casual employment.

Third, as services and production jobs were increasingly out-sourced, many workers were induced to become self-employed or work as independent contractors. For example, insurance brokers are now increasingly engaged as independent contractors rather than employees. They earn commissions on policies sold rather than salaries.

A fourth factor is that flexibility extends to pay and benefits. A number of incentive pay schemes such as performance bonuses and flexible benefit schemes were devised. During the boom days in the 1980s, Hong Kong workers expected raises every year. The only issue was the percentage of the raise over the wage for the previous year. By the early 2000s, workers faced across-the-board salary freezes and even pay cuts and reductions in fringe benefits.

Finally, work organization was restructured and work qualifications were upgraded. Workers were expected to work harder, constantly upgrade their skills, and become more functionally flexible. A government survey (Census and Statistics Department, 2000) indicated that 27% of all employed persons reported that they experienced more flexible and longer working hours; 20% reported higher intensity of work.

A significant difference between the pre-1997 period and the post-1997 period is that flexible work was no longer confined to small firms in the manufacturing sector. In the post-1997 era, flexible work penetrated into large firms in the private sector and into the civil service. It affected manual workers, technicians, white-collar clerks, and middle-class professionals. In order to regain competitiveness in the global market, corporate restructuring, streamlining, consolidation, utilization of high-tech machines and equipment, and downsizing appeared in full force among Hong Kong's large firms, leading to massive layoffs, short-term contracts, and part-time hiring. In 2001, for example, layoffs occurred at QPL International Holdings/ASAT Limited (600 technicians, craft workers, and clerks in March), Triumph International (400 craft workers in July), a bus company (500 drivers in July), KK Supermarkets (525 staff in June), The Bank of China (450 clerks and elementary workers in September), ASAT Ltd (about 600 in July), and PCCW (506 from senior to elementary occupations in December). Major redundancies were announced in the first 3 months of 2002 by Phoenix TV (over 400 in January), Motorola Semiconductor (700 to 800 engineers and employees from production and business development in January), and PCCW (858 in March).

The Hong Kong government quickly followed suit and implemented public-sector reform to trim the numbers, reduce the costs, and increase the productivities of civil servants. The growing budget deficit in the early 2000s provided the SAR government a strong rationale to carry out such reforms as restructuring, consolidation, subcontracting, and privatization, especially under the slogan of enhancing the competitiveness of the Hong Kong state and economy in the global market.

Increasing Misery of the Working Class

Lang et al. (2001), Chiu and Lee (1997), and Ho (2001) point to the increasing misery of the working class as a result of deindustrialization and flexible production. The first generation of female workers let go by the manufacturing sector had difficulty finding full-time, relatively high-paying employment. In Ho's (2001) study, Choi-Lin, who worked her way up from the lowest level on the production line when she was 15 to the craftsperson level in the garment industry, still sounded bitter when she recalled her job-seeking experiences after her factory closed in 1994:

> They [bosses] used to treat you like a treasure when they wanted you to work for them . . . . Now they acted as if you were grass. A few of them gave me the cold shoulder when I approached them for a full-time job after the factory closed, others told me to go home and take care of my children . . . . People in the service sector were worse . . . . Someone told me my skills were of no use to them and sent me home. Others just asked me to go home and wait once they learnt of my age, or that I am divorced. Of course they never called back. What made me feel bad was their attitude, they made you feel so useless, that I am old and useless

and sort of good for nothing. It is their attitude; they just ignore you, just want to brush you off.

Because they know the difficulties of finding jobs, workers are very worried about the instability of their employment conditions. They fear the possibility of losing their jobs at any time and believe their future job prospects are gloomy. One respondent sounded very disturbed:

Well they can always tell me that I do not need to go back [to work] in the morning. They can do this to me, and anything . . . . This is only a part-time job. We do not need to sign any contract . . . I don't think the job would last. They [the bosses] are already talking about moving out of Hong Kong . . . to where, I don't know, maybe China, most probably to China . . . . You know, I do not even know what will happen to me next (Ho, 2001, p. 125).

Female workers increasingly ended up in the flexible and casual work categories. Such jobs are characterized by instability, low pay, poor working conditions, and lack of benefits. Feelings of insecurity cause a lot of stress for casual workers:

Usually the time of my work is not fixed; they [factory owners] just call me when they want me, sometimes they might call me tonight and need me to work the next day. Sometimes they won't call me at all for weeks . . . . I was very anxious those days, waiting for the phone to ring, hoping that they would hire me; [I] didn't even want to go anywhere in case I might miss the calls . . . . They pay me by the hour when they have work for me. The hourly pay is not fixed also, it depends on the kind of work they want me to do, sometimes it's cheaper, sometimes a little more, it all depends on the kind of work they want me to perform each time (Ho, 2001, p. 126).

Workers ultimately lost their self-confidence and felt confused and demoralized. A female worker's perception echoed the feelings of other workers:

At that time [the boom phase] I never had to worry about my income . . . . Changing jobs was as easy as borrowing a light . . . . I was pleased with my own work, so were all the bosses I have worked for . . . . Who is to know that all this [working] experience is useless in helping me to find a job now? Do you know what they told me? "You are too old" . . . and I was only 42 at that time. Maybe it's true; maybe I have really fallen behind, not up to date anymore . . . . The skills I developed are no longer needed; there is no place for us any more (Ho, 2001, p. 128).

Displaced workers who are single mothers of nonworking children face the greatest difficulties. The case in Lang et al. (2001, p. 121) is illustrative:

One 42-year-old woman in our sample joined a metal products factory in 1970, at the age of 15, and then moved to a toy factory. But she lost that job in 1985 when the plant was moved to the Mainland. Next, she worked as a machine operator in a chemical products factory, but this plant was also moved to the Mainland in 1987. She then found work in a metal product factory, but again lost her job when production was moved to the Mainland in 1991. She tried working in a restaurant as a dim-sum worker, but found that her health was not adequate for the job, and since then she had been unemployed for 6 years. Divorced with two children at home, she had to rely on public assistance for three years. She would prefer a half-day job (since she still had an 11-year-old child at home), but was unable to find one.

Despite facing age and gender discrimination along with all the misery, frustration, and insecurity, Hong Kong manufacturing workers seldom exhibited an insurgent attitude or engaged in strikes and protests. Instead, they tended to adopt a resigned attitude, retreated involuntarily to the domestic sphere, and renewed their dependency on their husbands. This forced withdrawal from work is not a pleasant experience, a worker compared staying at home to "becoming disabled":

> I have had a working life for more than 20 years and suddenly there is no more work to do, it's like becoming an idiot, because there is too much dead time . . . . It feels like you're going to explode. Even if I don't get paid, I'd like people to give me something to work on, to make use of my time (Chiu and Lee, 1997, p. 40).
>
> I am now at home all the time and I feel so uncomfortable. There is pain here and there. When I was working, I was like an "iron woman." Staying home all day, getting bored and stuck, makes me feel sick (Chiu and Lee, 1997, p. 41).

It is interesting to note that deindustrialization in Hong Kong has not provoked the kinds of pressure on the state that appeared in other countries. Most Hong Kong factories relocated offshore are small and nonunionized; most workers are women who benefited from the favorable flexible labor market in the 1970s. Deindustrialization occurred concomitantly with expansion of the service sector during an economic boom. Subsequently, although Hong Kong's deindustrialization was completed with amazing speed, the process was quiet and produced few labor protests, little worry from the working class, and scant pressure on the colonial government to help the workers.

Labor Insurgency in the Old Sectors

Compared with the female workers in the manufacturing industries, workers in large firms in the private sector tried to put up a modest fight to protect their working conditions, wages, and benefits. In 1998, when Hong Kong Telecom (probably the largest private employer at that time) announced it would cut wages for its 13,800 staff and workers by 10% for 1 year and those who refused to accept the cut would be sacked, the union organized strikes and public demonstrations and initiated a public campaign against the company.

The union pointed out that the company was sitting on HK$15 million (about US$2 million) in cash and had just received HK$6.7 billion in compensation from the government for the surrender of its monopoly on international calls. After a prolonged struggle, the union eventually induced the company to withdraw its proposed wage cut.

The company returned with a new proposal to lay off workers the following year. On November 19, 2002, PCCW announced that workers would face pay cuts of at least 10% in the latest move by the telecom giant to reduce costs. The plan was outlined to 3,000 staff members after the announcement that a new subsidiary would be formed the following year to take over support and management work. Under the plan, 75% of workers would have to take pay cuts of at least 10% if they wanted to join the new company, Cascade Limited. Unionists claimed that cuts of 20% would be implemented for some workers. Those who rejected the proposal were to be laid off in January (*South China Morning Post*, November 20, 2002, p. 2).

A day later, PCCW suddenly made another announcement that it would fire 529 staff, concluding a massive lay-off program that cost almost 1,900 jobs over a 12-month period. "We are shocked," said Terry Ip, PCCW staff association chairman. "Just yesterday they found a new company and promised a good future, but today they slashed 500-plus staff" (*South China Morning Post*, November 21, 2002, p. 1).

Similarly, the civil workers' union tried hard to prevent the government from implementing salary cuts, privatization, and changing working conditions. The large government deficit meant that pressure mounted to privatize government activities. One example is the estate maintenance and management of the housing authority that affected some 9,000 caretakers, managers, and technicians working at the 165 public rental estates. In August 1999, the Alliance of Housing Department Staff Unions threatened a week-long strike when it was excluded from a working group studying privatization and a task force that would approve changes. Perhaps in response to this union protest, the chief executive, in his policy address in October 1999, tried to assure civil servants that the administration would attempt to avoid redundancies while pushing ahead with civil-service reforms and cost-cutting targets through interdepartmental redeployment, secondment, and employee retraining (*South China Morning Post*, 1999a and b).

In March 1999, the Civil Service Bureau published a consultation document proposing a major restructuring of employment practices that would make the civil service operate more flexibly. In June 2000, the government introduced a new entry system of terms of appointment for recruits in line with its aim of increasing the flexibility of the hiring system. Under the new system, most recruits were appointed on probationary terms for a specified period before being considered for appointment on prevailing permanent terms. Departmental and grade management staff would be responsible for monitoring and managing probationers and agreement officers. In July 2000, the government introduced a voluntary retirement scheme to enable existing staff at 59 grades and surplus (or anticipated surplus) staff to retire voluntarily with pension benefits and compensation.

On salary issues, moves to cut pay by 2% to 4% without an agreement in 2002 prompted 30,000 civil servants take to the streets in protest. In February 2003, the government made an agreement with the unions that civil servants' pay would be effectively frozen until the end of the year. Additionally, salaries would then be restored to 1997 levels within 2 years, i.e., the result was a 6% cut (*South*

China Morning Post, February 22, 2003). Although civil servants were willing to accept the 6% pay cut over 2 years, business organizations had yet to agree to accept a 1%-to-2% raise in profit taxes based on the fact that the civil servants' pay cut was not deep enough to solve the government budget deficit of HK$70 billion (US$9.8 billion).

New Labor Insurgency

The new round of government budget cutting led to new patterns of labor insurgency. On February 23, 2003, at least 10,000 foreign domestic helpers joined a march against the government's proposal to impose a HK$400 (US$50) levy on their wages. It was the biggest protest ever held by migrant workers in Hong Kong. Wearing red T-shirts, workers from the Philippines, Indonesia, Thailand, and Nepal waved flags, danced, and chanted "No to wage levy, no to wage cuts" in English and Cantonese as they made their way from Victoria Park.

Hong Kong employs about 237,000 foreign domestic helpers, of whom 148,000 are from the Philippines. The domestic helpers were against the proposal to cut HK$400 from their minimum monthly wage, bringing it down to HK$3,270 (US$417). Bishop Joseph Sen complained to the public that Hong Kong citizens should have shown foreign workers more gratitude because their services were much needed (*South China Morning Post*, February 24, 2003, p. 5).

On the same day, a coalition of 90 groups criticized the government for its plan to slash welfare payments by 11.1%; they accused the government of exploiting the poorest people in society. Dressed in black and sitting in front of crossed-out giant Chinese signs that read "Caring and Justice," dozens of representatives from social, labor, and religious groups protested against the decision to lower comprehensive social security assistance for about 260,000 families.

Chong Chan-Yau, Oxfam Hong Kong's executive director, said the government pledged to create a harmonious and caring society, but its actions violated its promises. He said the welfare cut would exacerbate class differences and deepen class conflicts (*South China Morning Post*, February 24, 2003, p. 3).

Two weeks earlier, 80 temporary workers held a public demonstration to protest the government's failure to renew their contracts. The workers were mostly middle-aged women who did cleaning work in public hospitals. They complained that the government would rather subcontract their cleaning jobs rather than re-hire them. They also argued that if they worked for the new subcontractors, their wages would further decrease from HK$6,000 (US$769) to HK$4,000 (US$513) a month to do the same jobs (*Ming Pao*, February 10, 2003, p. A2).

This case illustrates the common problem facing outsourcing. In the Hong Kong Women Workers' Association's survey of 150 cleaners working in public estates (1999), the majority were middle-aged women and many were new immigrants from mainland China. The monthly average wage of those working full time was only HK$3,613 (US$463). Most did not receive statutory benefits in the forms of holidays, paid annual and sick leave, and compensation for occupational injuries.

After the 1970s male-dominated labor movement in the manufacturing sector during the heyday of export-industrialization. In the early 2000s, the key actors in Hong Kong's labor movement shifted. In a new group: foreign flexible female workers in the service sector. Very often, instead of being led by the old, established labor unions, labor insurgency is now organized by independent unions and nongovernment organizations, or NGOs (groups of social workers, students, and religious leaders). Instead of large-scale labor protests, the new pattern takes the form of small-scale, scattered, and discontinuous protests.

The recent burst of labor struggles is a function of both the fermentation of discontent in the labor market and the efforts by the labor movement to mobilize hitherto marginal groups of workers. The presence of over 220,000 foreign domestic helpers, largely from the Philippines, Indonesia, and Thailand, led to the development of dense interpersonal and organizational networks among migrant workers, contributing to a sustained struggle protect their rights and against policy changes like the levy. As for women workers, although the majority remained unorganized, the rise of new forms of flexible employment gave rise to new attempts at organization. The labor movement attempted to organize the cleaning service and domestic workers, for example. The government's half-hearted attempts to retrain workers through funding union and NGO-organized retraining programs also inadvertently facilitated organizing endeavors.

There are, however, signs that workers' grievances against capital are sometimes displaced to become conflicts within the working class. A prime example is anti-immigration protest. Believing that the new immigrants stole their jobs, Hong Kong workers established various stereotypes of working-class immigrants from mainland China, labeling them lazy and uncultured and accusing them of burdening the Hong Kong welfare system. Mainland migrants were said to be likely to commit crimes and their children were prone to dropping out of school. The Hong Kong workers felt that the SAR state should have applied the brakes to the immigration of mainlanders to the territory.

Although the Basic Law (mini-constitution) of Hong Kong granted citizenship to mainland Chinese for reasons of family reunification, the SAR state appealed to the National People's Congress to repeal the provision, leading to a protracted battle with the "pro-right of abode" activists. The SAR state argued that an influx of 1.6 million mainland peasants and workers to Hong Kong for family reunions would ruin Hong Hong's economy. The state even took the drastic measures of arresting and sending overstaying family members back to the mainland in 2002. In 2003, the state further proposed that mainland immigrants had to stay in Hong Kong at least 3 years before they were eligible to apply for welfare, housing, and medical benefits (*Ming Pao*, January 27, 2003).

Most labor groups tried their best to foster more inclusive struggles against capital and are critical of the conservative counter-mobilization that scapegoats new immigrants. Interviews of local part-time domestic workers organized by the trade union federation, for example, suggest a surprisingly open-minded attitude toward the foreign domestic helpers who are often portrayed in the mainstream media as competing against local workers. Local domestic workers now perceive themselves as serving a very different niche from foreign workers (Chiu, Fung, and Choi, 2003). Although labor groups have been unable to forge solidarities across the two groups of workers, they have at least alleviated a possible schism. Other groups, notably some traditional trade unions and conservative political parties, are willing to profit from the anti-immigrant sentiments and campaigns against foreign workers. Whether the nascent labor insurgency degenerates into in-fighting between the working classes depends on how progressive labor groups devise strategies to forge a more inclusive movement.

Conclusion and Discussion

This chapter examines the changing patterns of flexible work in Hong Kong over the past four decades. We would like to highlight four points for discussion. First, this paper shows that although Hong Kong workers may have benefited historically from flexible work because of a tight labor market in a booming economy, they have suffered immensely and were demoralized when Hong Kong's economy declined.

The situation in the 2000s is particularly unfavorable to Hong Kong's labor because of the historical legacy of strong state–business bonds, the lack of collective bargaining, and the weak labor unions inherited from British colonialism. The Hong Kong case shows that labor's bargaining power cannot rely solely upon favorable market conditions during boom days; workers need to build up their class power by strengthening unions and labor legislation and engaging in social movements and party politics.

Flexible work has greatly changed the composition and nature of labor activism. In the pre flexible era, Hong Kong labor activists were usually male workers in the manufacturing sector. Since the spread of flexible employment, nonlocal female workers in the service industry have become active in labor protests.

A third factor is that flexible employment intensified sexism and gender inequalities in Hong Kong. Instead of promoting worker enrichment as claimed in the management literature, flexible employment puts women in a much more disadvantaged position in the labor market than they occupied earlier, our study shows. They are discriminated against from finding or holding good jobs; they are the first to be laid off and have been sent home to become full-time housewives.

Fourth, flexible work has drastically transformed the pattern of labor insurgency. On the one hand, flexible employment undermined labor insurgency because workers' commitments to strike were minimal. As flexible workers, they worked only part time and filled temporary positions. In addition, flexible workers may find it difficult to determine who the boss to struggle against is because he is often hidden behind layers of subcontractors. On the other hand, flexible employment provided new impetus to labor insurgency because flexible production broadened the composition of the working class to include nonlocal women.

In the era of flexible production, gender, ethnicity, and nationality have emerged as new sources of worker solidarity and militancy, opening up a new terrain of flexible labor protest in the 21st century that differs from the trade union politics practiced earlier.

In sum, this chapter shows that after globalization opened national frontiers for industrial restructuring and relocation and flexible employment spread from the manufacturing sector to the state sector, Hong Kong workers were in a much worse situation in the 1990s than they were earlier. Middle-aged female workers in particular were hit hardest in the new era of globalization and flexible employment.

However, despite weak unions and the lack of collective bargaining power, Hong Kong workers still joined protests against this assault by unrestrained market forces. Hong Kong workers in the state sector protested against cuts of their wages and benefits and the subcontracting of their work to the private sector. Domestic workers protested against cuts of HK$400 from their minimum wage. Many other small-scale protests related to work issues have been conducted over the past few years. However, SAR government never took these workers' protests seriously, either because of its close ties to big business or because of its proglobalization stand that views global-market competitiveness as paramount. Finally, the accumulation of conflict reached such a height that over 500,000 Hong Kong residents came out to protest against the SAR government on July 1, 2003.

The July 1 protest can be seen as a societal backlash against the *assaults of globalization's unrestrained market forces*. The protesters wanted to tame the market forces and to bring them under control, i.e., "re-embed" the market in society and in the state. The protesters demanded that the SAR government not cut so many jobs in the state sector and not over-cut its expenditures on welfare and social services. They also demanded that businesses not lay off workers when they earned big profits.

Hong Kong is not alone. Other states in Asia, such as South Korea, Taiwan, and mainland China, are also developing policies and programs to re-embed unrestrained market forces after they experienced societal protests. Because these attempts to tame unrestrained market forces have only started, it will be difficult to predict whether they will succeed. One thing is certain: As antiglobalization forces grow, globalization and flexible employment projects are increasingly put on the defensive. At the advent of the 21st century, it seems that the neo-liberalists are unwilling to back off their globalization agenda. Instead, they are trying their best to regain hegemony through any means, including using state terrorism and wars to reinvent empires!

References

Alasoini, T., 1993, "Transformation of Work Organization in Time-Based Production Management," *International Journal of Human Factors in Manufacturing*, 3: 319.

Avery, C. and D. Zabel, 2001, *The Flexible Work Place*, Quorum, Westport, CT.

Census and Statistics Department, 2000, Thematic Household Survey Report 1, Employment Concerns and Training Needs, Government Printing Department Hong Kong.

Census and Statistics Department, 2001, Special Topics Report 30, Social Data Collected via the General Household Survey, Government Printing Department, Hong Kong.

Census and Statistics Department, 2002, Special Topics Report 31, Social Data Collected via the General Household Survey, Government Printing Department, Hong Kong.

Chiu, S.W.K. and C.K. Lee, 1997, *Withering Away of the Hong Kong Dream? Women Workers under Industrial Restructuring*. Hong Kong Institute of Asia–Pacific Studies, Hong Kong.

Chiu, S.W.K., H.I. Fung, and F. Choi, 2003, *Disconnected Youth, Disgruntled Adults: Social Exclusion and Social Cohesion in a Life-Course Perspective*, Social and Economic Policy Institute, Hong Kong.

Gereffi, G., M. Korzeniewicz, and R.P. Korzeniewicz, 1994, "Introduction: Global Commodity Chains," in Gereffi, G. and M. Korzeniewicz, Eds., *Commodity Chains and Global Capitalism*, Praeger, Westport, CT, p. 1.

Gordon. D.M., 1996, *Fat and Mean: The Corporate Squeeze of Working Americans and the Myth of Managerial Downsizing*, Free Press, New York.

Harvey, D., 1989, *The Condition of Postmodernity: An Inquiry into the Origins of Cultural Change*, Blackwell, Cambridge, MA.

Ho, C.K., 2001, "Of Flesh and Blood: The Human Consequences of Economic Restructuring on Women Workers in Hong Kong," in So, A.Y. et al., Eds., *The Chinese Triangle of Mainland China, Taiwan, and Hong Kong*, Greenwood, Westport, CT, p. 117.

Hong Kong Catholic Commission for Labour Affairs, 2003, *Community Economic Development: A Way Out for the Unemployed and Marginal Workers?* Hong Kong. hknews@ahkcus.org

Jessop, B., 2002, *The Future of the Capitalist State*, Polity Press, Cambridge, U.K.

Kalleberg, A., 2000, "Non-standard Employment Relations: Part-time, Temporary and Contract Work." *Annual Review of Sociology*, 26: 341.

Lang, G., C. Chiu, and M. Pang, 2001, "Impact of Plant Relocation to China on Manufacturing Workers in Hong Kong," in Lee, P.T., Ed., *Hong Kong Reintegrating With China: Political, Cultural and Social Dimensions*, Hong Kong University Press, Hong Kong, p. 109.

Lee, K.M., 1997, "The Flexibility of the Hong Kong Manufacturing Sector," *China Information*, 12: 189.

Levin, DA. and S.W.K. Chiu, 1997, "Empowering Labour? The Origins and Practice of Joint Consultation in Hong Kong," in Markey, R. and J. Monat, Eds., *Innovation and Employee Participation through Works Councils: International Case Studies*, Avebury, Aldershot, U.K., p. 280.

Ming Pao

Ngo, H.Y. and Lau, C.M., 1996, "Labor and Employment," in Nyaw, M.K. and S.M. Li, Eds., *The Other Hong Kong Report 1996*, Chinese University Press, Hong Kong, p. 259.

Polivka, A. E., 1996, "Contingent and Alternative Work Arrangements Defined," *Monthly Labor Review*, 119: 3.

Polivka, A.E. and T. Nardone, 1989, "On the Definition of 'Contingent Work'," *Monthly Labor Review*, 112: 9.

Scandura, T.A. and M.J. Lankau, 1997, "Relationships of Gender, Family Responsibility and Flexible Work Hours to Organizational Commitment and Job Satisfaction," *Journal of Organizational Behavior*, 18: 377.

Skeldon, R., 1997, "Hong Kong: Colonial City to Global City to Provincial City?" *Cities*, 14: 265.

So, A.Y., "Hong Kong's Pathways to Global City: A Regional Analysis," in Gugler, J., Ed., *World City in Poor Countries*, Cambridge University Press, Cambridge, in press.

South China Morning Post

Wallerstein, I., 2003, "U.S. Weakness and the Struggle for Hegemony," Monthly Review, July–August, p. 1. Available at http://www.monthlyreview.org/0703 wallerstein.htm (accessed July 29, 2003).

Womack, J. P. et al., 1990, *The Machine that Changed the World*, Rawson Associates, New York.

Wong, H. and K.M. Lee, 2001, *Predicaments, Exclusion and the Way Ahead: A Qualitative Study of Marginal Workers in Hong Kong*, Oxfam, Hong Kong.

Yeung, Y.M., 1997, "Planning for Pearl City: Hong Kong's Future, 1997 and Beyond," *Cities*, 14: 249.

14

From the Third World to the "Third World Within": Asian Women Workers Fighting Globalization

GRACE CHANG

The present form of globalization has not produced enough jobs for all those who seek them or in the places where they are most needed. This is probably its biggest failure.

Juan Somavia
Director-General, International Labor Organization[1]

I want to begin to dispel the myths. It's not about mail-order brides. Hello, this is a global world . . . . We are a global population.

Mike Krosky
Owner, Cherry Blossoms[2]

Introduction

These observations on globalization probably could not have come from more distant corners. Juan Somavia's comment, addressed to representatives from 175 International Labor Organization member countries was intended to be sobering. He warned that the failure of globalization to create new jobs in developing countries has fueled and will continue to fuel massive migration worldwide. He estimated that about 500 million jobs will have to be created over the next decade just to accommodate the young people and women now entering the labor market.

In contrast, Mike Krosky's comment from an interview about his Cherry Blossoms business is positively celebratory. Krosky's business lists over 6000 women available for order through print catalogs and a web site, half of whom are Filipina. The next largest group is Indonesian, and the group showing the greatest increase comes from Eastern European countries. Krosky celebrates globalization not only because of huge business profits, but also for his personal

217

satisfaction as the happy husband of a Filipina more than 18 years his junior, whom he met through his own service.

Both these comments speak directly or otherwise to an important but often neglected aspect of globalization: migrations of Third World people from their homes as a result of the destruction wrought by globalization on their abilities to survive at home.

I want to address this dimension of globalization, particularly Third World women's migrations, and, like Mike Krosky, I want to begin to dispel the myths. I also want to address the reality that in today's globalized context, virtually all migration can be seen as coerced through economic means, through the institutionalized underdevelopment and impoverishment of Third World nations and people.

A few years ago I had the privilege of speaking on an International Women's Day radio program with Ethel Long Scott of the Women's Economic Agenda Project. Scott remarked that we must talk about globalization in its proper terms, as the *globalization of poverty*—that is, the creation, perpetuation, and exacerbation of poverty worldwide. Scott also cautioned listeners not to think that the ravages of globalization are confined "over there" in the Third World but to examine its impacts in our own communities of color.[3] Scott raised an important point missing from many debates surrounding globalization—that those in the Third World and those in the "Third World within" First World countries share these conditions and thus are central to the struggles against this globalization of poverty.[4]

I will examine how women of color and migrant women in First World host nations experience the impact of globalization on their lives and livelihoods daily and forge resistance to these impact daily. Specifically, I look at the struggles of Filipina migrant workers in the U.S. and Canada—women who suffer these impact on both ends of the global "trade route." I interviewed members of two migrant domestic worker organizations, one in Vancouver, Canada, and the other in Bronx, New York, who provide important models for critical gender analyses of globalization and organized resistance against it.

Many of us who attended the 1995 Non-Governmental Organizations (NGO) Forum on Women as members of the U.S. women of color delegation were humbled by our Third World sisters who danced circles around us in their analyses and first-hand knowledge of global economic restructuring and its impact. Poor women of color throughout the world suffer first and worst under globalization. They experience so-called "development"" and "free trade" as losses in status, freedom, safety, education, access to basic needs of food, water, housing, and health care—indeed, as assaults on their very survival. As the first victims of globalization, poor women of color are also the primary leaders in fighting back, in resisting the so-called "New World Order" that they know is not new at all but a continuation of neo-imperialist activities into the 21st century.

Global Economic Restructuring

At the Fourth World NGO Forum on Women held in China in 1995, women from Africa, Latin America, the Middle East, and Asia echoed the same truth in their testimonies: Global economic restructuring embodied in Structural Adjustment Programs (SAPs) strikes poor women of color around the world the hardest, rendering them most vulnerable to exploitation both at home and in the global labor market. Since the 1980s, the World Bank, International Monetary Fund (IMF), and other international financial institutions based in the First World have routinely prescribed structural adjustment policies to the governments of indebted countries as preconditions for loans. These prescriptions included cutting government expenditures on social programs, slashing wages, liberalizing imports, opening markets to foreign investment, expanding exports, devaluing local currency, and privatizing state enterprises.

Women have consistently reported increasing poverty and rapidly deteriorating nutrition, health, and work conditions as a direct result of SAPs. When wages and food subsidies are cut, wives and mothers adjust household budgets often at the expense of their own and their children's nutrition. As public health care and education vanish, women suffer from lack of prenatal care and become nurses to ill family members at home; girls are the first family members to leave school to help at home or go to work. When export-oriented agriculture is encouraged—indeed, coerced—peasant families are evicted from their lands to make room for corporate farms, and women become seasonal workers in the fields or in processing areas instead of land-owning farmers.

Lands once used to raise staples like rice are used instead for raising shrimp, oranges, and orchids—all for export, not for local consumption—or for golf courses and luxury hotels for tourists. Essentially, SAPs lead to destruction of both subsistence and social service systems in Third World nations so that women have no viable options to sustain their families and leave them behind to migrate in search of work. Usually women go from villages to cities within their home countries first and then migrate to the First World to pursue service work, sex work, and manufacturing jobs.[5]

Since the 1995 NGO Forum, women of color around the world have spoken in no uncertain terms to these continuing trends that globalization imposes on their lives.[6] They report the persistence of the most devastating impact of globalization on their abilities to support their children and families in the form of increased assaults on their reproductive rights. In short, globalization threatens the very survival of people of color by hindering the ability of their women to reproduce and maintain their families and communities.

In 1999, before the Seattle protests against the World Trade Organization (WTO), the Northwest Labor and Employment Law Office (LELO), a multi-racial community and labor organization, recognized the need for education to build awareness of these issues and the linkages between workers' struggles in the U.S. and abroad. LELO brought together several grassroots groups, including the Seattle Young People's Project, Committee Against Repression in Mexico, Community Coalition for Environmental Justice, and the Washington Alliance for Immigrant and Refugee Justice to form the Workers' Voices Coalition. The coalition sponsored the participation of eight women labor-rights organizers from Third World countries in the WTO protest activities and a post-WTO conference.

Cenen Bagon, a participant, responded to comments by Michael Moore, then WTO director-general, when he addressed the International Confederation of Free Trade Unions. Moore said, "There is also a darker side to the backlash against globalization. For some, the attacks on economic openness are part of a broader assault on internationalism, on foreigners, immigration, a more pluralistic and integrated world . . . ." Bagon, who works with Filipina and other immigrant women workers in Canada through the Vancouver Committee for Domestic Workers and Caregivers Rights, countered sharply:

> Moore and others like him, in his ideological dogma, forget to add, and I'm sure it's quite intentional, that what we are against are the realities brought about by trade authored by the backers of capitalist globalization . . . . And if these so-called leaders are really looking for indicators of whether their programs are truly creating economic improvements, they should look beyond the country's balance of payment and budget deficits and analyze how women are affected by these programs . . . . Supporters of structural adjustment programs should visit the night life in Japan, Hong Kong, and certain places in Canada and listen to the stories of Filipino and other women who unknowingly left their countries as entertainers and ended up being prostituted by their recruiters. They should also listen to the stories of domestic workers who left not only their countries . . . but their families and their own children, as well, to care for other women's children and households . . . .[7]

Bagon calls for world leaders to view the migration of women forced to leave their homelands and families because of the ravages of SAPs as true indicators of the impacts of global economic restructuring. Extending on this, the experiences of immigrant women workers can serve not only as measures of the effects, but as true indicators of the *intentions* of SAPs and other neo-liberal economic policies. The sheer magnitude of women's migration urges us to examine this phenomenon and view it as both an effect of globalization and as a calculated feature of global economic restructuring.

In other words, it is important to understand the economic interventions in Third World nations embodied in SAPs and free-trade policies as deliberate. They facilitate the extraction of resources, especially labor and people, from the Third World and their importation into the First World. In effect, they support trade in and traffic of migrant women workers and their exploitation at both ends of the so-called trade route. This trade or forced migration is orchestrated through economic interventions compelling migration from the Third World coupled with welfare, labor, and immigration policies in the First World that channel these women into service work at poverty wages in host or receiving countries.

I have argued elsewhere that structural adjustment in the Third World and welfare reform in the First World are inextricably linked; indeed, they are two sides of the same coin. For example, in the U.S., domestic forms of structural adjustment, including privatization and cutbacks in health care and the continued lack of subsidized child care, contribute to expanded demand among dual-career middle-class households for child care, elder care, home health care, and housekeeping workers. The slashing of benefits and social services under "welfare reform" helps guarantee that this demand is met by a pool of migrant women readily available to serve as cheap labor. The dismantling of public support in the U.S. in general and the denial of benefits and services to immigrants in particular act in tandem with structural adjustment in the Third World to force migrant women into low-wage service work in the U.S.[8]

Migrant women workers from indebted nations are kept pliable by both the dependence of their families on remittances sent home and by the severe restrictions on immigrant access to almost all forms of assistance in the U.S. Their vulnerability is further reinforced by First World immigration policies explicitly designed to recruit migrant women as contract or temporary workers yet deny them the protections and rights afforded citizens. This phenomenon is readily apparent in the cases of both U.S. and Canadian immigration policies structured to ensure a ready supply of women workers available for nursing aide, home care, domestic care, child care, and elder care work at low wages and under conditions most citizens would not accept.

"Filipinos for the World"

The massive migration of women from the Philippines to all corners of the First World illustrates clearly how structural adjustments imposed on the Philippines and welfare and immigration policies in First World receiving countries combine to make the global traffic in Filipinas an explicit government practice and highly profitable industry on both ends of the trade route. Every day, an average of 2700 people are estimated to leave the Philippines in search of work. Currently, more than 8 million Filipino migrant workers live in over 186 countries, and an estimated 65% are women.[9] Although the Philippine government denies that it has an official export policy now, an agency called the Philippine Overseas Employment Administration (POEA) was established in the 1970s to promote migrant labor with the stated goals of (1) earning foreign currency and (2) easing the Philippines' unemployment rate.[10]

Confining the analysis for the moment only to the benefits of this trade to the Philippine government and capital, the numbers are staggering. One woman migrating to Canada reported paying 1900 pesos at the embassy in the Philippines, 1500 pesos for a medical examination, and 5000 pesos to the POEA according to the research by the Philippine Women's Centre.[11] If we multiply this total 8400 pesos ($181 US) for typical bureaucratic expenses paid by one individual migrating from the Philippines by the average daily exodus of 2700 people leaving the country, the Philippine government receives the equivalent of almost half a million U.S. dollars in revenue daily for processing exports of people. Moreover, the remittances sent home to families by Filipino workers overseas infuse into the economy what amounts to the Philippines' largest source of foreign currency—far more than income from sugar and mineral exports.

Although the absolute numbers are remarkable, taken in context they are particularly telling. For example, in the year 2000, remittances from overseas workers were estimated at $6.23 billion officially, reported as channeled through the Central Bank of the Philippines. This does not include funds received through informal channels. The $6.23 billion represented 5.2% of the gross domestic product and exceeded the entire interest payment on the country's foreign debt that hovers around $5 billion a year.[12]

Philippine President Gloria Macapagal-Arroyo launched a program known as "Filipinos for the World" to celebrate and further institutionalize this exportation of workers for profit. Arroyo (unaffectionately referred to as GMA) persists in glorifying these migrant workers, following a long line of Philippines officials who once called women in particular the country's "modern heroes." In even more crass economic terms, GMA now calls them "overseas Philippines investors" and "internationally shared resources."[13] She is promoting her new labor export plan announced in June of 2002 as a push to have 100 million overseas Filipinos serving others across the globe. Arroyo's program will certainly serve her interests well. As one observer remarked, "Arroyo seeks not only the remittances from the migrant workers, but their absentee ballots to keep her in office and bolster her unstable position. She wants not only the dollars but the 8 million Filipinos abroad in her pocket at election time."[14]

It is particularly useful to examine the experiences of Filipinas trained as nurses who migrate to work in the U.S. and Canada. They provide cheap and highly skilled labor and also serve to further the neo-liberal agenda of privatizing health care. In both countries, immigration policy is structured to keep these trained workers underemployed and deskilled in exploitative situations closely resembling indentured servitude and debt bondage. Nursing schools graduating hundreds of thousands of registered nurses abound in the Philippines, but few graduates reside in their own country.

The Philippine Women Centre (PWC) of British Columbia, a group of Filipino–Canadian women working to educate, organize, and mobilize Filipina migrant workers in Canada, identifies this phenomenon as the "commodification of the nursing profession in the Philippines." The group observes that nursing training is promoted as "a quick route to work abroad," rather than as a means to serve the needs of Filipinos. As a result Filipina nurses are seen as exportable commodities.[15] A survey of members of the group revealed that 77% of participants studied nursing with the specific intention of going abroad, and 62% took entrance exams allowing foreigners to practice nursing in the U.S.[16]

Clearly, exclusion from both welfare benefits and workers' rights through immigration policy makes immigrant women workers available for—indeed, unable to refuse—low-wage service work in the U.S. In Canada, the connection between labor control and immigration policy is even more explicit because of the use of both immigration and nursing accreditation issues to prevent foreign-trained nurses from being able to practice nursing for several years after arrival in Canada. In tandem, the policies serve to exclude immigrant nurses from their professions and channel them into low-paid care work as nannies, domestics, and home support workers.

The Live-in Caregiver Program (LCP) is the immigration policy through which the vast majority of Filipina migrants enter Canada and become trapped in low-wage care work. Established in 1992 to facilitate the importation of primarily Filipino women, the program provides that a Canadian employer (individual or employment agency) may apply through the Canadian Employment Office for a prospective employee after showing that an attempt was made to find a Canadian to do the job. A job applicant must have 2 years of post secondary education, 6 months of formal training or 12 months of experience in caregiving work, and be in good health. Once matched with an employer, she must notify the Ministry of Citizenship and Immigration if she wishes to change employers. After 2 years of live-in work, a nanny can apply for landed-immigrant status, but during those 2 years she is considered a temporary migrant. Three years after applying for landed-immigrant status, she can become a Canadian citizen.[17]

The PWC undertook a community-based participatory action research project, interviewing 30 Filipina nurses who entered Canada via the LCP and performed domestic work. According to Cecilia Diocson, founding chairperson of the PWC, the interviews revealed that women with up to 15 years of nursing experience in operating rooms, cancer units, and other facilities were becoming deskilled while working as nannies and home support workers.[18] Others were indeed using their skills, working around the clock and performing nursing tasks, but they were not recognized or compensated as such. Many of their tasks included heavy lifting; transferring; personal care duties; administering medications; and tube feeding for elderly, ill, and disabled clients. One nurse, Mary Jane reported:

> Because of the LCP requirements, we become responsible for our employers 24 hours a day, but we are only paid for 8 hours, with no overtime pay. For some of us, we accompany our employers to the hospital and even sleep at our employer's bedside at the hospital.[19]

Many of those interviewed did not realize when they migrated that they would not be doing nursing work after they entered Canada through the LCP. Many believed that they would perform nursing in private homes or care for disabled children. Moreover, many did not know that working as a nanny would mean so much labor demanded of them beyond caring for children. For example, Pamela, a registered nurse in the Philippines who left three children behind to seek work in Vancouver, said:

> I thought being a nanny, as the dictionary says, is child's nurse. In the Philippines, a yaya [Tagalog for nanny] works for the kids only, right? They don't do other jobs in the house. They just change the kids, feed them and put them to bed . . . . When I came here, I was shocked. I said, why is it a package? Three children in a big house, 5 bedrooms, 1½ baths, and 3 living rooms . . . . I feel like I'm going to die. My female employer didn't work. She stays at home. Then, she said that I'm not clean enough. I told her that I have to prioritize the work and I asked her, what's more important, the kids or cleaning? . . . . It was so hard I quit.[20]

After Pamela quit, her former employer refused to give her a reference, nanny agencies would not accept her, and she decided to advertise for a job caring for the elderly. Several prospective employers who answered her ad sought caregivers willing to provide sexual services. After several such experiences and trying to work as a nanny for one more family, she found a job caring for a single woman.

Pamela supports her husband, who is a student, and her three children in the Philippines by sending a quarter of her wages home each month. She spoke of the hardships of separation from her family and her doubts and fears about reuniting:

> I'm confused whether I should get my family or not. The separation is really hard for me, but I also think if my family is here, my husband and I have to chip in. I fear that communication will be through messages on the refrigerator. We don't see each other any more. That's why sometimes I feel that maybe it's better for them to stay in the Philippines because they write to me and there's an attachment still. Here, it seems that you're not really intact.[21]

Mary Jane, another Filipina nurse working as a nanny, reflected on the pain of separation from her children and the great financial hardship of maintaining contact:

> My children are now 5 and 8. I spent so much money on the long distance because sometimes when I call, my child will say, "Mommy I still want to sing." You know, you didn't see your child for 4 years and she will tell you she wants to sing, you cannot say no . . . . I said I will call everyday so that [her youngest child] will not forget my voice. I only stopped calling because my phone bill is over $500.

For these women, the agony of separation from their own children is surely not diminished by caring for their employers' children. For many of the women interviewed, the hope of eventually being able to bring their families to join them in Canada influenced them to stay in unhappy and often abusive working situations in order to fulfill the 2-year live-in work requirement of the LCP as quickly as possible. The policy prohibits them from earning any extra income to supplement their low wages as caregivers and explicitly stipulates that working for anyone other than the employer named on the employment authorization is illegal, and unauthorized employment will not count toward satisfying the 2-year employment requirement to apply for permanent residence.[22] Thus, women are effectively kept bonded to the employers named on their original LCP employment authorizations at whatever wages and conditions the employer chooses to provide. As Pamela reports:

> Filipinos are abused because they are pressured to stay with the 24-month requirement . . . . You stay because it's not that easy to find an employer. And you get exploited and we are highly educated . . . . That's really racism.

In addition to these barriers that essentially lock trained nurses into nanny and home support work for at least 2 years, migrant Filipinas face more hurdles in trying to gain accreditation to practice nursing even after serving the 2-year live-in requirement. Applicants must take English tests that are irrelevant and extremely costly, about US $410. According to Leah Diana, a registered nurse and volunteer with the Filipino Nurses Support Group (FNSG) in Vancouver, Filipino nurses are usually educated in English, used English while employed in the Philippines and elsewhere, and passed mandatory English interviews before arrival in Canada. Diana says, "The English tests required are only based on the racist assumption that people of color can't speak English." These barriers are particularly outrageous when viewed in the context of Canada's recognized nursing shortage. A Canadian Nurses' Association study showed an expected shortage of 59,000 to 113,000 registered nurses in Canada by the year 2011.[19]

Cecilia Diocson reports that the mainstream, predominantly white nursing unions in Canada have not been good allies. They have not supported allowing Filipina nurses to practice despite shortages. Diocson expressed outrage that the president of a nursing union tried to pass this off as concern that "the Philippines needs them." She said:

> We responded, "Don't give us that kind of rationalization. The nurses are already here, and in crisis, and we are seeking solidarity. Is the real issue that we are non-white, from the Third World, and foreign-trained? Are you threatened by our presence?" It's so clear that this is just racism. Otherwise, they would support and struggle with us.

Beyond the presence of women of color born and trained in the Third World, the existence of a surplus of low-wage workers and ostensible competitors is perhaps most threatening. Migrant women workers are well aware that the Canadian government can and does use their presence in the country and their exclusion through the LCP from the nursing profession to render them available to do other low-wage care and service work while keeping Canadian citizen nurses wary of competition. As Gemma Gambito, a member of FNSG who graduated from nursing school in the Philippines in 1993 and went to Canada in 1997 under the LCP, says:

> Our presence in Canada is used to drive down the wages of Canadian nurses and health care workers. Once completing our temporary work contract and becoming landed immigrants, many become home support workers, nursing aides, or continue to do domestic work for low wages. A pool of highly skilled yet low paid health workers has been created by the Canadian government's LCP.[23]

The LCP and its attendant racism facilitate the privatization of health care and help ensure the lack of movement or alliance building for subsidized child care, health care, and other staples of feminist and worker agendas. Dr. Lynn Farrales, a co-chair of the PWC, observes that the LCP functions simply to bring in women who are educated and trained nurses to do domestic work and provide live-in child care and private home care for the disabled and elderly for less than minimum wage. Farrales says:

> Canada, a country without a national day care program and a health care system moving towards increased privatization, has established in the LCP a means of importing highly educated and skilled workers to fulfill the need for flexible and cheap labor in the spheres of child care and health care. The economic and social consequences of the LCP have been devastating for Filipino women. They are highly exploited, oppressed, and de-skilled. Despite being highly educated, many are trapped in minimum wage jobs after completion of the LCP, and are effectively legislated into poverty.[24]

Moreover, Farrales notes that these negative consequences extend to the next generation of Filipino youth as well, including the effects of years of separation of mothers and children and the systemic racism in Canadian institutions that Filipino–Canadian youths encounter. Because Filipino youths drop out of high school at high rates, they join their mothers working for low wages in the service sector. Thus, the Canadian government achieves what Farrales calls the "commodification of the migration of the entire family as a package deal of cheap labor."[25] Meanwhile, ironically, with rapidly privatizing health care and the continuing nursing shortage in the public sector, health care becomes inaccessible for working-class Canadians, including Filipina nurses and their families. Thus, the Canadian government provides middle- and upper-class Canadian citizens with quality, low-cost, in-home child care and health care, literally at the expense of Filipina women workers and their families, who cannot afford these services for themselves.

Filipina migrant workers understand all too well how the Philippine government benefits and profits from this trade in women and thus plays a calculated role in ensuring its smooth functioning. The following statement of the

PWC reflects this analysis of the past and current complicity of the Philippine government in this trade:

> The migration and commodification of Filipinos is sanctioned by official Philippine government policy. Known as the Labour Export Policy (LEP), this scheme of systematically exporting labour is part of the Structural Adjustment Programs (SAPs) imposed by the IMF and World Bank as conditionalities for borrowing. Ultimately, the LEP and SAPs are part of the neoliberal policies of the globalization agenda. The LEP seeks to alleviate the continuing problems of massive unemployment, trade deficits, foreign debt and social unrest . . . . The government relies upon the remittances of these migrants to prop up the economy and pay off the massive foreign debt owed to the IMF and the World Bank. Instead of selling coconuts and sugar, the Philippine government is now engaged in the sophisticated practice of selling its own people to industrialized countries.[26]

This statement reflects these women's clear recognition that the official Philippine government labor export policy is part and parcel of structural adjustment programs that wreak havoc on their lives and force them to migrate in the first place. The LEP institutionalizes the exportation of Filipina women to other countries for cheap labor and effectively guarantees that remittances from these migrant women workers are used to pay off foreign debt.

Turning the "New World Order" Upside Down

Carol de Leon is now program director for the Women Workers Project at CAAAV (formerly Committee Against Anti-Asian Violence): Organizing Asian Communities in the Bronx, New York. She grew up in the Philippines, where she was a youth activist until she left in 1987 to work abroad as a nanny. She recalls that when she was in Hong Kong she applied to go to Canada, but it did not materialize, and this was probably fortunate. In the mid-1980s, the Canadian government was "very lenient, inviting people to come into the country, so at the time it was so easy to find an employer and go to Canada." In the 1990s, the Canadian government instituted requirements such as educational background checks for 2 to 3 years of college education. She comments:

> It seems very appealing to go to Canada when you are in other countries . . . for a Third World woman to go there—but in reality that structure is not well-implemented. When you go there, you'll end up working for a family for 2 or 3 years, and if you are being exploited, you can't leave while applying for a change in status. So the employer has all of the control, because the worker will end up staying anyway.[27]

de Leon knows that she is lucky not to be speaking from the experience of being trapped as a live-in caregiver in Canada. Although some aspects of her initial experiences in the U.S. were very similar, she not only was able to escape these exploitative situations, but is now organizing women like her to mobilize against the common abuses they face.

de Leon says that although the U.S. has no program like the Canadian LCP, it has a formal legal structure for au pairs who are usually young students from Europe. She says employers can hire them through agencies and arrange for them to have connections to church and school here. She also emphasizes that these "young students are treated very well and respected for what they do, compared to immigrant women who work as professional nannies." Third World women working for corporate executives do not get working permits. de Leon says, "You just get a visa that is tied to an employer." She had a contract to work as a live-in nanny for a family; her working papers described her as a "personal servant to American family." She added, "I really hated that because it sounded like back in the days when women and men are being brought here from Africa against their will and became enslaved. To me, *servant* means *slave*, and I'm certainly not one." She started working a few months after arrival in the New York City suburb of Ardsley. The people and weather appeared strange. Her job conditions were "a nightmare—I did everything from waking up the children, giving them breakfast, walking the dog, shoveling the snow, and cleaning the house." She worked from 6:30 a.m. to 9 p.m. 6 days a week. After a year, she asked for another day off after noting that others had 2 days off. Her employer, who worked for Philip Morris Corporation, said that he had seen that the common practice in Hong Kong was only one day off and refused her request on that basis.

She took the initiative to call the labor department to find out about the minimum wage and overtime pay and asked her employer to adjust her salary. Again, her employer said that the contract they signed was based on earnings in Hong Kong. de Leon pointed out that she could not support herself on those wages. When she asked for overtime, saying she understood the law limited the workday to 8 hours, her employers demanded to know where she got the information. After telling them that her source was the labor department, they still refused, then gave her a $25 raise. de Leon calculated that her earnings after the raise amounted to $2 an hour when the minimum wage was $4. After that, she decided that she wanted to leave, but met the typical tactics of exploitative household employers:

> When I told them that I'd rather leave, they said I couldn't break the contract. I said that in a contract, either party can break the contract if you are not happy, so I'm giving you 2 weeks' notice. They insisted that I couldn't do it, and tried to manipulate me, asking where I was going, if I was going back to my country. To me, that's an implication that I was going to starve! I told her that it's none of her business.

Ultimately de Leon decided to stay because she signed a contract to work for 2 years—"the reality is that I felt I was legally trafficked." She remarks that women who are brought here by executives or diplomats have no way to network with others and no assistance from employers to find a community. Instead, she observes, workers are discouraged from meeting others and deliberately isolated in the suburbs, where they had no contact with other nannies, not even in the park. She adds that, "Without other people giving me support, I decided to stay and finish my contract and just survive," recalling that this also happened to her in Hong Kong. She was finally able to leave and find a live-out job from 11 a.m. to 7 p.m. that allowed her to start going to the park:

> That's when I realized that in this industry the majority of workers are women from the Third World. I met other domestic workers from all over the Third World. I realized that these conditions were widespread, whether you were from Indonesia, Malaysia, Philippines, Barbados, Guyana, Trinidad, most domestic workers face long hours, low wages, and isolation, and lack of control of our living and working conditions. Labor laws are not enforced in this industry. And labor laws simply do not protect our basic human rights to decent housing, food, shelter, and livable wages. And many laws, like those protecting workers against discrimination in the workplace, including sexual harassment and racism, specifically exclude domestic workers.

de Leon recalls many accounts of women who were subject to abuse and exploitation, worked long hours even when they were sick, and were forced to terminate pregnancies. After 7 years, she met people from CAAAV when they were handing out fliers in the park. de Leon approached them, "they took my number, and the next week I met with them and ended up going to weekly meetings."

Now, de Leon leads the Women Workers Project, which holds monthly meetings to improve working and living conditions among women in the domestic work industry. The project members began drafting standard guidelines and a pay scale to make recommendations for how much should be paid per child, for housekeeping tasks, etc.:

> We started looking at the industry, and realized that we had to be strategic about it, doing outreach with women from other ethnicities, and women really embraced it. We did a survey in 2000 in parks, indoor playgrounds, train stations, to see the conditions of women—who gets minimum wage, overtime pay, sick days, holidays. One woman who was being sponsored was forced to work 6 days a week, over 65 hours. She wanted to have one day to go to church. She started asking and showing papers from the labor department, and her employers were furious. Employers will try all their ways to not follow the regulations.

de Leon remarks on the lack of regulation of the industry: "We're not even protected from sexual harassment or any other abuses." Moreover, she notes that employers try many different tactics, including using race to divide household workers. For example, they make comparisons and say women from the Philippines are "better than from other countries, to create tensions between workers." They also "discriminate against us because of race, language, and immigration status."

Domestic Workers United, a project sponsored by CAAAV and Andolan, a South Asian workers' group, is pushing now for legislation that de Leon's group drafted. Led by a steering committee composed mostly of women from the Caribbean, the group used their research to design a standard contract and approached the New York City Council to pass a new law regulating the industry. Essentially, the law will regulate the Department of Consumer Affairs, the agency that licenses employment agencies recruiting and placing domestic workers. Seventy-five percent of domestic workers get their jobs through such agencies. The agencies should serve to protect these workers' rights, yet, de Leon says, when a worker has an abusive employer and calls her agency, "they advise you to stay for at least 3 or 4 months because they want to receive their fees from the employers." Otherwise, the agency will have to give the money back to the employer or provide another employee without a fee. de Leon explains, "What we are asking for is a code of conduct, so that the agency provides a contract with your work conditions, including minimum wage, 2 weeks' paid vacation, etc. and the agency should enforce it."[28]

The group introduced the bill in March 2002 and provided supporting testimony at a hearing in May with the chair of the committee on labor. Supporters like Councilwoman Gail Brewer said the bill should have been easy to pass because it involved no cost to the city. The group staged a city-wide action on October 5, 2002, starting with a rally at Washington Square Park, followed by a march to City Hall. Participants wore yellow rubber gloves and aprons, just as they did when they introduced the bill. Media coverage surpassed their expectations: although the turnout for the action was strong at 500, the press coverage put the numbers above 1000.[29]

de Leon reflects on the Women Workers' Project and the demands of the bill. She also describes the nature of her organization's work and, more broadly, the movement she is helping build. The measure is in some ways modest and yet revolutionary:

> The bill is very basic—how we should be treated, working conditions, minimum wage, overtime pay, legal holidays and sick days—but really, we want to turn the industry upside down and change the notions that immigrant workers are lazy and uneducated. Because it relates to history, because this country inherited this industry through American slavery and ideas that this is women's work, etc. We're calling for respect and recognition for women in this industry.

de Leon says the group continues to wait patiently for a meeting on the bill with the Department of Consumer Affairs but will stage another action if necessary. In the meantime, her project offers an immigrant rights law clinic through New York University students working with CAAAV to provide advice on negotiating with employers and maneuvering the healthcare system. The project also provides courses for nannies on child care, psychology, and cardiopulmonary resuscitation training leading to Red Cross certification.[30]

Similarly, while the PWC in Vancouver pursues its long-term campaign to dismantle the LCP, its members work to build the movement for immigrant workers' rights in Canada every day in myriad ways. For example, the PWC has rented a house for use as a drop-in center for members who yearn for camaraderie and some comforting elements of Philippine culture. Cecilia Diocson, founding chairperson and director, describes how the center serves as a place for women to congregate, eat, and talk with women in similar situations:

> The women started to educate each other, bringing their stories to discuss at the center. We have had a lot of successes in making these women more assertive in their employers' homes after gathering these stories over food. They report having to pay for their own room and board, sleeping in the garage without heat, and being "shared" by two employers. They say, "It's like being in prison from Monday through Friday." The majority work 14 to 16 hours and are underpaid. We found out that they are getting underfed too. They want rice at least twice a day, but lots of white employers don't eat rice, just pasta and potatoes. The regulars on Friday afternoon would be rushing to the kitchen, saying "I'm so hungry. I haven't had rice all week." They could hardly work because they were so hungry.

Clearly, the drop-in center provides more than a refuge for hungry workers. It serves as a space for these women to build a community base from which to organize. The effectiveness of the other work of the PWC is closely tied to this base, as much of it evolves from participatory research and is advanced through popular education including cultural events and political theater. The center has been able to conduct longitudinal studies, following women through 8- to 10-year time spans, to document the segregation and lack of mobility Filipinas face in the labor market in Canada.

The most recent research relates to the way the increasing number of Filipinas who enter Canada via the LCP led to growth over the past 20 years of the mail-order bride industry—"another category of slave," as Diocson says. The PWC also plans to launch a women's studies program with guest lecturers at the center for women who cannot afford to attend universities.[31]

At a recent international women's conference, Diocson presented an analysis of global migration and particularly the cases of Filipina women forced to migrate to Canada in the context of global capitalism. Her cogent analysis, both as a trained nurse who migrated from the Philippines and as a radical political organizer, is one of the most well-articulated analyses I have encountered in a variety of contexts. She commented about the LCP:

> Instead of instituting a universal day care system to address the needs of women who are leaving the home to join the workplace, the Canadian state's response to this economic restructuring is to import cheap but highly educated and relatively skilled foreign domestic workers. This confers several advantages both to the Canadian state and Canadians who can afford a foreign domestic worker . . . . [T]he Canadian state earns revenue through the processing of migration

documents and taxation of these foreign domestic workers . . . . [F]oreign domestic workers help provide a stable base of cheap "reserve army of labor" that keeps wages down and ensures continuous accumulation of capital . . . . Thus, the foreign domestic worker is functional to the maintenance of the existing capitalist system in Canada. On the other side of the ledger, the sending country also benefits much from its export of foreign domestic workers.[32]

In my experience, Third World women migrant workers have always been many steps ahead of us in formulating and articulating these analyses of globalization, perhaps because of its direct and dire impacts on the conditions of these women's lives. They have much at stake to develop strategies to resist these conditions effectively, and it is only fitting that those who have suffered first and worst under globalization will lead the way out from under its oppressive forces. The women of the Workers' Voices Coalition, the PWC, Domestic Workers United, and many other grassroots organizations are doing revolutionary work in the face of what they all know is surely not new under globalization. They remind us through their fierce struggles and sharp analyses that they will revolutionize not only their work force and their adopted societies, but the antiglobalization movement itself.

Acknowledgments

Portion of this chapter are reprinted from Chang, G., "The Global Trade in Filipina Workers," in *Dragon Ladies: Asian American Feminists Breathe Fire*, south End Press, Boston, 1997, p. 132; Chang, G., *Disposable Domestics: Immigrant Women Workers in the Global Economy*, South End Press, Boston, 2000, p. 123.

Notes

1. "Globalization's Inability to Create Jobs Fuels Mass Migration: ILO Chief," *Tehran Times,* June 13, 2002.
2. Nishioka, J., "Marriage by Mail: The Internet Makes It Easier for Potential Mates to Connect across Seas," *Asian Week,* July 29, 1999. [Cherry Blossoms is identified by all but Krosky as an international mail-order bride business.]
3. KPFA Radio, Morning Show with host Andrea Lewis, International Women's Day Program, 2001, guests: Grace Chang and Ethel Long Scott.
4. See "Third World Within" cited in *CAAAV Voice,* Special Issue on Women, Race and Work, Vol. 10, Fall 2000, p. 17. Cindy Domingo, founder of the Workers' Voices Coalition, in her call for seizing the moment after the Battle at Seattle, 1999, said: "We saw the profound deterioration in the conditions of immigrant and women workers worldwide as a direct result of free trade policies, globalization and privatization. In the United States, immigrant workers have become scapegoats for the failures of the global economy because U.S. workers don't see their interests as one and the same with workers in Latin America, Asia or Africa. The WTO coming to our city gave us a once-in-a-lifetime opportunity to draw links between conditions faced by working people in developing countries and those faced by immigrants and people of color in the United States," cited by Joy, K. in "Gender, Immigration and the WTO," *Network News,* Winter 2000, p. 12.
5. Testimony of representative of the International Organization of Prostitutes, Gabriela Workshop, September 3, 1995.
6. See Sandrasagra, M.J., "Globalisation Heightening Gender Inequalities," IPS, October 10, 2000; Tauli-Corpuz, V., "Asia-Pacific Women Grapple with Financial Crisis and Globalisation," Roundtable Discussion on the Economic, Social, and Political Impacts of the Southeast Asian

Financial Crisis, Manila, April 12–14, 1998, and Rural and Indigenous Women Speak Out on the Impact of Globalisation, Chiangmai, Thailand, May 22–25, 1998.

7. Testimony of Cenen Bagon, "Voices of Working Women," Proceedings of "Beyond the WTO: conference on Women and Immigration the Global Economy" organized by Northwest Labor and Employment Law Office (LELO) and Workers' Voice Coalition. Seattle, Washington, December 4, 1999. p. 16.

8. See Chang, G., "The Global Trade in Filipina Workers," in *Dragon Ladies: Asian American Feminists Breathe Fire*, South End Press, Boston, 1997, p. 132; Chang, G., *Disposable Domestics: Immigrant Women Workers in the Global Economy*, South End Press, Boston, 2000, p. 123.

9. Filipino Nurses Support Group, "Contextualizing the Presence of Filipino Nurses in BC," in *Advancing the Rights and Welfare of Non-Practicing Filipino and other Foreign-Trained Nurses*," proceedings of national consultation for Filipino and other foreign-trained nurses, December 7–9, 2001. The Philippines Department of Labor and Employment estimates that about 2748 Filipinos leave the country daily.

10. This number does not include women who are trafficked, illegally recruited, or migrate for marriage or students and tourists who eventually become undocumented workers. Data compiled by Kanlungan Center Foundation from Philippine Overseas Employment Administration and Department of Labor and Employment statistics, 1995; Vincent, I., "Canada Beckons Cream of Nannies: Much-Sought Filipinas Prefer Work Conditions," *Globe and Mail*, January 20, 1996, p. A1. Other authors more extensively address trafficking in women for the sex, entertainment, and mail-order bride industries. See Rosca, N., "The Philippines' Shameful Export," *Nation*, April 17, 1995, p. 523; Kim, E., "Sex Tourism in Asia: A Reflection of Political and Economic Equality," *Critical Perspectives of Third World America*, 2, Fall 1984, p. 215; Blitt, C., Producer, "Sisters and Daughters Betrayed: The Trafficking of Women and Girls and the Fight to End It," Video, Global Fund for Women.

11. Testimony of Pamela, "Filipino Nurses Doing Domestic work in Canada: A Stalled Development," Philippine Women Centre of British Columbia, March 2000, p. 20.

12. Philippine Overseas Employment Administration, 2000, bulatlat.com.

13. Presentation by Ethel Farrales, Filipino–Canadian Youth Alliance, Vancouver, "Link Arms, Raise Fists: U.S. Out of the Philippines Now!" North American Conference, July 6–7, 2002.

14. Comments of youth member of Overseas Filipino Workers' Organization, Vancouver, "Link Arms, Raise Fists: U.S. Out of the Philippines Now!" North American Conference, San Francisco, July 6–7, 2002.

15. Philippine Women Centre of British Columbia, "Filipino Nurses Doing Domestic Work in Canada: A Stalled Development," Vancouver, March 2000, p. 10.

16. Ibid., p. 16.

17. Ibid., p. 11.

18. Diocson, C., Philippine Women Centre of British Columbia, Vancouver, Phone Interview, August 2002.

19. Statement of Sheila Farrales, "The Use of Filipino Nurses in the Scheme to Privatize Health Care," Conference Proceedings: Advancing the Rights and Welfare of Non-Practicing Filipino and Other Foreign-Trained Nurses, Filipino Nurses' Support Group, Burnaby, British Columbia, December 7–9, 2001, p. 51.

20. Testimony of Pamela, "Filipino Nurses Doing Domestic Work in Canada: A Stalled Development," Philippine Women Centre of British Columbia, March 2000, p. 19.

21. Ibid., p. 20.

22. Ibid., p. 29.

23. Statement of Gemma Gambito, ibid., p. 61.

24. Statement of Lynn Farrales, ibid., p. 42.

25. Ibid.

26. Philippine Women Centre of B.C., "Filipino Nurses Doing Domestic Work in Canada: A Stalled Development," March 2000, p. 7.

27. de Leon, C., Women workers Project, CAAAV, Bronx, NY, Phone interview, September 2002.

28. de Leon, C., Women Workers Project, CAAAV, Bronx, NY, Phone Interviews, September 2002 and February 2003.

29. Alapo, L., "Bill to Protect Domestic Workers," *Newsday*, March 25, 2002; Greenhouse, S., "Wage Bill Would Protect Housekeepers and Nannies," *New York Times*, March 25, 2002;

Richardson, L., "A Union Maid? Actually a Nanny, Organizing," *New York Times,* April 4, 2002; Ginsberg, A., "Nannies March for Fair Pay, OT," *Daily News,* October 6, 2002; Ramirez, M., "Domestic Workers Seek Wage, Personal Protection," *Newsday,* October 6, 2002; Geron, T., "All in a Day's Work," *AsianWeek,* July 11, 2002; Lee, C., "Revolt of the Nannies," *Village Voice,* March 9, 2002.

30. de Leon, C., Women Workers Project, CAAAV, Bronx, NY, Phone Interview, September 2002.

31. Diocson, C., Philippine Women Centre of British Columbia, Phone Interview, August 2002.

32. Diocson, C., "Forced Migration: Perpetuation of Underdevelopment," paper presented at Ninth International Forum, Association for Women's Rights in Development, Guadalajara, Mexico, October 3–6, 2002.

15
Can U.S. Workers Embrace Anti-Imperialism?

BILL FLETCHER, JR.

Introduction

The period between September 11, 2001, and the invasion of Iraq raised many questions about the psyche of the U.S. public in general and the U.S. working class in particular. The ability of the Bush Administration to utilize fear and patriotism to refocus attention away from pressing domestic issues has been astounding. The Republican Congressional victories in November 2002 were nearly unprecedented and most likely would not have happened had the focus on Iraq not emerged during the preceding summer.

The widespread fear that resulted from the terror attacks on September 11 is understandable. The assault on civilians through the destruction of the World Trade Center and the use of civilian aircraft as weapons were certainly crimes against humanity. However, the ability of the Bush Administration to link all sorts of real and perceived threats to the personality of Saddam Hussein (and, before that, Osama Bin Laden), as well as to create what looks like a state of permanent war, has resulted in a situation of perpetual anxiety. It has also enhanced the foundation of a pro-imperial front, presumably representing the U.S. people, against the rest of the world. This front has led many people, including those of good intention, into believing that any and all concerns and disagreements expressed overseas or at home about the objectives of U.S. foreign policy are without foundation. Instead, it is argued, any and all methods to guarantee "our" security must be entertained, regardless of the cost.

For these reasons, the danger of a domestic police state has risen to levels not seen since the Nixon Administration. Additional dangers of a cowboy foreign policy in the interests of strengthening a U.S.-dominated global capitalist empire place the entire planet at risk and certainly do not increase security for anyone. In this situation, a fundamental question emerges: Can a working-class-based, anti-imperialist movement emerge that shifts U.S. foreign policy and, in the long term, lays the foundation for the transformation of the U.S.

This chapter is published with permission from the Monthly Review Foundation. It appeared in *Monthly Review* (July–August 2003).

state? In order to answer this question, we must ask ourselves some difficult questions about labor, race, and empire. It must be said at the outset that much of our focus will be on the organized sector of the U.S. working class in order to consider the strategic and tactical options for the creation of a new set of politics through a transformation of organized labor.

The Crisis of Contemporary U.S. Labor

The defining ideological feature of the modern U.S. labor movement is the Gompersian notion of trade unionism. Samuel Gompers, founder and long-time leader of the American Federation of Labor (AFL), rose out of the Cigarmakers' Union in the latter decades of the 19th century. Responding to the crisis in the Knights of Labor, a significant and more radically inclusive labor federation, Gompers argued that workers could be organized effectively only on a craft basis. Although he paid lip service to unskilled workers, Gompers' emphasis was on the skilled crafts. In constructing the AFL, Gompers built a ruling bloc that supported such a vision and soon surpassed the Knights of Labor in size and influence.

Gompers broke with the earlier U.S. tradition and that of Europeans in his opposition to a labor party for the working class. This view flowed from his belief that the role of the trade union was to fight in the interests of the workers in the workplace. Further, his philosophy dictated that the trade union movement accept the existence of capitalism and take no steps in opposition to it. Gompers' program came to be known as bread-and-butter trade unionism or job-conscious trade unionism, most notable for its claim to be pragmatic and not ideological. In the political realm, this meant that organized labor would not, to paraphrase Gompers, have permanent friends or enemies but permanent interests. At one level, that might sound quite class conscious, but Gompers was not speaking about the entirety of the working class—only of its organized, craft-based sector. When it came to political action, Gompers restricted the AFL to lobbying rather than political mobilization of the working class. In other words, Gompers insisted that the AFL engage only in traditional interest-group politics.

The roots of Gompers' philosophy of trade unionism were in his view of class and the state, and, by implication, race, gender, and U.S. foreign policy. Although once a socialist, he soon rejected any noncapitalist view of the future. The role of trade unionism was to improve the lives of those fortunate enough to belong to such unions. Gompers actually embraced a peculiar form of trickle-down thinking; what was won by the trade unions might eventually improve the lives of the unorganized sector, but the unorganized sector was not Gompers' concern. If they wanted improvements, they should have joined or formed unions.

Gompers' pragmatism reflected an exclusionary unionism, a view that the objective of unionism was to narrow the relevant population to that which could "cut the best deal" with capital. The AFL, from its beginning, excluded the bulk of unskilled workers, workers of color, and female workers. This "pragmatic" practice demonstrated the racism and sexism of the AFL.

Gompers also came to view the U.S. state as essentially an empty vessel that could be filled by any type of political or economic influence. The job of the trade union movement was to exert pressure on that state to benefit organized labor and, through the trickle-down effect, the whole of the working class. It was not necessary for the working class to challenge the capitalists for state power. The state could be influenced either by organized labor or by capital. It was up to organized labor to ensure the former.

The class character of the state was denied by Gompers. For him, the state was a class-neutral entity—a view that holds sway within much of organized labor even today. Gompers slowly and steadily abandoned concerns about matters of race and gender. After the great 1892 general strike in New Orleans, a strike that demonstrated the potential of a racially united labor movement, the matter of race and its significance declined in importance for Gompers. By the early 1900s, he had become an openly white supremacist.

It was a short step within Gompers' pragmatism from the repudiation of class struggle and the fight for power to the open embrace of capitalism and the government's efforts to strengthen U.S. business interests abroad. In other words, Gompers saw a unity between labor and capital; both continually sought a better economic climate.

In the realm of foreign policy, this view came to mean open, unconditional, and even rabid support for whatever the U.S. government did abroad. An early example of this was the AFL's embrace of the First World War and its support of the suppression of opponents of the war, such as the Industrial Workers of the World, a left-wing union that had considerable success organizing workers ignored by the AFL. For Gompers, the interests of organized labor were allied to a strengthening of capitalism and the success of U.S. foreign policy, regardless of the impacts on workers in other countries. The flag of an imperialist patriotism was to be the banner of the AFL.

Alternative politics challenging Gompersian trade unionism emerged after the founding of the AFL. The Industrial Workers of the World, organizations allied with the Communist and Socialist parties, independent left and progressive currents, and caucus movements of oppressed nationalities all significantly influenced both the discourse and the practice of U.S. trade unionism. Nevertheless, although this alternative politics was sometimes successful, the Gompersian view (often aided by a repressive state) has remained hegemonic. The reluctance and frequent opposition to tackling racist oppression (always with the excuse that this would create divisions); the tailing after the Democratic Party and, worse, the crass currying of favors from both major parties; and the consistent support of U.S. foreign policy in the name of patriotism have continued and have, in fact, strangled the development of the movement.

The Patriotism of Organized Labor

To further explore the consequences of organized labor's *pragmatism*, we must examine the notion of *patriotism*. According to the *American Heritage Dictionary of the English Language*, patriotism is "love of and devotion to one's country," but this is not the operative definition in U.S. politics. The operative definition is more akin to "support for the policies of one's government irrespective of the social costs, if said policies are justified as being in the interests of the nation–state." In the United States, this operative definition has been used primarily to suppress dissent.

Gompers wrapped organized labor in the operative definition. The AFL and later the AFL–Congress of Industrial Organizations (CIO) used it to crush opposition to its pro business, pro-imperialism policies. Most critically, two decades after Gompers' death, the operational definition was critical when the Cold War commenced and loyalty oaths were enacted into law. In the late 1940s, unions representing over one million workers were expelled from the CIO for failing to sign affidavits mandated by the Taft-Hartley Act signifying that their leaders were not communists. In order to justify and enforce these expulsions, patriotism was an effective means of intimidating opponents. Linked to this skewed view of patriotism was the notion promoted by the political right that antiracist activity was a sign of communist influence. This became the case within organized labor as well. The unions expelled from the CIO were those that had the strongest positions against racism within the labor movement.

The operative definition of patriotism, then, is a call for class collaboration and a repudiation of genuine international working class solidarity. In the realm of international affairs, for instance, the AFL and later the AFL-CIO supported foreign policies that accepted U.S. world hegemony and overseas trade union movements that opposed the political left. In other words, the operative definition of patriotism supported the empire; what stood domestically in opposition to the empire was seen as unpatriotic.

Organized labor, seeking to justify its own existence and withstand attacks from the capitalists, chose the expedient route of support for and advancement of the operative notion of patriotism. It supported policies that were antithetical to working class interests but often seemed to be in labor's (and especially labor's leaders') short-term economic interests.

A Race-Neutral Social Contract: Does a Rising Tide Raise All Boats?

Established trade unionism embraces the notion of a social contract between labor and capital within the context of the capitalist system. In embracing this conception, however, the leaders and members of organized labor put on blinders when it came to matters of race and gender. Not coincidentally, these blinders also inhibited their ability to see and understand the empire.

It is once again important to clarify terms. The early usage of the term *social contract* derives from the Enlightenment and the U.S. and French Revolutions of the 18th century. The term referred to a myth elaborated by the intellectuals at the service of the emerging bourgeoisie to the effect that a bond or contract had been implicitly made in the early years of humanity to end prehistoric barbarism. This social contract presumably recognized basic rights for all sectors of society and protected people against arbitrary rule.

Although the nascent bourgeoisie used the myth of the social contract in its struggle with absolute monarchies and feudalism, the term, in fact, justified the existence of classes and the relative role for each of them. This was true whether the social contract took the crude Hobbesian form or Rousseau's more revolutionary and egalitarian form.

In the 20th century, however, the social contract took on a new meaning, particularly in the aftermath of the Great Depression and the Second World War. It came to refer to the welfare state and the demand upon society to protect its citizens. Again, a myth developed that all sectors of society basically accepted the existence of a strong public sector, core social benefits for all, and trade unionism. In reality, these precepts were never fully accepted, nor was there ever consistent implementation of policies that would have made them a reality. What did exist, however, was a balance of forces in the class struggle that gave this new meaning of the social contract some plausibility.

Organized labor has typically seen the terms of the social contract as narrowly economic. Under Gompers' reign, those who were fortunate enough to be in AFL unions were seen as the beneficiaries of the social contract. The fate of those outside official trade unionism was left to chance. Over time, the views within organized labor changed and led to a greater concern for the conditions and futures of unorganized workers. This took the form of organizing the unorganized, particularly in the 1930s and 1940s, and later within the public sector, during the 1960s and 1970s, as well as fighting for progressive legislation.

Even during the New Deal, the social contract was never consistent. The trade union movement could perpetuate the myth of this contract only by its failure to address racial disparities in the working class and among the oppressed more generally. For example, Roosevelt's agricultural and labor programs overlooked black farmers and farm workers in the South and Asian and Chicano farmers and farm workers in the Southwest. Little was done later, during the "golden years" of U.S. capitalism (1945 through 1973) to address the secondary (poorly paid and insecure) labor market situation facing the majority of black and Latin workers.

The social-contract myth assumed that capitalism now had a human face and would be forced to respect all sectors of society. It also assumed that the conditions for the existing workforce would continually improve so that the living standards of their children and grandchildren would always be better. This was a white myth. Racial differentials in jobs, housing, education, and health policies always militated against full implementation of the social contract.

The existence of a relative privilege for whites over people of color created a myopia that reinforced the social-contract myth. The ability to rise from the poverty of the early years of immigration led many whites to believe that this society was and remains equitable in its treatment of its citizens. The social contract promised the continuance of this *modus vivendi*. Indeed, the racial nature of the social contract permitted the transformation of Europeans into white people.

In addition to its racial character, the social-contract myth also had an imperial quality. The great wealth of the U.S. was not simply the result of domestic economic performance and ingenuity, but also arose from its global power. By the end of the Second World War, the U.S. was the premier capitalist and imperialist power, and the dollar was the *de facto* international currency.

The U.S. used its international power to export its debt, gaining badly needed cash resources to sustain its economic stability. This imperial role, therefore, had more than a psychological impact on U.S. workers (and not only whites); it also exerted a positive material impact on the conditions of most of the U.S. working class and petty bourgeoisie. Defending this status quo became for many an essential component of the theories and practices of their lives and their organizations.

The racial and imperial nature of the social-contract myth and the failure of organized labor to challenge it undermined the ability of workers to conceive of themselves as having legitimate and independent progressive class interests. One of the most tragic examples of this took place after the Second World War, when the trade union movement failed in its effort to conduct a large-scale organization effort in the south (Operation Dixie) and subsequently failed to integrate itself into the emerging Civil Rights Movement. The bulk of organized labor, although bloodied by the defeat of Operation Dixie and the subsequent passage of the rabidly anti labor Taft–Hartley Act, believed that it nevertheless had an established place in the tripartite relationship of business, government, and organized labor—a place that dictated that labor promote U.S. capitalism.

A second tragedy revolved around the open support of U.S. foreign policy, even when that policy took direct aim at workers overseas. Examples range from support for the crushing of French dockworkers in the late 1940s to military coups in what was then British Guiana in 1964 and Chile in 1973. Despite the known impacts of such actions on the working classes of these countries, most organized labor members were prepared to serve as foot soldiers in the fight to promote U.S. interests. In its anticommunist crusade, organized labor could generally be counted upon to disrupt and attempt to destroy legitimate working class organizations, including those in Brazil during the 1980s (Central Unica dos Trabalhadores) and those in South Africa in the late 1980s and early 1990s (Congress of South African Trade Unions).

The impact of the racial social-contract myth on labor has become particularly critical in the past 25 years, with the collapse of the welfare state–New Deal consensus and its liberal conception of the social contract. Had the collapse of the welfare state and social contract affected only people of color, organized labor would still be facing a crisis, albeit one very different from what it is currently experiencing. Majority acceptance of the equitable nature of the U.S. imperial state would persist, at least to a degree. What is creating a larger crisis, however, is that the emergence of neo-liberal globalization guided by the U.S. imperial state has challenged the earlier notions of a racial deal for white workers.

A Challenge Emerges: Right-Wing Populism

Key to the complicity of most of the white working class, and most significantly its organized fraction, with U.S. racism and imperialism was a combination of two essential factors: (1) white racial privilege and the social bloc that it created and (2) the promise of improving living standards. These two factors, although related, must be distinguished. White racial privilege is not necessarily tied to the economic strength of the U.S. state. The privilege is fundamentally political and structural and refers to the enforced racial differential that exists between whites and nonwhites in U.S. society. This differential exists in both boom times and depressions, but it is enforced through the practices of both the state and civil society. It can be seen in the areas of employment, education, housing, health, and culture, as well as in arenas that include a high preponderance of people of color, such as entertainment and sports.

Living standards, on the other hand, correlate with the overall economic picture, the racial differential, and the status of the U.S. as the dominant imperialist power. Political decisions play a part in living standards, but the performance of the economy is directly affected by larger forces. The stagnation of the U.S. economy that began in the early 1970s was driven by economic and political factors. Specific political and economic actions were taken to deal with this stagnation and they affected the working class as a whole, usually with disproportionate suffering within communities of color.

The stagnating economy generated a significant drop in living standards for the bulk of the U.S. working class, and this sent reverberations throughout the entire society. At the same time, the victories of the social movements of people of color and women and changes in immigration patterns changed the tapestry of U.S. society. It took some time for people to grasp that living standards had permanently declined, but certainly during the 1980s and 1990s this came to be understood. By the 1990s, the established media paid heightened attention to this phenomenon and its impact on social sectors that had typically thought of themselves as impervious to economic decline.

One consequence of declining working class standards has been the rise of right-wing populism, not only in the U.S. but in most of the advanced capitalist nations. Its rise in the U.S. must be understood in terms of the crisis to the white racial bloc that unfolded at the same time neo-liberal globalization arose.

The challenge to the white racial bloc arose from both the victories in the antiracist struggle and the changes in imperialism. The victories in the domestic antiracist struggle created new and unprecedented roles for individuals of color. The appointments of people like Condoleezza Rice and Colin Powell represented a fundamental change at the top levels of power. These are not the traditional roles occupied by people of color in a Democratic or Republican administration. In corporate America, the rise of black CEOs in key companies such as American Express is also significant. The problem created for white America by these developments is summed up in the notorious questions of sports commentator "Jimmy the Greek" who bemoaned the future of white players with the advent of black quarterbacks: What happens to the hopes of the average white person? Does it pay to be white anymore?

The state and corporate onslaughts on labor that included the wholesale destruction of much of U.S. manufacturing and the constitution of closer intercapitalist and interimperialist alliances have meant that the U.S. workforce holds no special place for U.S. capital other than its role as consumer. The threat of movement overseas, not to mention its actuality, presented a major crisis of confidence in the status quo for the average worker. The loyalty that workers were led to expect from their employers simply does not exist. The loyalty is, as it always has been, to the almighty dollar.

The sense of betrayal goes to the core of contemporary right-wing populism. Despite his poor showings in the 2000 election, political commentator Pat Buchanan summed up the feelings of millions when he launched tirades at the allegedly traitorous companies that had abandoned the American worker. Buchanan's subtle anti-Semitism, racism, and nativism became the lens for his anticorporate (but certainly not anticapitalist) polemic.

The racial deal is now in shambles. Key elements of the white racial bloc sense betrayal, and white workers (as well as sections of the white petty bourgeoisie) cannot count on improved lives for their children. Thus, a combination of the objective economic decline in the living standards of the average worker and the readjustment in the racial deal has fueled right-wing populism. The anger this spawned, whether in the extreme form of the militia movements or in the more acceptable form of a Pat Buchanan, has become a pulsating pressure point within the U.S. social formation.

This right-wing populism is demanding a reinstatement of the white racial deal. Even in its most militant anticorporatism, it is not challenging capitalism; it is demanding a return to the mythical social contract. With regard to the international situation, at some moments this right-wing populism is isolationist and protectionist, whereas at other moments it is expansionist and jingoist. In both cases, however, protection of the U.S. state and its hegemonic role in the world are key: the U.S. first, and within the U.S. so-called natives, and among the so-called natives, whites. Patriotism, in its operative definition, then comes to mean defense of the empire against any and all potential threats.

Within the U.S. left, there have at various points been assumptions that its economic decline and specifically the decline in the conditions for its working class would engender a militant if not radical response. The assumptions may turn out to be true but not quite in the manner the left expected. Declining living standards do not automatically produce predictable responses. The left is seldom an immediate beneficiary. Any politics predicated on this assumption is a politics destined to destruction.

An additional complicating factor is the matter of the white racial bloc. The declining living standards understood through the prism of white racism and white racial privilege can easily be blamed on anyone and anything but the capitalists and the capitalist system. As we have seen over the past 20 years, the growing number of immigrants from the global South, whether documented or not, can be the scapegoats for the unraveling of the American Dream. Politically this has been in evidence in English-only and anti-immigrant initiatives.

One note should be added here. Right-wing populism does not find the same level of resonance among people of color. Part of the reason for this is obvious in that at the core of right-wing populism in the U.S. is white racism. Additionally, people of color in the U.S. have had the "advantage" of seeing the underside of the American Dream.

That said, two points are worth making. In the 1990s, with the rise of anti-immigrant sentiment and violence, populist sentiments arose among segments of communities of color. In the anti-immigrant Proposition 187 campaign in California in the mid-1990s, large numbers, although not a majority, within the African American, Chicano, and Asian electorates supplemented white fervor in favor of the reactionary proposition. In the competition for limited resources under capitalism, the worst sentiments started to surface. Years later, in the aftermath of September 11, there were calls to variants of right-wing populism within communities of color. In the name of patriotism, African Americans, for example, were called upon to march side-by-side with others in the so-called war against terrorism. Many African Americans embraced this call in the hope that they would finally be accepted as Americans. Things have not quite worked out that way, however.

As already noted, right-wing populism can also serve the interests of imperial expansion, as we have seen since September 11. Playing on both fear and the desire for revenge, right-wing populism merged with jingoism to support all sorts of adventures in the name of patriotism, security, and ensuring U.S. hegemony. The desire for revenge against al-Qaeda and all other groups and nations allegedly threatening the U.S. way of life can play itself out politically as support for war, militarism, and, indeed, political repression.

A case in point is the alliance between the reactionary Bush regime and the Teamsters Union under James Hoffa, Jr. The leadership of organized labor has been relatively paralyzed in addressing the emergence of right-wing populism. Trapped within the Gompersian paradigm, the bulk of organized labor has been unable to respond credibly to the new populism. It has been unable to address the sense of betrayal among many white workers, except rhetorically, because of its lack of deep critique of neo-liberal globalization, lack of a frank admission of the racial nature of the social contract, and lack of any coherent analysis of U.S. foreign policy. The irony of the current situation is that as we approached the invasion of Iraq, sections of the leadership of organized labor wished to take a stand against the aggression and found that their views were not necessarily mirrored by the membership. This gives new meaning to the notion of reaping what one sows.

The Gompersian paradigm has not only restricted organized labor from addressing race and gender, but it also has inhibited an ability to tackle the picture of global capitalism. Insofar as organized labor saw its role as helping promote a more humane, pro-U.S. global capitalism, it has found itself hamstrung in opposing U.S. foreign policy. Demands for organized labor to face up to its brutal history of support for U.S. imperialism have met with silence because there is no consensus on this history and whether it was correct to collaborate in these various atrocities. In the aftermath of September 11, it was nearly impossible to engage in a discussion of U.S. foreign policy and the simmering hatred engendered by the role the U.S. has played in the global South. The repression in the name of patriotism that spread nationally had its counterpart within the ranks of organized labor when it came to serious attempts to understand the tragedy of September 11.

Can Organized Labor Be Won to Anti-Imperialism?

This question has no clear answer. There are good reasons to believe that segments of the working class, including organized segments, can in the short run be won to a variant of anti-imperialist politics. In the long term, however, anti-imperialism must become the dominant view within the U.S. working class if any form of progressive, transformative politics such as socialism is to become hegemonic.

The Uruguayan writer Eduardo Galeano made the observation that in order for the global South to achieve the level of development of the global North, the solar system would need 10 more planets. This is a dramatic illustration of the skewed manner in which resources are distributed and used internationally. According to the United Nations, the richest fifth of the world's population consumes 86% of all goods and services whereas the poorest fifth consumes only 1.3%; wealth is polarized dramatically. Again, according to the United Nations, in 2002 the world's 225 richest individuals, 60 of whom are from the U.S., have a combined wealth of over $1 trillion—equal to the annual income of the poorest 47% of the world's population.

The imbalance in resources and wealth, a direct result of imperialism, is not referenced here to make a moral appeal or as an advertisement for the poor starving masses and the charity they need. Rather, in order for the U.S. working class to advance, and specifically in order for the trade union movement to transform itself, an appreciation of this imbalance must become part of the new politics it embraces, for these facts point to what for many people is an unsettling proposition: the need for global wealth redistribution.

In order to defeat right-wing populism within the working class and other sectors of U.S. society, a multi-pronged assault will have to be mounted against points of division. Cracking the white racial bloc and cracking imperial consciousness will be key to that assault. To the extent that segments of the U.S. working class see themselves as victims of the rest of the world rather than both pawns and victims in an imperialist game, right-wing populism can be counted on to gain strength.

In this context, the struggle for reparations—both domestically for African Americans and internationally for Africans—has an objectively anti-imperialist character. The demand for reparations begins the discussion about global (and domestic) wealth redistribution. This is not a demand that white people, or in the international context citizens of the global North, give up their toothbrushes and cars. It is a demand, however, that will necessitate changing the manner in which we live our lives in the global North. It is a demand that will need to be directed at governments, multi-national corporations, banks, and the real-estate industry for compensation for past atrocities and, in more general terms, reconstruction assistance to place peoples ripped out of history back onto a path of self-determined development.

Again, this is not charity. It is compensation for crimes committed. It is also a recognition that the global North generally, and the people of the U.S. in particular, cannot be trusted as long as they turn a blind eye to the wealth (and people) stolen from the rest of the world. This may sound moralistic, but it can be put in terms targeted to self-interest: There will be no security for anyone as long as wealth, resources, and power are distributed so unjustly.

Within the organized section of the working class, the struggle for reparations and global wealth redistribution should move from a demand of well-intentioned leftists to a political demand of the movement. Such a demand can take many forms; one is the struggle for a democratic foreign policy. In light of the Bush Administration's codification of the "New World Order" through the release of the new U.S. security strategy in the fall of 2002, the entire pretense of a peaceful, humane, and harmless U.S. foreign policy has been stripped away. The new doctrine proclaims for all the world to hear and see that the U.S. heads the global capitalist empire, that no other power will be allowed to contend with U.S. military might, and that the U.S. reserves the "right" to take preemptive military action against any nation or force it deems a threat to its interests.

Although the U.S. has historically engaged in much of what the new doctrine advocates, what is different is the blatant nature of the proclamation. What is also different is the flagrant disregard of the opinions and actions of key imperialist allies of the U.S. A case in point is the heated international debate surrounding Iraq. Although the Bush Administration succeeded like few before it in isolating the country internationally, what is striking is the arrogant denial of the importance of this isolation.

Developing anti-imperialism as a mass current within the working class, therefore, involves a fight for a democratic U.S. foreign policy. Of course, as long as the U.S. remains an imperialist power, its ability to have a democratic foreign policy will always have objective limits. Nevertheless, it is the fight that is critical in changing the consciousness of the U.S. working class regarding the role of the U.S. on the world stage. Such a struggle could include demands for reparations and reconstruction assistance; massive assistance to the Global AIDS Fund; renunciation of the national security strategy; withdrawal of military assistance from dictatorial regimes; removal of agricultural subsidies from U.S. agribusinesses; full repayment of dues to the United Nations; replacement of the World Trade Organization (WTO) with a democratic, multi-lateral trade institution; and other measures. In sum, this is a fight for altering the U.S. role within the international arena.

The fight for a democratic foreign policy has another side. For the working class to engage in this struggle represents a strike against the Gompersian dependence on one of the two established capitalist parties. Such a struggle brings to the fore the notion of an independent working-class view of the world rather than tailing after whoever happens to be the "best" Democrat. Trade union policy during the Clinton era demonstrated the bankruptcy of failing to have an independent stand. Even when the unions disagreed with Clinton regarding foreign policy (or domestic policy, such as with welfare reform), they had a deep fear of establishing independent terrain. This made it exceedingly difficult for the union movement to conduct a consistent struggle against Clinton's pro-globalization policies (with the exception of the WTO demonstrations).

Another challenge to the U.S. working class is protectionism. Protectionism can sometimes appear anticorporate, if not anti-imperialist, but it is actually neither. Although the working class is justified in its anger at the loss of jobs, rather than a protectionist response, the response must strike at capital and support workers overseas. As Jesse Jackson so eloquently demanded during his 1988 run for the presidency, we must have accountability—which could be described equally as a form of repair or reparation—on the part of capital when it vacates a neighborhood, community, city, or state.

This matter goes to another issue that extends beyond the scope of this chapter. With the loss of many value-producing jobs because of technological changes or moves offshore, the productivity gains by corporations must be shared. We cannot assume that high-paying jobs will return in the future.

Thus, to borrow from the ideas of the late Tony Mazzocchi, founder of the Labor Party in the U.S., there must be a redefinition of work along with a massive unionization effort to transform existing low-wage jobs into higher-wage employment.

A second response to the specific issue of the shifting of jobs overseas is true international labor solidarity. The growth of left-led trade union movements in places such as South Africa, Nigeria, Brazil, and South Korea represents a major development in the fight for global justice. Not only has it meant improvements in the living standards of workers, but it also has made it far more complicated for the capitalists to place workers in what has come to be known as a race to the bottom. The AFL-CIO under John Sweeney brought about considerable improvements in the international arena regarding to labor solidarity, but even here activity is inconsistent, with remnants of Cold War trade unionism continuing to sneak through. The choice for organized labor in the U.S. seems all too often to be one between the desire for respectability in bourgeois circles, with the accompanying fantasy of a return to the good old days of the New Deal's social contract, and genuine solidarity with foreign labor and other social movements.

One final arena implicit in the above is opposition to U.S. wars of adventure. Although it is conceivable that a scenario analogous to the Second World War may reemerge at some point, nothing like that appears on the horizon. Instead, and in line with the new national security doctrine, we are now witnessing the further militarization of the U.S. justified in the most cynical manner by alleged concerns about human rights, terrorism, and so-called rogue states. Liberal and progressive forces are constantly placed on the defensive when the political right demands that actions be taken against this or that state. Instead, we must "flip the script," so to speak, and ask the difficult questions about the objectives of U.S. policies and military actions. In order to do this, particularly in the post-September 11 environment, fear must be addressed directly. As long as fear of alleged and real threats dominates the national discourse, anti-imperialism will be suppressed.

The fear that most people experience today is the uncertainty of further terrorist attacks. This fear has been played upon by the Bush administration and the political right in order to increase militarization and domestic repression and to discourage popular examination of the deteriorating U.S. and global economies. This can and will be broken to the extent to which people come to understand the political nature of the terrorists (both clerical fascists and state terrorists) and the actions of the U.S. that have laid the basis for the sympathy that many of these terrorists receive.

Concluding Thoughts

The challenge to the U.S. working class and to organized labor cannot be addressed without some formal left presence. The emergence of anti-imperialism as a current rather than as a set of politics elaborated by a few individuals requires engagement in various political struggles, both within the trade union movement and more broadly. The movement against U.S. aggression in Iraq is precisely the sort of mass social phenomenon that can lay the foundation for an anti-imperialist movement. Even here, though, the measures will fail unless a more organized left presence ties the various strands together.

Discussion of the reconstitution of such a left goes beyond the scope of this chapter. Suffice it to say, however, that the development of genuine anti-imperialism is actually tied to a vision of a different world. Anti-imperialism in its best sense is not solely a reaction against the atrocities of the global North, but it is the suggestion that the world can and should operate on a fundamentally different basis. Creating and articulating such a vision should be the task of a genuine left. In the absence of such a left and a new vision, we will find ourselves facing and fighting endless resistance battles with little hope of final victory.

16

Why the Mexican Rural Sector Can't Take It Anymore

VICTOR QUINTANA

When Rural Areas Still Yielded Food Crops . . . and Votes

The countryside was the foundation of Mexico's national development from the mid-1930s to the mid-1960s. It produced cheap food for urban dwellers and raw materials for the steadily expanding national industries. Although the managed prices of agricultural products were kept low to the benefit of the industrial sector, Mexico's agriculture experienced the kinds of growth rates that current President Fox might want to insert in his pie-in-the-sky speeches about the future of Mexico.

By 1965, two factors led to the weakening of this positive pattern of economic development. One was the continued transfer of resources from the agricultural sector to other areas of the economy by way of state-directed underpricing of agricultural products; the other, was the political manipulation of the peasantry. To be sure, the rural sector produced the basic food grains for the national diet, but it was also the source of votes in elections.

The Partido Revolucionario Institucional (PRI) utilized the Confederacion Nacional Campesina to manipulate the peasants as a mass they could use for their own purposes and, through corruption and other methods of control, succeeded in stunting the growth of any efforts to develop an independent peasant organization.

The administrations of Luis Echeverría (1970–1976) and Miguel López Portillo (1976–1982) attempted to boost national agricultural production. They injected large sums of money in the rural sector and succeeded in stimulating production and growth. However, everything the PRI and its corporate agencies did on behalf of the rural sector was marred by the privileging of political dividends, corruption, and demagoguery on the backs of the peasants and in detriment of agricultural production.

Conversations with Chihuahua peasants reveal that their last good year was 1981, not only because it rained, but also because 1981 was the last year of government-supported prices and the national program of agricultural subsidies and supports.

Stages of the War against Mexico's Agriculture

1982 represented a breaking point in the development of Mexico's agriculture. In August, under cover of the declaration of Mexico's default on its foreign debt by its Treasury Secretary Silva Herzog, the first set of structural adjustment measures was enacted. The International Monetary Fund, the World Bank, and the U.S. Treasury Department, a triad representing the "Washington consensus," imposed the adjustments on Mexico.

Bad news for the many was good news for the few. The structural adjustment measures imposed by the nefarious triad were well received by a generation of technocrats educated in U.S. universities precisely with the goal of employing them in the imposition and administration of structural adjustment plans. Thus, beginning in 1982, we witness the first generation of measures imposed on Mexico's countryside, including the deregulation of price controls for agricultural inputs such as fertilizers, machinery, and fuels. Support prices were reduced and the government began to cut back on investments and expenditures on research, extension, and agricultural support mechanisms. Shortly thereafter, the national economy began to open up to imports of foodstuffs after Mexico's joining of the General Agreement on Tariffs and Trade (forerunner of the World Trade Organization [WTO]).

A second generation of such measures began with the coming to power of President Salinas de Gortari in 1988. One of Salinas's highest officials summarized the government posture toward the agricultural sector thus:

> In the Mexican countryside there is an excess of millions of peasants, because their contribution to the gross domestic product is out of proportion with its proportion of the total population. Therefore, we must reduce the rural population from its current 25 million to about 5 million.

There is little one could add to a clear and self-explanatory statement about what the central government had in mind for the peasants of Mexico.

Salinas continued the reduction of agricultural supports and reduced guaranteed minimum prices as well as the number of products thus protected. His strategy toward the rural sector was built upon the dual goals of privatizing agricultural landholding and negotiating a free-trade agreement with the U.S. He achieved the first goal by enacting an agrarian counterreform in 1992 with the support of both PRI and PAN (Partido de Accion Nacional) deputies in the national congress. Under the new laws, former ejido (commonly held) lands could be bought and sold, and corporations could purchase agricultural properties. Salinas's hope that this measure would attract foreign investment in agriculture proved false. Today less than 1% of foreign direct investment in Mexico is located in the rural sector.

Salinas's second goal became a reality with the signing of the North American Free Trade Agreement (NAFTA) in 1994. Eight years later, Secretary of Agriculture Javier Usabiaga recognized that the treaty was "poorly negotiated" and that the rural sector was not adequately protected, but in the Salinas years the first steps in the (limited) economic integration with the U.S. carried a consensus of many who bought into the schemes of Salinas. Only independent peasant organizations, the Frente Democrático Campesino in Chihuahua, and later the Zapatistas in Chiapas, stood in opposition to the Salinas policies.

The administration of Zedillo, who followed Salinas, continued the government's war against national agricultural activities. Zedillo eliminated the support prices for the few products that remained, continued the policy of importation of agricultural foodstuffs, looked the other way as imports surpassed officially established quotas, reduced the budget for agriculture, and dissolved CONASUPO (Companía Nacional de Subsistencias Populares), the major state-owned purchaser, distributor, and retailer of agricultural foodstuffs. Although claiming that the last measure was an effort at eliminating corruption, in effect it signified the elimination of the last remaining mechanism that allowed protection against market-price fluctuations for agricultural producers.

Two figures summarize the story of the change of official policy toward the countryside. Between 1982 and 2001, state investment in the rural sector was reduced by 95.5% and public expenditures for the sector diminished by 73.3%. Second, the credit made available to rural producers dropped 64.4% during the same period.[1]

The Ignored Warnings

Beginning in 1991, when the first discussions about a free-trade pact with the U.S. were initiated, serious warnings pointed to the perils of placing our rural sector in competition with the most powerful agriculture in the world. The figures in Table 16.1 show the clear asymmetries of the agricultural sectors of the three country signatories of NAFTA.

Basic differences in the availability of natural resources and the asymmetries in government policies of agricultural development and support account for the large differences in productivity. For example, in 2001, the subsidies received by U.S. agriculture amounted to 47.2% of the total value of the agricultural crop whereas subsidies in Mexico reached only 24.1% of the value of agricultural production.[2] U.S. government expenditures on agricultural research reached 2.6% of the gross domestic agricultural product. For Mexico, it was only 0.52%.[3]

Those figures were cited over and over by specialists at CIESTAAM (Centro de Investigación y Estudios Superiores sobre las Transformaciones en el Agro Mexicano), José Luis Calva at the Universidad Nacional Autonoma de Mexico, and also by peasant organizations such as the Frente Democrático de Chihuahua. The Frente organized demonstrations at border crossing points and in 1993 invited a delegation of U.S. congressmen to learn first hand the view of

Table 16.1 Comparative Available Natural Resources, Technologies, and Productivities of NAFTA Signatories

	U.S.	Canada	Mexico
Cultivated hectares per agricultural worker	59.1	117.2	3.1
Irrigated hectares per agricultural worker	7.4	1.9	0.7
Pasture hectares per agricultural worker	79.0	74.4	9.2
Forest hectares per agricultural worker	58.5	116.8	2.8
Tractors per agricultural worker	1.6	1.8	0.02
Kilograms of fertilizer per agricultural worker	6,114	6,352	209.6
Corn (tons per hectare)	8.4	7.3	2.4
Bananas (tons per hectare)	1.8	1.8	0.6
Rice (tons per hectare)	6.8	—	4.4
2001 value of agricultural productivity per worker	$67,871	$54,816	$3,758

Note: 1 hectare = 2.47 acres.
Source: Calva, J.L., "Brechas de Competitividad Agricola," El Universal, Noviembre 22, 2002. With permission.

Mexican farmers of the proposed treaty. Later, the Frente sent two of its leaders to Washington to make their views known to the U.S. House of Representatives.

Negotiation of NAFTA

NAFTA was negotiated in an undemocratic manner. Those who would be most affected were not involved in negotiations. Only a few representatives of large agribusiness concerns that stood to gain from the treaty, such as Bachoco, were consulted. The treaty was not discussed in the Mexican House of Representatives. It was ratified by Mexico's Senate, then controlled by Salinas's PRI party.

According to CIESTAAM a number fundamental deficiencies characterized Mexico's handling of treaty negotiations:

1. Mexico did not review the experience and problems arising from the treaty signed by the U.S. and Canada in 1989. If it had, it would have concluded that NAFTA Chapters 19 and 20 designed for problem resolution would be insufficient to resolve trade disputes and conflicts.
2. Mexico did not exclude any agricultural products from the scope of the treaty; Canada managed to exclude its dairy and poultry sectors. Mexico accepted high import quotas without tariffs for a large number of agricultural items without introducing into the treaty any provisions for suspensions, revisions, moratoria, or other instruments of protection.
3. An important juridical asymmetry was involved. While the U.S. negotiated an agreement, Mexico signed a treaty that had legal status

almost at the level of the national constitution and allowed little political "wiggle" room for modifications.

4. The U.S. was and still is in the strongest position to negotiate and evaluate the effects of NAFTA and, on that basis, to make beneficial revisions and adjustments.[4]

Agricultural Policies in Early Years of NAFTA

The agricultural segments of NAFTA set out a system of quotas, tariffs, quota-and-tariff combinations, and the progressive elimination of all barriers to agricultural products. NAFTA included a timetable whereby tariffs would begin to decrease and the quantities of items imported free of tariffs would increase simultaneously beginning the first year of the agreement. By 2003, all agricultural products, with the exception of corn, beans, powdered milk, and sugar cane, were to have been imported without restrictions of any kind. The four exceptions were to be freely imported by 2008 (the 15th year of the treaty).

Thus, Mexico had at least 9 years to put into practice an aggressive policy of agricultural development. It could have designed and applied public policy measures that would have allowed its farmers to reach higher levels of competitiveness and be ready or at least prepared to face the two phases of complete barrier removals in 2003 and 2008. What did the Mexican government do during that period? Did it use the time advantageously to strengthen Mexico's agriculture?

The evidence is telling: In the 9 years after signing NAFTA, the Mexican government cut back in real terms 65% of the budget for the agricultural sector. As a percentage of total government expenditures, the rural sector proportion decreased from 8.8% in 1994 to 3.5% in 2002. As a percentage of Gross Domestic Product it fell from 1.5% to 0.6%.

During the same period, the governments of Salinas, Zedillo, and Fox reaffirmed the application of the orthodox neo-liberal adjustment measures against the countryside. Minimum price supports disappeared, prices of fuels for irrigation shot up, and rural credit continued to shrink. At the same time, even though the treaty allowed Mexico to continue to protect corn and bean producers by way of quotas and tariffs, the government did not collect $2.8 billion in tariffs for corn imports and $77 million for bean imports. It also allowed the importation of 14 million tons of basic grains above the quota limits set by the treaty.[5]

During the same period, the U.S. engaged in everything except free trade. Contrary to its commitments to the WTO, it increased subsidies to its agricultural sector and flooded Mexico with low-quality products at prices below the costs of production. This practice of dumping prohibited under free-trade rules worked to the detriment of Mexican producers and applied to beef products, milk, dairy products, cotton, and apples.

Subsidies to U.S. agriculture were significant, increasing from $5 billion annually in 1994 to more than six times that amount, $32 billion, in 2000.[6] A comparative review of subsidies in the U.S. and Mexico reveals that the U.S. government provides support of $125 per hectare of land and, on average, $21,000 per farmer. In Mexico, government support is limited to $45 per hectare and $700 per agricultural producer. An additional comparison sheds further light on the situation. In 2003, the U.S. agricultural budget reached $118 billion compared with $4.5 billion in Mexico. In other words, the U.S. agricultural budget is 26 times larger than Mexico's, although in terms of absolute size, U.S. agriculture is only six times greater than Mexico's.[7]

Impacts of NAFTA on Mexico's Agriculture

The first major consequence of NAFTA was an increase in Mexico's dependence on foreign sources for its basic food needs. For Mexico's countryside, NAFTA has meant, first and foremost, the imports of foodstuffs. In the first 8 years of NAFTA, imports of agricultural products increased by 80% from $2.9 billion to $4.2 billion.[8] Additional figures indicate who benefited from NAFTA: From 1994 to 2001, Mexico's purchases of agricultural foodstuffs increased by 44% whereas its exports of the same products increased by only 8%. At the same time, U.S. sales to Mexico increased significantly—by 205% for fresh and dried fruits and by 84% for seeds and oils.[9]

The trend has accelerated over the period in question. In 2001, food exports increased only by 4% in relation to 2000, while food imports grew by 15.5%. In that year, the U.S. imported $5.2 billion worth of Mexican agriculture and sold $7.4 billion in products to Mexico.[10] Table 16.2 shows the evolution of the aggregate trade in food products for the U.S. and Mexico from 1995 to 2001.

A more detailed look reveals that of 10 basic staple foodstuffs (corn, beans, wheat, soya, sorghum, barley, sesame, rice, and safflower), Mexico imported 8.7 million tons in 1990. By 2000, the amount imported reached 18.5 tons, an increase of 112%, of which the U.S. supplied 90%.[11] Corn constitutes the basis of Mexico's diet. Before NAFTA, the largest amount of corn ever imported into Mexico reached 2.5 million tons annually. By 2000, imports more than doubled and exceeded 5.2 million tons. In 2001, the figure increased by an

Table 16.2 Post-NAFTA Agricultural Commerce between U.S. and Mexico

Year	Imports from U.S.	Exports to U.S.
1995	$3254 million	$3835 million
2000	$6420 million	$5078 million
2001	$7415 million	$5267 million

Source: El Financiero, Marzo 4, 2002. With permission.

additional 15% (more than 6 million tons).[12] This level of corn importation also meant that Mexico used $3.6 billion in foreign exchange dollar reserves in payment—ironically, an amount that nearly equals the entire government budget for the rural sector. Additionally, the Mexican government gave, in effect, a gift worth $1.9 billion to the giants in the import business by allowing the entrance of tons of corn without the stipulated tariff payments.[13]

Imports of beans also increased. In 1996, the U.S. exported 109,406 tons of beans to Mexico, and in 1998 the amount increased 60% to 170,737 tons which does not include large amounts of contraband that further threaten national production.[14] Some estimates place the illegal contraband alone around 200,000 tons annually—about three times the authorized nontariffed quota for 2002 of 65,239 tons.[15]

Of every 10 kg of rice consumed in Mexico between 1980 and 1990, 1.7 kg was imported; 1.2 kg of every 10 kg of wheat consumed was imported. Between 1994 and 1998, the dependency on foreign food imports increased to 5.3 kg of every 10 kg for rice and to 3.5 kg of every 10 kg for wheat.[16]

In actuality, the complete "liberalization" of trade in corn, beans, barley, rice, sorghum, and soya began in 1996 and not in 2009 as stipulated in NAFTA. During the first 5 years of NAFTA, Mexico imported on average 12 million tons annually of these grains, an increase of 66.6% over the 9 years preceding NAFTA. This again meant an outflow of $10.7 billion in foreign exchange reserves; this was 10 times the Procampo (Programa de Apoyos al Campo) budget and five times the SAGAR (Mexico's Agriculture Department) budget for 1999.[17] Between 1995 and 2000, Mexico imported 50 million tons of basic grains and became the top importer of basic grains in Latin America. This figure does not include the open or "technical" contraband.

Meat products did not fare any better. Today Mexico consumes twice the quantity of imported meats than it consumed before the signing of NAFTA.[18] During the first 6 years of NAFTA, beef imports increased by 200%, pork products by 300%, and eggs by 55%, chicken imports by 130,000 tons. Imported milk constituted 20% of national consumption.[19]

Mexican cattle farmers face the dumping practices of U.S. exporters, the tolerance of contraband by Mexican authorities, the disregard for quota limits, and low input prices enjoyed by their U.S. competitors. Not surprisingly, Mexico imported $1.03 billion worth of fresh and frozen red meats in 2001, 22.5% more than in 2000 and 442% more than in 1995.[20]

Established import limits of chicken and turkey have been consistently surpassed. In 1994, imports of chicken reached 65,000 tons though the quota limit was 25,000 tons. Imports in 2002 tripled the NAFTA-established quota of 30,700 tons. Excess turkey imports exceeded authorized amounts by two to two and a half times.[21] Imports of pork products increased by 2.2 times from 1998 to 2000 and reached 208,573 tons. Beef and lamb imports increased 1.5 times since 1994 and met 60% of internal demand.[22]

It could be argued that producers of fruits and vegetables benefited from NAFTA because exports to the U.S. increased by 76% for fruits and 26% for vegetables.[23] However, between 1994 and 2000, imports of canned vegetables and canned and dried fruits increased by 77% and 300%, respectively. This means that Mexico exports fresh fruit and it returns in processed form.[24] Apples represent a special case. Apples are very important agricultural items in states like Chihuahua. In 1997, imports amounted to 114,922 tons. By 2001, imports increased by 94% to 221,269. A tariff of 101% was supposed to go in effect at the beginning of NAFTA; this was modified to authorize a minimum price of $13.72 per imported box, somewhat above the wholesale price of Mexican apples. U.S. exporters were allowed to provide cash rebates to Mexican importers. In effect, this eliminated local producers from the competition and ruined them.[25] Thus, Mexico, one of the historically great agricultural civilizations of the world, has placed its food supplies in foreign hands. It now imports 95% of its edible oils; 40% of its beef, pork, and other meat products; 30% of its corn; and 50% of its rice.[26]

The future does not look brighter. According to the U.S. Department of Agriculture (USDA), Mexico will become a large importer of both raw materials and foodstuffs. Mexican imports of grains (corn, sorghum, wheat, and soy) were expected to grow by 31% from 18.3 million tons in 2000 and 2001 to 24 million tons by 2011 and 2012.[27] USDA predicts that imports of beef, pork, and poultry will increase by 86% from 2000 to 2011.[28]

The complete elimination of protection for 20 agricultural products beginning in 2003 is expected to double the agricultural trade deficit beginning that year, and the deficit will reach $10 billion.[29] Since NAFTA was enacted, Mexico has paid $78 billion for food imports, a figure larger than its national public debt. In 2002, Mexican food imports amounted to 78% of its petroleum exports.

A second major consequence of NAFTA has been the disappearance of profitability for national agricultural producers. As a consequence of unfair competition from foreign imports, the value of Mexican agricultural products plummeted. Between 1985 and 1999, in real terms, corn lost 64% of its value and beans lost 46%. This in no way meant that retail prices dropped for consumers. Between 1994 and 2000, the prices of staple consumer goods rose by 257% while registering a much lower increase (185%) in prices paid to agricultural producers.[30] As a result of plummeting profitability, producers abandoned agricultural endeavors en masse. The production of basic grains and edible oils that involved 14 million hectares or 70% of the country's cultivated area was the major loser under NAFTA.[31] Even the Consejo Nacional Agropecuario, an organization of large agribusinessmen, recognized that basic grain and livestock production were seriously affected by NAFTA.[32]

During the first 8 years of NAFTA, 1.6 million previously cultivated hectares used for corn, beans, wheat, soy, and cotton were abandoned. The loss of cultivated land was most pronounced in states with substantial numbers of peasant producers such as Veracruz, Oaxaca, Guerrero, Morelos, Michoacán, Querétaro, Puebla, and Guanajuato. In areas characterized by more-modern agriculture such as the Yaqui and Mayo Valleys, peasants opted to rent their parcels to large enterprises. The International Monetary Fund expects that 10 million hectares of grain crops will be abandoned in the next few years.[33]

To truly appreciate the social impact of the situation, consider the case of corn—a grain produced by 2.5 million peasants on parcels smaller than 5 hectares that yielded no more than 2 tons. These peasants formerly produced 75% of the country's total production of corn.[34] Not surprisingly, rural poverty has shot up in the past few years. The Department of Social Development acknowledged in the fall 2002 that, in terms of nutrition, poverty in the rural areas rose significantly from 35.5% in 1992 to 52.4% in 2002. Poverty and impacts on access to health and education grew during the same period from 41.8% to 50% of the population in the countryside.[35] Economist Julio Boltvinik analyzed these official data and figures from other sources to conclude that 86.2% of rural inhabitants live under conditions of poverty in Mexico.[36] Other comparisons also illustrate the dire situation of the rural sector, for example, the wide income disparity between population groups that depend on agriculture and those that do not. In the nonrural population, 74.6% of the people generate 94.3% of Mexico's total income; 25.4% of the total rural population generates only 5.7% of Mexico's aggregate income.[37]

Twenty-five million people live in the countryside, and 15 million of them face limited employment futures. Most of them no longer depend on agriculture. They rely on other sources for support, for example, the sale of their labor and handicrafts and other informal commercial activities.[38] In fact, 70% to 80% of the income of most small peasant families now originates in nonagricultural activities.

Even the World Bank recognizes that the current index of extreme poverty in the agrarian sector indicates a worsening of the situation in the past decade. One of every two rural dwellers survives in situations of dire poverty "in the midst of a vicious cycle in which the indiscriminate use of natural resources is the only avenue for the poors' survival."[39]

In 1998 and 1999, peasant families dropped their consumption of tortillas by 20.4% because of lack of cash to purchase them.[40] The 11 states with the highest proportions of rural inhabitants are threatened by insecurity of food supplies and malnutrition: Chiapas, Guerrero, Oaxaca, Puebla, Veracruz, Tlaxcala, Hidalgo, Durango, San Luis Potosí, Yucatán, and Zacatecas. Of the 113,000 municipalities within those states, 706 face inability to feed their populations. Other figures are equally dismal: Malnutrition affects approximately 44% of native Indian children under 5 years of age—a rate equal to rates in the poorest nations in Africa.[41] The average daily wage in the rural areas is 15 pesos, less than half the national minimum wage. Of people in the primary sector, 30% earn no income whatsoever, 39% earn less than minimum wage, and only 5.2% earn more than the minimun wage.[42] In the communal lands of the ejidos of Mexico, fewer than 50% of the houses have running water, only 16.5% are connected to sewers, and only 65% have access to electricity.[43]

Poverty, of course, is not merely malnutrition, lack of food, low income, or absence of public services. Poverty is many sided and multi-dimensional. For the Mexican farmers and peasants it also means forced migration—abandoning one's land and family. According to Mexico's Secretary of Labor, 1.78 million people have left the countryside since 1994. SEDESOL (Secretaria de Desarrollo Social) estimates that on average 600 peasants migrate from the rural sectors every day.[44] Migration means family disintegration, the forced separation of its members. It represents the tearing apart of the social fabric, the social networks that the rural communities constructed over a long time that somehow offered a degree of protection from exploitation and abuse and access to a few meager resources. Those networks become weak when only the elderly and children remain in the rural towns. The average age of the Mexican rural producer at present is 52 years.[45]

Winners of NAFTA's Onslaught on Mexican Agriculture

Although 3.3 million poor Mexican peasants suffer the impacts of NAFTA on agriculture, NAFTA has produced large winners as well, albeit a few. The winners are mainly large multi-national corporations and a few Mexican agribusiness enterprises. The most prominent are as follows:

- Grupo Bimbo: bread giant of Mexico. It benefits from subsidized wheat imports. Annual sales of $3.5 billion.
- Grupo Modelo: number one exporter of beer. Annual sales: $3.5 billion.
- Nestlé Mexico: a consortium producing diversified products including cereals, meats, coffee, chocolate, and milk and dairy. Annual sales: $2.3 billion.
- Grupo Maseca (GRUMA): number-one producer of tortillas and corn flour. Benefited immensely from 14 million tons of corn imported above and beyond the limits established by NAFTA. Annual sales: $1.9 billion.
- KOF–Coca Cola–FEMSA: number-one producer of beverages in Latin America. Produces and distributes beer, soft drinks, and containers. Operates the OXXO chain of convenience stores. Benefits from imports of fructose. Annual sales: $1.9 billion.
- Sabritas–Pepsico: number-one producer of chips and snacks in Mexico and Central America. Annual sales in 2001: $1.8 billion.

- Unilever and subsidiaries: producer of a wide variety of prepared food products such as soups, salsas, ice cream, condiments, and juices. Annual sales: $1.2 billion.
- Grupo Lala: number-one producer and distributors of milk in Mexico. Benefited greatly from imports of grains and cattle feed. Annual sales: $1.2 billion.
- Grupos Pulse y Savia: develops, produces, and markets seeds for fruits and fresh vegetables. Annual sales: $1.2 billion.
- Bachoco: monopolizes large-scale production of poultry and eggs. Benefits from imports of sorghum and corn. Annual sales: $1 billion.
- Pilgrim's Pride of Mexico: subsidiary of the Pilgrim's Pride International poultry giant. Annual sales in 2000: $280 million.[46]

Another entity that could be added is Cargill, which receives a large share of the Mexican government's supports for the marketing of corn internally. Cargill is also one of the main exporters of U.S. corn to Mexico.

Renegotiation of NAFTA

Mexico has a possibility of establishing a moratorium and renegotiating the agricultural aspects of NAFTA in accordance with its Constitution, international law, and even Chapter VIII of NAFTA. The procedure would be as follows: In accordance with Articles 131, 39, and 73, Sections XXXIX A and E of Mexico's Constitution, its Senate would declare a social, economic, and ecological emergency. Next, as permitted under Chapter VIII of NAFTA, a provisional 3-year suspension of agricultural commitments would go into effect. The suspension would affect food chains defined as basic and strategic for Mexico's food security and sovereignty as per Chapter XVII of the Law of Sustainable Rural Development. The defined food chains include corn, beans, wheat, sugar cane, rice, sorghum, coffee, poultry and eggs, milk, beef, pork, and fish.

At the same time, the national Congress would issue a decree instructing the Executive Branch to begin renegotiation of the agricultural segments of NAFTA. Mexico could also utilize Article 162 of the Vienna Convention pertaining to international treaties. This article allows any agreement or treaty to be subject to modification if conditions of signatory countries change significantly. It is the case that U.S. subsidies to its agriculture were significantly less when NAFTA was signed than they are today and that Mexico's agriculture budget was significantly higher than it is today. Mexico can demonstrate that conditions have changed in a pronounced manner and insist that a revision and renegotiation of NAFTA is in order.

Negotiation Issues

The issue is not throwing NAFTA completely overboard or attempting to achieve agricultural autarchy and suspend agricultural exchanges with the

U.S. and other countries in toto. NAFTA has caused great harm to many
small producers in the U.S. and led to the displacement and migration of
hundreds of thousands of Mexican peasants and farmers. Therefore, it is in
the interests of both Mexico and the U.S. to seek renegotiation of a number
of aspects of NAFTA:

1. The exclusion of corn and beans, the basic staples of the Mexican
   diet, from NAFTA's process of trade liberalization. This is fundamental to Mexican national security and the preservation of genetic
   resources and because of the multi-functional impact of peasant
   production of corn and beans.
2. The reintroduction of quotas and tariffs on the imports of products
   that affect agricultural food chains classified under the law of Sustainable Rural Development as basic and strategic for Mexico's food
   security and sovereignty. In addition to corn and beans, they include
   sugar cane, rice, wheat, sorghum, coffee, poultry and eggs, milk, beef,
   pork, and fish. Maximum volumes of imports without levies should
   not exceed 5% to 20% of local production, depending on item, and
   additional amounts should be subject to tariffs.
3. Enforce the application of health and sanitary rules that pertain to
   imported foodstuffs. Enforce the identification of genetically modified foods.
4. Eliminate all unfair trade practices, such as internal U.S. subsidies
   that allow dumping, that is, exporting below costs of production and
   special subsidies to U.S. exporters.
5. Negotiate two additional agreements that parallel NAFTA. The first
   would guarantee that Mexican migrants to the U.S. would be entitled
   to all rights as workers and residents. The second would establish a special fund to compensate regions, products, productive chains, and individual and social producers that suffer from relative disadvantages.[47]

Toward an Inclusive, Sustainable, Sovereign Agricultural Policy
Mexico needs more than simply protecting its rural sector and allowing it to
continue age-old bad agricultural habits. What we need is a complete structural
reform with the goal of developing a solid, prosperous, and economically and
ecologically sustainable agriculture. A restructured rural sector should be able
to produce healthy and accessible foods for all Mexicans, guarantee the nation's
food security, and treat our peasant brothers and sisters as priority agents in a
process of inclusive development.

Such restructuring requires long-term planning. The Campo No Aguanta
Mas (the countryside can't take it anymore) movement proposed a 20-year
project to be carried out by a central government commission that should
include representation from the executive and legislative branches, organizations

of rural producers, peasants and indigenous groups, institutions of higher learning, and research centers. A framework for the structural reforms is already provided by the Law of Sustainable Rural Development.

According to José Luis Calva, five fundamental instruments for an aggregate policy of rural development to be put into practice are:

1. A policy of support prices for basic agriculture. This policy would provide certainty based on long-term profitability and expectations that investment in agriculture would allow producers real possibilities for accumulation, technical improvements, and credit availability.
2. A long-term program of support for research, agricultural and animal extension programs, and technical husbandry that would produce considerable impact on production and productivity.
3. Substantial increases in public resources devoted to infrastructure to allow better utilization of natural resources, for example, increases in irrigated acreage and better use of water supplies.
4. Provision of a fresh new supply of credit to agricultural areas, with preferential interest rates granted to small producers of basic products, along with resolution of the enormous indebtedness that has become an enormous obstacle to continued agricultural production.
5. Maintenance of employment and income opportunities for the rural sector; promotion of and support for small peasant proprietors.[1]

All these points and more were incorporated into a major unity document released on March 24, 2003 by the four large rural associations: Movimiento El Campo No Aguanta Mas, El Barzón (representing indebted peasants), Confederacion Nacional Campesina, and the Consejo Agrario Permanente. The document is titled "A proposal of a national agreement for the rural sector: Towards the development of rural society and food sovereignty with peasant men and women as the fundamental elements of a national project in the 21st century." It resulted from peasant mobilizations arising from the elimination of all entry restrictions on food imports within the NAFTA agreement in January 2003. It is to date the most complete, broad, strategic, and united effort of Mexico's associations of agricultural producers.[48]

Notes

1. Calva, J.L., "Disyuntiva Agrícola," *El Universal*, November 8, 2002.
2. Calva, J.L., "Brechas de Competitividad Agrícola," *El Universal*, November 22, 2002.
3. Cruz, M.A. and R. Schwentwisus, "Desastroso Impacto del TLCAN en el Sector Agroalimentario," CIESTAAM, Mexico City, p. 3.
4. Ibid, p. 2.
5. Ibid.
6. Movimiento El Campo no Aguanta Mas, Comunicado de Suspensión Provisional de las Disposiciones Más Lesivas del Apartado Agropecuario del TLCAN a Partir del 1o, January 2003, p. 2.
7. *La Jornada*, May 15, 2002.
8. *La Jornada*, July 8, 2002.

9. Ibid.
10. *El Financiero*, March 4, 2002.
11. Verduzco, J.J.F., research cited in *El Financiero*, September 18, 2001.
12. Suárez, V., ANEC, data cited in *El Financiero*, September 11, 2001.
13. ANEC, *La Jornada*, September 12, 2001.
14. *La Jornada*, September 26, 2001.
15. *El Financiero*, March 4, 2002.
16. Flores, J.J., *El Financiero*, September 18, 2001.
17. Suárez, V., ANEC, *In Proceso*, July 15, 2001.
18. *La Jornada*, July 8, 2002.
19. *La Jornada*, September 20, 2001.
20. *El Financiero*, March 4, 2002.
21. *La Jornada*, July 9, 2002.
22. Ibid.
23. *La Jornada*, July 10, 2002.
24. Ibid.
25. *Diario de Chihuahua*, February 27, 2002.
26. *La Jornada*, August 16, 2000.
27. *El Financiero*, March 4, 2002.
28. Ibid.
29. *La Jornada*, February 15, 2002.
30. Cruz, M.A. and R. Schwentwisus, op.cit., p. 7.
31. *El Financiero*, September 18, 2001.
32. *La Jornada*, February 15, 2002.
33. *La Jornada*, July 8, 2002.
34. ANEC, *La Jornada*, July 18, 2001.
35. *Reforma*, October 16, 2002.
36. Boltvinik, J., "Economía Moral, El Campo No aguanta mas," *La Jornada*, February 7, 2002.
37. *El Financiero*, September 27, 2001.
38. *La Jornada*, May 26, 2001.
39. *La Jornada*, July 28, 2002.
40. *El Financiero*, July 18, 2001.
41. *La Jornada*, February 20, 2002.
42. *Milenio*, April 8, 2002.
43. Ibid.
44. *Reforma*, October 16, 2002.
45. *El Financiero*, May 22, 2001.
46. Licona Ocaña, I., "Comercialización y Distribución, Pilas de los Gigantes," *Revista La Buena* Cepa, Febrero–Marzo 2003.
47. Suárez, V., "Que Renegociar en el Capítulo Agrícola del Tratado?", *La Jornada*, January 29, 2003.
48. Movimiento El Campo No Aguanta Mas, El Barzón, Consejo Agrario Permanente, Confederación Nacional Campesina, Propuesta de Acuerdo Nacional para el Campo: Por el Desarrollo de la Sociedad Rural y la Soberanía Alimentaria con Campesinos, como Elementos Fundamentales del Proyecto de Nación de México en el Siglo XX!", (fotocopias), March 24, 2003, Mexico City.

Index

Greece, 5
  foreign domestic workers in, 110
Green Gang, 174–175, 176, 178–179
Grupo Bimbo, 258
Grupo Lalac, 259
Grupo Maseca (GRUMA), 258
Grupo Modelo, 258
Grupos Pulse y Savia, 259
Guatemala
  household income distribution, *47*
  trade in goods as percentage of GDP, *40*
Guinea Bissau, 56
Guomindang, 174, 178–179

H

Haiti, spread of AIDS in, 75
Hebrew Coachman's Group, 191
High-wage countries, 6
Histradut, 188
HIV/AIDS infection, 79–83
Homosexuality, 77
Honduras, trade in goods as percentage of GDP, *40*
Hong Kong; *see also* China
  cession to Great Britain, 167
  citizenship in, 212–213
  civil service employment in, 203–204
  emigration and immigration, 204
  flexible employment in, 200–201, 206–207
  flexible production during economic decline, 205–207
  flexible production during economic expansion, 200–201
  handover to China, 205
  labor importation, 205
  labor insurgency in, 209–213
  labor market, 204–205
  labor unions, 202–203
  migration, 205
  misery of working class, 207–209
  outsourcing, 211–212
  policy on domestic workers, 110–111, 211–212
  ports, 21
  service sector, 204, 205–206
  small and medium (S&M) firms, 201–203
  transition period from mid-1980s to mid-1990s, 204–205
Hong Kong and Shanghai Banking Corporation, 168
Hong Kong Telecom, 209–213

Hothouse agriculture, 136–138
Household income
  inequality in, 7
  in Latin America, *47*
Human Development Index, 47
Hungary, 56

I

Identities, 7
Ill-gotten funds, 59
Illiteracy, 47
Immigrants
  and globalization, 139–140
  India's policy on, 98–99
  undocumented, 14
  and US industrialization, 138–139
Immigration
  in Europe, 134–136
  and sex commerce, 74–75
  and terrorism, 98–99
Imperialism, 55–57; *see also* Globalization; Neo-liberalism
  anti-imperialism, 244–247
  and class war in Latin America, 57–58
  combined and uneven economic development from, 61–62
  globalization as, xiv-xv
  impact on labor, 57–58
  and marginalization of immigrants, 139–140
  migration and citizenship, xxii-xxvi
  military component of, 57
  and neo-liberalism, 59–60
  pillage and exploitation in, 58–61
  resistance to, 169–171, xxvi-xxxii
  ruling class, 62–63
  and rural labor, 67–69
  and social contract, 240
  stages of, 59–60
  theories, xvii-xix
  and working class, 65–67, xix-xxii
Imports, 18, 254–256
Income
  global, *51*
  in Latin America, *47*
  unequal distribution of, 5
India, 89–90
  automobile industry, 91
  Bangladeshi immigrants in, 98–99
  citizenship in, 97–100
  cross-border terrorism, 98–99
  economic liberalization, 90–93
  middle class, 90–93

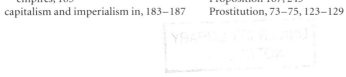